DATE DUE

JUL 26 2018			
AUG 25 2018			
SEP 29 2018			
		PRINTED IN U.S.A.	

Free the Beaches

Free the Beaches

*The Story of Ned Coll
and the Battle for America's
Most Exclusive Shoreline*

ANDREW W. KAHRL

Yale UNIVERSITY PRESS/NEW HAVEN & LONDON

Published with assistance from the
Mary Cady Tew Memorial Fund.

Yale University Press books may be purchased in
quantity for educational, business, or promotional use.
For information, please e-mail sales.press@yale.edu
(U.S. office) or sales@yaleup.co.uk (U.K. office).

Set in Minion type by Newgen North America, Austin, Texas.
Printed in the United States of America.

Library of Congress Control Number: 2017952545

ISBN 978-0-300-21514-4 (hardcover : alk. paper)

A catalogue record for this book is available from the
British Library.

This paper meets the requirements of ANSI/NISO z39.48-1992
(Permanence of Paper).

10 9 8 7 6 5 4 3 2 1

For my parents

Contents

Introduction

I t was a hot and hazy August afternoon in the summer of 1975. The line was long, and tempers were short. Outside the entrance to Hammonasset State Park, sunburned arms dangled from the sides of cars, children's heads rested on windows, and idle drivers burned fuel that a year earlier they could buy only on certain days of the month. At least it was a Monday. Had it been a Saturday or Sunday, the guard would have told them to turn around and go home. On weekends, the beach routinely filled beyond capacity by noon. The previous summer, park officials had turned away over five thousand persons in a single afternoon.

On the beach a cacophony of laughter and shouting—a girl shrieking as she was dunked underwater, a mother calling out to her son from the shore, her patience growing thin—echoed off Long Island Sound's placid waters. To a passing boater, the throngs of bathers crowded onto this checkerboard of beach towels made for a jarring sight. For miles to Hammonasset's east and west stood well-manicured, spacious, and lightly used town and private beaches, yacht clubs, and summer "cottages" (which more often resembled mansions), offering postcard-worthy images of a Connecticut that only a tiny fraction of its population would ever enjoy. Which was why hundreds of people waited for the chance to spend a day on an overcrowded stretch of shore with gravely sand, dilapidated changing rooms, and few amenities. In this state of over three million people and 253 miles of coastline, it was one of the few beaches open to the general public.

Holding up traffic that afternoon was the state's Democratic governor, Ella Grasso, riding shotgun in a baby blue police cruiser, followed by a pool of reporters and a team of officials from the state's Department of Environmental Protection (DEP). Fifteen cars in all. They were here on a "fact-finding" mission, the public was told. The governor wanted to meet and speak with regular folks about an issue of great concern: the severe shortage of publicly accessible beach space in the state. To show she cared, the governor took off her canvas shoes, rolled up her slacks, and waded out into the water for a photo op with a gaggle of children. Such was the extent of her concern. Speaking to reporters afterward, Grasso made it known that no matter how great the demand or how stark the disparities in access, when it came to the coast, "town beaches are the property of towns" and "private beaches are private property." And in Connecticut, "private property is inviolate."[1]

For the "besieged and beleaguered" residents and summer homeowners of the state's Gold Coast—where the wealth was old, the right to property sacred, and the beaches off limits to the urban poor—these were reassuring words in troubling times.[2] They served as a direct rebuke of the man who had, for the past five seasons, turned their beaches into battlefields and forced Grasso to take her veritable stand in the beach house door. For that man, Edward T. "Ned" Coll, it constituted a declaration of war. And, as his mounting list of adversaries could attest, the anti-poverty activist-turned-class-warrior was ready for a fight.

Throughout the summer, they came—often unannounced—to the private beaches and public-in-name-only beaches that dotted the state's shoreline. They came by land, in rented school buses filled with eager children and determined mothers. They came by water, in rowboats and inflatable rafts. Once, they even came by air, hiring a parachutist to descend onto a private beach from a plane that carried a banner reading "Free America's Beaches." Leading the charge was a man whom one reporter said "seemed like a young lieutenant about to lead his troop into a battle that was going to be fun."[3] And indeed, that was why they came to the beach: for fun. But it was where they came from that turned what was for millions of Americans an unremarkable ritual of summer into a protest against racism and privatism and a public demonstration of the relation between the two.

"It was amazing," Tom Condon said of one of the most remarkable stories he covered over the course of his forty-plus years as a reporter. "He [Coll] would show up at an all-white beach with a busload of black kids [and say] 'here we are!' And challenge anybody to throw them out." "It was," Condon remarked, "a bold and incredible kick in the teeth of the structural racism" that pervaded upper-class New England towns, one that "forced people to think [not only] about racial segregation, economic segregation, [but also] the whole question of [whether it is] fair to give what is arguably a public resource and put it in private ownership." To Joanne West and others who had marched with civil rights protestors, worked in poverty-stricken black and brown neighborhoods, and grown disgusted with the smug elitism and faux liberalism of Gold Coast residents, Ned Coll's decision to challenge the local ordinances that effectively rendered Long Island Sound off limits to the urban poor was a stroke of genius. "[These] rich people had so much and they wouldn't give nothing. And these are innocent little kids [and] all they wanted to do is play in the water. . . . It was a brilliant idea."[4]

"We used to call him 'straight up and down,'" Ralph Knighton, who as a child growing up in Hartford's public housing projects in the 1970s was on those trips to the beach, said of Ned Coll. "He was *straight up* with whatever he felt and thought and he was *down* to do anything he needed to do to prove his point."[5] And in a place—New England—that placed a premium on propriety, where the Irish families he grew up with hung "lace curtains" in their windows and taught their children not to make waves, that made Ned, in the eyes of many, a "nut," a "certified whacko," "crazy as a loon."[6] "The man's eyes tell the story," Connecticut governor and Ned's arch-nemesis Thomas Meskill once said of him. Few people who lived in Connecticut in the 1970s did not hold a strong opinion about the man who roiled the state with clever verbal assaults on the wealthy and with inventive, outlandish, and always unpredictable protests against the litany of injustices suffered by the poor in this, the most unequal state in America. Regardless of where they stood, Ned

Exercising their legal right to the wet sand portion of the shore, children
from Hartford's North End play at the private Madison Beach Club
(figure 1) while local law enforcement and club members look on
(figure 2, right). *Photos © Bob Adelman. Courtesy Bob Adelman.*

forced them to take a stand. He "forced himself onto the consciousness." He was "someone who was always out there, stirring the pot."
"There was nothing fake about him." Even people who questioned his
sanity could be moved to quit their jobs to work for him, simply because, as one former associate put it, "What he was saying needed to be
said [and] what he was doing needed to be done."[7]

For a brief moment in the early to mid-1970s, Ned Coll and the
organization he founded seemed poised to accomplish great things. Less
than a decade after the young Irish Catholic college graduate abruptly
quit his job at an insurance company in Hartford and founded the anti-
poverty/social activism group he called Revitalization Corps in 1964, it
had grown to include chapters across the nation, from inner cities to
college campuses, with a team of volunteers, from college students to
ex-felons and former drug addicts to white suburban housewives, numbering in the thousands. In 1972, he ran for president and despite being
too young to occupy the office, was able to make it into a nationally tele-

vised debate during the New Hampshire primary, where, seated next to
George McGovern, Ed Muskie, and other major candidates, he held up
a rubber rat to protest urban poverty. The issues Ned championed and
the work Revitalization Corps performed ran the gamut—from tutoring
low-income children and helping young men and women find jobs, to
fighting slumlords and price-gouging merchants, to protesting austerity-
minded politicians and indifferent bureaucrats, to providing free lunches
to hungry children and boxes of clothes to needy parents. It was, as one
of his former associates described, "activism triage." "Every day was like
an adventure. . . . If you needed help, he was going to help you." To Earlie
Powell and countless other black mothers living on Hartford's North End,
the city's black ghetto, "Ned Coll was like a little welfare department."[8]

    At a time when anti-poverty and welfare rights organizations pro-
liferated across the nation, Revitalization Corps stood out. Founded on a
mission to wage a war on apathy, it placed as much emphasis on changing the lives and outlooks of the nation's privileged as it did on serving
the poor. In words and actions, Revitalization Corps took the emerging
discourse on cultural deviancy that policymakers and social scientists
used to explain the persistence of poverty in black America and turned

it on its head. It was middle-class white Americans, Ned argued, who suffered from damaged psyches as a result of racial segregation. It had rendered them numb, cold, and uncaring, disengaged and disinterested in the lives and struggles of others. This included the wealthy, socially liberal people of coastal Connecticut, who professed concern for the less fortunate while constructing structural and—on the shore—physical barriers to a more integrated, equitable society.

Ned was far from the only white liberal of this era to see summer vacations and places of outdoor recreation as having the potential to break down racial divisions and foster a more inclusive society. For over a half century, New York City's Fresh Air Fund had been calling on wealthy white families who lived or owned summer homes in the suburbs and rural areas to provide a vacation from urban life to underprivileged children. Like the Fresh Air Fund, Ned assumed that the fresh air and open spaces of suburban America offered something that black and brown youth were sorely lacking and in desperate need of. But unlike the Fresh Air Fund, he also believed that white Americans had as much to gain from—and were also in desperate need of—spending time in urban black neighborhoods and in black families' homes, meeting and getting to know fellow parents, bearing witness to their struggles and strivings, finding common humanity. And, in contrast to other organizations dedicated to facilitating interracial contact and exposure, he was not content to simply wait for a few well-meaning white families to volunteer their time and open their homes.[9] Instead, Ned decided to confront privileged white America directly and without warning, in the very place where people go to escape from and forget about the problems ailing society: the beach. Carrying a busload of children from Hartford's North End, Revitalization Corps arrived in shoreline towns and private beach communities unannounced, demanding access to the beach, and challenging vacationing families and local residents to do their part in the making of a more equal, integrated society. But instead of open arms, Ned and his busloads of children were greeted with closed gates, slammed doors, and threats of arrest.

What began as a charitable endeavor turned into a cause, one that would bitterly divide a state, draw an unprecedented degree of public

scrutiny to the exclusionary practices of its wealthy communities, inspire countermeasures aimed at fortifying the state's sand curtain, and
raise a host of legal questions over who, exactly, owned the beach. From
1971 through the end of the decade, summers along the Connecticut
shore were a time of tension and unrest. Residents of wealthy towns like
Madison and Greenwich learned to dread the sight of a broken-down
school bus—inflated rafts, tires, and rowboats tied to its roof—loaded
with children, life jackets swung around their necks, their heads stick-
ing out the windows, their faces filled with joy and expectation. Town
officials hastily passed new ordinances. Law enforcement scrambled to
block beach entrances. Local and, before long, national news reporters
rushed to capture the drama. When it came to generating headlines, Ned
never failed to deliver. His protest tactics became the stuff of legend. His
witty, sharp denunciations of haughty, overprivileged homeowners and

Members of Revitalization Corps march for open beaches in the town of
Old Saybrook, Connecticut. *Photo © Bob Adelman. Courtesy Bob Adelman.*

arrogant local officials always made good copy. One reporter called him "a human quote machine."[10] Seasonal and year-round residents of shoreline towns, on the other hand, denounced him as a "publicity-seeking brat" and "patronizing do-gooder." They charged him with "emotional blackmail." They said he exploited children. They accused his organization of child abandonment. Mostly, they tried to ignore him, a tactic that Ned made nearly impossible. Today, they try to forget him.[11]

For the black and Puerto Rican mothers and children who went on these trips, it was an experience that remains etched in their memories. Four decades later, Earlie Powell still laughs when she thinks of the looks on those white folks' faces when she and dozens of children in cutoff jeans, T-shirts, and other makeshift swimsuits came ashore. She proudly recalls saying in response to their protests that the beach was private, "You don't own this ocean! The ocean belongs to all of us. . . . Now if you want to get up and get your chair and move on, that's fine, 'cuz I'm going to enjoy it for the day. You can come back tomorrow if you want to."[12] And she'll never forget the racial hostility—both subtle and overt—on display in some of America's wealthiest, most educated, and most liberal communities. Trips to the beach left an indelible impression on the children as well. For most of them, it was the first time they had ever visited a beach or seen firsthand the vast expanse of the sea. For many, too, it marked their first introduction to white liberal racism. This came in the form of white parents hastily, and without explanation, summoning their kids to come inside or pulling them away from their new black playmates, of adults trying desperately to avoid eye contact as they struggled to explain why others couldn't come on *their* beach, or of being subjected to humiliating questions from persons— young and old—who rarely ever saw a person of color. During one of those trips to the beach, a young Lebert Lester, the child of a Jamaican immigrant and black woman from North Carolina who lived on Hartford's North End, was building sand castles with a blonde-haired, blue-eyed girl whose parents owned a summer cottage on the shore. As they were digging a trench, Lester said the girl asked him "how come I didn't just wash off my skin. I looked at her like 'what the heck is she talking about?'" Moments later, the girl's father "grab[bed] her by the hand"

and told her it was time to leave. Still confused, later that evening Lester asked his parents what the girl meant, at which point his mother sat him down and "started explaining racism" for the first time.[13]

Throughout the twentieth century, the Connecticut shore held a mirror to the society it surrounded. After the extension of a commuter railroad line from Manhattan into Fairfield County in the mid-nineteenth century, prosperous suburban communities began to take shape along the western half of the state's shore. With the rise of the automobile in the early twentieth century, towns such as Stamford, Greenwich, and New Canaan emerged as bedroom communities for Manhattan's business and professional class, forming what came to be known as the Gold Coast. The mass production of the automobile not only sped the suburbanization of Fairfield County, but also led to the growth of summer vacationing in "the country," the collection of small villages scattered along the shore. Beginning in the 1920s, developers began to acquire vast swaths of undeveloped waterfront property and to secure charters from the state legislature for the development of private beach associations that offered homeowners their own private beaches and, in some cases, private security forces.[14]

These trends accelerated in the decades following World War II. Federal programs such as the Federal Housing Administration and, later, the Federal Highway Act facilitated the mass exodus of people and capital from central cities. Throughout Connecticut the white ethnic neighborhoods of cities like Hartford and New Haven emptied into surrounding suburbs. In New York City, corporate executives, lawyers, and professionals migrated to Fairfield County, which absorbed the vast majority of the fifteen hundred corporate firms that relocated to the state in the 1950s and experienced some of the largest population growth in the nation.[15] As the state's white population prospered, the number of families owning vacation homes along the shore soared. During these years, Connecticut's state legislature approved dozens of private beach association charters. Nationwide, the seasonal and year-round populations of shoreline towns soared, and the amount of undeveloped, open land along the shore dwindled. By 1967, the public could claim ownership of

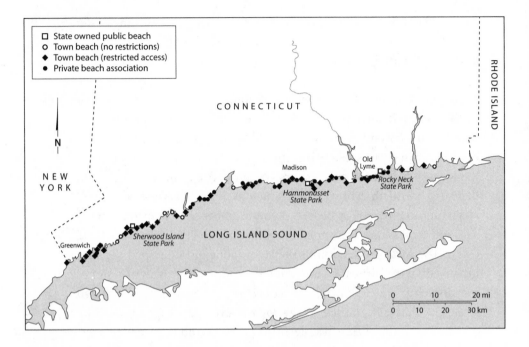

Location of beaches along the Connecticut shoreline
and their accessibility to the general public.

only 2 percent of the 59,157 miles of shoreline in the continental United
States, over one-half of which was under military control and restricted
to the public. Of the 21,724 miles of U.S. shoreline that the federal Bureau of Outdoor Recreation classified as suitable for recreation, approximately 86 percent was under private control. By 1970 over 95 percent of the nation's coastlines suitable for recreation were closed to the
general public. "We are becoming a landlocked people," Texas senator
Ralph Yarborough warned in 1969, "fenced away from our own beautiful shores, unable to exercise the ancient right to enjoy our precious
beaches."[16] The problem was most acute in the Northeast, where, the
Department of Interior estimated, 97 percent of the region's 5,912 miles
of recreational shoreline was "inaccessible to the general public."[17]

As people privatized the shore, the shore itself changed. The public trust doctrine defines the foreshore as public land, a legal principle
that dates back to the Roman era and was incorporated into American

jurisprudence from English common law at the founding of the republic. But the line separating public land from private property along the
shore could more accurately be described as a moving target. That's because beaches exist in a state that marine scientists describe as "dynamic
equilibrium."[18] With each passing season, the shape of a beach changes.
Erosion can steadily transform yesterday's real estate into tomorrow's
seabed. A single massive storm can, in an instant, render a shoreline
unrecognizable. The most expensive and comprehensive attempts to
freeze the shoreline in place are no match against the mighty sea. This
did not stop coastal towns and beachfront homeowners from trying.
Along Long Island Sound, fences extended across rocky cliffs, and groins
and jetties carved up and disfigured sandy beaches, all designed to keep
people out and all inflicting damage on coastal processes, habitats, and
ecosystems.[19]

The state's public beaches, especially, bore the signs of the state's
social divisions and inequalities. While well-heeled towns replenished
their beaches with fresh sand and worked to keep the waters off shore
clean, in older industrial cities such as New Haven and Bridgeport,
public beaches suffered from water pollution, erosion, spotty maintenance, and general avoidance. Throughout the 1960s, scores of city
beaches closed due to underfunding and overpollution. Nationwide,
as people, employers, and taxes fled to the suburbs, cities struggled to
maintain, much less expand, public recreation programs and facilities.
Excluded by ordinance, distance, and absence of public transportation
from suburban shores and lacking public places of their own, residents
of underserved, low-income urban neighborhoods sought relief from
the summer heat by surreptitiously turning on fire hydrants—which
became a flashpoint of conflict with police—or by playing along the
banks of dangerous, often polluted urban waterfronts—which resulted
in shocking numbers of drowning victims, most of them children, each
summer.[20]

For African Americans living in Harlem, New Haven, or on Hartford's North End, the summer months brought into focus a larger set of
social and environmental inequalities and injustices endemic to postwar metropolitan America. Throughout the 1960s, groups of concerned
parents and community organizations struggled to force cities to clean

up and fence off the polluted bodies of water that snaked through their neighborhoods and secure funding for parks and recreational facilities. Their pleas, however, could barely be heard above the din of bulldozers clearing land for interstate highways and public housing projects. When the National Advisory Commission on Civil Disorders (the Kerner Commission) released its report on urban violence in 1968, it listed the absence of safe, healthy, and attractive places of play high among the grievances of residents of neighborhoods that experienced civil unrest. In several cities, anger over inadequate or dangerous recreational space or lack of access to cooling waters on brutally hot summer days sparked uprisings.[21]

Beneficiaries of unprecedented levels of federal and state funding for outdoor recreation over the previous decades, the predominantly white suburbs of the Northeast responded to the mounting unrest of urban black populations and the concerted efforts of civil rights organizations to loosen the white noose that kept people of color locked in urban ghettos by tightening restrictions on access to public spaces in the suburbs, especially public beaches. In the suburbs of Long Island and Connecticut's Gold Coast, restrictive beach ordinances proliferated in the 1960s. "It has become virtually impossible for a city-dweller to venture into the suburbs and find an inexpensive, pleasant place to swim, sun, or relax within a single day's drive," the New York Times reported in 1972. "For hundreds of thousands of sweltering New Yorkers . . . the experience is a little like being trapped in a desert in the middle of an oasis."[22] Exclusionary ordinances ranged from the blatant (outright denial of access to nonresidents) to the thinly veiled (exorbitant beach access fees for nonresidents) to the subtle (limited parking or bans on street parking and bans on the wearing of swimwear on town streets or eating on the beach). It was no secret whom these towns were seeking to keep out. "One would have to live in a vacuum," one legal expert commented, "not to suspect that many beach restrictions are based in part on racial motivation, intermingled with the idea of building a wall between city and suburb."[23]

In a state where extreme wealth and equally extreme poverty resided in close proximity, beach access restrictions complemented, reinforced, and helped to naturalize the barriers dividing thriving suburbs from dying cities. Cities suffering from some of the highest and most persistent poverty rates in the nation were mere miles from some of the wealthiest zip codes, priciest real estate markets, and best public school districts in America. While exclusionary zoning ordinances kept the numbers of low-income minorities residing in Gold Coast towns to a minimum, resident-only beaches and similar restrictions on public access to public space kept them out entirely.[24]

This was how Jim Crow had long worked in the Northeast, through ostensibly color-blind and race-neutral land-use regulations and the privatization (in fact if not in name) of public space, all of it cloaked in the region's "tradition" of privileging private property rights, local autonomy, and "home rule." It proved to be a sturdy foundation. As the civil rights movement fought to dismantle racial apartheid in America, these forms of segregation also proved much harder to undo. Ned Coll was among the few who tried.

This is the story of a man who fought to defend the public's right to public space and the principles these places embodied and who, in so doing, exposed the limits of white racial liberalism in its birthplace, New England. It is also the story of people who turned a place synonymous with freedom and openness—the beach—into one of the most exclusive and exclusionary stretches of land in America and in the process wreaked havoc on the very environments they wanted to themselves. And, it is the story of a place—the Connecticut coast—that came to reflect and embody the lived experience of privilege and poverty in modern America and whose history raises important questions concerning the fate of democracy and the planet in an age of extreme wealth inequality, questions that grow more pressing as the racial crisis in America deepens, the gap between rich and poor widens, and the temperature of the oceans rises.

New England's Sand Curtain

If a man with a family wants a nice, quiet place to swim on
Long Island Sound, he'd better buy a cottage on the shore.

Hartford Courant, *August 17, 1959*

T he novelist Ann Petry "didn't learn about Jim Crow in Alabama or Georgia or Mississippi." She "learned about it in
Connecticut . . . at a Sunday School picnic" on a private beach.
As a "colored" girl growing up in Old Saybrook, Connecticut,
a quiet, rustic seaside town on the eastern half of the state's shoreline,
Petry only rarely caught a glimpse of the sea. Blocking her view were
summer mansions—which, no matter the size, were called cottages—
whose owners claimed dominion over the beaches that fronted their
homes. Her first visit to the beach came on a field trip with her Sunday
school in 1915. "The sun was shining," she remembered. "The sand was
white. The water was very blue. . . . The sudden shock of the cold salt
water made us laugh." After splashing in the Sound's gentle surf, she and
a group of girls walked back to their spot on the beach. There, a group
of older children "of the very wealthy people who owned the big houses
that lined the beach" were waiting for them. The largest boy in the group
pointed to the four-year-old Ann, the only "colored" girl in the class.
"What's she doing on our beach? She's a nigger." Ann's Sunday school
teacher tried to keep the children distracted, gathering them in a circle

and leading a sing-along, while the group of local boys ran to summon the private security guard whom their families hired each summer to protect their properties—in particular, *their* beach—from trespassers.[1]

Ten minutes later, a big "red-faced man" came marching toward the circle of singing children. "No niggers allowed on this beach," he barked at Ann's Sunday school teacher. "I'm the guard here. And there's no niggers allowed on this beach. It's writ in the rules." Before the teacher could muster a response, he warned her, "If you don't get off the beach I'll call up the sheriff." By then the singing had stopped. The children sat, legs crossed, toes dug in the sand, in awkward silence. Finally, the teacher spoke. "Come children. We have to go." Ann's class-mates began to cry. "But the picnic—" one protested. "The hot dogs," added another. "The marshmallows to toast—" It was no use. They had no right to the beach. It was private property, after all, and they were subject to the rules of its owners. "So we ended up eating our hot dogs and our untoasted marshmallows on the Sunday School lawn. We ate in a clammy silence."[2]

Like Petry, the future civil rights activist, politician, and judge Constance Baker Motley also first learned about Jim Crow while attempting to access the state's shoreline. As an African American teenager in New Haven in the 1930s, Motley said she experienced comparatively little discrimination in her day-to-day life. But when she accompanied a group of white friends to a beach in Milford, Connecticut, Motley encountered, for the first time, a color line drawn in sand. Her friends, she recalled, "had been there previously, but when I appeared with them there was suddenly a membership requirement."[3]

In New England and across America, this was how many black children first encountered the color line: during the summer and at the beach. "Recreational facilities," the historian Rebecca de Schweinitz notes, "were one of the most common ways that young people collectively experienced Jim Crow."[4] During the first half of the twentieth century, the Connecticut shoreline also became the place where new forms of privatized government and ostensibly race-neutral forms of discrimination and exclusion proliferated and became woven into the fabric of the state's legal and political culture.

For centuries, beaches have been considered public property. As noted in the introduction, the public trust doctrine defines the foreshore as public land.[5] In 1892, the U.S. Supreme Court validated the public trust doctrine's core principle with its decision in *Illinois Central Railroad v. Illinois,* where it held that land covered by tidal water belonged to the public, with the state acting as a trustee. States were obligated to maintain that trust and protect the public's right to access the shore in perpetuity. Each state, however, marked the line separating public land from private property along the shore at a different spot—some drew the line at high tide, others at low tide, still others at the vegetation line—and devised different definitions of what constituted legitimate use of the public's shore.[6] Some states conceived of the public's right to the foreshore in broad terms. Other states hewed closely to the public trust doctrine's original intent. Massachusetts and Maine, for instance, held that the public's right to the foreshore applied only to fishing and navigation (and not to sunbathing, swimming, or walking); that private ownership extended down to the low-water line; and that the recreational use of private property was tantamount to an unconstitutional taking of private property. Connecticut drew the line between public and private property at the mean high water mark, and its courts recognized swimming and recreation as legitimate uses of public trust lands.[7]

While the state's supreme court upheld the public status of the foreshore, the actions of shoreline developers, backed by the state legislature, made it increasingly difficult for members of the public to enjoy their beach access rights. Beginning in the 1880s wealthy families began building summer cottages along remote sections of shore in the state's eastern half. In 1885 the state legislature granted a charter to a group of families who owned cottages in Old Saybrook. The charter granted the Fenwick Association the power to levy its own taxes and enact zoning restrictions.[8] During the late nineteenth and early twentieth centuries other small groups of families successfully petitioned the state legislature for charters to form what came to be known as private beach associations. Many of these early beach associations formed as an expeditious way of meeting the basic needs of summer homeowners in remote, undeveloped areas of the states lacking in basic infrastructure and services.[9]

James Jay Smith saw that beach association charters could also serve as an instrument for manufacturing and preserving exclusivity. In 1880 Smith started his own real estate investment and development firm and began buying properties in major U.S. cities. By the 1890s he had become a major dealer of real estate on Chicago's West Side and by 1908 was marketing waterfront lots along the Hudson River on New York City's Upper West Side. In 1909 Smith opened a real estate office in Old Saybrook and began buying up farmland and dense forested areas along the eastern half of the shore. With only a model for future development in hand, Smith petitioned the state legislature to grant special charters to imagined communities with evocative names such as Point O' Woods, White Sands Beach, Cornfield Point, and Grove Beach.[10]

With these charters, fortified by a host of deed and zoning restrictions and given concrete definition by a set of common, shared amenities and a form of private governance, Smith's company marketed the ultimate luxury—a summer cottage by the sea—at a price affordable to many middle-class white families. In addition to giving its members the power to tax property owners and control land use, beach association charters also dictated the terms of membership and the election of officers, which included a board of governors, president, vice president, secretary, treasurer, and tax collector. Beach association charters also contained strict regulations on housing construction and land use, prohibitions against commercial activities and a whole host of other "nuisances," and exclusion of nonmembers from streets and land held in common by association members, including parks and, especially, the beach.[11]

Once chartered and populated, Smith's beach associations had the power to perpetuate a certain identity and status. Like most homeowners' associations formed in the first half of the twentieth century, deed restrictions explicitly forbade the sale of lots to blacks or Jews. Deeds in beach associations also contained provisions that owners of lots must be members of the affiliated beach club, with membership in the club determined by a board of governors. This provision helped to ensure that members could determine who could acquire property and become a part of a beach community and meant that most beach associations became closely associated with certain ethnic groups and religious denominations.[12]

Smith became a prolific developer of shoreline real estate. Prior to his arrival in Old Saybrook, there were fewer than a dozen beach associations in the state. Between 1920 and 1950 the James Jay Smith Company chartered and developed thirty-four private beach associations. By the late 1920s Smith was developing vacation home properties all along the eastern seaboard, from Maine to Florida.[13]

Across New England, private recreational land development became a booming industry. By 1930, privately held summer homes and lots accounted for over 60 percent of all recreation land in Connecticut, a total of 264,517 acres valued at over $130 million. By the late 1930s, the state's recreation industry generated an estimated $500 million in annual revenue. A substantial portion of this acreage, and a majority of its

Chalker Beach
Old Saybrook, Conn.

Postcard of Chalker Beach, a private beach association
formed in 1931 in the town of Old Saybrook.

total value, was concentrated along the western half of the Connecticut shoreline. Summer homes in Fairfield County alone accounted for over 50 percent of the total valuation of private recreational property in the state and a quarter of the total acreage. Fairfield County also accounted for nearly one-half of all yacht, boat, beach, and lake clubs in the state. Not coincidentally, Fairfield County also had, by a wide margin, the lowest percentage of total recreational land open to the public (6.1 percent) of any county in the state.[14]

Here, along what came to be known as the Gold Coast, exclusion and exclusivity reigned over the land and shore, extending beyond private beach associations to include the public beaches of shoreline municipalities. By the mid-1920s, the portions of Fairfield County's shoreline open to the public teemed with visitors during the summer months.[15] Many were coming from the cities of Bridgeport and New Haven, where heavy industry hugged the shore, polluted the waters, and robbed the cities of any viable public beach space, or from Manhattan and the Bronx, also bereft of sandy shores and safe waters. Wealthy families brought domestic servants with them to their summer seaside cottages, and these servants in their off-hours congregated with other "colored" workers on town beaches. There, out-of-towners and seasonal workers jockeyed for space with local residents—in particular locals who did not own a summer cottage along the shore or belong to a private beach or yacht club. For them, the public beach offered the closest approximation to the luxuries enjoyed by their well-heeled neighbors, even as the seaside mansions off in the distance and the steady parade of yachts that floated by served as constant reminders of just how humble those accommodations were by comparison.

As private beach associations proliferated and the Northeast's overall population swelled, even this small luxury seemed, to shoreline residents, under threat. "Unless something is done in the near future," a resident of the shoreline town of Madison fumed, "every foot of shorefront property will be gobbled up and there will be no more chance for the residents of a Shore Line town to go bathing than there is for those who dwell in inland communities—and that will be an outrage."[16] To protect what they had, shoreline residents worked to severely limit the accessibility of public beaches to the general public. In 1930, Westport passed an ordinance that restricted parking privileges along the beach to residents only. The following year, it enacted an outright ban on nonresident use of town beaches on Saturdays, Sundays, and holidays.[17] Three years later, Darien adopted an ordinance limiting parking privileges at the town's beach to residents only. The ordinance, as its author explained, aimed to "effectively keep out all but residents and taxpayers of the town."[18] In 1944 Greenwich purchased 147 acres on Greenwich (or Tod's) Point for the purpose of creating a public beach. The Lucas Point Association, owner of a narrow piece of land (known as a driftway) that led to the point and that provided the only point of access from the mainland, acceded to Greenwich's plans to build a road to the point on the "[condition] . . . [that the town] limit the use of the area to Greenwich residents."[19] At a subsequent town meeting, Greenwich's board of selectmen passed an ordinance specifying that only "residents, taxpayers, lessees and their bona fide guests of the [t]own" were permitted use of the new beach.[20] In effect, Greenwich crafted it own, narrower definition of "the public," one that included municipal residents only. Two years later, in a separate case involving a dispute over beach access restrictions, the state supreme court declared that while a town park is "primarily for the benefit of the inhabitants of the municipality . . . it is also for the use of the general public."[21] Despite the decision, Greenwich continued to bar nonresidents from its beaches on the basis that the special act passed by the state assembly in 1919 authorizing the town to maintain parks and beaches "for the use of the inhabitants of said town" meant that these spaces could be made available only to town residents. Nearly fifty years would pass before someone challenged the town's legal rationale for maintaining public beaches for residents only in court.[22]

It was not the number of visitors that local residents of shoreline towns wanted to limit but rather the type. The earliest attempt by the residents of Madison to limit public access to the town's beach, for instance, came in response to complaints about its use by the summer vacationing families' "colored help," who, local white residents charged, "congregate in large numbers, at times becoming boisterous to the annoyance of nearby cottage residents."[23] All along the Northeast corridor, seaside towns enacted policies or stealthily adopted practices aimed at limiting the ability of "undesirables" to access public beaches and segregating shorelines by class and race.[24] In the town of Long Branch, New Jersey, officials instituted a policy requiring beachgoers to first purchase a ticket that allowed them to access one of the town's four beaches. Which beach they could enjoy was at the seller's discretion. Without exception, African Americans received tickets for Beach 3 only. In Asbury Park, New Jersey, beach attendants permitted blacks to use only one heavily polluted section of the beach, where, one writer complained, they were "herded together like cattle" and forced to bathe "where the sewer is dumped into the ocean."[25] In most cases, segregation was enforced informally, through hostile treatment and black beachgoers' desire to avoid an unpleasant experience. In Branford, Connecticut, the town's small black population learned by word of mouth to avoid the public beach. As one unnamed black resident explained, "I heard they did everything possible to discourage Negroes from using it, and I see no sense in looking for trouble."[26]

When African Americans did successfully challenge discriminatory beach access ordinances and practices, municipalities responded by privatizing public space. In the late 1930s, NAACP attorneys Randal Tolliver and Leon Scott successfully sued Westchester County, New York, over its Jim Crow public beach policies. In the years that followed, the county steadily divested itself of places of public recreation. By 1960, six formerly public beaches had become private clubs. Along the city of New Rochelle's nine miles of waterfront, there were only two public beaches. City officials worked to keep it that way, actively thwarting efforts to convert undeveloped waterfront property into public beach space and instead rezoning it for private development.[27]

By 1938 over 82 percent of all recreational land in the central and southwestern portions of Connecticut was privately owned. What little remained open to the general public was not only "insufficient for the demand," but also comparatively unappealing. The only state beach along the western half of the Connecticut coast at Sherwood Island State Park—which, incidentally, local residents fought tooth and nail to prevent from being created in the 1930s—consisted "entirely of cobbles" and coarse, rocky sand and, as a result, "receive[d] a very small attendance."[28]

If good fences did not make private homeowners good neighbors, they ensured that the homeowners would enjoy good beaches. And for them, that's all that mattered. For beach associations, the private beach was sacrosanct, their *raison d'être*. Keeping the public out became one of the primary tasks of beach associations and an abiding obsession of residents and officials alike, inseparable from their desire to protect a community's "character" and enhance property values. Boards of governors, as one report described, "work[ed] feverishly and with splendid dedication to preserve the pristine beauty of their private beaches and to frustrate invasions by those destructive gangs of 'beer-drinking bums'" that members feared could invade their shores at any moment.[29]

Their single-minded focus on privatizing the shore, though, rendered shoreline towns and beachfront homeowners—and the shore itself—more vulnerable to a far more menacing, destructive foe: nature. On September 21, 1938, a Category 3 hurricane slammed the Connecticut shore. The Great New England Hurricane of 1938 (nicknamed "the Long Island Express") claimed the lives of nearly seven hundred people and destroyed over fifty-seven thousand homes, and it remains to this day the most powerful and deadliest storm to have struck New England in its recorded history. On the eve of the storm, an uncoordinated assemblage of jetties, breakwaters, and seawalls extended along the Gold Coast. Further east, in the state's central section, a frenzy of summer home construction had turned hundreds of acres of fragile wetlands into real estate and stripped the shore of its natural defense mechanisms.[30] By disrupting natural processes of erosion and accretion, fences, jetties, groins, and other structures built by homeowners and beach associations slowly destroy the very coastlines they were designed to protect. In its natural state, the sand on any beach is in a constant state of movement, migrating up and down the shore, depending on water currents and the angle at which waves hit the shore. This process is known as littoral drift or longshore transport. Structural barriers that run perpendicular to the shore, such as jetties, attempt to halt this process and capture and hold sand in place. But in so doing, they disrupt and alter the shape of neighboring beaches and the shoreline as a whole. Officials in the Army Corps of Engineers blamed the "deterioration and gradual loss of beaches" on "the nearly continuous development of the entire water front, and the resultant protection of areas previously eroding and furnishing material to the littoral drift supplying neighboring areas."[31]

The massive damage the 1938 storm inflicted on the Connecticut coast offered an important (if unheeded) lesson: measures designed to limit public access to the beach and transform formerly public lands into private real estate were not only antisocial but also environmentally destructive. While surveying the damage the storm had inflicted on the town of Madison, State Parks and Forest commissioner A. M. Turner found summer cottages situated on narrow ribbons of land between the beach and interior wetlands. These areas were "manifestly unsuitable for private development" but, he lamented, "probably will be [developed] again before anything can be done about it."[32] Along the Gold Coast, beach fortifications and obstructions exacerbated the damage to the ecology of the coast's beaches and tidal marshes by limiting their capacity to naturally migrate. Places such as Pine Creek Point in the town of Fairfield exemplified the reckless development that had taken place over the first half of the twentieth century. On this narrow sand spit, which in its natural state was subject to rapid and extreme changes in shape, sat a cluster of cottages. No sooner had a single-lane road been laid and the cottages sold than nature began to fight back. Erosion quickly gobbled up the sandy beach and threatened the structural integrity of the buildings. "Underground gas and water mains serving the area have already been exposed and destroyed," an official in the Army Corps of Engineers reported in 1949. "The area is extremely unstable and should never have been developed as a residential area." Instead, he recommended the area be abandoned and "allow nature to take its course."[33]

In Connecticut, as elsewhere, wealthy beachfront homeowners and exclusive shoreline towns had little patience for such pesky facts of nature, no more so than in the aftermath of a "natural" disaster. In the 1938 storm's aftermath, shoreline homeowners and municipalities, which had for the past decade resisted attempts by the state and federal government to devote public funds to the improvement and expansion of public recreational facilities along the shore, begged for state and federal assistance. Over a chorus of protests from taxpayers' leagues and people from across the state, who argued that coastal communities and individual homeowners should bear all the costs of post-hurricane recovery and who were quick to point out the hypocrisy of wealthy homeowners "reaching for . . . aid with one hand and voting agin it with the other," the state agreed to pay 50 percent of the cost of rebuilding seawalls, jetties, and breakwaters damaged or destroyed as a result of the hurricane.[34] Beach associations' stance on the legal status of a beach tended to reflect the physical condition of the beach. When a beach appeared stable and shoreline property secure, the lines separating public and private property, and private rights and the public interest, were clear and irrevocable. When a storm laid waste to the shore or when erosion ate away at the shore, those lines became blurred, and distinctions between public and private collapsed.

Beach associations could be autonomous, self-sustaining communities merely asking to be left alone one day and vital public assets worthy of support and protection the next, as circumstances demanded. Following Hurricane Carol, which struck the Northeast in late August 1953, for example, shoreline communities clamored for federal aid to combat erosion. Federal law, however, restricted funding for erosion control projects to publicly owned beaches and shores.[35] So long as they remained, in effect, private property owners' associations and not municipalities and insisted on designating their beaches off limits to the public, beach associations remained ineligible. In response, beach association officials lobbied for amendments to federal laws that would allow the federal Beach Erosion Board to participate in erosion control projects at private beaches, calling them "great recreational resource[s]" vital to the "public interest."[36] Norris L. Bull, the head of the Federation of Old Lyme Beaches, went so far as to make the case, in a letter to Senator Prescott Bush, that "*there are no private beaches in Connecticut, literally speaking.*"[37] What's more, he argued, private beaches *do* serve the public—or, at least, that segment of the public that could afford to rent a cottage by the shore. Just as "*publicly-owned* beaches get protective works when recommended by the U.S. Beach Erosion Board and approved by Congress," so too should "so-called 'private' beaches, WHERE THE PUBLIC RENTS ITS SUMMER COTTAGES." "Private beaches make available to the public a substantial portion of [their] recreational facilities at the shore."[38]

Persons not fortunate enough to own or rent a cottage by the shore found these arguments preposterous. When Connecticut governor Abraham Ribicoff held a conference in the town of Clinton in the spring of 1955 to discuss erosion control, the question of "spending . . . Federal funds on privately owned property," as one observer described it, elicited "the biggest grumble" from attendees.[39] "My personal experience [trying to find a place to fish along the state's shore] has been very discouraging indeed," Hartford resident Orlando Lorenzetti told Ribicoff in a letter expressing his opposition to proposed changes to state laws that would allow for greater funding for erosion control at private beaches. "What difference would it make to me, and many other hundreds of thousands, who neither own property, nor are able to get to probably 70% (just a guess) of our shore line beaches because of private property signs."[40]

In Hartford and Washington, policymakers struggled to reconcile the public's reluctance to fund shorelines they were barred from enjoying with the outsized influence of beachfront property owners and members of beach associations, who were, by and large, wealthy, well connected, and organized. Between 1949 and 1955 the estimated total annual income derived from shoreline activities in the state—which included home construction, cottage rentals, resort businesses, beach clubs, and local merchants—doubled, from $25 to $50 million.[41] This growth fit a nationwide trend that saw coastal populations and seasonal economies explode in the post–World War II years. As they did, lawmakers increasingly bought into the argument that protecting this highly valuable, and uniquely vulnerable, property did serve the public's interest. In 1956 Congress passed Public Law 826, which authorized the use of federal dollars and the participation of federal agencies in erosion control projects aimed at protecting private property when such protection was deemed to serve the public's interest.[42] Following the law's passage, beach associations in Connecticut clamored for funding and assurance that the funding would come with no strings attached. Writing to Ribicoff a year later, representatives for the Laurel Beach Association in Milford inquired about the availability of financial aid to control

severe erosion of its shoreline, "bearing in mind that, to us, it is manda-
tory that we retain our rights and privileges as a private beach."[43] With
the funding stream's dam removed, the line separating the public from
the private was restored and the sand curtains rehung.

But as the numbers and political influence of beach associations
grew, so too did tensions with residents of shoreline towns. The so-called
"bums" that private beaches fought to exclude, critics noted, were often
residents of the towns that paid the salaries of the constables that beach
associations demanded be stationed on their beaches during the summer
months. Even among their fellow members, beach association officials
were sometimes described as petty tyrants and derided as "Friday Night
Mayors."[44] Local year-round residents resented the "have-it-both-ways"
attitude of beach association officials and summer residents, who demanded that towns provide the same level of public services available to

As private beach associations proliferated, "Private beach, no
trespassing" signs became a familiar sight along the Connecticut
shore. *Photo © Bob Adelman. Courtesy Bob Adelman.*

other homeowners while at the same time claiming the right to exclude
the general public from using the roads and beaches public tax dollars
helped to provide. Beach associations, in turn, bristled at paying local
property taxes that went to support services few if any of their members
used, such as public schools. Complaints by summer homeowners of
unfair assessments by local officials became common. Some beach associations succeeded in getting the state assembly to amend their charters
so that they could self-assess the value of their real estate, a move that in
turn led town officials to charge beach associations with a form of tax
evasion via fraudulent and deliberate underassessment. Other beach associations locked horns with town officials over tax exemptions. In 1961
the state supreme court rejected a lawsuit filed by the Laurel Beach Association against the town of Milford seeking to have its beaches, docks,
and recreational lands declared exempt from taxation on the grounds
that they were "used for a public purpose."[45]

As local municipalities clamped down on beach access and as efforts by
the General Assembly to acquire and expand state beaches languished,
the private development of the state's shoreline proceeded at a rapid
clip. By the late 1960s the state was home to 54 beach associations and
an estimated 184 private clubs and residential nonstock corporations
situated along the shore. By 1965, Connecticut had lost over half of the
26,500 acres of coastal wetlands in the state at the turn of the twentieth
century to development. Twenty-nine percent of those losses occurred
between 1958 and 1967 alone. Writing in 1961, Connecticut governor
John Dempsey warned, "The time is not far off when the last remaining open area on Connecticut's shoreline is usurped for some private
purpose." During these same years, publicly accessible sections of the
state's shoreline disappeared. By the late 1960s all but 7 of Connecticut's
253 miles of coast (and 72 miles of beach) were in private hands or effectively limited to residents of coastal towns.[46]
    During these decades, a host of new federal and state programs di-
rected money toward the acquisition, development, and improvement
of beaches, parks, and playgrounds across the country. In 1958, Congress
established the Outdoor Recreation Resources Review Commission
(ORRC), which was charged with compiling an inventory of areas in

need of recreational resources in America.[47] The 1961 Federal Housing Act established the Open Space Land Program, which provided financial help to communities to acquire and develop parks. In 1962, President John F. Kennedy established the Bureau of Outdoor Recreation, a division of the Interior Department, charged with assessing the nation's recreation needs and coordinating with states and municipalities on the acquisition and development of recreational lands. In 1965, Congress passed the Land and Water Conservation Fund Act, which provided grants to states and local governments to plan, acquire, and develop recreational projects. All of these programs focused on conserving open space in rural and suburban America.[48]

The brief period of robust federal government support for outdoor recreation and leisure bypassed inner-city neighborhoods and effectively excluded black people. Between 1962 and 1970, only 6 percent of all federal expenditures on outdoor recreation and open space acquisition (or $17.7 million) were devoted to low-income neighborhoods.[49] In spending on water-based recreation, state governments disproportionately focused on developing areas and providing facilities (such as boating marinas) that bore few rewards for, and had little relevance to, urban black communities. City governments invariably channeled funds toward beautification projects in wealthier urban neighborhoods to stem the tide of white migration to the suburbs.[50] In other instances, urban neglect was built into the funding structure of federal programs. The Land and Water Conservation Fund, for example, distributed 40 percent of its funds in equal amounts to each state; of the remaining 60 percent, no state could receive more than 7 percent of the total annual appropriation. As a result, states such as Wyoming received $6.44 per citizen while New Jersey and New York received $1.00 and $1.26 per citizen respectively. The federal formula for distributing funds within a given state also conspired against urban centers, requiring funds to be distributed equally among counties irrespective of population.[51] As cities' tax bases shrunk, fewer of them could even afford to meet the 50 percent matching fund requirement.[52] "It is . . . no accident," one government report on urban recreation commented, "that most Americans perceive the better life to be the exclusive offering of suburban municipalities."[53]

Federal housing policies, local ordinances, and real estate industry practices ensured that the "better life" to be had in the suburbs would be unavailable to people of color, except in a service capacity. Throughout the 1940s and 1950s, most of Greenwich's small African American population worked as domestic servants and lived in servants' quarters on white-owned estates. Black families seeking to become Gold Coast homeowners (as opposed to working in white families' homes) encountered a host of formal and informal barriers. Realtors adhered to "gentleman's agreements" not to sell homes to racial or religious minorities, a practice dramatized in the eponymously titled 1947 film. Set in Darien, Connecticut, *Gentleman's Agreement* depicted the struggle of a white journalist posing as Jewish in finding a home in the town's "restrictive" neighborhoods.[54] In the decades that followed, anti-Semitism in Gold Coast housing markets decreased considerably. A 1964 study of Greenwich's housing market by the Anti-Defamation League of B'nai B'rith reported that "Jewish couples were treated as cordially and helpfully as . . . white non-Jewish couples" and "were shown substantially the same homes in the same neighborhood[s]."[55]

African Americans, on the other hand, continued to suffer rampant discrimination in Fairfield County real estate markets. Realtors refused to show homes to black couples, regardless of income or status. In 1953, Brooklyn Dodgers star Jackie Robinson and his wife, Rachel, were thwarted in their attempt to purchase land to build a home in New Canaan and were shunned by realtors in Greenwich. Only after area newspapers began reporting on the case of the man who had broken the color barrier in baseball but who couldn't break into Fairfield County's housing market were the Robinsons able to purchase a home in the less exclusive town of Stamford. Still, by the mid-1960s, Fairfield County's black population remained miniscule and mostly confined to isolated residential areas near downtown business districts.[56]

As a means of restricting access, preserving neighborhood exclusivity, and limiting negative publicity, Gold Coast towns discovered that large-lot zoning proved far more effective. After the U.S. Supreme Court authorized municipal zoning in its 1926 decision on *Euclid v. Amber Realty Co.,* wealthier towns across metropolitan America established minimum lot size requirements and placed restrictions and outright prohibitions on multi-family units. In suburban Boston, historian Lily Geismer found, "wealthier towns during the interwar period ... adopt[ed] rigid zoning and municipal planning laws to preserve both their physical characteristics and economic exclusivity."[57] For established towns seeking to ensure a high-income populace and preserve some of their rural characteristics in the midst of rampant suburbanization, minimum lot sizes held a special appeal. "By the simple design of large lot zoning," a pair of real estate economists wrote in 1961, "suburbanites believe that a municipality can achieve its developmental goals in a single stroke. The community will be beautiful, its taxes will be low, and 'undesirables' will be kept out."[58] Often, it was the imminent threat of "undesirables" that compelled towns to take action. Mount Laurel, New Jersey, the township at the center of a pivotal case challenging the constitutionality of exclusionary zoning in the 1970s, enacted its first zoning law in 1952 in direct response to a proposed labor camp for migrant workers.[59] As the New York metropolitan region continued to expand outward in the years following World War II, cities and towns in Fairfield County enacted ordinances limiting lot sizes to no less than two acres and, in many neighborhoods, four acres. Other exclusionary measures included minimum floor space requirements on new housing construction, bans on multi-family dwellings, caps on the percentage of rental units in a town's total housing stock, and requirements that multi-unit developments include such luxuries as tennis courts and swimming pools, a regulation that one critic likened to requiring a hungry person "to put caviar on their bread or have no bread at all."[60]

Exclusionary zoning ordinances proliferated after the U.S. Supreme Court declared one of the chief legal instruments of residential segregation—racial covenants—unenforceable in its 1948 decision, *Shelley v. Kraemer*. During the 1950s, the average lot size in the suburban counties of the New York City metropolitan area (which included Fairfield County) doubled. Between 1960 and 1967, over 150 municipalities in New Jersey amended local zoning ordinances to increase minimum lot sizes. In Connecticut, the absence of a state income tax, a feature that attracted so many high-income earners to Fairfield County from New York City, also exacerbated the exclusionary impulses of its municipalities. With state government generating little in revenue, local governments relied heavily on property taxes. This, in turn, led cities and towns to practice various forms of "fiscal zoning" designed to protect and enhance property values (and tax revenues) while limiting expenditures on local services, in particular public schools. By 1970, nearly one-third of Greenwich's 30,700 acres zoned for residential use required lot sizes of four or more acres. Eighty percent of New Canaan's housing market was zoned for two- or four-acre minimum lots. State-wide, more than one-half of all land zoned for residential use during the 1960s had minimum lot requirements of 1–2 acres. In the south-western portion of the state, over three-fourths of land was zoned for one acre or more.[61] Exclusionary zoning was most pronounced along the state's shoreline. A study by the fair housing advocacy organization Suburban Action Institute classified the zoning ordinances of every city and town along the state's shoreline, with the exception of Fairfield and Stamford and the port cities of New London and Bridgeport, as moderately or severely restrictive.[62]

Exclusionary zoning ordinances effectively priced moderate- and low-income homebuyers out of certain neighborhoods and, in some cases, entire municipalities. In the process, exclusionary zoning created communities free of poor people and people of color (except in a service capacity) and blind to poverty. In New Canaan, one report noted, "Housewives can be seen daily picking up or dropping off their black domestics at the railroad station."[63] The children of affluent white couples struggled to grasp what it meant to be poor. A high school teacher in New Canaan told of a student who once tried to write a story "about a family that was very, very poor." The family was so poor, the student wrote, "the father couldn't afford a car and he had to take a taxi to work everyday."[64] Along with federal housing policies and private industry practices, local zoning ordinances kept the state's black and Spanish-speaking populations concentrated in urban areas and helped make Connecticut one of the most racially and economically segregated states in the nation by the early 1970s.[65]

In addition to rendering the poor and people of color invisible, the use of zoning powers as an exclusionary device allowed its practitioners to plead color-blind innocence whenever charges of racism arose. In 1955, the all-black congregation of Harlem's St. Thomas Episcopal

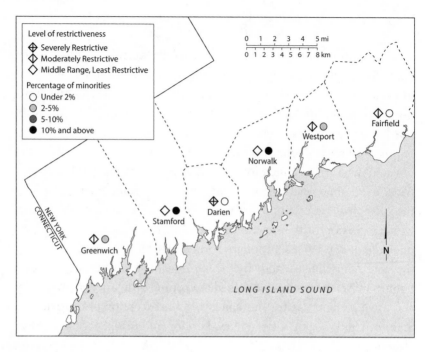

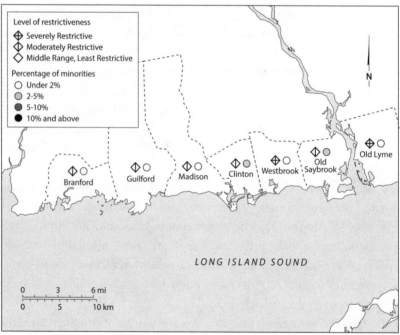

Findings of 1978 study by the Suburban Action Institute on the relationship
between zoning restrictions and racial diversity in the towns along
Connecticut's Gold Coast (figure 7) and central region (figure 8).

Church used a "straw buyer"—a person who purchases (often in secret) property on behalf of someone else—to purchase a twenty-one-
room estate in Darien that it intended to use as a summer day camp for
inner-city children. Shortly after learning of the property's purchase,
the town's board of selectmen passed an amendment specifying that
land uses must "be in harmony with the appropriate and orderly development of the district in which [the land is] located."[66] The town's
planning and zoning commission subsequently deemed the proposed
day camp inharmonious. In what became a ritual reenacted by zoning
commissioners across postwar suburban America, the town's chairman
of the planning and zoning commission professed, "These amendments
have nothing to do with race, religion, color or creed. They are designed
to protect our homeowners whoever they may be."[67]

Private beach associations and other communities governed by
property owners' associations could afford to be less circumspect in
maintaining racial exclusivity. In 1955, William Philpot, an African
American minister from New Haven, purchased a summer cottage on
Andover Lake. But for the next twelve years he and his family were unable to enjoy the lake that fronted their home; it was reserved for members of the Andover Lake Property Owners' Association only. Philpot
applied for membership four times and each time was rejected. Following his fourth unsuccessful application, the property owners' association passed a bylaw requiring people turned down for membership
to wait five years before reapplying. Officials in the state's civil rights
agency denounced the action as clearly racist in motive but claimed
the agency was powerless to do anything about it. The state's attorney
general, Robert Killian, rejected calls from the NAACP to revoke the
organization's charter, claiming to lack the authority. Only after the state
superior court ruled in 1967 that Philpot had acquired an implied easement upon his purchase of the cottage could he and his family legally
access the lake.[68]

"No one can get elected [in Connecticut] unless he swears on the
Bible, under the tree at midnight, and with a blood oath to uphold
zoning," one Greenwich homeowner sarcastically remarked.[69] He was
only slightly exaggerating. In 1967, Hartford-area representative Norris

O'Neill introduced a bill in the state's General Assembly that would have prevented towns from requiring lot sizes of greater than one acre. Gold Coast towns erupted in outrage. This bill, which was pushed by the "homeowners–civil rights" lobby, strikes "a blow against free enterprise and capitalism," Georgiana Weldon of Bridgeport wrote to Governor John Dempsey.[70] It will "eventually destroy local governments, which [have] been a source of strength in Connecticut and New England since the revolutionary days," Harold A. Huckins Jr. of New Canaan predicted.[71] Not to be outdone, Marie Lloyd of Westport wrote that it "eventually will lead to dictatorship."[72] Of the hundreds of angry letters that poured into the governor's office and found their way onto the opinion pages of local newspapers, many disavowed racism and took pains to differentiate class-based from race-based exclusion. Opposition to the bill, one resident of the opulent Round Hill section of Greenwich argued, "has nothing to do with racial or religious factors. It's just economics." He continued, "It's like going into Tiffany and demanding a ring for $12.50. Tiffany doesn't have rings for $12.50. Well, Greenwich is like Tiffany."[73] No matter the motive, the strength of the opposition was intense. In Weston, an overflow crowd jammed into the town's junior high school, where residents unanimously passed a resolution expressing their opposition to any changes to the local zoning powers. As one resident put it, "Our children's education, our property values, the quiet and tranquility of our surroundings, indeed, the very atmosphere we breathe are all at stake."[74] The bill went nowhere. As did another bill proposed in 1970 (modeled on Massachusetts's 1969 Anti-Snob Zoning Act) that would have allowed developers whose projects were rejected by local zoning boards the right to appeal to the state's Department of Community Affairs.[75]

Opponents of statewide restrictions on exclusionary zoning often referred to the state's celebrated tradition of local democratic rule. Local control and municipal autonomy had long been hallmarks of politics and governance in Connecticut. Among the state's 169 towns and cities, regional coordination was rare and regional administrative bodies virtually nonexistent. In 1957, the state moved toward greater political autonomy for local governments with the passage of the Home Rule

Act. Three years later, in 1960, the state abolished its county government system. Such trends would only accelerate in the years ahead, when, as the historian Thomas J. Sugrue notes, "a shift in political culture led to an even greater reassertion of local control."[76]

It was no coincidence that white homeowners and affluent municipalities embraced political localism at the very moment when the powers of the federal government and judiciary were being used to dismantle the legal, political, and economic foundations of Jim Crow–style segregation. Indeed, what the political scientist Margaret Weir labeled "defensive localism" was just that: defensive.[77] It was deployed by localities in response to immediate threats (real or imagined) to property and power from outside.

Those seeking to desegregate the suburbs, in turn, continued to search for undefended fronts that could be used to challenge broader exclusionary practices. In 1966, a group of New Haven residents believed they had found one: the beach. That year an interracial group of women led by Sarah Cogen, the wife of the general counsel of the city's redevelopment authority, tested the legality of the exclusionary ordinances used by shoreline towns in Connecticut to bar outsiders. After being denied access to town beaches in East Haven, Branford, and Madison, Cogen, along with Ruth Holle and Barbara Louis, filed a lawsuit in state court. More than securing the right to the beach, the women hoped to use the case to challenge a host of other, ostensibly race-neutral, mechanisms of exclusion, including those used by local school systems. Writing to ACLU attorney Spencer Coxe, Yale law professor and adviser to the litigants Clyde Summers commented, "It has been our thought in proceeding with this litigation that it might provide an opening wedge to more broad principles. We conceive of it as the easiest case in what may be a series of cases which will proceed to test . . . certain exclusionary arrangements or de facto local preference principles of public schools."[78]

The group soon learned, however, that challenging the constitutionality of beach access restrictions was anything but easy. Indeed, shoreline towns had acquired and developed their public beaches with the possible threat of future litigation in mind. All three towns named in the suit had, over the years, deliberately avoided taking any state and federal funds for their beaches, acceptance of which would have made them vulnerable to a lawsuit from members of the general public whose tax dollars had helped to pay for the facility. So when the group of women from New Haven filed suit in 1966, town officials and local residents quickly fired back. "The town bought it [the beach] and the residents paid for it," East Haven selectman Dominick Ferrera told a reporter.[79] The claim was not entirely accurate—every coastal town had been the beneficiary of civil engineering projects paid for through federal dollars—but the narrative of self-reliant towns under attack from litigious outsiders stuck. "This misguided threesome," Old Saybrook resident Henry P. Bakewell Jr. wrote, "will not earn themselves any plaudits from respectable citizens by operating under the all too common contemporary philosophy that 'what's mine is mine and what's yours is mine.'"[80] Branford resident Regina Beauton was more blunt: "If you don't pay, you don't get in. So, until you pay taxes in our town, stay away and leave us alone."[81] So unpopular was the women's stance among people on the shore that candidates in that summer's primaries competed to come up with the most extreme position against public beaches, with one candidate calling on the state legislature to pass a bill allowing all towns in the state to restrict use of recreational facilities to residents only.[82]

After filing suit, the women struggled to assemble a legal team. ACLU legal director Melvin L. Wulf believed the case had merit: "Restricted suburban beaches no doubt discriminate de facto against Negroes." And he believed that a successful outcome could have larger ramifications. "The way into suburban schools," he remarked to ACLU's general counsel Osmond Fraenkel, "is through the Long Island Sound." But Fraenkel disagreed. Beach access, he told Wulf, was a "legislative problem" and a minor issue at that. "Why can't New Haven do something about acquiring a beach for its own residents[?]"[83] Fraenkel himself—as well as Wulf and fellow counsel Edward J. Ennis—resided in Westport, which discriminated against nonresidents. "So we all may have some kind of conflict of interest," Wulf sighed.[84] The ACLU declined to join the case. When New Haven Superior Court judge Joseph

Klau tossed out the first suit, against Madison, in 1969, the women did not appeal and quietly dropped their other suits against Branford and East Haven.

At the dawn of the 1970s, the legal foundations of the state's sand curtain appeared structurally sound, fortified by decades of careful planning and constant vigilance. From the beach, the people and problems of the city continued to cast only a faint echo across the water.

T W O

What Am I Doing Here?

E dward T. "Ned" Coll was born in 1941, the youngest of Daniel
and Claire Coll's five children and their only son. He grew up
in a middle-class Irish Catholic neighborhood on Hartford's
South End. His father was a first-generation Irish immigrant
and first cousin of Eamon de Valera, who led Ireland's War for Independence and would later serve as the nation's prime minister and third
president. Daniel served in World War I, where he received a Purple
Heart after suffering exposure to mustard gas. Blinded for months and
physically and emotionally scarred for life, Daniel became, in the years
following the war, a vocal advocate for disabled veterans and perennial
Republican candidate for local office. An energetic speaker and prodi-
gious writer of poetic verse, Daniel Coll became noted for giving fiery
speeches championing the interests of veterans and, later, offering bitter
denunciations of the New Deal, as well as penning dozens of poems on
issues of the day.

When he was in fifth grade, Ned suffered a seizure while playing
with a group of children in his family's home in Hartford and was subsequently diagnosed with petit mal epilepsy. Doctors began experiment-
ing with various medications while advising his parents to keep Ned
from engaging in strenuous activity and avoiding stressful situations.
His mother was panic stricken and, throughout his childhood, lived in

a constant state of fear over her son's health. Ned "grew up quickly." Perhaps due to his mother's treatment of his illness and her demeanor, Ned
never showed much "interest . . . in lots of kids' things," his sister Joyce
remembers. "He was serious, too serious sometimes."[1] Following doctors' advice, Ned's mother made it her mission to ensure her son would
enjoy a life of middle-class comfort in a low-stress and well-compen-
sated profession—like insurance, the city's main white-collar industry.
"Her dream," as Ned put it years later, "was that Junior goes to college,
gets out with honors and gets a job with an insurance company."[2]

All, it seemed, was going according to plan. In 1958 Ned graduated from high school and that fall enrolled in Fairfield University, a
small, all-male Jesuit school. At the time Ned matriculated, it had been
in existence for only seven years. Ned immersed himself in campus life.
He founded the university's press club; was a charter member of the
school's Cardinal Key Society; helped launch a club for undergraduates
from the Hartford area; and served as chairman of the school's speakers'
bureau, the literary editor of the school yearbook, and class historian.
During his senior year, Ned was inducted into the school's Honor Society and received an award for outstanding service to the university from
the Student Council.[3]

The year before Ned arrived on campus, a young professor named
Walter Petry joined Fairfield's faculty. Born in the West Indies and raised
in Harlem, Petry was the nephew of the author and Connecticut native Ann Petry. At the time of his arrival at Fairfield and for years to
come, he was the only minority faculty member on campus. Hired
to teach the history of Western civilization, Petry nevertheless found
ways to incorporate diverse voices into the school's otherwise orthodox
curriculum—and expose his students to different people and perspectives. Petry began leading groups of students on day trips to New York
City. "We would take the train down to 125th Street and we'd just walk
through various parts of Harlem," Petry remembers. The goal, as he
put it, was to simply expose his white, middle-class suburban students
to "the reality of urban life and [of] blacks." It was not uncommon for
the groups of students to be on the receiving end of verbal harangues
from street corner speakers. Early in his college career, Ned accompanied Petry on one such trip. He had never been to Harlem before—or

EDWARD T COLL, B.S.S.
English
38 White Street
Hartford, Connecticut

Second Honors 3; Cardinal Key Society 2,3,4, Editor of The Key 3,4; MANOR 4, Literary Editor 4; Sodality 2,3,4, Chairman of Speakers' Bureau 3,4; Student Council 2; Sophomore Raffle Chairman; Public Affairs Club 4; Stag 1,2,3,4; Democratic Club 3,4; Kennedy for President Club 3; Freshman Orientation Comm. 3, Stag Night Chairman 3; Junior Weekend Comm. 3; St. Ives Guild 4; Winter Carnival Comm. 4, Publicity Chairman 4; K. of C. Ignatian Council 4; Intramurals 1,2,3, 4, Capt. 1,2; Hartford Area Club 1,2,3,4, Corresponding Secretary 2, Recording Secretary 4, Scholarship Chairman 4.

Ned Coll's 1962 senior yearbook photo at Fairfield University. *Courtesy Fairfield University Archives and Special Collections.*

any predominantly black neighborhood, for that matter. He took him to places like the National Memorial African Bookstore, the revered black nationalist institution owned and operated by Lewis Michaux. On one occasion, Petry remembers, "A black guy came up to Ned [in the bookstore]—it was always three or four students [in a group]—and said 'something stinks around here.' And he was looking at Ned, the white guy." Ned "understood what that meant," and he didn't take offense. Almost by instinct, he took the message to heart "that there was a race problem [in America] and he was a part of that problem. He, Ned, the white man."[4]

Ned would later credit Petry with having "opened my eyes to the realities of black life in America" and for having inspired him to become an activist.[5] For his part, Petry sensed there was something unique about the feisty young Irish American student who seemed to hang around after class to talk—hang on his every word, in fact—and dutifully follow him on trips to Harlem. "Ned was different" from other politically engaged students. "He was not interested in ideology, he was not interested in politics. He . . . simply . . . wanted to engage directly in solving problems."[6]

In the spring of 1962, Ned graduated from Fairfield with honors in English. He returned home and, just as his mother expected, began his climb up the corporate ladder. He took a job as a public relations manager for Phoenix Insurance. The job seemed to play to his strengths: his people skills, his talents as a public speaker, his sharp wit and gift for the clever turn of phrase. And it provided all that he could—or was supposed to—hope for. "I was making money. . . . It was just what my Irish mother wanted."[7] Claire could already envision her son someday "retir[ing] and liv[ing] down in Palm Beach."[8]

On November 22, 1963, Ned was at his desk in a downtown Hartford office building when he heard the news. John F. Kennedy, the Irish Catholic president whom he had come to idolize, had been assassinated in Dallas, Texas. Throughout the downtown business district, workers trickled out onto the city sidewalks, stunned in disbelief, many in tears. Strangers stopped to console each other. "The city was a sea of white handkerchiefs," Ned remembers.[9] Days later, he would be in Washington, DC, for the funeral, where he met Ireland's president and his second cousin, Eamon de Valera. He stood among the crowds that watched the horse-drawn carriage carry the casket to Arlington Cemetery. As he rode the train back to the Insurance City, he couldn't shake the feeling of a life unfulfilled and of his own responsibility to help keep the spirit of Kennedy's New Frontier alive. When he returned to work, shock and despair still pervaded the office. Ned's changed demeanor was, on this morning, unremarkable. Everyone was still in mourning. But for Ned, it wasn't just the tragedy that had unfolded in Dallas that was eating away at him that day. It was a sense that the comfortable life he had laid out before him suddenly seemed so undesirable, so unfulfilling. "I asked myself, 'what am I doing here?'"[10]

It was the same question Earlie Powell had been asking herself ever since she had first stepped off the train in Hartford a year ago. Born in 1944, Powell had grown up in a shotgun house on a sharecropping plantation outside of the small town of Grant, Alabama. She had entered adolescence as the Civil Rights Movement began to shake the foundations of Jim Crow. Like in other counties across the Deep South, her school district had attempted to head off the threat of integration by hastily improving the quality of "colored" schools. Earlie would be one of the first in her family to attend and graduate from high school. Previously, the schooling of "colored" children had effectively ended at eighth grade. Still, many things remained the same—such as work opportunities for young black girls, which were limited to field labor or work in a white family's home. Earlie chose the latter. While in high school, she worked in the home of an elderly woman who paid her three dollars a week and furnished her with an old dress to wear on the job. Clad in hand-me-downs, Earlie learned to jump at the sound of the bell her employer rang to summon her and sneak in schoolwork during rare moments of rest. She, like so many of those who joined the Great Migration, longed for something better, for the "warmth of other suns."

Sundays at least offered a brief respite from drudgery. "I used to sing in the club from church," Earlie said. It was the highlight of her week. "We went to church and we didn't do nothing else." One Sunday in the spring of 1961, Earlie's final year in high school, a couple of young women from Birmingham came to her church. One approached Earlie after church. "This girl said to me, 'They have an agency where you can go away and you can make money.' And I said, 'How much money?' She said, '$25–$30 a week.' I said, 'What?!?!'" Next, Earlie asked, "Where?" "The North," the girl responded.[11]

"I decided I wanted to get away from the Southern life," Earlie recalls. "I wanted to learn what the people were doing in the North and how they were making it." She completed high school, graduating in

May. In June, she contacted the agency that placed young black girls from the South in the homes of wealthy white families in the North. The agency sent her a bus ticket and an address. Her destination: Hartford, Connecticut, to work in the home of a family named Schweitzer, where she would be paid twenty-five dollars a week, minus the weekly installment payments for her thirty-dollar bus fare, which she owed to the agency.[12]

When she stepped aboard that bus, Earlie also joined the last wave of migrants to flee the rural South. She came to a city populated with generations of black people who had made that same journey over the previous decades. The outbreak of war in Europe in 1914 had set in motion the greatest internal migration in American history. In Connecticut, the Great War was a boon for the state's arms and munitions industry, which grew rapidly and drew much of its labor from the Italian and Polish immigrants who worked in the state's tobacco fields, located in the rural areas north of Hartford. Tobacco growers, in turn, looked south for a new source of cheap labor, sending agents into southern towns to recruit workers. Offering free transportation north and the promise of good wages, labor agents recruited tens of thousands of rural blacks to central Connecticut in the first decades of the twentieth century.[13] Beginning in the 1950s, they began to heavily recruit laborers from Puerto Rico, eventually making Hartford home of one of the largest Puerto Rican populations in the continental United States outside of New York City.[14]

During the first wave of the Great Migration (1910–1920), Hartford's black population increased 140 percent, the largest percentage increase of any northern city's black population during that decade. As black migrants poured into Hartford, a clearly defined black "ghetto" began to take shape on the city's North End. A 1921 survey of residential patterns found that despite the influx of black migrants, the black population in four of the city's wards sharply decreased during those same years as racial prejudice combined with the proliferation of racial covenants forced blacks out of predominantly white and immigrant neighborhoods—and into the waiting arms of slumlords, who profited handsomely from the city's dual housing market. By the 1930s 80 percent of the city's black population lived within a forty-square-block area on the North End. There, new arrivals to the northern city were forced to devote up to 50 percent of their monthly income toward rent on apartments that, in many cases, lacked running water, indoor plumbing, or reliable sources of heating. Those fortunate enough to own properties in this section of the city accumulated fortunes from the meager incomes of black migrant families. Capitalizing on high demand from a captive market, slum owners turned bedrooms into one-room apartments, refitted closets as kitchens, forced multiple families to share a single bathroom, neglected basic maintenance, and ignored tenants' complaints.[15]

No sooner had the city's black population growth slowed during the Great Depression, the United States' mobilization for World War II, and the resultant high demand for workers in the state's defense industries, instigated another wave of black migrants into the city. From the 1920s to the 1960s the population of the North End quadrupled.[16] Between 1941 and 1943 alone, an estimated two thousand black families moved to Hartford. And still the color line held firm, as did the profitability of slum housing. By one estimate, 80 percent of rental properties on the North End annually generated rents in excess of 25 percent of the owners' initial investment; more than one-half returned over 50 percent each year, and one-third returned more than 100 percent. Slum owners spent some of that excess capital buying political influence over the city's Bureau of Code Enforcement, which dismissed the thousands of complaints filed by North End tenants each year.[17]

While the neighborhood's population had quadrupled since the 1920s, the city's sanitation department continued to collect garbage only once a week. Tenants often complained that landlords failed to even provide garbage cans for overcrowded apartments. Garbage piled high in alleys, on front stoops, in backyards, in tenement hallways. On hot summer days, the stench of trash and raw sewage from broken toilets and busted pipes was unbearable.[18] Fresh or putrid, air itself was a precious commodity. North End apartments provided, on average, roughly one-half of the cubic feet of air per resident as required under the state housing code. African Americans infected with tuberculosis, the city's health department found in 1937, were nine times more likely to die from the disease than the rest of the city's population, while black persons infected with syphilis were twenty-three times more likely to succumb to the illness. Many areas deemed suitable for black residence on the North End also tended to be low-lying and flood-prone, such as the notorious neighborhood known as the "Bottoms," where mosquitoes bred and each spring rising waters routinely threatened to inundate homes.[19]

And then there were the rats, which proliferated in such a welcoming environment, taking up residence in the walls and unlit hallways of crumbling tenements, terrorizing residents, and spreading disease. Rats the size of cats scurried across apartment floors, chewed through walls, and crawled across beds and into babies' cribs. They tended to attack babies and small children, their razor-sharp teeth inflicting deep slicing cuts that left victims scarred and disfigured. They transmitted Weil's disease, salmonella, rat-bite fever, and murine typhus. Each year dozens of infants and children were admitted to area hospitals for rat bites, while the city's health department received, on average, over four hundred complaints of rat infestations in tenements. For these accommodations, most tenants on the city's North End paid more, sometimes considerably more, than it would have cost to stay in a room in a downtown hotel.[20]

"The most concrete fact of the ghetto," social scientist Kenneth Clark wrote, "is its physical ugliness—the dirt, the filth, the neglect." Forced to live in a "rat-infested tenement, [a black person's] sense of personal inadequacy and inferiority, aggravated by job discrimination and other forms of humiliation, is reinforced by the physical reality around him."[21] This physical reality, along with its attendant dangers, humiliations, and profiteering, was the result of federal policies. In 1937 the Home Owners' Loan Corporation (HOLC) designated much of the city's North End a "slum area" and awarded it the lowest grade (D) in the agency's new lending classification scheme. The North End was "redlined," effectively ineligible for the federally insured home mortgages from the Federal Housing Administration (FHA) that were fueling growth and opportunity in Hartford's booming suburbs.[22] Banks and federal housing officials didn't just redline neighborhoods. They also redlined people, turning the products of residential segregation and slumlord exploitation—overcrowding, rapid deterioration of housing stock, high rates of illness and disease—into racial traits. Such redlining not only deprived black neighborhoods of access to the credit needed for capital investment. It also further stigmatized ghetto residents and ensured that few of them would be able to escape its confines, in effect validating white homeowners' prejudices and giving white suburbs a financial incentive to resist neighborhood integration.

As the boundaries of Hartford's ghetto hardened, as housing options dwindled and the cost of living escalated, the city's blacks learned to endure. They learned to fend off the rats that scurried across their floors, treat the rashes and other illnesses that routinely afflicted them and their children, cram three to four children into a single bed, and make do without hot water or functioning toilets or reliable heating. They learned how to live as much of their lives outdoors, on the city's streets, which afforded them no less privacy than they could find indoors and more air to breathe and room to move. Hartford had 2,117 acres of park space in forty-six locations throughout the city, which equaled 13.4 acres of open space per 1,000 residents, the most of any city in the nation.[23] All the open spaces were open to the general public, without regard to race. But as the city's black population swelled, informal racial codes enforced by young white men severely restricted the outdoor public spaces that African Americans could use. A black kid could never quite be sure of which parks he or she was permitted to use. Better to remain safe by playing in a trash-filled alley or in the streets of one's own neighborhood than risk being humiliated, assaulted, or worse in a public park. Rather than round up enough money for admission into one of the city's public swimming pools and then risk being turned away at the gate or assaulted once inside, why not cool off and splash around in one of the ornamental fountains downtown until a cop chases you away? Or find a remote spot along the Connecticut or Park Rivers and claim it as your own. Even the gully between Tower and Cleveland Avenues or the unfilled ravine on the corner of Hampton and Montiville Streets after a heavy rain will do. Fun is where you find it.

Of course, playing in the streets was not safe, a fountain was a poor substitute for a pool, and the shifting currents of the city's rivers carried the risk of drowning (all the more threatening given that few children on Hartford's North End had ever received a swimming lesson) and brought bathers into contact with water-borne pathogens. Between 1900 and 1960, the volume of industrial and urban waste put into rivers and streams in the United States increased by 550 percent. "There has been a serious neglect of youth needs," a 1945 report by the Hartford Negro Citizens' Council on the social and economic conditions of Hartford's black population concluded. "Recreational programs for boys and girls are almost non-existent." The solution, according to the North End's most ambitious, far-reaching reformers: level the tenements, put the slumlords out of business, fill in the ditches, sweep the trash-strewn alleys, and start anew.[24]

"Clear the slums!" "The slums must go!" Wipe those miserable "dwellings unfit for human habitation" off the map. These words echoed from the offices of the Hartford Housing Authority, formed in 1938.[25] For black civic leaders and persons stuck in overcrowded slums, the city's plans for urban renewal seemed, in their broad outlines, to offer them a chance to start anew, to finally become truly free, after two long, frustrating, trying decades in the urban North. Clearing the slums promised to free them from the shackles of disease and delinquency; it promised to break the vicious cycle of poverty; it promised deliverance from the predatory slumlord. It promised.[26]

On a sunny autumn afternoon in September 1941, a crowd of over five hundred persons gathered on Hartford's North End for the laying of the cornerstone at the Bellevue Square housing project. State and city dignitaries came. Public housing officials from cities across Connecticut came. The mayor and a state senator delivered addresses. The Reverend William K. Hopes delivered a prayer. The Hartford WPA band performed. As Americans readied for a war they would soon enter in Europe and the Pacific, state senator Alfred M. Bingham reminded the assembled crowd that there was a war going on at home too. And in this war, "a public housing project such as Bellevue Square is as important in its way as a battleship." "Here will be 500 families more with a stake in the democratic way of life, a stake that they lack so long as their country allows their children to grow up in unhealthy back alleys." Here, in the heart of the most depressed area in the city, would rise a new North End and a renewed black populace, free from the scourge of disease, delinquency, and crime. It was, as one of the city's most prominent black attorneys put it, "an occasion of thanksgiving for a new national policy of which [Bellevue Square] is a symbol."[27]

Bellevue Square would come to symbolize a lot of things over the course of its troubled history, but on this occasion, it symbolized progress, tangible evidence that the hopes and dreams of those African Americans who had been recruited to work and live in this city over the previous decades might soon be realized. As the audience listened to Senator Bingham deliver his speech, the enthusiasm of some might have been tempered once they ran the numbers in their heads: an estimated twenty-five hundred persons in five hundred units on twelve and one-half acres. What building materials were they planning to use, exactly? The size and extent of the project's playground and recreational offerings seemed a bit less than advertised. Nevertheless, those in attendance, many of whom expected to be first in line for an apartment after having been displaced from the tenements that had formerly stood there, surely nodded their heads in agreement when Hartford Housing Authority chairman Berkeley Cox predicted, "The neighborhood is going to be better after this project is built. I am sure of that."[28]

From its inception, the Hartford Housing Authority pursued a policy of racial segregation in its public housing assignments. White applicants could choose from several different unit types in Nelton Court, Dutch Point Colony, Stowe Village, and (following its conversion from defense worker to low-income housing in 1947) Charter Oak Terrace.[29] In all of these projects, units were set aside for white applicants and remained empty until filled, meaning that white applicants never had to wait for a unit and had plenty to choose from. Despite far greater demand, African Americans, on the other hand, were subjected to lengthy waits before a unit became available. In the meantime, they were forced to scramble to find the barest of accommodations in a rental market that was rapidly shrinking as the city leveled block after block of dilapidated housing on the North End and landlords and realtors steadfastly held the color line in the city's suburbs.

Hastily built in order to alleviate the overcrowded conditions on the North End and long waiting list of black applicants for public housing units, Bellevue Square would come to embody, in concrete form, the Jim Crow logic of the city's public housing administrators. The housing

authority adorned Bellevue Square with only the barest essentials. It neglected to paint hallways or decorate the grounds. Unlike at the projects
reserved for whites, it failed to provide basic services such as garbage
removal. Instead, tenants had to haul their trash to one of six incinera-
tors located on the project's outskirts. Hot water was in short supply,
available only between the hours of 1 a.m. and 6 a.m., according to one
complaint filed with the city's Board of Inquiry.[30] The housing authority's promises of a robust recreational youth program for tenants failed
to come to fruition. The roughly thirteen hundred youth in Bellevue
Square had to make do with a single cheaply built, sparsely equipped
playground.[31]

In 1949, the Connecticut General Assembly amended the state's
public accommodations law to outlaw discrimination in public housing
projects. At the time of the act's passage, virtually all of the public housing projects in the state were segregated by race. The law empowered
the state's civil rights commission to investigate complaints by public
housing tenants and pursue charges.[32] The city's housing authority subsequently adopted what it called a policy of "planned integration."[33] In
practice, this meant setting a quota for the number of African American families admitted into each housing project, with racial quotas for
black tenants varying from 5 to 30 percent.[34] Like white Southern school
districts' interpretation of "all deliberate speed," "planned integration"
bought housing officials the time they needed to formulate a new set
of instruments for maintaining segregation. For years afterward, the
city's "white" projects were only nominally integrated, housing small
numbers of black families, always clustered together in one corner of a
project, while large numbers of units in white sections were allowed to
remain unoccupied.

Planned integration soon gave way to outright ghettoization. As
white families secured FHA-insured mortgages and moved into new
homes in the suburbs, African Americans quickly moved to occupy
areas formerly reserved for whites. Between 1965 and 1968, the ratio of
non-whites living in Charter Oak Terrace rose from 25 to 42.3 percent.
Stowe Village, which had relaxed its quota in the early 1960s, was by
1968 over 95 percent non-white.[35] The North End's Nelton Court, one-
half white in 1965, was roughly 31 percent white by 1969. Dutch Point

Colony saw its non-white tenant population rise from 26 percent in 1965 to nearly 40 percent in 1969.[36] Nationwide, the number of whites and middle-income persons in public housing fell sharply in the second half of the 1960s. Simultaneously, changes in federal housing policy forced local housing authorities to slash their budgets and resulted in a virtual freeze on new construction or repair and rehabilitation of existing structures.[37]

Hartford's housing projects soon began to resemble the overcrowded tenements from which many of their tenants had only recently fled. Completed in 1954, by 1967 the units at Stowe Village were infested with cockroaches and teeming with rats. Tenants reported to the housing authority of waking to find roaches crawling over "infants in their cribs."[38] The housing authority laid the blame on tenants, who, it claimed, failed to practice good housekeeping. Tenants, in turn, demanded the authority collect garbage more than once a week and use a more potent extermination spray; many suspected that the spray in use was purposely watered down as a cost-saving measure. The project's physical deterioration should not have come as a surprise. From its very inception, Stowe Village and other public housing units had not only been constructed on the cheap, but were also situated in areas of the city that had, for good reason, long been shunned by builders and were wholly incompatible with multi-unit housing. Both Dutch Point Colony and Charter Oak Terrace had been built in low-lying parts of the city that were routinely subject to flooding. In the ten years prior to the construction of Charter Oak Terrace, the land had been inundated with floodwaters on three separate occasions.[39] The site chosen for Stowe Village, meanwhile, was considered a mud hole and had previously been listed on city maps as a "dump." The site's sub-standard soil conditions (which included numerous quicksand pits) delayed construction and sent costs skyrocketing.[40] Even before the first tenants moved in, officials in the housing authority noted the entire site suffered from poor drainage, which resulted in large pools of water forming after moderate rains. After completion, the units' basements routinely flooded; in many, 2–4 inches of gray, slimy standing water became an almost permanent feature. Tenants referred to their basements as the "sewer" and donned gas masks and boots before venturing down with one of the pumps supplied by the housing authority.[41] Such an environment, of course, provided an ideal breeding ground for rats. The city never got around to placing sidewalks along the streets leading to and from Stowe Village, forcing the over one thousand school-age children living there to walk along a busy thoroughfare and cross a dangerous intersection on their way to the neighborhood's elementary school each day.[42]

When she first arrived in Hartford, Earlie Powell wasn't thinking about rats or children or the living conditions of the city's black population. Like many young black girls who had come to Hartford through placement agencies, she had a place to stay—in the servant quarters of a spacious home in West Hartford, far from the dilapidated tenements of the North End, far from the housing projects in which, despite everything, black families still competed for a coveted spot, far from other black people in general. Everything about her new surroundings— and the new family she had come to work for—was different—and unsettling. Gone were the racist epithets that routinely dropped from the mouths of her former employers in Alabama. Gone, too, was the warmth of home. There was a coldness to the way white people interacted in the North that seemed to match the chill in the air. Ned liked to joke that the "best way to scare someone in [Hartford] is to say Hello to them."[43]

Earlie could understand. The Schweitzers were quiet. The husband worked long hours as an attorney. His wife seemed perpetually tense, cold, and mean, her face a permanent scowl. Their college-age sons came home on occasion but acknowledged Earlie's presence only long enough to dump a pile of dirty laundry at her feet. And the food! Gone were the rich, hearty meals—biscuits and gravy, fried chicken, collards—that nourished and sustained her back home. In their place, the Schweitzers offered Earlie poached eggs, toast and juice, bagels and lox. Within two months of her arrival, Earlie had lost twenty pounds; her jawbone began to jut out from her cheek. Earlie feared she was dying. So did the small circle of young black women whom she had gotten to know through the agency and whom she took the bus into the city to meet on Friday nights. They gave her the name of a black doctor who practiced on the North End. But the Schweitzers would not hear of it and insisted on taking Earlie to their family doctor. Something must be wrong with her, Mrs. Schweitzer explained to the physician. "She's lost so much weight . . . [but] she's not doing anything strenuous. The only thing she does is take the dog to the park."[44]

Earlie bit her lip at such an outrageous remark—she did back-breaking labor all day and into the evening. But that was nothing new. It was definitely not the work she performed that had caused her to fall ill. After a quick examination, the doctor concurred. "There is nothing wrong with her. Her resistance is down, she is dehydrated, she is not used to eating [the type of food you are serving her]," he told Mrs. Schweitzer. "She's been eating [one] way all her life, and all of a sudden, she changed over to this. . . . She has to get back to eating foods." After they arrived home from the doctor's office, Mrs. Schweitzer said to Earlie, "I'm going to take you to [the supermarket], and you go in and pick up whatever you want." She drove Earlie to the store, handed her a blank check, then left to run errands. "So I got me some cornmeal, I got some buttermilk, I got some seasoning so I could make some cornbread, and I bought some collard greens, and I bought the meat to cook it with, and I bought some chicken." Mrs. Schweitzer returned to the store. Earlie was waiting outside with a grocery sack under each arm. They drove home. Mrs. Schweitzer let Earlie out and told her she'd be back in a couple of hours. "So that gave me a lot of time" to make a home-cooked meal.[45]

"Oh man, I got some of the finest pots [the Schweitzers] had," Earlie remembers. "Put my meat on, cooked my meat. Made my collard greens, fried my chicken. By the time I got through cooking, sat down and ate, here she comes." Mrs. Schweitzer had returned home. "I was just cleaning up the kitchen, fixing to put all my stuff in the refrigerators." When she walked into the kitchen, Mrs. Schweitzer froze. "What's that smell?" she asked Earlie. "Don't tell me that you cooked pork in my house!" "Excuse me?" Earlie said, confused as to what she had done wrong. "This is a kosher house!" Mrs. Schweitzer screamed. Still dumbfounded, Earlie sputtered, "Well, I didn't know." In truth, Earlie didn't even know what "kosher" meant. "She didn't tell me!" In a fit of rage, Mrs. Schweitzer began tearing down the curtains, rolling up the rugs, and throwing pots, pans, plates, and silverware in the garbage. She warned Earlie not to dare take them out of the trash. When her husband came home, Earlie remembers, "she gave him a fit." Three weeks later he died of a heart attack. Earlie was convinced the stress from the ordeal killed him.[46]

After Mr. Schweitzer's death, "I was so scared to stay there," Earlie said. She enlisted her friends in the city to help her find a new job. She told Mrs. Schweitzer, "I can't stay here any more. I am really afraid of you." Two weeks later, Earlie began work for a new family. "They paid me a little bit extra" and were a little bit nicer. But Earlie couldn't stand to live under another white family's roof much longer. She saved enough money to rent an apartment on the North End. She landed a job working the assembly line at Pratt and Whitney aircraft, met a man, got married, and got pregnant. Earlie's new life in the urban North was just beginning.[47]

It had been months since Kennedy's assassination, and Ned still couldn't shake that empty feeling every morning when he walked through the front entrance of Phoenix Insurance. "Is this it?" he asked himself. He had grown disgusted by the values that middle-class white society, and his mother in particular, attempted to impart on him. He looked around and saw fellow college grads who were "more concerned about getting a nice, security-oriented job where [they could] 'ride the elevator for nothing,' escape into suburbia, have two kids, and let the rest of the world go by."[48] He began walking the streets of Hartford's North End, like he had done on those trips to Harlem in college, observing its conditions and the spirit of its people. He began getting involved in civic organizations. In February 1964, he secured a two-year appointment to the Hartford Human Relations Council. He began writing letters to the editor, like his father had done for years. But instead of railing against New Deal liberalism or women in the workplace, Ned spoke out against the passive prejudices and corrosive indifference toward the black urban poor among New England's white middle class. The stereotype of the North End as a "'hell-hole' made of wild savages, drug addicts, and lazy, hostile people," widely shared by the young white professionals among whom he worked and lived, was a "cancerous myth," he wrote.[49] Rather than fear and avoid the ghetto, he called on young college grads like himself to get to know its people and their daily struggles. If every middle-class white man and woman gave a little bit of time, even just a couple of hours a week, the problems that plagued the inner city could be solved.

Ned, though, was not content to give just a couple of hours of his time. By the fall of 1964, he was determined to devote his life to rekindling the flickering spirit of public service and social activism he had come to believe the slain president had embodied. In November, he abruptly quit his job, withdrew his $1,200 in savings, and ran a classified ad in the city's two daily newspapers: "Volunteers to serve in local-style peace corps type program. All ages. Serve three hours a week. Project dedicated to J.F.K." He called it the Revitalization Corps.[50]

"My mother almost dropped dead when I quit that job," Ned recalls. "She thought I was crazy."[51] Claire Coll was, indeed, convinced that her son had lost his mind and was determined to get him the help he needed. One afternoon while Ned was at his parents' home on Hartford's South End, she summoned the police, who handcuffed Ned and transported him to the Norwich State Hospital's psychiatric ward for evaluation. She called local reporters who had written stories about the local lad who had given up a promising career to help the poor and told them her son was "unstable" and to pay him no mind.[52] She raged against Walter Petry—that "nigger" professor, she called him—who, she was convinced, had poisoned her son's mind. "She blamed me, this nigger, for Ned's change in life," Petry recalls. "She hated me." Petry, along with a colleague, visited Ned at the state hospital. "He was in perfectly good humor and laughing about his crazy mother."[53]

Ned got out after a few weeks and went straight back to work on building his organization and, he hoped, inspiring a movement. He chose a motto: "Let us not merely reflect; let us project."[54] He rented a shabby storefront in a working-class Italian neighborhood on the city's South End, "not far from my [parents'] home."[55] But far from the North End, in what blacks considered hostile territory. "I ran into a lot of reaction in the South End," Ned recalls, "because there was a great resistance toward blacks, particularly among the Italians. A couple of windows [of the storefront] were broken, things like that."[56]

But Ned was not deterred, nor was he all that interested in challenging the city's working-class white ethnics to do more to help others. They were struggling too. The real problem, as Ned saw it, was in the suburbs, where self-identified white liberals seemed content to sit back and watch as lives were destroyed by grinding poverty in the cities they had left behind. These were the people he wanted to reach. The suburbs, Ned believed, made their inhabitants indifferent to the struggles of others, fearful of change, and hostile to new ideas. What suburbanites—and America—needed was a "unified and constructive movement to counteract the national menace of public lethargy and apathy."[57] Ned wanted to build "a bridge between the city and the suburbs; between middle class and poverty."[58] He wanted to find a way "to keep both ends stimulated and awake."[59] To that end, Revitalization Corps aimed to offer a "grass-roots channel for the city dweller and the suburbanite to tackle a dual poverty: basic poverty conditions in Hartford's neglected areas, and the growing cancer of the 'poverty of purpose' that flows from the average middle-class home."[60]

Ned's pitch was simple: you don't need to join the Peace Corps or VISTA to contribute to the betterment of society. Just donate two hours a week. (Later, he upped it to three hours a week.)[61] It was the least that persons "who live in one of the wealthiest sections of our country" could do.[62] In letters to the editor of local newspapers and in speeches before country clubs and suburban church congregations, Ned tried to goad and shame suburbanites into action. Too many of you are "out to take everything from a democracy and contribute nothing."[63] "The suburbanite father who only shops or works in Hartford must realize that he has a social responsibility to our core city."[64] "What will you say when your child someday asks you, "Dad, where were you when Negroes and Puerto Ricans needed help?"[65]

Volunteers began to trickle into Ned's South End storefront. People like Susan Heslam, a schoolteacher in her midtwenties who lived in Enfield, Connecticut. Heslam explained, "I heard Ned talk in a coffeehouse. [Afterward], I went to the office to see him and he took me to a PTA meeting."[66] Heslam began driving twenty-five miles from her home into the city several times a week to volunteer. "At first I had to hustle to find things for [the volunteers] to do," Ned remembers. He put people to work "collecting books for the poor, organizing block dances for teenagers."[67] He began organizing tutoring sessions for children and leading field trips to museums and attractions outside the city.

By the end of Revitalization Corps's first year, Ned had enlisted over five hundred volunteers for his cause.

Ned had also blown through much of his savings. He learned to live on ten dollars a week. When bills needed to be paid, he worked as a substitute teacher in the city schools. But mostly he put his skills as a salesman to work on wrangling donations from civic organizations, businesses, and individuals and obtaining free airtime and coverage from media outlets. Ned "haunted newspaper offices and radio stations, begging [for] space and time."[68] He gave talks to the city's Rotary Club, the Jaycees, and anyone who would listen. He asked priests if they could spare a room for tutoring during the week and school principals if they could loan out a classroom after school. "People would duck when they saw me coming," he joked.[69] He secured a slot hosting a Sunday evening radio program called "Challenge," where for one-half hour each week he spoke of the need "to mobilize adults and students of all ages" to fight apathy.[70] At the time, Charles Towne was an assistant managing editor for the *Hartford Courant*. Initially, he dismissed Revitalization Corps as "just another hare-brained scheme."[71] But Ned won him over, and before long, the city's leading newspaper was devoting ample coverage to the fledgling organization and its various initiatives. The first time Ned approached Dan Lieberman for a donation, the downtown department store owner couldn't get rid of him fast enough. "The last thing Hartford needed was one more bunch of do-gooders, trying to save the world," he thought.[72] But Ned won him over as well. The formerly skeptical businessman began making an annual donation.

Ned had a harder time, initially, establishing ties with Hartford's African American community. First, there was the problem with the location of Revitalization Corps's headquarters. If Ned wanted to make inroads with the city's blacks, he would need to come to them. He did. Ned spent days on end walking the streets of the North End, stopping and talking to strangers at every chance, strolling into barber shops and diners, and attempting to join in whatever conversation was taking place at the time. He'd hang around places like Tom's Gas Station, a black-owned business that doubled as a social space where African American men gathered after work and that had become, by the 1960s, a veritable black community institution; any prominent black political and civil rights figure or celebrity who came to Hartford made a point of dropping in. He began searching for a place on the North End to relocate his fledgling operation, eventually securing a lease on a run-down building on Main Street, in the heart of black Hartford's commercial district. Consisting of a "couple of shabbily furnished rooms," the new headquarters had little to offer aside from space and a strategic location. But the location was exactly what Ned wanted. It brought him closer to the people he was trying to reach, in contrast to administrators of the city's official anti-poverty agency, the Community Renewal Team, whose shiny, nicely furnished headquarters could not have seemed more disconnected from the realities of ghetto life.[73]

"In the beginning," the community organizer Saul Alinsky wrote, "the incoming organizer must establish his identity or, putting it another way, get his license to operate. He must have a reason for being there—a reason acceptable to the people."[74] Initially, few on the North End were prepared to issue Ned his license, and they resented his presence in black social spaces—places where blacks could take a rest from white racism and from dealing with white folks—hostile, solicitous, sympathetic, or otherwise. When Ned strolled into places like Tom's, North End resident Riley Johnson remembers, "A lot of people would run and hide." When he wasn't hanging around, Ned himself became the topic of conversation. At first, "A lot of people didn't understand him. People would ask, 'Who is this white guy coming around here.' . . . People were skeptical." Some speculated that he was an undercover FBI agent. Eventually, though, Ned "knitted himself into the community."[75]

It took time, and it was hard earned. Years before Alinsky penned *Rules for Radicals,* a book that Ned would later credit as a major influence on his organizing strategies, Ned seemed to intuitively grasp its lessons. He "learn[ed] the local legends, anecdotes, values, idioms. He listen[ed] to small talk. He refrain[ed] from rhetoric foreign to the culture." Most fundamentally, Ned did not, as Alinsky later warned, "try to fake it." He was always "himself."[76]

But it was less his demeanor and sincerity and more his actions that earned Ned the trust and support he sought. Just as his college professor had observed years earlier, Ned was solely interested in addressing problems and meeting immediate needs. Such as the problem

of unemployment in a city that was hemorrhaging jobs. In the summer
of 1967, Revitalization Corps launched an eight-week leadership training program for children in grades seven through nine each summer. It
took participants on field trips to corporate headquarters, factories, hospitals, and other major employers in suburban Hartford. It hosted an
annual Career Day for high schoolers. It ran a program that taught office
and clerical skills to teenage girls. When a local typewriter manufacturer
closed its Hartford plant, the Corps launched a program to provide laid-
off workers assistance finding new jobs. It ran a program in the state
penitentiary that aimed to prepare prisoners for life on the outside and
encourage employers to hire ex-convicts. If a slumlord failed to provide
tenants heating oil in the winter, Corps volunteers rounded up sweaters
and blankets and notified authorities. When the Hood Milk Company
stopped delivering to North End residents, the Corps picketed its corporate offices while helping local residents organize a food co-op. When the
holidays rolled around, Corps volunteers got busy rounding up gifts to
distribute to needy children. When residents complained of price gouging by local merchants, Revitalization Corps set up a program to drive
inner-city mothers to grocery stores in the suburbs, where prices were
lower. Ned had no philosophy and followed no playbook. When he saw
a problem, he tried to solve it. After doing what he could, he moved on
to the next problem. It was his most enduring strength—and, for many,
his most endearing quality. Wherever there was a need, he was there.[77]

In the hallways and community spaces of Hartford's housing
projects, word of Revitalization Corps's services spread fast. In the Rice
Heights housing project, a neighbor alerted Earlie Powell to the free
clothes Revitalization Corps distributed to needy families. Powell had
recently moved into public housing with her three young children, including one infant, and was struggling to support her family with the
wages she earned working on the assembly line at Pratt and Whitney.
One afternoon, she casually mentioned to a fellow tenant her struggle to
save enough money to buy some warm clothes for her newborn. "I'll get
everything you need for the baby and more," Powell remembers being
told by the neighbor. "I could get him dressed at least five or six times
a day if I wanted to, that's how much clothes that lady got for me from
Ned Coll."[78] Earlie began sending her older children over to Revitaliza-

tion Corps's headquarters after school for tutoring and other activities. Soon after, she too began to hang around the office, talking with Ned about her struggles, frustrations, and hopes, volunteering on various projects. Ned was drawn to, and drew strength from, Earlie's "humor, personal contact, hope," her smarts, her ability to size people up, to "know who's [full of] shit and who's not" and not hesitate to say so. To him, Earlie personified "absolute true soul."[79]

Through the energy, organizational skills, and networks of women like Earlie Powell, Revitalization Corps found its footing and sense of purpose. As it did, Ned began to look beyond his hometown and toward the place that first kindled his activist spirit—Harlem—as he began the work of creating an organization and a movement national in scope. In the fall of 1966, he took his first steps toward that goal, renting a storefront on Seventh Avenue in Harlem (a block from the National Memorial African Bookstore that Ned had first entered as a student) and opening a second Corps chapter. He simultaneously acquired office space on the Lower East Side, which he used to recruit volunteers to tutor children in Harlem.[80] He entered Harlem in the midst of heated protests over the fate of the block where Michaux's bookstore stood and the adjacent corner, known as African Square, which the state of New York planned to level and replace with a new state office building, sparking months of protests and occupation of the site by groups of black nationalists.[81]

Ned made a point of keeping the door to the Revitalization Corps headquarters in Harlem wide open all day. He needed people to stroll in off the street. He needed people to stop and look at the flyers posted all over the front windows, asking Harlemites to "Join the War on Apathy."[82] He needed to earn the trust of parents so that they would feel comfortable allowing their kids to come there after school. He needed local reporters—here in the media capital of the world—to pay him some notice. He needed to distinguish his organization from all of the federal and local anti-poverty programs operating in the city. And he needed to do so while remaining independent of the red tape and bureaucracy that he had come to see as obstacles to action and an invitation to cronyism and corruption. Revitalization Corps would not be feeding at the trough of the state, would not depend on the government to pay the bills and keep the lights on, and would not join forces with other organizations. To Ned, bureaucracy bred corruption, coalition meant capitulation, and coordination was just another way of saying, "Shut up and do what we say." Revitalization Corps was founded on a feeling, guided by the needs of the moment and governed by instinct and spontaneity, and it would remain so throughout its existence. Its programs and activities evolved in relation to the needs of the communities it served. Every Wednesday evening, it held an open-door meeting at its Harlem office, where local residents spoke of their hopes and desires, challenges and frustrations, to Corps staffers and volunteers. In these meetings, parents like Florence Brown, a mother of six who lived blocks from the Harlem office, spoke of her dealings with rapacious and uncaring landlords who ignored her pleas to deal with rat infestations and peeling lead paint, of the abusive police officers who prowled the neighborhood, of the horrific conditions her incarcerated son was forced to endure at the Attica State Prison. To the idealistic white volunteers who enlisted in the Corps, these meetings became a weekly seminar on what it meant to be black and poor in urban America.[83]

News reporters struggled to explain what, exactly, Revitalization Corps did and what it stood for. But that didn't stop them from reporting on it. Soon after Ned began operations in Harlem, the *New York Times* and the *New Yorker* ran stories on the idealistic young white man who had stopped climbing the corporate ladder and started working in the ghetto. In September 1967 the nationally broadcast *Huntley-Brinkley Report* on NBC profiled Revitalization Corps.[84] The media were fascinated with this private Peace Corps that seemed to be doing so much with so little. "He works 16 hours a day without pay and he looks it," a profile of Ned in *Parade* magazine read.[85]

Ned believed in the power of the media to advance a cause, and the critical role powerful and well-connected white people could play in allowing black voices to be heard. As part of his effort to drum up coverage of his fledgling organization, he assembled an advisory board consisting of prominent Northeastern white liberals, including Arthur Schlesinger Jr., the Pulitzer Prize–winning historian and former special assistant to President Kennedy; former Kennedy speechwriter Ted Sorensen; Robert Lindsay, the brother of New York mayor John Lindsay; and Carter Burden, a New York socialite and legislative assistant to Senator Robert Kennedy.[86] Their support, Ned believed, would lend his organization credibility and strengthen their hand when applying pressure to local officials, landlords, and employers.

Such support also, though, threatened to reinforce white stereotypes about black inferiority and incapacity for self-help. At the turn of the twentieth century, urban Progressive reformers had diagnosed crime, violence, and social deviancy among white immigrant populations as a product of their social environment while deeming these very same conditions among black migrant populations to be racial traits. As the historian Khalil Gibran Muhammad writes, white Progressives judged blacks to be "their own worst enemies," immune to the types of social interventions prescribed for white immigrants.[87] Now, nearly a half-century later, a more racially enlightened white public had come to accept the notion that impoverished, "culturally deviant" blacks could be rehabilitated, but only under the guidance of whites.

But the press's fawning coverage of Revitalization Corps during its early years also spoke to white Americans' growing rejection of President Lyndon B. Johnson's War on Poverty. No sooner had Johnson begun to explain to the American people that "freedom was not enough," that it could not simply "take a person who, for years, has been hobbled by chains and liberate him, bring him to the starting line of a race and then say, 'you are free to compete with all the others,' and still justly believe that you have been completely fair," than an anti-liberal narrative of the New Frontier's demise—the loss of innocence of the early 1960s—at the hands of Johnson's Great Society began to take hold.[88] It went as follows: instead of asking Americans what they could do for their country, Great Society liberalism encouraged people to ask government to do something for them. Instead of a government that served the interests of the people, Great Society programs had given us a government of unaccountable, wasteful, and selfish bureaucrats who were more interested in lining their own pockets and rewarding favored constituents. Great Society liberalism was creating a nation of malcontents. What was needed was a restoration of the civic virtues of volunteerism, of charity rather than bureaucracy, a War on Poverty administered by citizens and private organizations reliant on the support of donors rather than large, impersonal, and permanently funded public institutions. Private, grassroots social welfare groups like Revitalization Corps became a convenient foil for critics of federal anti-poverty programs. One report described Ned as living "hand to mouth," caring only about the poor whose lives he hoped to improve.[89] Another remarked that Revitalization Corps's entire budget for the year 1966 was less than it cost to train one person to work for the inner-city youth anti-poverty program Job Corps.[90] With only thirty-one dollars in its treasury, another profile of the organization noted, the Harlem chapter paid the rent on its storefront "from profits made on the fish fry."[91] Want to make a difference? Don't look to Washington. Just get up and get involved.

Across the country, many did. Ned's ability to attract media attention to his cause and supply reporters with a bevy of sound bites fueled the public's curiosity and interest in Revitalization Corps's charismatic founder and his inchoate mission. By 1966 Ned reported receiving on average six requests per week to open new chapters in other cities. That year, a chapter opened in Miami, Florida, as well as in Bridgeport, Connecticut. Chapters formed on college campuses across the country. By the spring of 1967, there were Corps chapters in operation at Iona College, Brooklyn Community College, Trinity College, the University of Hartford, and Ohio State University. In May 1967 a couple from Los Angeles who had read about Ned flew to Hartford to meet him in person and returned home to launch a new chapter in Watts.[92]

In November 1967, Ned gave his pitch to a group of students crowded into a classroom at Yale University. It's not enough for privileged white college students to "feel sorry for the people in the ghetto," he told the audience. You need to get to know them, on a personal, intimate level. While social scientists and the public take a clinical approach to the problems of urban poverty and social marginalization, he went on, "We've forgotten to build a lab in the streets." Edward Forand and John Meininger sought to do just that. That fall the two Yale undergrads founded a Revitalization Corps chapter on their campus. They wanted to do something to "change the system which turns out bureaucrat upon bureaucrat," Forand said. Soon after forming the chapter, Forand, Meininger, and four fellow classmates spent a weekend living with and getting to know several Harlem families. They spent the night in their homes and tried to become familiar with the conditions and concerns facing their community. On Saturday, the students took a group of children to the Yale-Columbia football game and afterward held a party for the Harlem families back in their neighborhood. The following morning, they brought a group of seventeen children and fifteen adults to New Haven to visit the Yale campus.[93]

Later that fall, Yale students led Revitalization Corps's drive to send material support to Mississippi's besieged and beleaguered rural black population. Another long, cold winter was approaching, and the people of the Mississippi Delta were in desperate need of food and clothes from outsiders, as state and local officials continued their efforts to prevent the allocation of food and basic provisions to the state's poor.[94] Ned dubbed the initiative IGAD (I Give a Damn). At Yale and other college campuses in the Northeast, volunteers gathered hundreds of clothing items and books. Over Thanksgiving break Yale undergrad Bruce Keary drove a truck filled with food and clothing to Tougaloo College in Jackson, Mississippi, where a group of students had founded a Corps chapter that fall, for distribution among families living in the Delta. After Thanksgiving break, the Corps's Yale chapter resumed its collection drive. At Yale, forty-five volunteers got nearly three hundred students to donate several hundred clothing items. Boston College's campus chapter brought in a similar haul. The United Transport Company of Hartford loaned Ned a truck to carry over one ton of supplies down south, on the condition that the Corps not publicize its destination or the nature of its trip beforehand. The company feared that its truck would get firebombed.[95]

That December seven men and women huddled into the truck for the long drive to Mississippi. Ned was behind the wheel. On board were Forand, David Tine (the Boston College chapter director), and four other students. It was an interracial group driving a truck loaded with supplies and bearing a Connecticut license plate. Once they entered Mississippi, the question was when, not if, they would be pulled over by a state trooper. And indeed, an hour into their journey through Mississippi, along a dark, desolate highway, the group was pulled over for no apparent reason. At that moment, the images of Michael Schwerner, James Chaney, and Andrew Goodman—the three students who had been arrested in Neshoba County and subsequently murdered in June 1964—flashed across Ned's mind. Conditions had changed, if ever so slightly, in the years since that atrocity had cast the eyes of the world—and forced the FBI to descend—onto the Magnolia State. Now, the state troopers had been reduced to practicing more subtle modes of intimidation—in this instance, a lecture and presentation of a book describing all of the supposed atrocities committed by Northerners who had come to aid black Mississippians in recent years. After this bizarre exchange, the group was allowed to continue its journey.[96]

At Tougaloo's campus, Corps volunteers were warmly greeted by some and shunned by others. One traveler later described being berated by one of the school's white faculty members, who told the group that it could never grasp the scope of the problems facing black Mississippians in one weekend. The students tried. Each student lived with a family in the Delta for the weekend and witnessed firsthand a level of poverty few could have imagined possible in the richest nation in the world. A family of sixteen crowded into a two-room shack. Entire communities dependent on rainwater for cooking and cleaning, struggling to survive the winter months on scraps of vegetables grown on small plots of land. The visitors came, as one later described, "face to face with the people and not the statistics, in meaningful communication among human beings rather than the endless and finally meaningless talk of politicians and schoolboys."[97] In total, Revitalization Corps delivered over eighteen thousand pounds of food, clothes, and books to Mississippi that winter.

Even as Corps volunteers worked to help the poor, Ned kept his sights on another, more pernicious form of poverty—the poverty of purpose—that had spread like a disease across white suburban America. In this war on poverty, Ned hoped to place children on the front lines. Operation Suburbia, as he dubbed it, aimed to bring urban minority and white suburban children and their parents together during the summer months and, through healthy social interactions, facilitate greater understanding and empathy.[98] "Kids," Ned explained, "are a marvelous bridge across barriers. They can be a catalyst."[99] In Harlem, he enlisted volunteer Elizabeth Skinner, a native of England who had arrived in

New York City with her mother and sister in 1965 and began working for the Corps soon after to recruit families from suburban New York and Connecticut.

Elizabeth did not have to spend much time explaining the concept behind Operation Suburbia to the white families whose phones she rang and doors she knocked on. Middle- and upper-class whites in the Northeast had a rich tradition of treating the problem of urban poverty with a summer vacation. In 1877 the Reverend Willard Parsons had begun soliciting members of his congregation in the rural town of Sherman, Pennsylvania, to contribute to a fund to provide vacations for

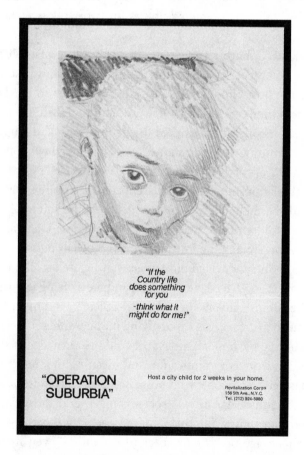

Poster soliciting support for Revitalization Corps's Operation Suburbia, launched in 1966. *Courtesy Ned Coll and the Library of Congress.*

the disadvantaged children of New York City. The Fresh Air Fund was
an enormous success; in 1888, the *New York Herald Tribune* assumed
control over the charity. The charity tapped into wealthy whites' sympa-
thy for the plight of underprivileged urban youth and their view of New
York City's slums as incubators of disease and criminality. "A dollar a
day," 1920s Fresh Air Fund solicitations read, "keeps some child away
from the city streets; from the torrid heat of New York summers; from
ill-health."[100] Connecticut played host to more of these children than
any other state. Host committees formed in summer vacation communities along the Gold Coast, quiet country towns in the state's interior,
and leafy suburbs outside of Hartford and New Haven, placing dozens
of inner-city children in families' homes for two-week stretches during
the summer months.

Operation Suburbia was similar to the Fresh Air Fund except for
one crucial difference. "We have the [white] family come and meet the
family [of the host child] in the city."[101] In contrast to the Fresh Air
Fund, where inner-city children were brought directly to the host communities and its organizers worked to ensure minimal disruption to a
host family's routine, Revitalization Corps challenged white families to
confront their fears of the urban ghetto and encouraged them to develop
meaningful relationships with the parents of the children they planned
to host and maintain those relationships after the initial visit. White
parents and children from the suburbs, Ned surmised, had as much to
gain from experiencing life in the city as the urban poor gained from
visiting the countryside. Ned didn't just want white families to feel like
they had done a good deed; he wanted to initiate a dialogue, to get, in his
words, "the suburbs involved in urban problems. And by involvement
we don't mean just paying taxes or giving money, either."[102] Ned appreciated the intangible opportunities that could be provided to disadvantaged children from communication and meaningful interaction in social settings between people who possessed power, resources, and what
one social scientist later called "social capital" and those who lacked
it. "It's through things like this," he commented, "that ties evolve—
jobs for a teen-age brother or sister in a family—even men get job
opportunities."[103] Also, unlike the Fresh Aid Fund, Revitalization Corps
volunteers conducted extensive interviews and vetting of the families

who volunteered to participate in the program. As Elizabeth Skinner explained, "We wanted to make sure that their objectives and interests were not patronizing" and that the children would find an "embracing situation and safe environment."[104]

In the spring of 1966, Corps volunteers went door to door, placed ads in church bulletins and newspapers, and made radio announcements seeking to sign up families for Operation Suburbia. "When is the last time you met a North End family?" Ned asked prospective participants.[105] Ned appealed to white liberal parents who "[didn't] want their own children to grow up in a vacuum, never meeting Negroes."[106] A case supervisor at the state welfare department who worked with Corps on the program explained, "What we're hoping to do is break down barriers which seem to be present in most suburban areas, where it's cause for comment if a Negro simply walks down the street."[107]

The number of white families volunteering to host a child far exceeded Ned's expectations, as well as demand. The first summer, seventy-five families signed up to host one of fifty children. Mary Tyan was among those children. For a week in the summer of 1966, the young African American girl stayed with the Grimshaws in Windsor, Connecticut. She played with the couple's three-year-old daughter and accompanied the family on a trip to their summer cottage on the shore. Lucia Dowdell stayed with the Keifer family at their home in Wethersfield, where she played croquet for the first time.[108] Harlem resident Ruth Pressley and her seven children spent the weekend at a white family's home in suburban Hartford. It was the first time any of the Pressley children had been outside of the city. Everything about the place seemed different: the grass, the open fields, even the grilled hamburgers and hot dogs. When asked about the best part of their visit, seven-year-old Mary Pressley said it was enjoying a barbeque and "not having the police knock at the door and question you about the fire."[109]

Back in Harlem and on Hartford's North End, the fires of discontent burned, and as another long hot summer approached, they seemed poised to spread.

THREE

Rats Cause Riots

Summertime and the livin' is easy. . . . In suburbia, plans are being
made to prepare the beach cottage, paint the boat at the lake,
get the shots for the passport. . . .
In the city . . . [t]he heat in the crowded apartments will keep people out
on the street until late at night. The smell from garbage in yards will drive
children to play in the road. . . . Heat, helplessness, depression and frustration
will rub together like tinder sticks . . . and the whole country will watch to see
if that dreaded word will appear in the morning paper . . . RIOT!

Hartford Courant, *June 22, 1969*

It was just after noon on Sunday, May 11, 1969—Mother's Day—
when people began assembling at the edge of the Flatbush Avenue
Bridge in Hartford. Forecasters expected the temperature to reach
60 degrees by midday. Another long, hot summer was drawing
near, and for the parents who lived in the Charter Oak Terrace housing
project, that meant another summer of living in fear of the death trap
that snaked through their neighborhood. That afternoon they gathered
for a vigil in memory of the seven children whose lives had been lost
to Park River in the previous years. Mothers, fathers, brothers, sisters,
cousins, ministers, teachers, and community leaders donned black armbands and carried signs that read "River of Tears," "We Love Our Chil-

68

dren Too," "We Demand Action Now!" and "To Hell with Promises."[1]
Prayers and hymns mixed with shouts of protest and the anguished cries
of the bereaved. Larry Taylor's father laid a wreath on the spot where his
son had drowned in 1963. Sobbing, Patricia Alexander explained to a reporter, "It's a river to drown in," before being overcome with emotion.
"They should call it a dead river," another man muttered in disgust.
Gathering themselves, the protesters joined hands and marched across
the Flatbush Avenue Bridge, singing "We Shall Overcome."[2]

Barbara Henderson was quite prepared to lay down her life to force
the city to take action. A year earlier the deaths of two children in the
river had led the Charter Oak tenant, an African American woman and
mother of seven, to help form the Association of Concerned Parents.
The group members, which consisted of poor white and black parents
from the only integrated housing project in the city, began lobbying city
and state officials to do something to protect their children from the river's dangerous currents. They organized meetings in the housing project
rec room; crowded into city council meetings waving signs that read
"Count Lives, Not Dollars" and "Safety First, Then Beauty"; and waited
anxiously to meet with officials in the Hartford Housing Authority, city
engineers' office, the Greater Hartford Flood Commission, the Public
Works Department, the state highway department, the mayor's office,
the governor's office—you name it.[3] Even as relations between white
and black tenants deteriorated and acts of interracial violence became
a regular occurrence at Charter Oak, they all shared a concern about
the safety of their children during the summer months. For once, at
least, the parents of Charter Oak Terrace were not "fight[ing] with each
other" but instead "[were] joining together."[4] Speaking as one voice, the
parents demanded that the section of the river that ran past the housing
project be covered with a conduit. The city made a vague promise to
lower the river's depth and place high fences along its banks. In return,
Henderson promised to counsel patience among fellow tenants.[5]

One year after the Mother's Day vigil, the river was as deep and as
accessible as ever. Henderson had heard all of the excuses before: the
matter required further study; the excavators had to finish their work
downstream before they could remove the dams; the cost was too prohibitive; perhaps the tenants should do a better job watching over their

children. She was fed up with talking, and she could sense that tensions and frustrations were about to boil over. "They holler about burning[,] they holler about rioting—this is what causes riots," Henderson warned. "I look like a fool because I said to wait, to trust the establishment. No more. It's time for action."[6]

In the days and weeks that followed the Mother's Day vigil, protests at the Flatbush Avenue Bridge grew larger, more disruptive, and more confrontational. At the start of the afternoon rush hour, protesters assembled on the bridge, tying up traffic for miles on one of the main arteries leading to the all-white suburbs west of the city. Drivers, most of them white and male, angrily laid on their horns. Henderson stood at the front of the pack and stoically stared them down while fellow protesters chanted and waved signs. Members of the newly formed Hartford chapter of the Black Panther Party came to show their support. Ned Coll was there, too, carrying signs and shouting to any reporter within earshot that if it were rich children drowning in Park River, action would have been taken long ago. On one afternoon, a driver attempted to force his way through. He got within inches of the assembled body of protesters, revved his engine loudly, and issued a string of obscenity-laced threats. Henderson didn't budge. Those standing next to and behind her didn't either. A police officer arrived on the scene and attempted to coax the protesters off the bridge. Henderson refused to move. Only after several more squad cars had arrived, and long after the dinners of those white-collar workers stuck in traffic had gone cold, did the crowd disperse. "It had all the ingredients needed for a pre-riot season warmup," the *Hartford Courant* wrote the following day, "and it was enough to send shivers through City Hall."[7]

For urban black parents, activists, and children alike, the annual search for a place to play and to cool off on hot summer days, and the all-too-often tragic results of such a search, brought a host of outrages and injustices into focus. The brand-new public swimming pools and robust summertime youth recreational programs available in white suburban neighborhoods came to symbolize the uneven development and unequal provision of public services in the northern metropolis. Conversely, the polluted, disease-carrying rivers and shorelines of many urban black neighborhoods came to embody public officials' indifference to the health and safety of their residents. As municipalities, homeowners' associations, and private clubs hung sand curtains along their shorelines and as the disparities in the quality and quantity of public outdoor recreational spaces in suburbs and cities grew more pronounced, the frustrations of the urban poor—isolated and alienated—grew more volatile, and summers in the city became longer and hotter.

On November 1, 1963, nearly six hundred tenants in Harlem stopped paying their rent. Organized by tenants' rights activist Jesse Gray, the Harlem rent strike came in response to slumlords' indifference to the wretched conditions tenants were forced to endure: lack of reliable heating or hot water, broken pipes, dangerous wiring, cracking walls, and rats. Especially rats. When the slumlords sued to have the tenants evicted, Gray called on strikers to gather up dead rats and bring them to civil court so they could be introduced as evidence. Tipped off to Gray's plans, courthouse guards searched tenants' bags and confiscated eight dead rats outside the courthouse. But the plot to smuggle dead rats into court had served its purpose. The following morning, the striking tenants who had deposited rotting rat carcasses on the steps of a New York City housing court made front-page news in the city's daily newspapers and may have swayed the judge hearing the case, who ruled in the tenants' favor.[8]

In February 1964, Gray applied pressure on the state's governor, Nelson Rockefeller, to take action to curb the plague of rat infestations in the city's poorest neighborhoods by calling on Harlemites to mail small plastic rats to the governor's office. If the sight of dead, stinking rats had shocked the public, the hundreds of plastic rats dumped on the governor's doorstep only elicited laughs. The governor and the press corps in Albany treated "Rats to Rockefeller" as a joke. To roars of laughter from reporters, Rockefeller announced that he had rerouted some of the plastic rats to Mayor Robert Wagner's office in Manhattan. "I'm not going to let them pass the buck up to Albany," Rockefeller said, grinning from ear to ear. The state and the city took no action to combat rat infestations, while the city's slumlords defied court orders and continued to squeeze as much profit from crumbling buildings as they could.[9]

Later that summer, Harlem went up in flames. The 1964 Harlem "riot" began—as was so often the case—following the shooting of an unarmed black teenager by a cop. Four days of civil violence ensued, resulting in 1 death, 118 injuries, 465 arrests, and between $500,000 and $1 million of property damage. Historians would come to mark the 1964 Harlem riot as the start of America's long hot summer.[10] If the strong arm of the state in the form of trigger-happy police had provided the spark, the bemused indifference of high-ranking officials to the deplorable living conditions Harlem residents were forced to endure stoked the flames. To the children of Harlem, Hartford's North End, and other urban ghettos of the Northeast, the rat was the stuff of nightmares, the pest that spread disease and attacked sleeping children, leaving them scarred and deformed. But to governors, mayors, senators, congressmen, and much of white America, the rat was a joke.

Fleeing in terror from the vermin that stalked the hallways and scurried across the floors of their apartments, children of northern ghettos found little relief outdoors. Under city planner Robert Moses, New York City had invested heavily in the expansion of summer recreational facilities, but most of those dollars had gone toward white neighborhoods or to places such as Jones Beach on Long Island that were virtually inaccessible to the urban poor. Moses infamously directed engineers to construct the overpasses leading to Jones Beach low enough that buses could not make it through, ensuring that the only members of the public there would be those who owned an automobile. In contrast, Harlem and heavily black sections of Brooklyn saw little in the way of public investment in outdoor recreation. Their parks and playgrounds, strewn with trash and broken bottles, became places children were taught to avoid.

Summers in Harlem mirrored trends in cities across the nation. In his 1967 report on "Recreation and Civil Disorder," the pioneering urban recreation planner Richard Kraus found that "in most cases Negro neighborhoods possessed the oldest, most limited and run-down recreation facilities" in the city, often "amounting to little more than a bare blacktop or concrete area."[11] Another study found that "as the percentage of blacks [in an area of a city] increases, [the number of] outdoor recreation facilities, park and recreation personnel . . . and the number of volunteers . . . decreases."[12] Recreational inequality, others pointed out, endangered the lives of inner-city residents, especially youth, not just their quality of life. Kenneth Clark, for instance, tied the inadequacy of inner-city parks and playgrounds to the disproportionate number of pedestrian accidents involving children at play in urban black neighborhoods. In New York City, persons under the age of twenty-five were almost twice as likely to die as a result of being hit by an automobile in Harlem than anywhere else in the city. During 1964 alone, the Harlem Hospital Center received 215 children who had sustained injuries from being hit by an automobile, and these included 94 serious injuries and 5 fatalities.[13]

These and other preventable tragedies became more frequent during the summer months, as social activity shifted outdoors and the supervision of children decreased. City officials seemed to make a priority of safeguarding children in white neighborhoods by providing street lights and crosswalks, well-equipped playgrounds, and swimming pools. But not in Harlem, where the streets were the playground and fire hydrants the swimming pool. Across urban America, police and citizens battled over the right to outdoor public space during the summer months. On a sweltering hot summer day on Chicago's West Side in 1966, violence erupted after police officers turned off a fire hydrant that children were using to cool off. The kids had few other options. The closest public swimming pool was located in an Italian neighborhood where any black person who dared to enter could expect to be assaulted. Public health officials had forced the closing of the nearest beach along Lake Michigan due to overpollution. After officers shut off the water, black youth began shouting back. Why didn't the cops turn off hydrants in white neighborhoods? one kid asked. "We run this. You niggers don't run nothin' around here," the cop barked. Moments after the officers had left, another youth shouted, "If they can keep theirs on, we can, too," and proceeded to unscrew a hydrant cap.[14] When the cops returned, they were pelted with bricks, rocks, and bottles. Within minutes dozens of squad cars flooded the West Side. Cops clubbed protesters indiscriminately and fired into crowds. Blacks fought back with whatever weapons were at their disposal. Violence and civil disorder raged for three straight days. In the aftermath black residents took pains to emphasize to reporters and inquiring public officials alike that while the closing of a fire hydrant triggered the "riot," the lack of water recreation facilities did not alone explain black unrest. At meetings in community centers and church basements in the days that followed, "Westsiders stood up to proclaim that hydrants in Chicago, like hamburgers in the South, were only superficial elements of a problem that had its roots buried in the soil of a greater discontent," the *Chicago Defender*'s Betty Washington wrote.[15] Martin Luther King Jr., who was in Chicago that summer to wage his ill-fated open housing campaign, echoed those sentiments, emphasizing that the "lawlessness" found on the streets of Chicago and cities across the country was a consequence of the "vicious system" of racist abuse, denial of opportunity, and a host of exploitative practices carried out by whites who had made a "mockery of the law" and that such mockery invited violent retaliation.[16]

The events that had precipitated civil violence in Chicago and other cities seemed to confirm to many white public officials that the problem of long, hot summers was summer itself. In the wake of the 1966 Chicago riot and others sparked by conflicts over access to water for recreation, many came to believe that urban unrest could be extinguished (both literally and figuratively) by dousing the ghetto in water. In Chicago, Mayor Richard J. Daley ordered the installation of spray nozzles on West Side fire hydrants, promised to look into providing police protection for black youth at neighborhood swimming pools, and ordered the immediate purchase of ten "mini pools" to be placed in vacant lots in the city's black neighborhoods.[17] Days later the Federal Office of Economic Opportunity rushed through a $400,000 anti-poverty program to provide swimming pools for "disadvantaged youth" in over forty cities across the country. "We shall continue . . . to try to lessen these tensions by . . . opening up recreational areas, swimming pools, [and] supervised play . . . facilities," President Johnson told reporters the following spring.[18] By the summer of 1968, the city of Chicago had placed thirty-two new portable, above-ground swimming pools and thirteen spray pools in black and brown neighborhoods.

New York City's parks commissioner, August Heckscher, similarly believed that the city could avert future crises by providing poor neighborhoods with more outdoor recreational space. "Is there any better way to keep [the city] cool than to get its citizens out under the shade of the trees and into the waters of pools or ocean?"[19] His boss, Mayor John Lindsay, agreed, and during his first term in office he implemented a program to place "mini pools" measuring twenty by forty feet in riot-torn neighborhoods and to convert abandoned lots into "vest pocket parks," consisting of a few benches and picnic tables and some play equipment on an asphalt surface.[20] Lindsay's office appropriated $1.5 million for its 1967 "Keep Cool" program (to be spent on, among other new amenities, spray caps for fire hydrants).[21]

Throughout the 1960s public recreational planners in cities across the nation increasingly took a more active role in devising preventative strategies for summertime unrest. Numerous articles in recreation industry publications and entire annual meetings of the National Recreation and Park Association were devoted to addressing issues such as "Recreation and the Urban Crisis," "The Park and Recreation Profession's Responsibility in the Ghetto," and "Programs That Work in the Ghetto and Why."[22] A generation of freshly minted graduates of urban planning programs became experts in keeping inner cities cool during the summer months, and now they were on call to dispense sage advice to desperate and confused urban governments.

Cities were open to anything as long as it was inexpensive and could be implemented on short notice. In Los Angeles, the police and fire departments outfitted a fleet of buses and hired a crew of drivers to transport young people to beaches. Pittsburgh rushed through funds for the construction of twenty-five above-ground swimming pools in predominantly black neighborhoods. Officials in Oakland, California, received plaudits from the National League of Cities, the Department of the Interior, and the Department of Housing and Urban Development (HUD) for their innovative repurposing of the land beneath newly completed expressways and freeway interchanges as playgrounds and "tot lots." HUD secretary Robert Weaver called this repurposing an "innovation" that provided "low-income famil[ies] . . . the opportunity . . . to enrich their lives with constructive use of leisure time and . . . an environment that lifts the human spirit."[23] Within the year, other cities that had also completed freeway construction projects that ran straight through the heart of black neighborhoods began placing swing sets, slides, and teeter-totters "adjacent to, underneath, and above expressways and highway interchanges."[24]

In response to urban blacks' demands for jobs, justice, and an end to wanton police brutality, the government gave them pools and told them to play under a freeway. Few features of the 1960s urban landscape better symbolized white liberals' narrow understanding of black discontent and cynical, insulting gestures toward inner-city communities than the ubiquitous "mini pool" or the under-expressway "tot lot." In many neighborhoods, small, hastily assembled above-ground swimming pools were one of the few tangible signs of government action in the wake of protests and civil disorder. These facilities were, as Kraus admitted, simply "a means of social control," a way to "keep angry and frustrated black youth active"—and distracted.[25]

Fittingly, these new facilities provided only the barest of accommodations. In New York City, the pools scattered throughout "hot spots" in Harlem and Brooklyn were so small and overcrowded that bathers reported they could only stand in the water and splash around. The sides of the pools, a narrow band of concrete and chain-link fence, provided only a platform to leap into what locals derisively called "giant-sized urinals."[26] The city did not even provide changing rooms. At least local residents used the mini-pools, which were filled with children on hot summer days. The same could not be said of vest pocket parks, another hallmark of New York City's response to summer unrest. In a city where social activity took place on the streets, the vest pocket park, tucked in between buildings and shrouded from public view, was incompatible with summer life in Harlem but highly conducive to criminal activity. In some neighborhoods, parents organized to prevent the city from converting lots into pocket parks, arguing that these secluded areas invariably became magnets for "winos, peeping toms, drug users, and lovers."[27] Far safer to have their children play on the sidewalk and in the streets, where at least the eyes of the neighborhood were watching. But on their front stoops and along the city's sidewalks, residents of Harlem were most susceptible to abuse from police, who seemed to make it their mission each summer to clear the streets and force people inside. A thirty-three-year-old man from Harlem described a scene that led to the anger and frustration that became such a common feature of the summer months. On the sidewalk, he explained, "A bunch of us could be playing some music, or dancing, which we have as an outlet for ourselves. We can't dance in the house, we don't have clubs or things like that. So we're out on the sidewalk; we might feel like dancing, or one might want to play something on his horn. Right away here comes a cop. 'You're disturbing the peace!'"[28] Another man, age thirty-five, added, "Last night, for instance, the officer stopped some fellows on 125th Street. . . . The officer said, 'All right, everybody get off the street or inside!' Now, it's very hot. We don't have air-conditioned apartments in most of these houses up here, so where are we going if we get off the streets? We can't go back in the house because we almost suffocate."[29]

In Hartford, housing conditions on the North End continued to deteriorate. In the summer of 1964 dozens of children in an apartment complex came down with rashes from parasitic mites that lived off rats.[30] Economic exploitation remained a fact of life. Retail and grocery stores on the North End charged on average 3.5 percent more for items than their counterparts in white neighborhoods, a study conducted by the Associated Press and published in the summer of 1966 found.[31] In Charter Oak Terrace in the city's southwest corner, tenants were forced to shop at a lone supermarket, where, as one observer described, "the meat has turned grey and much of the cheese has molded, and yet the prices are higher by 20 or 30 cents than the average supermarket."[32] On the North End, most of the businesses were owned by whites. The city's police department, likewise, had few blacks on the force. Its officers indiscriminately harassed and detained young black males and seemed, to many on the North End, to "function only to protect property . . . and keep the ghetto contained."[33]

By the summer of 1967, the North End was a tinderbox awaiting a spark. It came the night of July 12, when the black owner of a restaurant summoned police after a customer, twenty-four-year-old William "Billy" Toules, reportedly "used some bad language" in speaking with one of his waitresses.[34] Physically handicapped and lacking the use of one arm, Toules was well known in the neighborhood and, despite his occasional drunken benders, was not seen as a threat to others. Before officers arrived, Toules had left the restaurant, but the police found him

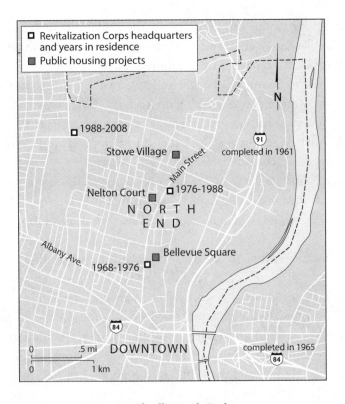

Revitalization Corps headquarters
and years in residence
Public housing projects

1988-2008

Stowe Village   completed in 1961

Main Street

91

Nelton Court   1976-1988

N O R T H
E N D

Albany Ave.

Bellevue Square

1968-1976

84

0   .5 mi   DOWNTOWN   completed in 1965

0   1 km   84

N

Hartford's North End.

at his home, returned him to the restaurant, and after the owner had
positively identified Toules, arrested him for breach of peace. When he
showed signs of resisting arrest, the officers threw him to the ground
and violently cuffed and tossed him into a squad car. A crowd of onlookers witnessed Toules's arrest. Word soon spread that a pair of cops
had viciously beat a disabled black man. As the night went on, the crowd
swelled. Around 11:40 p.m., someone tossed a Molotov cocktail into a
neighborhood supermarket, setting off a fire that consumed the structure. Others subsequently began hurtling rocks at other storefront windows. The following morning, the mayor and city council held emergency meetings with prominent black leaders and a group of young
black men from the neighborhood. The group of black youth aired a
list of grievances, from area stores' price gouging and refusal to hire
blacks to routine harassment and mistreatment by police. One of the

youth spokesmen noted the relationship among these problems; an arrest record was one of the main reasons given by area employers for their failure to hire blacks. When asked by Mayor James Kinsella what could be done to keep youth off the streets and restore peace, another youth suggested keeping the city's swimming pools opened until 10 p.m. That afternoon, the city announced later hours at city pools, effective immediately. This measure did not cool tensions, as violence, property damage, and standoffs between young black men and police continued into a second and third night before eventually subsiding. The usual explanations from incredulous white officials and moralizing black leaders soon followed—the tensions were orchestrated by "outsiders" or caused by that combustible mix of "hooliganism and hot weather."[35]

As city officials struggled to restore calm to the North End, violence erupted in the Charter Oak Terrace housing project south of downtown, where a series of incidents between the children of white and black tenants quickly spiraled out of control, resulting in a series of firebombings of apartments carried out by boys ages twelve to fourteen. Reports of violence and property destruction against black tenants in the project had been on the rise since 1965, when the city's housing authority abruptly ended its segregation policy and began housing new black tenants next door to whites. Police, however, dismissed these incidents of violence and property destruction as the doings of youth "out for kicks."[36] City officials, likewise, continued to dismiss the concerns of both white and black parents in Charter Oak Terrace about the depth, dangerous currents, and lack of adequate fencing around the section of the Park River near their homes.

The summer of 1967 was the hottest one yet. Massive uprisings in Detroit and Newark shocked white America and led President Johnson to form the National Advisory Commission on Civil Disorders and push Congress to take action against one of the sources and symbols of inner-city unrest: the rat. The proposed Rat Extermination Act would have provided cities $40 million in aid to combat the pest. Days before the vote, an eight-month-old black infant in the District of Columbia died after being attacked by a rat in his crib. It was estimated that, annually, more than fourteen thousand Americans, mostly babies and small children, suffered rat bites. The previous year, seven U.S. cities

had accounted for approximately one thousand reported cases of rat
bite. (Health officials agreed that the numbers of victims were far higher
since many persons were reluctant to report being bitten.) "It is one of
the cruelest manifestations of the urban slum," said New York congressman William Fitts Ryan. "For the mother who has to leave the young
children alone in her house, the rat is a danger that the mother thinks
about in dread." "The people in these areas face the threat of diseases
borne by rats, they fear for their children's safety in the night, and they
experience the disgust—and yes, the horror—of the constant presence
of these noxious, vicious, disease-carrying animals," Pennsylvania congressman William Barrett added.[37]

But many lawmakers treated the bill as a joke and spent their time
during debate to come up with clever ways to deride its authors and
dismiss their concerns. Mississippi congressman William M. Colmer
dubbed it the "civil rats bill" (hearty laughs). Representative Delbert
Latta of Ohio chimed in: "How about including mice? Every house-
wife has trouble with mice" (guffaws). "What about country rats?" Iowa
congressman Harold Gross asked. "Why not just buy some cats and
turn them loose on the rats?" Florida Representative James Haley joked.
Or invest in rat traps and cheese instead, Representative Samuel Devine
of Ohio added. Mississippi congressman John Bell Williams suggested
the government instead offer a bounty on rats: "25 cents a rat. It would
put youngsters to work, and get rid of poverty and rats at the same
time." After wiping away the tears from laughter, 207 congressmen cast
"nay" votes on consideration of the bill. The "scratching . . . tumbling,
scrambling sound" of rats scurrying up walls and across floors, the New
York columnist Jimmy Breslin wrote after the bill's defeat, "is something
that is heard by people in every poor neighborhood in every city in the
Nation. And it is one of the reasons why this is our longest of summers. Last week, the House of Representatives thought it all a cause for
laughter."[38]

As congressmen chuckled, cities burned. Coming in the midst of
the hottest summer of unrest to date, Congress's failure to take action
to combat the plague of rats in America's cities was, to Jesse Gray, particularly galling. Weeks after the House had voted down the bill, he and
a busload of activists from New York headed to Washington and, as the

House was about to adjourn for its summer recess, forced their way into the House gallery, where they shouted at lawmakers and chanted, "Rats cause riots!" Capitol police swarmed the gallery, clubbing protesters with blackjacks and arresting eight, including Gray.[39]

To Ned, it was no surprise that lawmakers—whether in Washington or Hartford—dismissed the severity of the rat problem or any of the other threats to public health and quality of life facing residents of ghettoized urban slums. They were so far removed from the lived experience of poverty that they could barely conceive of rats being anything more than a minor nuisance, something tenants should take upon themselves to handle. "It would be interesting," Ned mused, "if local political officials or the Chamber of Commerce decided to live in these shacks for a two-week period. Perhaps the Governor's mansion could even be moved. If this did happen white Hartford would get a better picture of the frustrations of the black man's fight for survival in a nation that has already gotten three centuries of free labor from his ancestors."[40]

But aside from those brief moments when they stared in horror, suburban whites mostly just looked away. And stayed away. Or, rather, sped past. Completed in 1965, Interstate 84 cut a wide concrete swath through the center of Hartford, severing the North End from the city's downtown. This was by design. The Federal Housing Administration's underwriting manual recommended the use of "natural or artificially established barriers" to protect areas of a city "from adverse influences." Across postwar urban America, interstate highways redrew the boundaries of ghettos and fortified racially segregated housing markets. The redrawing allowed slumlords to liquidate deteriorating properties and replenished the market of captive tenants. Over 88 percent of non-white families forcibly removed from the neighborhoods near downtown Hartford to make way for I-84 moved into the North End. One report found that families forced to move from urban renewal areas in Hartford paid on average $1,200 more in annual rent in their new locations.[41]

The white commuters who drove over and around the North End each morning and afternoon, however, remained willfully blind to the destruction and despair exacted on urban black populations in their name. Ned remained convinced that whites' strategic avoidance of black spaces and black people lay at the heart of the crisis facing the nation. Ensconced in their "suburban ghettos," suburban whites' racial imaginations ran wild, nourished by a steady diet of negative images spoon fed by sensationalistic media and unimpeded by any meaningful contact or interaction with people of color. And as the structural barriers to suburban integration grew stronger and more resilient, fear turned into apathy and the marrow of hate calcified into a thick shell of indifference. By the late 1960s, the white-collar families of America's suburbs increasingly articulated what the historian Matthew D. Lassiter describes as a "'color-blind' discourse of suburban innocence" that denied any complicity in the ghettoization of black America, disavowed any obligation to address the mounting crises facing America's cities, and demanded the "right" to be complacent.[42]

Whites' complacency, Ned argued, fueled black unrest. "Violence in the streets," he often remarked, "starts with the yawn in the suburbs."[43] Just as white suburbia must recognize its role in creating and sustaining the ghetto, it must also, he warned, shed any illusion that it could remain immune from its ills. "If comfortable white parents in the Greater Hartford community think their children will not be affected by the further decline of Hartford's poverty belt, they are mistaken."[44] White America ignored the problem of urban poverty and black anger at its own peril.

When the Kerner Commission released its much-anticipated report in February 1968, Ned saw this as the moment when white America would be awakened from its slumber. Contrary to the expectations of the Johnson administration officials who formed the commission and authorized the study, the authors of the Kerner report dismissed in its opening pages the notion that urban unrest was instigated and orchestrated by leftist radicals. Rather, riots erupted in cities across America because white police officers beat and harassed black citizens; because urban schools were segregated, overcrowded, understaffed, and underfunded; because employers and industries had left the inner cities, reducing urban blacks, especially young black males, to a state of persistent unemployment and underemployment; because blacks still remained stuck in exploitative housing markets, discriminated against by lenders, locked out of suburban real estate markets, and forced to pay exorbitant

rents to live in crumbling, overcrowded apartments or the new verti-
cal ghettos built by public housing authorities; and because cities failed
to even provide their neighborhoods with safe, decent places of public recreation. The shock that greeted the report's release among white
Americans only served to underscore the authors' warning that America
was fast becoming "two societies, one white, one black—separate and
unequal."[45]

Most of white America did not know, and did not want to know,
the reality of life in urban black America. The Kerner Commission
wanted white America to look in the mirror, to recognize that "white
society [was] deeply implicated in the ghetto. White institutions created
it, white institutions maintain it, and white society condones it."[46] So,
too, did Ned Coll. He treated the report as gospel and, in the months
that followed, preached its findings and conclusions to audiences across
Connecticut. The report seemed to endorse and provide confirmation
for arguments that he had been making to middle-class suburban white
New Englanders for years—namely, that their apathy and indifference
to poverty and unequal access to jobs and education within urban black
communities were as damaging (and damnable) as the vicious—and
southern—forms of racism that so many of them disavowed. This report,
Ned said, "should hit the average citizen with the fact that he is a white
racist if he remains passive."[47] It captured, in powerful, uncompromis-
ing words, what he referred to as the "cancer of white racism" that had
spread throughout the suburban North, a disease that, as he put it, was
"subtle and passive," its chief symptom a feeling by its sufferer that "he
is not personally responsible for prejudice."[48] The Kerner Commission
report promised, Ned hoped, to give the lie to white America's claims of
innocence. But unless it was followed by active and ongoing engagement
with the people living in riot-torn neighborhoods, the report threatened to become just another study, spawning theories among some and
sowing fears among others, but offering little of tangible significance to
those whose anger and frustration it purported to address.

On the eve of another summer, Revitalization Corps's programs
and projects increasingly made addressing the sources of urban violence
their explicit aim. Weeks after the release of the Kerner Commission
report, Ned announced plans for a jobs program directed at Hartford's

"hard-core" unemployed. Dubbed a "Riot of Involvement," it aimed to enlist representatives from over one hundred of the state's main industries to visit Revitalization Corps's Hartford headquarters and conduct job interviews. Behind the scenes, Ned lobbied area businesses to relax their policies against hiring convicted felons and high school dropouts. He pressed companies to address prejudicial hiring practices and structural barriers to black employment within their industries.[49]

Along with these pleas for concern and reform came the warning that without action, they could expect to see Hartford erupt in flames that summer. "The North End is tense now. The action that will loosen it up is if these guys get jobs. If they don't get them, they'll be on the corner this summer and there will be an explosion here," Al Cooper told a reporter. Cooper knew what he was talking about. Shortly after his release from an eight-year prison term in the Connecticut State Penitentiary, Cooper began working as a field rep for Revitalization Corps in Hartford. He hung around the neighborhood bars, corners, and poolrooms, keeping an eye and an ear on local happenings, feelings, and sentiments. He did what Ned was increasingly unable to do as he darted back and forth between Hartford and Harlem throughout the week— that is, feel the pulse of the city's black community. His background and close ties to the North End made Cooper a very effective spokesperson and recruiter for Revitalization Corps. That spring, while Ned traveled to corporate offices and tried to convince executives to hire from the vast pool of unemployed black males, Cooper rounded these young men up off the streets, helped them fill out job applications, and worked to prepare them for interviews with companies such as Fenn Manufacturing, Aetna Life and Casualty, and Southern New England Telephone Company at the Corps's headquarters.[50]

By late March 1968, the headquarters in Hartford and Harlem buzzed with activity and seemed possessed with an optimism that comes when a group can begin to sense that tangible results and real change lay ahead. Maybe, Ned mused, the Kerner Commission report would finally arouse white America from its slumber, get it to appreciate the complexity and the urgency of the problems facing black urban America, and join the Corps in its "war on apathy." Perhaps America's day of racial reckoning was at hand and that spirit of civic involvement that seemed so radiant at the dawn of the 1960s could yet be rekindled. Signs of hope seemed to flower from all corners. Earlier that month, Lyndon Johnson, whose disastrous escalation of the war in Vietnam had divided the nation, had announced to the nation that he would not seek another term. The man seeking his party's nomination, Bobby Kennedy, not only embodied the ideals of his slain brother, but he also seemed, at least to pundits, to be the one person who could bind the nation's racial wounds; bridge its class and cultural divisions; and bring urban blacks, blue-collar whites, Eastern intellectuals, and pious Catholic Midwesterners into the same tent and help them see their mutual interests and shared destiny.

Bobby Kennedy liked what Ned Coll was doing. His Senate office provided the Harlem chapter group tickets to plays and other cultural activities.[51] In February 1968 he spent an afternoon at the Revitalization Corps headquarters in Harlem listening to Ned and other workers describe projects that the Corps was carrying out. Afterward, he praised them for making a "direct commitment" to confronting the urban crisis and described their programs as "practical and vital" toward meeting the "tremendous challenge" facing the nation.[52] As Kennedy barnstormed across the country that spring, drawing increasingly larger and more diverse crowds of young, old, white, black, and brown, it seemed as if America might yet overcome the crisis; that out of the darkness of war, poverty, and injustice a new day, and a renewed determination to solve the nation's problems and live up to its ideals, might dawn. Instead, the nation plunged further into darkness.

Ned spent the afternoon of Thursday, April 4, 1968, in his disheveled office in the Corps's Hartford headquarters. With his scuffed-up brown leather shoes perched atop a desk piled high with papers, he worked the phones, calling local businesses, begging secretaries to patch him through to a chief executive so that he could personally request the executive's cooperation in that spring's "Riot of Involvement." Over in another corner of the office, Al Cooper and two other young black workers were sitting on folding chairs, drawing up lesson plans for tutoring sessions. Around nine o'clock in the evening, they began to hear shouts of anger and cries of rage coming from outside; a crowd was gathering just up the block, on the corner of Main and Pavilion Streets. They could hear owners of other storefronts on the block furiously pounding nails into boards that would cover their windows. It wasn't long before they heard the news: Martin Luther King had been assassinated in Memphis earlier that day. Soon, they could hear rocks crashing through storefront windows and sirens blaring. Fire trucks summoned by false alarms were pelted with rocks. Police knew better and instead began erecting a barricade around the entire North End. If anguished blacks were going to vent their anger, let them do it in their own neighborhood. The cops' job that night was to just keep black rage contained, channeled inward, away from downtown.[53]

By ten o'clock, the crowd at the corner of Main and Pavilion, yards away from Corps headquarters, had swelled to over one hundred persons. Further up the street, the Reverend J. Blanton Shields, a local black minister, had climbed aboard a sound truck furnished by the police and begged for calm, his amplified words periodically interrupted by the sound of a rock or bottle smashing against the truck's side. Before Ned, Cooper, and the others in the office even had a chance to absorb the news, a group of around fifteen young black men stormed the office, kicked open the door, and began moving on Ned. "You killed our King!" they shouted at the white man who had made the North End his home and its people his mission. Caught in that situation, the stereotypical white liberal would've cowered in fear or run. He would've shown, then and there, just what blacks could truly expect from him in a crisis, when racial lines in the sand were being drawn. But Ned didn't do that. He shot out of his chair, marched toward the door, looked the group straight in the eyes, and shouted, "Get the hell out of here! He was our King, too."[54] Moments after it seemed the Corps office would be ambushed, the group of young men fell silent, exited the room, and went back out into the night.

For the next two days, the North End burned. Police fired round after round of tear gas canisters into crowds. By Friday evening John Barber, the leader of New Haven's Black Panther Party, was standing guard outside Hartford's police headquarters, demanding the ouster of the city's chief of police, John Kerrigan. "We don't have too much power," he shouted from a loudspeaker, "but we do have a lot of matches."[55] On Sunday morning, the North End mourned. But by the early afternoon, groups of teenagers were racing up Main Street, smashing windows, shouting epithets at police. Through it all, the Revitalization Corps storefront remained unscathed. Later that day, Ned and roughly 150 persons, mostly white, marched through downtown, clad in black armbands. Ned walked alongside Mayor Ann Uccello. At one point along the route, they were heckled by a group of neo-Nazis cheering King's death and shouting, "Heil Hitler."[56] The following week, Ned and a group of Corps volunteers and North End residents drove to Atlanta for King's funeral. As Ned drove into the city, the passengers listened to a local radio station. A white caller phoned in to request that it play the song "Bye, Bye Blackbird" to celebrate King's death.[57] Less than a week ago, Ned had dared to believe that America was poised to exorcise its demons. That now seemed hopelessly naïve.

King's death and its aftermath only lent greater urgency to Revitalization Corps's mission. In the weeks that followed, Ned deliberately focused his efforts and energy on reaching the city's white suburban population. He gave speeches to students at high schools in some of Hartford's most exclusive suburbs and tried to explain the realities of daily life in Hartford's ghettos and help them to comprehend the rage that followed King's assassination. He hastily assembled picnics and outdoor gatherings where families of diverse backgrounds could come together and engage in a dialogue over the meaning of King's life and death and begin to map a way forward for Hartford and the nation. On weekday afternoons, he stood outside high schools in the wealthy suburbs of West Hartford, handing out pamphlets about Revitalization Corps and, speaking from atop the roof of a sound truck, gave rousing speeches encouraging students to become agents of change in the inner city that summer. But he could sense that his words were increasingly falling on deaf ears.[58]

Ned struggled to enlist white volunteers for Operation Bridge, a tutoring program that required participants to spend time tutoring underprivileged children in the children's homes and get to know the children's parents. He could sense that fear of riot-torn black neighborhoods was giving way to contempt, that the actions taken by suburban municipalities and white neighborhoods in Hartford, Boston, and cities across the nation made it clear that middle- and working-class whites were becoming increasingly, and more openly, hostile to the black freedom movement's aims and demands, intent on consolidating their gains and preserving the privileges they had secured from the postwar liberal state and then dismantling it before it had a chance to extend its reach into black and brown America. Working frantically to build bridges between these "two societies, separate and unequal," all Ned could see around him were others building walls—around their schools, their neighborhoods, their public places of recreation, their tax bases.[59]

In Hartford, a crumbling bridge and the dangerous currents over which it passed neatly symbolized the deteriorating living conditions of the urban poor in this age of metropolitan fragmentation. In the first week of May 1968, both nine-year-old Frank Sarubbi and seven-year-old Robert Gallagher drowned in the Park River near their families' homes in the Charter Oak Terrace housing project. They were the seventh and eighth children to drown at that exact section of the river in the past sixteen years. Both had been using the river and its banks as their de facto swimming pool and playground. Following Gallagher's death, area residents began to organize a boycott of the neighborhood elementary school, and over three hundred residents packed the Charter Oak Terrace Community Center for an emergency meeting with state and city officials.[60] For two hours parents berated officials for their indifference to their children's safety. Tears streaming down her face, her voice cracking, Mrs. Joseph Moquin, the white mother of Sarubbi, pled with officials to take immediate action to cover the section of the river that ran past the project and to station a police officer on the crumbling Flatbush Avenue bridge to guard a gaping hole in the structure that was large enough to swallow a child. "I vow to my dead baby that if I have to walk the leather off my shoes I'll see to it that the [Park] river is covered," Moquin promised the assembled officials. The audience broke out in cheers when another speaker said that the city would act "only when some big shot's kid drowns there." Boos rained down on councilman Frank DeLucco, who suggested the parents were to blame and recommended the tenants form their own patrol force, and on Greater Hartford Flood Commission director Philip Smith, who told the crowd that its demands were too cost prohibitive.[61]

Following the meeting, the Association of Concerned Parents drew up a list of demands and made plans to stage protests on the bridge in the coming days. The group named Barbara Henderson its chairman. As parents marched along the bridge carrying signs that read, "Fill the river and save our children" and "Let's prevent another tragedy," workers from the Department of Agriculture and Natural Resources hastily erected a fence along the riverbanks, the Public Works Department patched holes in the bridge, and city officials issued vague promises to lower the river's depth.[62] The police department agreed to place an officer on patrol at the bridge for the summer, with instructions to arrest and hand over to the juvenile justice system any child found playing near the river.

Being young, dark-skinned, and poor in Hartford had never seemed more dangerous. Between 1959 and 1968, fourteen children three years old or younger died from lead poisoning in Connecticut. All but four of the victims were black or Puerto Rican.[63] In June 1968 alone, six children on the North End, all two years old or younger, were hospitalized for lead poisoning. The city's health director advised parents to situate cribs away from walls and stick a pacifier in their kids' mouths to lessen their temptation to eat paint chips.[64] Residents of the North End's housing projects, meanwhile, were learning to cope with another nuisance: tear gas, the riot-control method of choice for the city's police department. In late June, police swarmed the Bellevue Square housing project after reports of a disturbance in a grocery store parking lot and fired several canisters of tear gas into a crowd.[65] It became a familiar scene: a personal dispute or disturbance involving a few individuals attracted the attention of police, who responded by deploying anti-riot weaponry, which in turn drew large crowds of protesters angry at police overreaction. Mass arrests and additional rounds of tear gas followed. Rinse the tear gas from your eyes and repeat.[66] That summer alone, officers fired tear gas into crowds on the city's North End on at least twelve separate occasions. Several incidents resulting in the deployment of tear gas on crowds were sparked after police attempted to arrest persons for turning on fire hydrants to cool off. During one such incident, indignant crowds responded with chants of "Water power!" and "We pay taxes."[67]

The only effort by the city that summer to clean up and improve the physical environment of the city's black neighborhoods was one

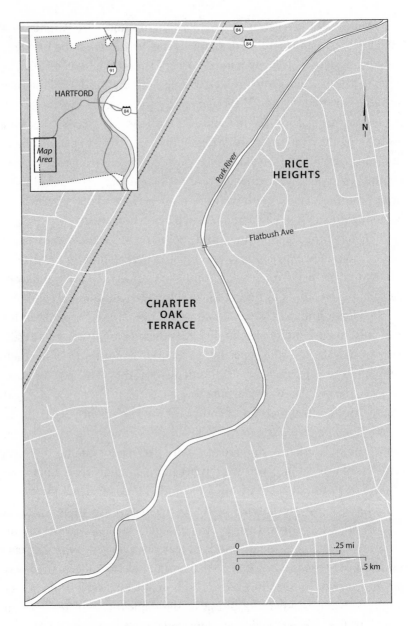

Charter Oak Terrace and Rice Heights public housing
projects, located adjacent to the Park River, site of several
drowning deaths of children in the 1960s.

aimed at ridding the North End of the weapons residents wielded against police cruisers: bricks and rocks torn from the sides of cheaply built housing projects and taken from the vacant lots of slums torn down by the city. Few officials bothered to notice the irony. A principal source of unrest—bad housing, made all the worse by a slum clearance program that failed to accommodate displaced residents—had provided the North End with the tools to attack the symbols of their oppression.[68]

While crews from the Public Works Department attempted to clear housing projects, vacant lots, and demolition sites of bricks and loose debris, a group of civic leaders considered possible diversionary tactics. That summer the Hartford Chamber of Commerce and Connecticut General Life Insurance Company sponsored a series of block dance parties in the North End and at Charter Oak Terrace. For two hours on summer nights beginning in July, local soul and R & B bands performed in parking lots of high schools and housing projects for crowds numbering in the thousands, and employees of Connecticut Life and other corporate sponsors sold fifteen-cent hot dogs and five-cent Pepsis. That is, until a fight between two groups of neighborhood teenagers broke out one evening as an otherwise peaceful audience, which included mothers, fathers, and children, watched Tony Bowen's Soul-Choppers perform. Squad cars swarmed the school parking lot and sprayed the entire crowd with tear gas. The show ended, and residents stumbled home blindly, their eyes burning, many burning with rage at an all-too-typical overreaction by the police. The following morning, organizers met and decided to cancel future events.[69]

Every attempt to manage unrest seemed to backfire or serve merely to illustrate white America's failure to comprehend the nature of unrest. In industrial waterfront cities, public health officials felt pressured not to declare urban beaches unsafe for bathing, regardless of pollution levels and risks to bathers, out of fear that would-be bathers would decide to riot instead. Testifying before a Senate subcommittee in 1970, a former official in the New Haven Health Department disclosed that over the previous summers, public health officials in the cities of Norwalk, Bridgeport, New Haven, and New London had decided to keep polluted beaches open to the public out of fear of "possible rioting in the slums of nearby cities" if they were closed—despite the fact that persons swimming in these areas risked "gastric disturbances" and "non-paralyzing" viral infections.[70] They seemingly had no other choice since, as he explained, "Public bathing areas in Connecticut . . . are usually restricted to use by residents of the municipality where the beach is located. Residents of cities along the Connecticut shore are not permitted the enjoyment of bathing in the cleaner waters of the suburban shore towns but must be content with the less desirable and more polluted facilities of harborside beaches."[71]

In the wake of the King assassination, New York City hastily adopted a program of mass evacuation and temporary relocation of urban youth from the city's roughest neighborhoods. It was called the Open Space Action Institute, and its goal was to get as many kids out of the city and into the "natural" settings of state parks in upstate New York as possible. Every day that summer, sixty or so buses rolled through the neighborhoods of Bedford-Stuyvesant, East New York, and Harlem, picking up kids off the streets and transporting them to places such as Bear Mountain State Park for a vigorous, tiring afternoon of hiking and exploring. These places, one bemused program director commented, "might as well have been in California to these youngsters," so ignorant they were, white officers presumed, of the world outside the urban ghetto.[72] At the end of a long day in the great outdoors, the buses returned to the city and deposited the children back on the street corners where they had found them that morning, filled with positive experiences or, at the very least, they hoped, too tired to go out. Regardless, officials in the newly created city agency credited the summer program with "help[ing] to 'cool it' during the summer."[73]

In 1968 two new Revitalization Corps chapters opened in Newark and Red Bank, New Jersey. That summer volunteers at the new chapters paired forty black children from Newark, Red Bank, and Harlem with families who owned summer vacation homes along the Jersey shore in the towns of Sea Bright and Monmouth Beach. Trouble began almost from the moment the families arrived with black children in tow. Neighbors shunned them. Restaurants where they had eaten on many occasions in the past refused to seat them. Beach clubs where they were members refused to admit them. Even the town's public beaches turned them away, ostensibly because their guests were nonresidents.[74]

Vacationing white families on the Jersey shore treated the arrival of forty black kids as an invasion and responded accordingly. Host families were shattered and distraught and the children confused, some said traumatized. Other charitable organizations caught in such a dilemma invariably issued apologies and promised to do a better job of notifying local officials and residents next time. This is certainly how groups like the Fresh Air Fund operated. Everyone in the wealthy "friendly towns" in Connecticut knew on which summer weekend all the poor black kids from the city would be playing on *their* beach. This was not how Revitalization Corps operated. Rather than retreat, Ned went on the attack. He contacted media outlets throughout New Jersey and New York and detailed the allegations of local residents. He worked to expose the heretofore hidden practices that rendered these ostensibly public beaches off limits to people of color. He made it his mission to shame and embarrass these towns, to draw public attention and scrutiny to forms of bigotry that many Americans, especially whites in the Northeast, preferred to believe existed only in the South.[75]

The story didn't register with the national media, but the experience sparked an outrage in Ned that would never fully be extinguished. Up until then, he had worked to convince privileged whites to question their stereotypes; shed their fears; and give their time, money, and energy toward improving the lives of others. But he had always operated under the assumption that these were fundamentally good people, just blind to the others' misfortunes. On the Jersey shore, however, Corps volunteers encountered forms of racism that were at once highly personal and deeply institutionalized, woven into the fabric of summer life and formalized through policies meant to bar "outsiders." Direct appeals to whites' consciences, Ned was beginning to realize, were alone insufficient. No amount of volunteer work in the ghetto, tutoring programs for black children, or other charitable endeavors could cure the disease—white supremacy—that afflicted the nation.

Ned needed to be more like the residents at Charter Oak Terrace— like Barbara Henderson, whose tenacity and fearlessness forced those in power to listen and take action and inspired and empowered others to also speak truth to power. As head of the Association of Concerned Parents, Henderson kept the pressure on city officials to follow through on their promise to lower the Park River and repair the Flatbush Avenue bridge throughout the winter and spring of 1969. When spring rolled around and the city had done nothing to make the area safer for children and families, she prepared the troops for battle. "It's time for action," Henderson told fellow tenants in late April 1969. "If it takes demonstrations, we'll demonstrate." If we need to stage a sit-in at city hall, the state highway department, the governor's mansion, "we'll sit-in."[76] She fired off telegrams to Governor Dempsey, Hartford's congressman, and Connecticut's two senators, recounting the tragedies of past years and the unfulfilled promises of the previous summer. Henderson summoned officials from the mayor's office and highway department to a meeting at a local church. There, an engineer from the highway department offered up a host of excuses for the delay, most of which were at odds with the excuses given by a representative of the Greater Hartford Flood Commission a week earlier. Both bemoaned the poor relations between the two agencies and chalked the delays up to bureaucratic politics.[77] Henderson was having none of it. "We don't want another, 'let's sit down and talk.' We want something to happen. The last time two kids drowned. We're not going to wait until they start dropping in fours, fives, and sixes."[78] At the meeting, Henderson announced plans for the Mother's Day vigil and promised that this would be just the first "mild step" away from talk and toward action.[79]

Actions—not words—got results. After protesters blocked traffic on the Flatbush Avenue bridge during rush hour and held demonstrations in front of the governor's mansion, Governor Dempsey, Mayor Uccello, and officials in the Flood Commission and State Highway Department held emergency meetings to find an immediate solution to the crisis. Exacerbated by bureaucratic delays and seemingly endless internal debates over costs, contracts, and liabilities, on May 26 the governor ordered the removal of three coffer dams downstream. By May 30, the depth of the river at the Flatbush Avenue bridge had dropped thirty inches. That summer the city installed a new fence to keep kids from swimming in the river and hastily assembled temporary above-ground swimming pools at Charter Oak Terrace and the city's other public housing projects.

"Probably if the people of Charter Oak Terrace draw any conclusions from their dealings with the establishment," a local report commented, "it will be that demonstrations and at least implied threats get action. Patience and rationality and the rest of it seem to have no effect."[80] It was a lesson Ned was learning and would soon begin to apply.

Let's Share Summer

The higher up the economic ladder you get, the less likely you are to say "nigger." But you'll say the same thing when you say, "I'm sorry this is a private beach" . . . which often times is more consequential because you've got the money and the wealth and the power to make it be that way.

Russell West, Revitalization Corps staffer

Russell West still remembers the moment when he decided to join Ned Coll's war on apathy, even if the details are now, some fifty years later, a little fuzzy. It was sometime in the late 1960s, and Russell, his wife, Joanne, and their two children were living in Bristol, Connecticut. Russ had recently taken a job in sales at Proctor and Gamble's New England headquarters after having spent the previous eight years selling cookware door to door. Joanne worked part time at her mother's business and raised their two daughters. They had taken part in some anti–Vietnam War marches and strongly supported the Civil Rights Movement but did not consider themselves activists. One night, their daughter Jessica curled up next to her father as he watched the evening news. Russ remembers, "There had been some particular atrocity against peaceful demonstrators . . . [shown] on the evening news, and . . . there was a black preacher on there, and I can still hear his words. . . . He said, 'White America: it's time for you to choose. Either you're on our side or you're on their side.' My daughter looked up at me and said, 'Dad, are we on his side?' . . . I paused long enough to let her know I was not [going] to answer flippantly, and I looked her in the eye and said, 'Jessica, yes we are.' "[1]

Russ had heard of Revitalization Corps and connected—on a gut level—with its energetic founder. "What he was saying needed to be said, what he was doing needed to be done, and I wanted to be a part of it." He liked that Revitalization Corps was "an action group . . . not a study group or committee." Joanne, too, was immediately struck by Ned's energy and ability to inspire people to action. "He was a dynamo."[2] Days later, Russ strolled into Revitalization Corps's Hartford office. Within a month, he and Joanne were volunteering several hours each week to Corps projects. Ned knew he had a natural salesman on his team and quickly put Russ to work soliciting white suburban families to participate in his latest initiative: providing summer vacations for underprivileged children. In an appearance on the NBC *Today Show* in April 1971, Ned announced plans to bring one hundred thousand children to the Connecticut shoreline that upcoming summer and made a direct appeal to privileged white Americans to "share summer."[3] It was a line he borrowed directly from the Fresh Air Fund, as was his pitch to white audiences, which stressed the negative aspects of urban life and warned of more long, hot summers to come unless families opened their hearts and their summer homes to those less fortunate.

Russ understood the point Ned was trying to make and the purpose of the program. Still, "I wondered about the value of such things" and whether the program reflected the " 'white man's burden' mentality."[4] He wasn't alone. As Revitalization Corps expanded its outreach into the suburban Northeast, many openly questioned the effectiveness of interpersonal strategies for solving structural inequality. "What is this supposed to prove?" wondered one man who attended one of Revitalization Corps's picnics for inner-city youth at a park in Bloomfield. "Many of these kids still have to go home to overcrowded tenements tonight." Ned dismissed the misgivings of middle-class whites as mere rationalizations for their own apathy and inaction. He could not, however, so easily dismiss the criticisms leveled by blacks over what many perceived as Revitalization Corps's missionary-style approach and negative assumptions about urban life. Rather than break bread with white folks in the suburbs, blacks called for community control, black empowerment, and liberation from white liberal paternalism. Many white liberals, it seemed, were more than happy to oblige. "They heard the word 'black power,'" Ned remarked, sarcastically, "and they ran from the ghetto."[5]

Al Cooper pegged Ned as a typical white liberal that the North End could do without. An ex-felon who had turned his life around in prison, Cooper became one of Revitalization Corps's earliest workers. In early 1969, though, he abruptly quit the organization, convinced that Ned was an "opportunist" who was "taking advantage of the black community." Depressed and disillusioned, Cooper began drinking heavily. One evening in April 1969, Ned returned to the headquarters on Main Street to find an inebriated Cooper disrupting a tutoring session for elementary school children. "I said 'hey, you're not gonna be here with these kids, you're drunk.' I think he figured [because I'm] white [I] wasn't going to stand up to him. So he attacked me." Cooper landed several punches to Ned's face before someone was able to pull him away. But Cooper soon broke free and came after him again, this time pushing Ned against a wall and holding him by the throat. "I had trouble breathing and I thought I was dying," Ned later testified.[6] Another worker was able to free Ned from Cooper's grip, and Cooper subsequently fled the scene.

"So then," Ned stated, "I had to make a choice, what do I do about this? This man tried to kill me, a black man, and I'm running a black program in a black neighborhood." To back down in these moments, to show fear, or to simply flee was not only a sign of weakness, Ned concluded. It was a sign of disrespect. It was, he believed, the essence of white liberal condescension: to treat an adversary with "kid gloves" because he or she was black, to not even bother to engage in a fight, to stand silently as one was being attacked and disrespected, like a parent would act toward a child throwing a temper tantrum, and then mete out punishment afterward (in the form of the withdrawal of funds, the withholding of services, or simply a retreat to the comforts and privileges of white suburbia). Instead, Ned pressed charges against Cooper and later testified against him in court. "That's when I learned not to be a candy-ass liberal," Ned later said.[7] In the years that followed, Ned never hesitated in responding to criticisms from local black leaders and community members as he would respond to any other adversary. If he believed someone was "full of shit," Ned said so, to the person's face. Even critics granted, Ned was *straight up*.[8]

And *down*. Indeed, it was not Ned's authenticity that led people on the North End to respect him and accept the presence of Revitalization Corps in the community. It was the work it was performing, day in and day out, much of which was increasingly being led and carried out by a growing circle of black women. While it was white volunteers like Russell West who were sent to knock on doors in West Hartford, on the North End, it was black mothers like Earlie Powell, Florine Cooper, and Ola Grady who were enrolling children in the Corps's tutoring program, who distributed food and clothing to needy families, and who chaperoned groups of children on trips outside the city. Contrary to many critics' assumptions, it was black mothers like Powell who pushed Revitalization Corps to devote its time and energy to getting kids out of the city during the summer months and exposing them to unfamiliar people and places. "I thought that it was very, very important at that time to get our kids some experience, getting out to see how other people even live[d]. A lot of kids weren't used to that, and all they did was probably stay right up in the [housing projects] or work all day, playing around in the yards."[9]

As they ventured further outside the city, though, Powell and fellow volunteers encountered increased hostility from communities who would have preferred that "ghetto children" remain in the projects and who were willing to employ extreme measures to keep summers to themselves. As they did, Ned's modest pleas for privileged whites to share summer with the poor turned into a crusade to take summer back from those who had expropriated its most sought-after space and most defining symbol: the beach.

When he began soliciting support for his summer campaign, Ned reached out to charitable organizations in shoreline towns. In Old Saybrook, Ned forged ties with the local chapter of the Jaycees, an auxiliary of the Chamber of Commerce whose membership consisted of young, civic-minded men. At the time, David Royston was a recent graduate of Georgetown Law School who had opened up a practice in town. He was also a former classmate of Ned's at Fairfield University in

the early 1960s. He admired Ned's tenacity and dedication to community service, and he and his wife, Eunice, agreed to host children from
Hartford in their home. Their guests enjoyed picnics and swam at the
beach. Some of them seemed, at times, more perplexed than impressed
by the well-heeled town's recreational amenities, more accustomed to
a playground paved with asphalt than one blanketed with sand. At one
point during the visit, one child asked Royston, "Is it okay if I go out
and play in the parking lot?"[10]

For every family like the Roystons, there were a dozen more that
were not about to let a poor child—or the problem of poverty—
interfere with their summer vacation plans. As Corps volunteers went
door to door in West Hartford, they heard husbands, fathers, wives, and
mothers offer any number of excuses for not being able to help, often
prefaced with an expression of support for the Corps's mission. Some
said they had no plans to vacation that summer; others denied owning
a cottage along the shore; still others expressed interest but when dates
were proposed, said that none fit their schedule. Others asked if they
could simply write a check instead. By midsummer, it became clear that
the number of children who signed up for the program vastly exceeded
the number of white families who had agreed to participate. As he struggled to enlist volunteers, Ned began to question whether these voluntary
arrangements merely reinforced the existing nexus of power, rendering
a trip to the beach a privilege granted by the wealthy to the poor rather
than a right shared by all.[11]

It bothered Ned that in places like Old Saybrook, the charitable
support and time a few families provided seemed to let everyone else
off the hook. He needed to test out a new strategy, one powerful enough
to penetrate the sand curtains that hung across the state's shoreline. He
needed to find a way to force the rich to see the poor, to bear witness
to their humanity, and to recognize how the privileges of wealth and
whiteness (among them the right to claim ownership over the beach)
negatively impacted the lives of everyone else. More important, he
needed to find an issue that would capture the public's attention and
galvanize others to take action.

Ned's frustration, combined with his ingenuity, became the mother
of invention. Instead of waiting to be invited, why not just show up, he

thought. "Surprise," he later explained, "gives us a chance to confront people who haven't been asked before, to say, 'This is not a discussion next week or a committee meeting next month, it's a chance to do something right here and now.'"[12] By barreling into quaint shoreline towns unannounced and unloading a bus full of kids from the projects rather than soliciting volunteers and making arrangements ahead of time, Ned aimed to, as he put it, "confront . . . people's consciences. We're not giving people a direct opportunity to pass the buck."[13]

On a Friday morning in July 1971, a school bus pulled up in front of the Corps headquarters in Hartford. Dozens of children, along with a group of parents, piled in and headed to the shore.[14] Their first surprise trip to the beach was uneventful. It was an overcast day in Old Saybrook. Few people were on the shore, and those who were seemed unperturbed by the uninvited visitors. Still, the children felt awkward, unsure of what to make of the white faces staring at them. As one girl recalled, "When we first got out there on the beach and those white people were staring at us, I felt like it was all kind of crazy, sort of a bad dream—you know, 'what am I doing here?' But Ned Coll said to me, 'Don't just stand there, Lorraine, go up and talk to someone.' And I did and most of the people were real nice, and after a while I began to think it was a good idea after all."[15]

Weeks later, Ned led another expedition, this time to Westport's Compo Beach. As the children disembarked from the bus, carrying "battered suitcases and shopping bags of belongings," volunteers canvassed the beach in search of families willing to welcome a child into their home for the weekend or longer. They got few takers and many cold shoulders. One volunteer was reportedly "reduced to tears by an angry resident's tirade on blacks and public welfare." Ned was furious, and more determined than ever to confront people's consciences and dare them to pass the buck.[16]

The following weekend the Revitalization Corps bus headed to the town of Clinton, a quiet shoreline town in the center of the state. From the moment of its arrival, confusion reigned. First, beach officials tried to prevent the bus from entering the parking lot, claiming the public beach was reserved for local residents and invited guests only. Ned refused to back down and eventually cajoled his way into the lot. Once they got

Children and staff outside Revitalization Corps's headquarters on
Hartford's North End. *Photo © Bob Adelman. Courtesy Bob Adelman.*

inside, Ned told the kids to fan out across the beach and ask families
if they could spend the weekend at their home. Volunteers were told
to stay back and supervise the children from afar. Persons who would
think nothing of slamming the door in the face of an adult volunteer,
Ned surmised, would be hard pressed to rudely reject a direct request
from a child, especially one who seemed to be alone. He was wrong.
Persons on the beach that afternoon did not hesitate to express their
outrage at the imposition the Corps's arrival placed on town facilities.
Nor did some of them shy away from open expressions of racial bigotry.
One woman reportedly sought out a volunteer and loudly berated her

for, as she put it, "bring[ing] a busload of niggers and dump[ing] them on our beach."[17]

Ned's tactical decision to send the kids out without chaperones by their side also exposed him to a charge of child abandonment, one that would dog him and his organization throughout the decade. People told stories of children left on their own, wandering along the sides of roads, carrying shabby suitcases or bags of clothes slung over their shoulders; of being harassed in their homes by volunteers, who appeared on their doorstep on a Friday night and tried to force them to take in one or more children for the weekend; of suspicious characters who "took notes on why they wouldn't [take a child] and [jotted down] their address." The "following week [our] house [was] broken into," one complainant told an investigator, who later passed along his findings to Governor Meskill.[18]

Children and parents from Hartford en route to the Connecticut shore. *Photo © Bob Adelman. Courtesy Bob Adelman.*

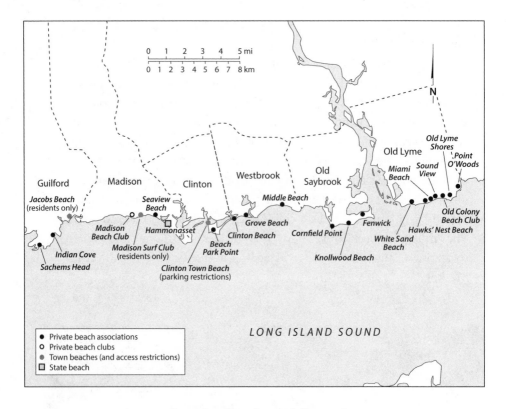

Central region of coastal Connecticut.

The negative reaction the Corps received in Clinton paled, though, in comparison to the response among summer residents of private beach associations. In mid-August, Revitalization Corps staged its first unannounced visit to a private beach on the state's eastern shore. Founded in 1927, Old Lyme Shores had become a haven for "lace curtain" Irish families, most of whom hailed from suburban Hartford.[19] Over the years it developed a reputation as one of the more exclusionary (if not exclusive) beach communities among the nine located in Old Lyme. Its members did not descend from old monied New England families; when compared to many of the other beach associations in Connecticut, the homes at Old Lyme Shores appeared very modest, the families who flocked there each summer decidedly middle class. Many of the families had only recently purchased their homes; for them, the purchase of a summer cottage signaled their arrival among a select set. Indeed, nothing symbolized their achievements more than the beach that fronted their summer homes. And nothing seemed more vulnerable to attack—from the forces of nature, as its members devoted an increasingly larger share of their tax revenues toward protecting the beach from erosion, and from the masses, who by day nonchalantly strolled along their shore as if it were theirs and by night engaged in unspeakable acts and all forms of debauchery. Or so they imagined. A few stray beer cans proved to be sufficient evidence to sustain such charges.

As soon as they arrived at Old Lyme Shores, Ned sensed the residents' hostility—to the imposition, to their presumptuousness, to their mere presence. As they disembarked from the bus, a middle-aged white woman glared at them from her white clapboard cottage, hands on her hips, teeth clenched, brow furrowed.[20] As the children got to work building sandcastles, hunting for crabs, and tossing balls, white mothers dashed out of their homes and grabbed their own kids off the beach. Men and women shouted at the unwelcome guests to leave. Older white kids and teenagers heckled, taunted, and shouted racist epithets. "You'd think the black panthers had arrived en masse. Or the Red Chinese," one white homeowner commented. "Not an incredibly cute group of six and seven year olds."[21]

Soon after the kids hit the beach, Old Lyme's first selectman, Merle S. Bugbee, called in the state police. Within minutes, two beach patrolmen, one squad car, and two state troopers were on the scene, warning Ned that they would all be arrested for trespassing if they did not leave.[22] Only association members and their invited guests were allowed on the beach. Ned tried to persuade the officers and assembled crowd of onlookers to allow them to stay, to no avail.

But just as Ned began to summon the children and head back to the bus, Forry Laucks, a petite, quiet woman who had spent every summer at Old Lyme Shores since childhood, stepped off her porch and walked toward the beach. All of the children and Corps staff members, she told the officers, were her guests. They could all stay, and the officers and state troopers could leave. Her neighbors were incredulous. "You cannot overload your house, madam," a flustered Fennessey Canty blurted while waving her finger. "We cannot allow it." Other neighbors joined Canty in imploring Laucks to change her mind, and when she refused to back down, they bitterly denounced her for what they described as a selfish, inconsiderate act. Laucks said she could not understand "this big fear." She simply wanted to allow the children to enjoy a day at the beach and thought it would "do the kids down here good to meet some of these children." One by one, other neighbors stepped forward to stand with Laucks and welcome the children to the beach and into their homes. In all, most of the children who wanted to stay overnight did. But those families who welcomed them found themselves shunned by their neighbors. The Sunday morning after the confrontation, the priest at Old Lyme's Catholic church gave a sermon that, as attendees later described, condoned the actions of those persons who had fought to keep the uninvited guests off the beach and assured them they had done nothing wrong.[23]

Others disagreed. In the days that followed, all of the region's major newspapers ran stories on the confrontation at Old Lyme Shores and included every unflattering detail of the actions taken by beach association members to keep black youth off the beach. "They had a chance to perform a great act of Christian charity and they blew it," Old Lyme resident Jere Smith remarked.[24] Mary Ann Smith, whose family hosted four children, later bemoaned, "I can't help but think what a glorious weekend it would have been if those wonderful kids had been greeted with the love that our four little houseguests later showed us." She called her summer community "sick" and oblivious to "the festering situation of segregation" in America.[25] Sandra Joncus, whose family hosted two children, expressed gratitude to Coll for helping her "overc[o]me [her] inertia" toward helping the less fortunate. "It takes an extra push to bridge the gap between what ought to be and what is . . . and to bring some of us procrastinators to the point of action."[26] Pitney-Bowes executive Jerry Loiselle, whose family also hosted children during the August visit, commended Ned for drawing greater attention to the challenges facing small-town New England, where racism was prevalent but, unlike in "places like Birmingham, Alabama, where the problems of integration are a very visible matter," remained "below the surface."[27]

Those members who had fought to keep the kids off the beach remained defiant, even as they stressed their nonracist motives for opposing the visits. Some argued that the unplanned visits established a dangerous precedent and set a bad example. Fennessey Canty called Ned's actions as "border[ing] on anarchy." "If situations similar to this are allowed to continue," she predicted, "we could lose our property rights." Ned should be teaching these children that in order to own a home in a beachfront community and enjoy the privileges that go along with it, "They have to learn, earn, and work," another woman added. Instead, he is "teach[ing] . . . children to break the law." Others objected to the manner in which Ned solicited support. "Personally, I like to be romanced a little before I give to charity," Frank Arioli, the beach association's vice president, commented. Many tried to turn the tables and accuse Ned of being indifferent to the needs of children by using them as props in his political cause. "Where are the child protective agencies," Barbara S. Sherman wondered. "Why haven't they stepped in to prevent further exploitation and embarrassment of Hartford's ghetto children, transported to [the] beach and distributed . . . like oranges."[28]

Ned and five of the parents who had chaperoned the trip tried to arrange a meeting with local officials to clear the air but were rebuffed. The head of the beach association's board of directors told them they had nothing to discuss. "They hid from us," Ned said of the board members. "They didn't want to meet the parents of the children. The[y] . . . couldn't look these women in the eyes."[29] Instead, town and beach association officials scrambled to tighten existing beach access laws and enact new ones before the Corps staged a return visit. The day after the Corps's visit, Old Lyme's Board of Selectmen called a special town meeting to discuss public and private beach access laws. Members of Old Lyme Shores crowded into the town hall and demanded that officials hire extra officers to police private beaches and arrest trespassers. A state trooper promised that in the future, state troopers would stop any buses from entering private beach associations without members' permission. The Board of Selectmen passed a resolution stating that outside groups could not bring children to town beaches without permission. A week later, the Old Lyme Shores Association held an emergency meeting. Dozens of members rose to advocate, as one person described, "for tighter security, more guards and gates." Boos rained down on members who had hosted children when they rose to speak. The board voted to form a committee to revise the beach charter to prevent nonmember access.[30]

That November, a consortium of local committees, social clubs, and community organizations representing shoreline towns met to discuss and formulate plans to both prevent Revitalization Corps from ambushing local beaches *and* prevent another round of negative publicity. The challenge was in finding a way for shoreline towns and private beach associations to appear supportive, at least publicly, of the Corps's mission of providing opportunities for urban black youth to access the coast while at the same time ensuring that beach exclusion laws remained intact and local communities wielded control over the numbers of visitors and timing of visits. They proposed the formation of a local information center that would connect families who were interested in hosting children with the Hartford office of Revitalization Corps, which would provide the names of children who wished to visit the shore. The information center would handle all arrangements, including the dates of visits and transportation to and from the shore. This, its supporters argued, would ensure that no family would be put in the position of having to turn a child away, and no child would have to experience the feeling of rejection.[31]

It was a classic white New Englander subterfuge: a measure designed to preserve exclusion and privilege disguised as an offer of assistance and expression of concern. And Ned was having none of it. He rejected the proposal out of hand. When negotiations proved fruitless, officials in Old Lyme tried an end run around Ned, entering into negotiations with Hartford officials to establish a program that would bring groups of twenty inner-city children ages six to thirteen down to the shore for one of three midweek sessions of the town's choosing. They called it Vacations Offered to Hartford Youngsters (VOHY), perhaps the most uninspiring name and most forgettable acronym ever conceived.[32]

At the beginning of the summer, Ned had aimed to simply provide a trip to a beach to as many North End children as he could. In that respect, the summer was a resounding success. In total, Revitalization Corps made fifteen trips to the shore that summer, bringing over one thousand children. "We would have 48 or 50 kids on one bus," Powell remembers. "So we had six buses, and do you know how many kids that is? That's 300 children [per trip]." Revitalization Corps never came close to meeting the demand. "Them kids was dying to go!" "Ned sent that bus out there at 7 o'clock in the morning. They would be already at my door, waiting for that bus to come. They'd jump right on it. . . . I think I said to Ned more than once, 'This was a blessing from the skies,' because some of these children would have never got to a beach."[33]

By summer's end, Ned had come to see these trips as providing more than a day at the beach for the kids. They also subjected to public scrutiny exclusionary policies and practices that served to perpetuate inequality and forced communities that had remained aloof to the nation's racial crisis to take a stand and individuals of good will to do their part. He called the surprise visits "probably the most effective tactic we've used." And he was unapologetic in enlisting children to advance the cause. "You bet your life I'm using kids!"[34] They were the ones being denied the opportunity to enjoy what the American public had come to regard as a rite (and right) of childhood: a day at the beach.

Plus, the approach worked. At every stage of the Civil Rights Movement, children and the rights of childhood figured prominently in protest rhetoric and tactics. And with good reason. As Rebecca de Schweinitz points out, "Linking African American civil rights to ideas about childhood and to images of young people helped make the movement meaningful, even compelling, to blacks as well as to a white American public not yet committed to the idea of racial equality."[35]

The Corps's unannounced visit to Old Lyme Shores accomplished one of Ned's main objectives—raising public awareness of his "war on apathy"—even as the experience led him to question whether it was apathy he was battling on the shore. When it came to the public's right to access "their" beaches, the residents of elite shoreline towns and members of private beach associations were far from apathetic. Indeed, the speed at which they had moved to prevent the Corps from returning showed just how active and engaged these communities were on matters of integration and diversity. A vocal, energetic majority of them were actively opposed to public access and prepared to fight "outsiders" and intimidate their neighbors to protect their beaches from such "outsiders." That summer, Ned saw how the state's sand curtain was

drawn and maintained, and he would never see the beach and the people who claimed it as their own the same way again. What had begun
as a modest, and seemingly noncontroversial, effort to provide impoverished children a day at the beach was morphing into a cause, one that
threatened to become a protracted legal struggle—over the status of
beaches as property and over the question of whether towns could deny
the general public access to public property.

The incident at Old Lyme marked a turning point for Revitalization
Corps and for Ned personally. It signaled his embrace of confrontation
and provocation. It also marked the moment when Revitalization Corps
joined the national fight for open beaches. In 1959, Texas became the
first state in the nation to explicitly guarantee the public's right to access
the state's sandy beaches. The Texas Open Beaches Act guaranteed the
public's right to the area between the mean low tide and the vegetation line, ordered the removal of all barricades along the shore, and severely restricted further beachfront housing construction.[36] Upon being
elected to Congress in 1968, the author of the Texas bill, Robert Eckhardt,
proposed a national open beaches act modeled on the Texas legislation.
In 1969, Eckhardt introduced a bill before Congress that would have
established, under federal law, the "free and unrestricted right to use
[beaches]"; prohibited "fences, barriers, and other restraints on the use
of the beaches by the public"; and empowered the Interior and Justice
Departments to enforce these rights. In addition, the bill would have
provided states with federal funds to condemn land for easements that
would ensure public access. That same year, Oregon became the second
state to guarantee the public's right to access all sandy beaches along its
coast when the state's supreme court upheld a bill passed by the state's
legislature on the basis that the public enjoyed a customary right to the
dry, sand portion of the shore.[37]

By the late 1960s federal policymakers were awakening to the dire
conditions of the nation's shorelines and waterways—and to the inter-
connected nature of the challenges facing ocean and Great Lake ecolo-
gies. In 1968 the President's Council on Recreation and Natural Beauty
released its report on the state of the American environment, *From Sea
to Shining Sea*. Its authors cataloged, in devastating detail, the frenzy of

unplanned coastal development in the decades following World War II that had resulted in "natural shorelines . . . being fenced, bulldozed, paved, and built upon" and had replaced "tidelands, beaches, dunes, and seacliffs . . . with shacks and chalets, hamburger emporiums and parking lots, highways and billboards, power plants and even oil derricks." To reverse the trend toward destructive coastal land-use practices, the report argued that more—not less—of the shoreline should be made available to the general public. Efforts to reshape the shore had been done by and in the service of private property owners and commercial interests. As the public became excluded from its shores and alienated from coastal environments, these practices threatened to become more widespread and to elicit less public opposition. As such, the report concluded, any attempt to build a cleaner, more sustainable future for the nation's coasts must include a vigorous campaign to expand public beach access. "It is time to proclaim the principle that all Americans—of present and future generations—have a right to enjoy the shoreline experience," the report declared, "and that ocean and lake shoreline[s] with high-quality scenic and recreation values are natural resources to be conserved and not destroyed."[38]

The following year, the U.S. Commission on Marine Science, Engineering, and Resources issued its report, "Our Nation and the Sea." Known as the Stratton Commission (after its chairman, Ford Foundation chairman Julius Stratton), it likewise identified the absence of a centralized coastal management agency whose powers superseded the narrow concerns of local authorities as the chief obstacle to more sound, sustainable coastal environmental policies and practices. "The key to more effective use of our coastland," it wrote, "is the introduction of a management system permitting conscious and informed choices among development alternatives, providing for proper planning and encouraging recognition of the long-term importance of maintaining the quality of this productive region in order to ensure both its enjoyment and the sound utilization of its resources."[39]

In cities and towns across coastal America, fights pitting beachfront homeowners and real estate developers seeking to fence off portions of the beach against citizens and a growing number of advocacy groups demanding access erupted with growing frequency.[40] Out of these local

skirmishes and discreet contests over coveted patches of sand began to
emerge a movement, national in scope, for restoring what proponents
characterized as the public's "ancient and well-established . . . right" to
the nation's beaches.[41]

Ned resumed that fight the following spring, when he rented a
cabin on Shore Road in Old Lyme and turned it into a campground
for inner-city youth and headquarters for a summer-long campaign to
open the state's shoreline to the public. By June they had cleared the
grounds and hung a massive banner announcing Revitalization Corps's
arrival in front of the property, just in time for the arrival of summer
cottage owners.[42] For both seasonal and year-round residents, Revitalization Corps's opening of a summer campground in town promised to
reopen wounds that had still not healed. The annual ritual of electing
board members to private beach associations, once a celebratory occasion that marked the beginning of the summer season, now became the
scene of petty skullduggery among rival groups. At Old Lyme Shores,
those in the vocal majority who had opposed Ned's "invasion" the summer before enacted measures meant to strengthen their hold on power.
They curtailed the ability of property owners to vote via proxy and
placed restrictions on who could speak at board meetings, moves aimed
at silencing, as one critic put it, those association members who held
views "not in conformity with their own."[43] Once folksy, carefree board
meetings turned tense, as officials tried to rush through business and
hastily enact controversial items without debate. Some members walked
out in disgust. Many families were still not on speaking terms.

The hostility of local residents to the Corps's presence was palpa-
ble. Each weekend, a new group of children from Hartford arrived, and
each afternoon, they spread out on the town's public beach or walked
and played along the wet sand portion of private beaches. Mother and
Corps volunteer Florine Cooper likened a walk down the beach to the
parting of the sea. Wherever she went, people would "grab their chairs
and children and leave."[44] On the beach, Earlie Powell recalled, white
parents taught racism to their children. "We could go to the water, and
the people would get their kids in the house; they didn't want their kids
outdoors when we were around. . . . Some of our kids . . . would say,
'hi,' and the little [white] kids would be waving, but the [white] parents

would [say], 'Come in the house!' . . . They were scared of us. They didn't want their kids near none of those kids. . . . It was sad. It was just like, 'What? I can't believe this is happening.' But it was happening." And because it was, the job of Corps workers and volunteers was to shield black children from racist abuse. "We as grown-ups knew what was going on," Powell said. "So we would kind of hold our kids and keep them tight so we could watch over them."[45]

In this climate, those who supported what Revitalization Corps was doing, the principles it stood for, and the dialogue it hoped to instigate, fell silent. Local officials, fearing the wrath of angry constituents, failed to speak out against the incessant verbal abuse and hostile treatment of black parents and children by residents. Throughout the summer, Ned staged public events that, almost by design, exposed the cowardice of local officials. In July he invited thirty-two town selectmen and officers in local beach associations to a barbeque picnic at the Corps's summer headquarters. "I'm really trying to get things in a positive mood," he told a reporter.[46] He "hoped to use the picnic to acquaint officials with the corps program."[47] Dozens of parents and children were on hand. A group of inner-city mothers prepared food. Only one invitee came: Marjorie Schmitt, a selectman from Guilford. Later that month, Ned invited seventy clergymen from area churches to another picnic. Only two came. (One of the two was later censured by his congregation for doing so.) Throughout the summer, the cottage was subject to incessant harassing phone calls. In late August, it was broken into, ransacked, and vandalized.[48]

Ned was determined to make local officials fear the bad publicity of forcibly preventing children from enjoying a day at the beach more than the organized resistance of a noisy bloc of seasonal homeowners. Some, like Clinton's First Selectman Margery C. Scully, tried to outmaneuver Ned while keeping hostile forces within her community at bay. In late July 1972, Clinton officials learned of Ned's plans to stage an unannounced visit to their town beach the following month. Initially, Scully tried to upstage Ned by extending an invitation for Hartford youth to come to the beach on several predetermined days in August. She expressed hope that such a move would "help us solve—before they begin—some of the problems which other towns have experienced. . . .

I hope this is a way to avoid trouble."[49] She was wrong. The move back-fired. Ned didn't take the bait, just as one of Scully's fellow selectmen, Hubert Adams, predicted. Such a plan, he told Scully, failed to recognize the entire purpose of these visits, "which is to shock middle America into what is going on."[50] Local residents, meanwhile, were outraged that Scully would open up the town's beaches to "ghetto youth" on *any* day. For several days, Scully's office was inundated with phone calls from angry constituents. One resident promised to initiate impeachment proceedings against her if she followed through on her plans.[51] Another expressed his amazement that town officials and local residents would even contemplate welcoming Coll back "after that lowdown act of invasion" the previous summer.[52] Scully quickly backtracked and scaled down her invitation to Revitalization Corps to one designated day: Monday, August 28. On that day, Scully stressed, "The corps would not . . . be permitted . . . to solicit, from town residents, weekend accommodations for the children."[53] "They are to come for the day and leave when the beach closes."[54] "Any double crosses" by Coll, Selectman Stephen Jackson added, "and the beach will be closed."[55]

Clinton officials had good reason to fear being double-crossed. Ned had developed a habit of announcing deals before they had been completed and interpreting vague promises as firm commitments. Public officials quickly learned that no conversation with Ned was off the record and that any expression of support for the Corps's mission would surely be shared with the public. It was all part of Ned's strategy of forcing people in positions of power to take a stand, to goad them into action or expose them as cowards and hypocrites. It was the art of deception in the cause of truth and transparency. And it enraged those who tried to negotiate with Ned to no end. Like Grant Harris, the president of the Black Point Beach Association, who in July agreed to meet with Ned to discuss Revitalization Corps's request to allow a group of campers to stay overnight on its private beach. The meeting was cordial. No matter how controversial he became, in one-on-one meetings, Ned could be incredibly charming and disarming. Harris tried to flatter Ned, telling him how much he admired his work and wanted to do all he could to help him fulfill his goal of providing summer vacations for urban youth. Ned responded by saying he could start by agreeing to allow

one hundred children to spend the night at Black Point Beach sometime later that summer. Harris promised to take the matter up with his
board of directors and assured Ned he would get back in touch with
him shortly. "That ought to keep him off our backs," Harris might have
thought as he walked an ebullient Ned to the door. He had given Ned
the run-around, and by all indications, Ned never caught on. All that
was left was a timely follow-up call informing Ned that, unfortunately,
the board could not find any day during the remainder of the summer
that fit its members' schedules. Perhaps next year?, he would suggest.
Either way, Black Point's president would have accomplished his main
objective: preventing his community from becoming the target of future protests.[56]

When Harris reached the Black Point's main office the following
morning, his phone was ringing off the hook. "Black Point Beach Group
Will Host Youngsters" read the headline in that morning's *Hartford
Courant*.[57] Shortly after meeting with Harris the previous day, Ned had
contacted Tom Condon, the *Courant* reporter who covered shoreline
communities, to announce the agreement he had supposedly reached
with Harris earlier that afternoon. The article that appeared the following morning provided the details, along with a quote from Ned praising
Black Point for its generosity of spirit and calling on other beach associations to follow its lead. Black Point homeowners were stunned—and
enraged. Angry calls poured in, some threatening Harris and his family
members with physical violence. Harris hastily called a press conference, where he denied making any deal and denounced Ned's previous
statements as "ill-timed, unauthorized and erroneous." "At no time,"
Harris stressed, "did the Board of Governors or the association in any
formal way endorse Coll's bringing children to the beach club." He went
on to denounce Ned as "thoughtless. He's created a tense antagonistic
situation where none existed before and where none need have existed."
Harris, an elementary school principal, was particularly incensed at
being put in the position of having to either deny children access to
Black Point's private beach or risk the venomous outrage and ostracism
of friends and neighbors. He stressed his love for kids. He questioned
Ned's motives. "It seems to me that with this publicity release he's revealed purposes other than giving ghetto children relief at the beach."[58]

And Harris employed the increasingly standard canard used by opponents to defame Ned: he accused him of abandoning children.

More nasty, bitter disputes with shoreline town and beach association officials over what Ned invariably called "misunderstandings" followed. In Old Saybrook, Ned tried and eventually lost the patience of its first selectman, Raymond Kotowski, after purportedly twice requesting and twice failing to show for meetings. After the second time he failed to show, Kotowski denounced Ned's actions as a "disservice" to whites and blacks alike; promised not to allow his office "or the town of Old Saybrook to be used by [Coll] as a springboard for sensationalism or as a headline seeking tool"; and warned him that "responsible town officials will not tolerate the transportation of minor children, under your auspices, into areas owned or under the control of the town of Old Saybrook, without having responsible adult citizens of Old Saybrook as an escort or host." If Ned failed to abide by these rules, Kotowski promised, he would be arrested and charged with endangering the lives of children. "The people of Old Saybrook are compassionate and understanding and are always willing to help and share with our less fortunate brothers. . . . If the less fortunate of this world are to enjoy any of the fruits or labor of the people of Old Saybrook, it will be because of their kindness and generosity and not because of Ned Coll."[59]

In the midst of this tempest, some local officials were beginning to find their sea legs. Others remained adrift, just praying for an end to summer. In Clinton, Selectman Scully's capitulation failed to appease those who opposed any concession to Revitalization Corps's demands. "Inviting the invaders for a day at the beach after that invasion last year is like inviting an assailant to dinner after being assaulted by him," Clinton resident Robert Olson wrote. "Why not proclaim August 28 Ned Coll day and have a parade and services at the beach. At this time change the name to Ned Coll Beach. After all his corps captured it without a struggle."[60] Other residents, meanwhile, said Scully's earlier backpedaling had merely emboldened the town's vocally antagonistic (to others, openly racist) faction opposed to allowing any outsiders onto its beaches. Resident Paul Bristol said he was horrified by what he'd heard openly expressed by his fellow citizens, "saying things that make Archie Bunker seem like Mary Poppins."[61] Dorothy Reba asked, "Have we become so greedy that we resent one day's use of the beach by those who aren't fortunate enough to live along the shoreline?"[62]

"Well, yes, we have," many replied, by their actions if not their words. In the days prior to Revitalization Corps's planned visit to Clinton, opponents made plans to stage a massive act of civil disobedience to protest the town's decision to allow urban black youth the use of its beach for one afternoon. After the Corps's bus passed through the town beach's gates, a group of persons planned to form a cavalcade and march en masse to the entrance and demand free admission themselves. The whole plan was based on the mistaken belief that the Corps group was being admitted free of charge. In fact, private donors had arranged to cover the expenses. But no matter. The plan never came to fruition, but a group of protesters did come, hoping to serenade the bus filled with children, ages ten and younger, with boos, jeers, and catcalls as it crossed Waterside Lane Bridge and entered the beach grounds.[63]

True to form, the Corps buses arrived two hours late, by which time many of the protesters had drifted away. In their place came numbers of locals who wanted to show their support for Revitalization Corps's mission. Volunteer and civic groups brought sandwiches and drinks for the visitors. White parents brought their children to play. Teenagers who believed in civil rights and racial equality came. As she awaited their arrival, Scully grinned and shook hands with supporters and tried desperately to appear calm before the television crew that was on hand, waiting in anticipation that Ned might do or say something outlandish or spark a confrontation. Ironically, Clinton's town beach was, on this day, covered in mud washed ashore from an ongoing dredging project that had kept attendance low all summer. The weather that afternoon was awful. As one report noted, "Winds whipped sand into a stinging spray, the water into a chop and the air had a slight chill." The children who streamed out of the buses that afternoon did not seem to mind. Some rushed straight into the surf; others headed for the playground set. Groups of older kids picked teams for pick-up basketball and volleyball games. A music teacher from the local elementary school led a group of children in song. Counselors from the town's recreational board taught kids how to fish. Tears of joy streamed down the face of a white mother as she watched her son meet and play with children of a different race for the first time. "I'm so proud of them," she told a reporter. "That's just beautiful." Despite the weather, one Clinton area teenager said, "It was the best day of the whole summer." Another wondered "what all the fuss had been about." Scully was beaming with pride.[64]

Others still stewed in anger. "Why were townspeople not called to vote on bringing the children into the beach?" Donald Chartier asked. "What right had the Board to use taxpayers' property and money for a picnic?" Chartier's wife added, "We heard Mrs. Scully on television say how marvelous the town of Clinton thought the visit was. I am part of the town and I don't think it was marvelous. . . . You invited them once; next time it will be more kids from Hartford and some from New Haven. This is only the beginning."[65]

In Old Lyme, local residents wanted to be sure that the end of summer also meant the end of Revitalization Corps's presence in town. As the temperature cooled, the Corps's trips to the seasonal cottage on Shore Drive grew less frequent. In early October, Ned and others boarded it up for the winter. They kept the Revitalization Corps banner hanging from the roof. Around 1:35 a.m. on the morning of November 12, flames burst out from the building's windows. Less than seventy-five feet away sat the local fire station. For nearly an hour, the fire burned unabated before firefighters showed up. By then, half of the building had been destroyed; the rest had suffered heavy smoke damage. Ned found the fire department's slow response highly suspicious; it was not the first, nor would it be the last, time local authorities in shoreline towns had failed to respond to or investigate crimes against Revitalization Corps persons or property. "Here was a cottage that was used for kids," Ned said as he fought back tears. "A lot of people, including parents and kids, worked hard to paint it and get it ready, and then, apparently, some one comes along and sets fire to it."[66]

They had come to the shore seeking relief and renewal from the Sound's waters. Instead, they found fire. Next time, Ned knew what to expect—and what to deliver in return. The war for the shore had just begun.

FIVE

Gut Liberalism

What we are fighting is not poverty. We're after negativism and fear. . . .

The problem is that whites are making judgments from a distance.

They are reading James Baldwin instead of meeting Mrs. Baldwin.

Ned Coll

B y the early 1970s Ned found himself increasingly at war with
the persona the general public had foisted upon him: a liberal
do-gooder whose work the Establishment could get behind
because it seemed worthy and, compared to the alternatives,
nonthreatening. White liberals in suburban Hartford spoke admiringly
of his work ethic and spirit—his sixteen-hour workdays, his numerous
"operations"—and his determination to tackle poverty and prejudice on
a case-by-case, person-to-person basis. Ned's calls for people in power
and of privilege to do more for others, and for those wanting a more
equal society to focus on helping the individual, resonated loudly and
seemed to drown out his more fundamental critiques of how power and
privilege operated and on the structural forces that produced inequality.
To its supporters and admirers, Revitalization Corps's ethos of volun-
tarism and civic engagement lit the path toward a more just, equitable
society. To its critics, it constituted a way for white liberals to feel better
about themselves, a form of penance for the privileges of whiteness that
ultimately served to uphold the status quo.

The problem for Ned was that the message people heard and came to embrace or reject was not his message. So in awe of Ned's devotion to the poor, members of the Establishment tended not to dwell on his underlying critique of liberalism and biting criticism of white liberals longer than it took to write a check or donate a pile of clothes or box of canned goods. Few stopped to consider what vision of Kennedy's Ned was referring to when he invoked—as he did at every opportunity— the name of the slain president. Revitalization Corps's mission was the fulfillment of the challenge President Kennedy had set forth in his inaugural address—a citizenry guided by the maxim of self-sacrifice for the common good ("Ask not what your country can do for you, but what you can do for your country"). This challenge began, but did not end, with two hours of volunteer work each week.

Such small steps, Ned had hoped, would become the catalysts for a transformation (or as he saw it, a revitalization) of the nation's values, away from the crass materialism and instant self-gratification promulgated by Madison Avenue and from sacrifice-free brand of growth liberalism espoused by the slain president's successor, Lyndon B. Johnson. For a brief moment, it seemed to Ned as if Robert F. Kennedy might rekindle his slain brother's more demanding version of liberalism and might be the one to start telling the young men and women of its swelling colleges and universities and the home-owning families of a suburban nation that, yes, they needed to do more for others and, no, they did not get to where they were by their own pluck and hard work alone. They also had the massive expansion in the welfare state under the New Deal to thank—and now it was time to pay it forward. In 1968, Bobby Kennedy seemed ready to tell privileged white Americans what so many other liberal politicians feared to say: the ideals liberals espoused came at a cost, and society's most privileged, most fortunate, should be expected to pay it. Before an audience of medical students at Indiana University in the spring of 1968, candidate Kennedy called for an expansion in social security and Medicare benefits. A skeptical student asked Kennedy, somewhat sarcastically, "Where are you going to get all the money for these federally subsidized programs you are talking about?" Without hesitation, Kennedy shot back, "From you. You are the privileged ones." It was, to Ned, Kennedy's finest moment and remains to this day Ned's favorite quote, one that he mentions in virtually any conversation on what liberalism should be and what liberals should stand for.[1] Bobby Kennedy, Ned mused to one reporter, "never let an audience off the hook before reminding them of their personal responsibility to other people."[2]

Though no one knew it at the time, that impromptu moment in an Indianapolis auditorium in 1968 marked the end of an era, the last time an unabashedly liberal politician could tell inconvenient truths about wealth and inequality, about the hard work and common sacrifice the achievement of a "great society" entailed, without its being treated as an act of political suicide. Never again would a liberal politician so willingly admit and offer a full-throated defense of liberalism's costs, conceding to what its detractors had been saying all along (that "somebody's gotta pay for all this") and then turn the tables on those critics and challenge them to explain exactly why they shouldn't pay. It was no coincidence that that moment came—and went—in 1968, just as the era of postwar prosperity came to an end and the "age of limits" began. As America entered the 1970s and as the nation's economy began to slow and then crater, the promise of growth liberalism was replaced, in American voters' minds, with the zero-sum game caricature of liberalism that the resurgent Right would come to lambast, with much success, for decades to come: big spending programs paid for through higher taxes, a state functioning merely to distribute wealth from the top to the bottom, to the benefit of the "undeserving" poor and to the detriment of hardworking, income-earning (white) Americans and the nation's economy as a whole.

In 1970 open hostility to the welfare state and vile contempt for the poor had not yet taken hold in Connecticut as it had in other parts of the country. Still, Ned was always quick to note that Revitalization Corps did not collect a dime of taxpayers' dollars and was unencumbered by the red tape and bureaucratic inefficiencies of federal programs implemented under the Great Society. Opinions on Revitalization Corps became a Rorschach test for views on the welfare state as a whole. For conservative critics of the welfare state, especially, groups like Revitalization Corps seemed to prove the viability of a privatized welfare system, one in which help for the poor came solely from the voluntary contributions of private citizens and businesses. Such was the view of Ned among Hartford's business community at the turn of the decade. Here was a young man who, personal politics aside, deserved their support and whose success served a larger purpose.

By 1970 Ned had become a darling of the Hartford dinner-speaking circuit, the fiery, idealistic but seemingly harmless activist, the safe alternative to the dangerous radicals from the New Left, the type of young man the city's business class and political Establishment thought would make for a good "voice of a generation." He seemed like a throwback to a more innocent time in America—the early 1960s, before the sixties became "the sixties." Maybe it was his uncanny resemblance to the Kennedys. Or that he eschewed anti-war rhetoric (not out of support for the war in Vietnam but rather because he believed the anti-war movement had shuffled the crises at home to the margins). Maybe it was because, in an age of doubt, Ned wore his Catholic faith on his sleeve. Whatever it was, people in power seemed to like him.

For a time, Ned seemed happy to play the part, just as long as a donation or contribution of goods or services was waiting at the other end and his integrity and independence remained intact. But it was becoming increasingly difficult for him to ignore the fact that such praise of Revitalization Corps notwithstanding, the city's Establishment blithely ignored the substantive message he sought to convey. His appeals for support and passionate calls to fight racism and poverty in Hartford before Establishment audiences had generated rounds of applause but little action. In the years since he had opened that first storefront in Hartford, patterns of residential segregation had hardened, and rates of poverty in the city's black and brown communities had remained persistently high. Rats continued to infest North End apartments and public housing. Black children were getting sick from lead poisoning at alarming rates. City and state leaders were consistently slow to take action and seemed utterly oblivious to the impact of policy actions on the poor. How much longer could Ned sustain his energy, his sense of optimism, his radiant positivity? At what point would his public persona, and the endless stream of positive publicity his initiatives generated, become a liability and obstacle to achieving his goals? When would he crack under the pressure to remain the anti-poverty activist who posed no threat to the Establishment? When would he muster the courage to spit hot fire at those in power instead of giving them a gentle nudge? When would he be as brave as his heroes, John and Bobby Kennedy, once were—or as he imagined they once were?

During these years, Ned's horror at the resurgent Right, which was preaching a message of intolerance to diversity, callous indifference to the less fortunate, and bellicose militarism at home and abroad, was matched only by his disgust at what he judged was myopic navel-gazing and the self-absorbed intellectualizing of injustice among those that comprised the liberal elite or the academic liberalism of social scientists who channeled public resources and energy toward studies when the real work was in the streets. He called it the "paralysis of analysis," and he had no time to entertain their pet theories, be a part of their fact-finding committees, or participate in their interminable discussions about what was ailing America's cities. "Philosophical discussion is all right up to a point, but it's time we got into the action stage." Liberals, he charged, had become "a walking, talking satire on research projects—while they've been researching, we've been out there."[3] In these perilous times, voices for social and economic justice needed to spend less time talking and more time doing. These "armchair liberals," as Ned despairingly labeled them, "just talk to each other at cocktail parties about what they want to hear."[4] They can expound at length on theories of inequality, but when it comes to doing the hard work of building a more equal society, their time is short. They can eloquently express their sympathies for the poor and outrage at their plight but shy away from actually helping those in need. "It's popular to be a liberal these days, but not many persons get out and do anything about it. The philosophy is fine—but few people are willing to take the time to work."[5]

In some respects, Ned's analysis of the nation's political situation mirrored that of the new president, Richard M. Nixon. He agreed with Nixon that the nation's silent majority, its vast white middle class, housed in the nation's booming suburbs, would determine the course of the nation's future. It also echoed Alinsky's prescription, which called for radicals to "fan the embers of hopelessness into a flame to fight" among a white middle class that was "numb, bewildered, scared into silence." "That is where the power is."[6] It was to their concerns, their views, and their fears that persons and movements on the Left had to appeal. Such was the reality of life in a representative democracy. To forsake any attempts to reach them, to focus solely on reclaiming and rebuilding the city was not, in Ned's view, an act of resistance or the start of a revolution. It was an admission of defeat. It let middle-class whites off the hook. Having grown up in a typical middle-class New England household, where race existed only as other people's problem and one which whites could easily ignore, Ned knew all too well that without constant engagement with the white silent majority, without a direct confrontation of whites' consciences and insistence that they see, hear, and feel the lived experience of racial inequality, the plight of the nation's urban black poor would quickly slip back into the recesses of white America's collective consciousness. Like a new language, an equal society demanded constant repetition and immersion. And like a new religion, the precepts of racial justice could catch hold only through evangelism and the belief made manifest through actions.

Ned also believed, like Nixon, that the nation's silent majority was more responsive to fear than to hope. By the early 1970s Ned's speeches to businessmen's organizations, suburban schools, and other conservative white audiences framed the issue of black poverty in terms of their personal safety and national security. Like the authors of the Kerner Commission report he so admired and quoted at length every chance he got, Ned told audiences that white racism created and perpetuated the ghetto and white America would ultimately reap the whirlwind of a "separate and unequal" America. White indifference had allowed these problems to fester, and no wall between the city and the suburbs would be tall enough to keep the consequences of whites' inactions contained.[7]

In place of "armchair liberalism," Coll offered what he called "gut liberalism"—short on words, even shorter on theories, long on actions.[8] Beliefs that came from the gut, from instinct, didn't come with a position paper and didn't need to be grounded in theories or backed by mounds of evidence. Gut liberals didn't "watch Walter Cronkite or read Dick Gregory for answers"; they knew "the real answer is to get personally involved in the problems of the streets."[9] If it came from the gut, it would be manifested in a person's every action, without words, without

any need for justification. It just was. The person whose liberalism resided in the gut did not fall prey to cynicism or lapse into an apathetic
stupor, as seemed to be the case with so many on the Left at the time.
The liberal operating from the gut who read about price gouging in
ghetto supermarkets didn't just express disgust or reflect on how economic exploitation fueled urban unrest. The gut liberal got into his or
her car, drove into the ghetto, and offered mothers on public assistance
rides to suburban grocery stores, where they could buy food and other
essential items at a lower cost and cut into the ghetto merchant's profit
margins. Such was the thinking that led Coll to launch "A Choice," a
program that enlisted suburban housewives with cars to run trips to and
from suburban shopping centers for North End mothers on welfare.[10]
Youth unemployment in the North End remained shockingly high, and
city officials were unwilling to do anything about it. Coll's gut liberal
instinct led him to launch Project Concern, which placed area youths in
apprenticeships at local businesses, where they could learn a marketable
trade. The city's housing projects lacked air conditioning and suffered
from poor ventilation, making summers not just unbearable but also
potentially deadly for infants and the elderly. Working from the gut,
Coll canvassed area businesses and banged on the doors of homes in the
city's wealthier neighborhoods, imploring them to donate box fans or
window AC units. Gut liberalism responded to immediate crises with
quick action. It lacked an organizing principle other than improving the
lives of others in a direct and immediate way. The opening of new Revitalization Corps chapters across the country, the support of thousands
of workers and volunteers nationwide, demonstrated, to Ned at least,
the success of his model for social action and of his ability to motivate
and inspire others to take action. It also emboldened him to think that
perhaps he shared more than an Irish ancestry and old-school liberal
values with the Kennedy brothers.

By 1970 Revitalization Corps had established itself as a truly national
organization with signs of becoming a national movement. New chapters continued to open across the country. In Des Moines, Iowa, Drake
University student Jack Hatch formed a chapter, the sixteenth college
chapter and first in the upper Midwest. Within months Hatch recruited

seventy-five members and was running a tutoring program in local schools, sponsoring a march against hunger, and hosting a career day for teenagers in the city's poorest neighborhoods. In February Ned traveled to Iowa to give a talk at Drake University as part of a speaking tour of the Midwest. In Chicago, he met with former Illinois governor Otto Kerner, the lead author of the report on urban violence that had become Coll's personal manifesto, and Robert Johnson, the editor of *Ebony* and *Jet* magazines. At Macalester College in St. Paul, Minnesota, Coll met with former vice president and presidential candidate Hubert H. Humphrey and secured from the former (and future) politician-turned-college professor an agreement to serve as the honorary chairman of his next major initiative.[11]

Ned called the initiative Revitalize Urbia. Its goal was to make suburban Americans active participants in the fight to save America's cities and, indeed, to reframe the entire discussion of the "urban crisis" around the interdependency of cities and suburbs, their shared fates, and shared responsibilities. Ned wanted no less than to have the American public think of the urban crisis as a metropolitan crisis and come to see the changes taking place outside of the city as deeply, inexorably, linked to the series of crises that enveloped cities, from job losses to declining tax revenue, from failing schools to police-community tensions. Revitalize Urbia was his attempt to constructively engage suburban families in the pursuit of solutions, to get them to invest in saving American cities. "The city and suburbs cannot live without each other," Ned said at the press conference to announce the program's launch. "The sooner suburban parents become personally involved in saving our cities, the sooner their children will turn toward building America, not blaming it."[12]

The weekend of March 12–15, Ned hoped, would be the start of a national movement. If Revitalize Urbia could be said to have had an end goal, it was the full implementation (and at least full public awareness) of the recommendations of the Kerner Commission report. To that end, Ned called for nationwide demonstrations demanding the federal government implement its recommendations. He encouraged businesses to distribute copies to employees and host discussions of its contents and schools across the country to teach and discuss it.[13] On

Thursday evening, March 12, Ned and Corps volunteers and supporters gathered on the steps of West Hartford's town hall and held a two-hour candlelight vigil. The choice of location was appropriate for an occasion aimed at raising awareness of urban problems in suburbia. In the 1920s and again in the post–World War II era, suburban West Hartford had experienced a boom in residential housing construction and population growth, absorbing waves of white-collar workers in the city's insurance industry and becoming a chief destination for middle-class white families leaving the city. As West Hartford's property tax base grew, the suburb became noted for the high quality of its public schools, services, and amenities—and for its miniscule non-white population, which remained until the 1980s under 1 percent of the total population.[14] This small percentage, of course, was no accident. Most of the new residential developments built in West Hartford in the 1940s contained racially restrictive covenants barring sales to African Americans, and such covenants remained enforceable until the Supreme Court's 1948 decision in *Shelley v. Kraemer*.[15] Into the 1970s, West Hartford realtors, as a matter of course, refused to show homes to black homeseekers. The lack of diversity, Ned believed, only fueled white racist stereotypes of black people. As he told a reporter, West Hartford was "chosen because of the tremendous fear toward Hartford's North End that exists there, largely based on stereotyped images of violence without personal knowledge of its causes."[16]

For two hours on a seasonally chilly night, over one hundred people assembled in front of West Hartford's town hall. While a crowd kept vigil, smaller groups held teach-in sessions, others listened to a folk singer perform, and others went door to door seeking to collect five thousand pieces of sports equipment for inner-city youth.[17] The following morning, a group of one hundred Corps supporters stationed in Washington, DC, began a seventy-two-hour fast and vigil in front of the White House. At nine schools in Hartford and surrounding suburbs, students watched films on black history and culture and held discussions and debates over the Kerner Commission report. On Saturday morning, while groups of white and black teenagers painted the homes of elderly persons on Hartford's North End, groups in several U.S. cities made preparations for evening vigils and protests. In Washington, a group chanted and held signs outside the U.S. Senate chambers in the Capitol building. In Philadelphia, protesters marched in front of Independence Hall.[18] In both Chicago and New York, protesters targeted the offices of the city's major television networks, which, Ned charged, "have given the American public a distorted image of black America with their over emphasis and exaggeration of acts of violence and giving a limited view of the causes."[19] In place of sensationalism, Ned and those supporters who assembled outside called on the major networks to host a televised "job-a-thon" with a goal of securing employment for one hundred thousand urban youth across America.[20] To culminate the weekend of engagement and activism, Ned called on suburban whites to attend services at an inner-city church and for blacks in the city to venture to the suburbs and do the same. He called on all of the city's ministers to make the lessons of the Kerner Commission report a focal point of their sermons. In total, only six churches in the Hartford metro area heeded his call.[21] At a time when protests—against the war, for civil rights, for women's liberation, among others—were erupting daily and had become a familiar feature of American life, the national launch of Revitalize Urbia barely registered and, outside of Hartford, received scant attention from the press.

Ned hoped his next big announcement would generate more waves. On April 8, 1970, he called a press conference at the Hartford Hilton to announce his candidacy for the Democratic nomination for Connecticut's First Congressional District, which encompassed the city of Hartford and most of its surrounding suburbs, including West Hartford.[22] He hired a seasoned veteran of Connecticut politics as his campaign manager, began holding fund-raising parties in the homes of supporters, met with local business and trade groups, and ran advertisements with eye-catching statements like "Politics Doesn't Have to Be Boring."[23] Behind the scenes, he tried to run a conventional campaign. On the stump, he tried to appear as anything but the ordinary politician. At a meet-the-candidate forum, he dispensed with the usual listing of credentials, qualifications, and policy proposals and instead launched into a stem-winding speech on the disease of apathy that gripped America. Nodding to his opponents, Ned remarked, "The country doesn't need a lot of polite people with a lot of credits. We've got to get involved. If liberalism is going to mean something it's going to have to be communicated, and this can't be done without real involvement in the problems by all people."[24]

Ned began to pick up high-profile endorsements. The New York City journalist and RFK biographer Jack Newfield endorsed Ned, saying, "He is one of the few insurgent politicians who can build a link or bridge between idealistic students, the blacks and the poor whites."[25] Corps advisory board member Arthur Schlesinger Jr. publicly endorsed Ned and raised money for the campaign. Next to Vietnam, Schlesinger told voters, the greatest challenge facing the country was the "task of reconciliation within our national community. . . . No young man has done so much in the Kennedy spirit to heal the division of this country."[26] James Wechsler, editor of the *New York Post,* endorsed Ned. "His creativity, energy and ability to relate to both the problems of the city and suburbs is unique and sorely needed in Congress."[27] His message of engagement and reconciliation resonated with some white suburban voters. "For it is only when we have men like Ned Coll serving in public office," West Hartford's Evelyn J. Lavelle told a reporter, "that the angers of this country will be quieted, the wounds healed, and we will have a better and more peaceful world in which to live."[28]

Ned's campaign stressed his brand of gut liberalism and sought to distinguish it from the moderate, corporate-centered liberalism of his Democratic opponents and the social-scientific, academic liberalism emanating from New England's elite colleges and universities. "Ned has steered away from the unproductive theorizing that failed our country in the last decade," campaign manager Robert D. Shea claimed. "His emphasis has been on action, not words, on eyeball-to-eyeball communication in the street, not on developing catchy phrases designed to solve our ills."[29] Ned "stimulates people to get going—get involved, check up and ask what you can do for your country, not what your country can do for you," said supporter Lee A. Reidy.[30] "Listen to Coll," one supporter urged. "In a time when the term 'empty rhetoric' is heard opprobriously from all sides, Ned Coll gives the lie to that noxious phrase." As one of his campaign posters put it, "Coll Is Different."[31]

In Connecticut politics, the only difference that mattered was Ned's outsider status within the Democratic Party machine. No amount of endorsements from newspapers or high-profile figures could over-come this. Party regulars still wielded total control over the selection of the party's nominee, with a primary election held only when more than one candidate received at least 30 percent of the delegates' votes at the convention. At the First Congressional Democratic Convention later that spring, Ned and his supporters could only shout from the rafters as delegates conducted a series of roll calls to determine the nominee. Through five roll calls, Ned received zero votes. The nomination even-tually went to William Cotter, the state insurance commissioner, fol-lowing a primary election. Wasting no time, Ned immediately declared himself an independent candidate for the office and quickly rounded up enough signatures to get his name on the fall ballot.[32]

Ned seemed confident that the public would come to embrace his message. He predicted "It will be easier to get 80,000 votes in an election than to get 20 per cent of those delegates."[33] His band of dedicated sup-porters, likewise, refused to succumb to cynicism over the state's corrupt and undemocratic process for choosing candidates. Even as pundits dis-missed his candidacy as a long shot, dozens of young people beat the pavement. A young woman reportedly quit her job to work full time on the campaign. So devoted to Ned's cause, his campaign manager stayed on and paid for all of the campaign expenses out of his own pocket.[34]

Once in the political arena, though, Ned began to show a vicious, vindictive side of his personality that, at the time, starkly contrasted with his message of reconciliation. Playing the role of the spoiler in a three-person election, Ned attacked both candidates mercilessly. He publicly dismissed the Democrat Cotter as a "flunky for the insurance compa-nies" and took delight in hounding his campaign at every turn.[35] He and his supporters showed up at Cotter campaign events with a loudspeaker attached to the hood of Ned's car, whereupon the insurgent candidate would level a series of attacks on his opponent and attempt to drown out whoever happened to be on the stage. Against his Republican op-ponent, Hartford mayor Ann Uccello, Ned launched attacks that came across as churlish and sexist. He described her views as "simplistic," described some issues as "over her head," and lambasted her "stun-ning ignorance" on others. At a candidate forum in Bloomfield, Ned accused Uccello of "hiding behind [her] incompetence for years" and then added, "hiding behind [her] skirts too." Boos and hisses from the audience followed.[36]

Ned put all of his seemingly boundless energy into the campaign, all the while continuing to coordinate the Corps's various activities and initiatives. In late September he collapsed from heat exhaustion while campaigning and was hospitalized. On election night, fifty supporters and campaign workers gathered at the Coll for Congress campaign headquarters, a dingy, unfurnished room above a construction company's warehouse. Ned received 5,732 votes. His campaign failed, as the Democratic Party had feared, to swing the election to Uccello, as Cotter won comfortably. Ned had spent over $11,000 on the campaign and had borrowed heavily from friends to finance the final months.[37]

Still, Ned saw it as money well spent. He had brought scores of young people into the political process and throughout the campaign had used his candidacy, and the press it attracted, to force the other candidates to address issues they would have preferred to ignore—like police brutality, poverty, and joblessness on the North End. At the same moment he was coming to see beach access as an issue that could bring larger injustices into focus, he came to appreciate the power of political candidacy (no matter how long the odds) to raise public awareness and serve as a vehicle for building a movement.

Ned's defeat in the November elections did little to dim his reputation as a young man on the move, destined, perhaps, for greatness. Months after the election, he was named one of the ten Outstanding Young Men in America by the U.S. Junior Chamber of Commerce (Jaycees), at the time considered to be a highly prestigious honor. His selection garnered front-page headlines in Hartford's newspapers. At the awards ceremony later that year, Ned stood beside fellow awardees Elvis Presley (at the ceremony, Ned strolled up to the King, extended his hand, and jokingly asked, "It's Presley, isn't it?") and Nixon press secretary Ron Ziegler (whom Ned took every opportunity to needle throughout the ceremony over his boss's indifference to the poor) and listened to U.N. Ambassador George H. W. Bush deliver the keynote address. Ned expressed ambivalence over being given an award from an organization he greeted with "suspicion" and associated with the type of "docile complacency" he fought against.[38] At the same time, he knew an award from such a pillar of the Establishment would indeed come in handy as he tried to coax donations out of Establishment institutions.

Soon, financial support began to pour into the Corps's shabby storefront on Main Street. In June 1971 Ned received a $9,500 grant from the Rockefeller Foundation to expand Operation Bridge, Revitalization Corps's tutoring program in Hartford.[39] By the time classes started that fall, Ned had enlisted over one thousand tutors to work on the city's North End. He hoped to add another four thousand before the school year ended. The news he received later that fall would go far toward reaching that goal. In November Revitalization Corps was awarded a second grant from the Rockefeller Foundation, this one for $150,000. The award was big news in Hartford.[40]

Along with financial support, volunteers from across the country continued to trickle into the Corps's headquarters in the early 1970s. In May 1971 four young men from California showed up. They came after hearing about the Corps, an organization that shared their principles but asked its members to do the "hard work for peace either in Vietnam or at home," a notion they found lacking among the youth movements on the West Coast.[41] There was a group of nuns from Wisconsin. There were dozens of young women, many from Catholic colleges and universities in the Northeast, driven by a radical vision of social justice but driven away from New Left movements. There were a couple of blue-collar young men who believed in liberalism but despised liberals.[42] Coll was different, they had heard.

As the 1972 election cycle approached, Ned set his sights on a larger stage: the presidency, not that he believed he could win the presidential election. At the age of thirty-two, he was ineligible to hold the office. Running a campaign for president, however, was another matter. Thanks to an oversight by state election and Democratic Party officials in New Hampshire, as well as several other states, nothing barred him from getting onto the primary ballot. All he and his band of supporters needed was to collect at least five hundred signatures from eligible voters in each of the state's two congressional districts.

Characteristically impetuous, Ned didn't decide to mount a campaign until Sunday evening, January 2. The deadline for submitting the required signatures was that Thursday, January 7, at 5 p.m. On Sunday evening, Ned, a couple of college-aged volunteers, and several women from North End housing projects, drove to Nashua, New Hampshire. The following morning, they began a furious drive to collect signatures. In a rural state and with little time to spare, Ned's campaign crew members went anywhere they could expect to find a crowd of people. They stood outside the factories and mills around Manchester during shift changes, soliciting signatures from workers as they filed past the gates. They stationed themselves on street corners during the noon lunch hour or outside supermarkets and laundromats in the afternoon. At the crack of dawn, they were at coffee shops and doughnut stands. In the evening, they canvassed bars and bowling alleys. One young woman stayed overnight at a twenty-four-hour service station in the off-chance of catching a few passing motorists. Over in Durham, a group of students at the University of New Hampshire fanned across the campus, collecting signatures from newly enfranchised college students eighteen years or older. By Wednesday night, they still had three hundred signatures to collect. On Thursday, with the temperature barely reaching zero by midday, volunteers made one last push in Manchester, the state's most populated city. It would be close. Even if they collected enough signatures that afternoon, Ned still needed to drive north to the state capital, Concord, and file in person at the office of the secretary of state before 5 p.m. With less than one hour before the deadline, Ned strolled into the office of the secretary of state and presented lists containing 1,040 signatures.[43]

"We made it!" Ned exclaimed to a Hartford reporter over the phone later that night.[44] The following day, he staged a press conference at the Revitalization Corps headquarters in Hartford to announce his candidacy and answer the question on everyone's mind: why? With television cameras running, Ned stood behind a makeshift podium in a cramped room. Posters and press clippings adorned the unpainted walls. Ned, one report noted sarcastically, wore an "establishment" gray-flannel suit, maroon patterned tie, and blue shirt.[45] Only his scuffed, unpolished brown leather shoes distinguished Ned on this morning from the regular, garden-variety politician of his day. Once he began to speak, however, it was clear that Ned had no plans to moderate his tone to appeal to the New Hampshire electorate. He spoke "in a rush of words," one report noted, about the campaign he planned to run and what he hoped to accomplish. "A vote for me will be a vote against politics as usual." That much was certain.[46]

Reporters couldn't seem to understand why Ned was in the race and what he hoped to accomplish. Ned, for his part, struggled to articulate a clear rationale. He wanted "to have an effect on things in America, to help people to get involved." "Basically, what I'm trying to do is to bring the whole question of social action and personal involvement into the campaign of 1972." "I'm a catalyst," he explained. By running, with passion and desire, for an office he had no chance of occupying, he hoped to serve as an inspiration for others to get involved in civic life. "We've got to bring back spirit to this country," he shouted, punching his fist in the air. We cannot allow ourselves to become a nation of cynics, passive critics of the crises unfolding before our eyes. He wanted to cure liberalism from its "paralysis of analysis," to reclaim the meaning of liberalism from today's liberal. Liberals "have given up hope and become cynical and complacent," Ned charged. They preferred to spend their time "mocking [vice president Spiro] Agnew" instead of "selling [their] beliefs." Fixated on big ideas and grand visions, they had forsaken the hard, day-to-day work that making a better world entailed. Referencing the work Revitalization Corps carried out, Ned commented, "The orthodox liberal would sneer at a clothing drive—but we help people."[47]

While liberalism slept, far Right reactionary movements were on the march. As the decade wore on, the downtrodden, blue-collar whites who filed out of those factories in Manchester after every shift, whose wages remained stagnant while the cost of living rose, who watched with alarm as their industries found new ways to shrink the cost of labor, drank the poisonous tonic of racist demagogues who told them to blame their troubles and anxieties on racial minorities and the white radicals running amok on America's college campuses. In the war going on in America, "between blue-collar and white-collar, between young and old, between black and white," liberalism was losing—decisively.[48]

To win the war at home, Ned argued, liberals needed to rebuild the New Deal coalition and appeal directly to the concerns of white blue-collar workers who had, in his estimation, "been written off by pseudo-liberals."[49] The nation's leaders, meanwhile, needed to start asking citizens to sacrifice their time, energy, and, yes, their wealth and income, for others—just as Kennedy once had done and what the current and former president had carefully avoided doing. The "tragedy of Nixon," Ned told reporters, "is that he has asked too little of the American people. Johnson did the same thing."[50] Before the cameras, Ned was again trying to channel the Bobby Kennedy of his imagination, the politician unafraid to tell an audience of educated, privileged white Americans that they should be paying more in taxes toward social programs that benefitted the lives of others less fortunate. They could, and they should. Ned remained consumed by this singular vision of John and Bobby Kennedy—the hectoring, moralizing leaders who comforted the oppressed and shamed the privileged. He would spend his life struggling in vain to recreate this imagined America of his adolescence, a society that valued, above all, self-sacrifice, radiated positive energy and spirit, believed that government was us and, as such, could do great things, and never succumbed to cynicism. It was no coincidence that this America, which never truly was, took shape in Ned's mind in the aftermath of the tragedies of 1968 and under the dark clouds of Nixon's America, a time when idealism had been replaced with cynicism, belief with doubt, and active engagement with passive criticism.

Something had happened to America in the four years since the nation's attention had last focused on the Granite State. In the winter of 1968 the voices of liberalism still seemed to possess energy and vitality, earnestness, a sense of purpose, and a genuine hope that, in spite of it all, the forces of good would ultimately prevail. The past four years seemed to have thoroughly extinguished that flame. Those kids who had "got clean for Gene" (McCarthy) in 1968 had, it seemed, since dropped out of politics, withdrawn from the world, and sought personal fulfillment instead of societal transformation. "The McCarthy thing," Bill Gallagher, the former press secretary for the senator's 1968 New Hampshire campaign told Hunter S. Thompson, had been "a bad trip." Disillusioned, "[Gallagher] had dropped out of politics with a vengeance," the Gonzo journalist reported. "He no longer cared who was President."[51]

People like Gallagher seemed to represent an entire generation—Ned's generation—of once idealistic, now dispirited youth. He was shocked, Ned would later tell a reporter, at "how passive students have become, . . . how many people have given up—not only as to the future of the country but in their own ability to affect the future in any way. There's a tremendous amount of hopelessness" in America today.[52]

If today's youth no longer cared who was president, Ned reasoned, maybe the best way to reach those without hope was to ask them to vote for someone who had no hope of becoming president. The day after his press conference in Hartford, Ned headed back to New Hampshire and rented a storefront in downtown Manchester. The following day, Ned gave his first campaign speech, fittingly, to an audience of disenfranchised inmates at the state prison in Concord. He was still over $8,000 in debt from his 1970 congressional campaign. He had hoped to spend no more than $100 of his own money on the New Hampshire primary. With no money to spend on advertisements and no campaign manager, he and his supporters would have to find ways to make their way into the news cycle.[53]

One media outlet that made a point of ignoring Ned was William Loeb's *Manchester Union-Leader*. Loeb had used his publication as a platform for his extreme brand of right-wing politics. In an age when most media outlets disguised the political biases of their owners and editors, Loeb proudly—and aggressively—advanced his. Loeb was a particularly contemptible figure who reveled in the politics of personal destruction long before it became fashionable. Hunter S. Thompson described Loeb, perhaps unfairly, as a "neo-Nazi" and the *Union-Leader* as "America's worst newspaper"; the latter, most of his fellow reporters on the campaign bus agreed, was a fair observation.[54] Ned called the *Union-Leader* "garbage," and he and his supporters proceeded to stage daily protests outside its headquarters—that is, when they weren't following Maine senator and presumptive front-runner Ed Muskie around the state, trying to goad him into agreeing to a debate.[55] All around Manchester, the Coll campaign carried a large wooden cross that read "End the War in America" and listed the number of policemen killed in the previous year and the number of prisoners killed at the Attica Prison uprising.[56] Carrying their cross, Ned and his supporters marched in the Manchester Winter Carnival parade, where they followed a Marine color guard, whose members were incensed to have a "bunch of peace creeps" behind them.[57]

Ned treated his run for president as an extension of the work Revitalization Corps was doing in the cities. He turned his campaign into a workshop in participatory democracy. Each weekend, several black and Puerto Rican families from Hartford traveled up to Manchester. For many, it was their first encounter with the American electoral process. "We would take a busload" of folks from the projects up to New Hampshire, Earlie Powell remembers. "We worked hard [up there]. People believed in Ned because he did a lot for us. . . . [He] made sure our kids got bread to eat; [he made] sure you got clothes on your back, you had a nice Christmas. . . . You had people saying, 'Oh yeah, I'll go [campaign for Ned]. I'll come, when ya'll going?'"[58]

Running a campaign he was sure to lose, Ned staked out policy positions that no serious candidate would have dared to embrace. In a state notoriously hostile to taxes, whose motto was "Live Free or Die," Ned called for the introduction of a state income tax—both in New Hampshire and in Connecticut. "We must help people who need basic services," he told a reporter.[59] He showed up at a candidate forum hosted by the Citizens for Public Prayer and told the assembled audience, "Religion should seek to improve the world by its example, not by forcing its prayers into public schools," and he later added, "Freedom of religion implies freedom from religion."[60] More remarkable, though, was just how conventional most of Ned's positions and proposals were. He called for a consumer bill of rights modeled on the one proposed by the consumer advocate Ralph Nader. He wanted more educational television programming. He called for a national health care system like the one proposed by Senator Ted Kennedy. He called for better pay and more professional training for police officers. And, of course, he called for immediate action on the findings and recommendations of the Kerner Commission report, which, he argued, "should be required reading in all the schools and colleges in the land."[61] To the casual observer, the thirty-two-year-old anti-poverty worker and activist could, at times, be mistaken for a legitimate candidate for national office.

But then there were incidents like the one that took place at a high school in a small town in the state's southwestern corner that served as a reminder of just how audacious a candidate with literally nothing to lose could be. Ned had caught wind of an upcoming appearance by Connecticut governor Thomas Meskill, whom Ned had grown to despise. The Republican Meskill, accompanied by his wife and daughter, planned to speak at several rallies for President Nixon, who was facing a nominal challenge for the nomination from the party's far Right by Ohio congressman John Ashbrook. Somehow, Ned got hold of an advanced copy of Meskill's itinerary. At noon on the Friday before the primary, Meskill was set to give a speech to students at Monadnock High School in the town of Swanzey. Ned arrived at the school ahead of the governor's entourage, and as the students were filing into their seats in the library, he grabbed the open microphone and launched into a speech. The governor arrived to find that he had been ambushed. The students sat, spellbound by the wildly energetic speaker. Ned didn't skip a beat and continued speaking as if he were the main event. The school principal, deeply embarrassed, tried to keep his composure and prevent the event from descending into chaos. He grabbed a placard near the stage and furiously scribbled a message for Ned. It said, as one reporter at the scene recounted, "in essence . . . to quit talking." Before law enforcement arrived, Ned put the microphone down, stepped off the stage, and exited the school out of a back door. The flummoxed governor tried to crack a joke. "It's Connecticut day in New Hampshire," he exclaimed, before launching into a canned speech on Nixon's record in office. The deflated crowd of students stared back with blank expressions, wishing that the other guy were still speaking.[62]

The most noteworthy event of the 1972 New Hampshire primary was Ed Muskie's implosion and subsequent nosedive in the polls. After having been relentlessly attacked and his wife subjected to vicious rumors and innuendos at the hands of Loeb's *Manchester Union-Leader*, the Man from Maine made the fateful decision to deliver a speech aboard the back of a flatbed truck in front of the paper's headquarters. As snow blew in his face, Muskie denounced Loeb as a "gutless coward."[63] Then, with cameras rolling, Muskie paused and appeared to choke up. Some later speculated that a snowflake had landed in his eye. Regardless, the damage was done. That evening and the following morning, newspapers across the country reported on Muskie's weepy, teary-eyed defense of his wife. His campaign reeling, his fitness for office suddenly in doubt, Muskie hastily agreed to an eleventh-hour debate with the other candidates, set for the Sunday evening before the election. With little room to negotiate, Muskie agreed to debate all of the candidates on the ballot, including Ned.

Ned seized the spotlight with both hands. By luck of the draw, he was the first candidate to speak. His three-minute opening remarks were typically rambling and unfocused, if lively and engaging. He tacked back and forth between calls for Americans to "get involved" and wage war on apathy to criticisms of his fellow candidates' inattention to the conditions in America's inner cities and suffering of the nation's poor.[64] As the red light began flashing, alerting Ned his time was up, he concluded by saying, "The number one killer and cause of violence is the rat," whereupon he reached into his suit jacket and pulled out a large rubber rat, dangling it by the tail above his head.[65] The audience gasped. Ned didn't blink.

The night was his. If press accounts of the debate are any indication, after Ned pulled out the rat, the pool of reporters quickly lost interest in the other, eligible, candidates and instead waited, with baited breath, for Ned's next opportunity to speak. He didn't disappoint. Though he "failed to respond directly to most of the questions," Ned put on a performance few in the audience or at home, and certainly none of the other candidates, would soon forget.[66] He repeatedly referred to the right-wing mayor of Los Angeles, Sam Yorty, whose long-shot candidacy was heavily promoted and bankrolled by the *Manchester Union-Leader*, as "Mayor Loeb." Later, he called Yorty "the most progressive voice for ancient history." The rat made several appearances throughout the ninety-minute debate. It served as a symbol of poverty, of violence, of the root causes of the prison riot at Attica, of "all that is wrong in this county," and of the right-wing press. At one point, Ned held up the rat and told the audience, "I have a copy here of the *Union-Leader*."[67]

That was not all. Ned said what the country needed was "leadership not bullship." He mused about filling his Cabinet with the likes of Ralph Nader. And he never missed an opportunity to pile on the

Presidential candidate Ned Coll holding a rubber rat
to protest urban poverty during a 1972 Democratic
primary debate in Durham, New Hampshire. *Copyright
© Associated Press. AP Photo/J. Walter Green/FILE.*

beleaguered Muskie. Afforded the chance to speak immediately after Muskie had offered another of his equivocal statements on the war in Vietnam, Ned turned to the senator and said, "You sound like Richard Milhous Muskie."[68] The audience erupted. Muskie, Ned recalled, "turned red as a fucking beet."[69] In general, one reporter noted, candidate Coll came across as "unanimously disdainful of his opponents," with the exception of Senator George McGovern, whom at one point in the debate Ned praised for his early opposition to the war in Vietnam. As he did, the camera panned over to McGovern, seated next to Ned. "The senator looked stricken with sudden pain."[70]

The following morning, Ned Coll and his rubber rat were the lead story in newspapers across the country. "Political Unknown, 32, Steals TV Spotlight in New Hampshire Race," read the headline in the *Chicago Tribune*. "For those who may have gone to the refrigerator for a beer when candidate Edward Coll came on the screen, you missed some great television," *Boston Globe* political editor Robert Healy wrote. It was, Healy concluded, Ned's "finest hour." (Others might have called it his finest fifteen minutes.) The *Guardian* of London begged to disagree, deeming instead the rat "the star" of the debate. On a night when the other candidates came off as uninspiring and undignified, "Only Mr. Coll," the *Guardian* declared, "came away unscarred. . . . Thanks to Mr. Coll's rat, which he waved in front of the cameras whenever the discussion seemed to him to be in danger of becoming irrelevant, the debate was never dull, but it rarely rose much above the level of farce." Hundreds of newspapers across the country ran the AP photo of Ned dangling the rubber rat before the shocked audience or the one of all five candidates seated next to each other at the debate's conclusion: Muskie trying hard to appear presidential yet seemingly aware that his goose was cooked; Yorty and Indiana senator Vance Hartke beaming, just happy to be there; McGovern calm and relaxed; and Ned, glowering, lips clenched, arm extended in the air, rat in hand.[71]

Two days later, voters in New Hampshire went to the polls. Ned received 256 votes, less than 1 percent. The story of the night was Muskie's precipitous fall from front-runner status, but "the rat" wasn't far behind. The morning after the primary, Ned appeared on the NBC *Today*

Show, where he was asked to wave the famed rat for the cameras. He obliged. It was, in all likelihood, the first time a presidential candidate who had received less than 1 percent of a primary vote and who was ineligible to hold the office had appeared on a major television network the following day. Ned was under no illusion as to the reason for his notoriety. It certainly had nothing to do with his anti-poverty work or his thoughts on the state of the nation. It was for comedic relief. Those "assholes," he later remarked, referring to the press, "didn't understand what I was saying about racism."[72] Didn't understand or just didn't care. While members of the media flocked to Ned, some of his more prominent one-time supporters ran from him. Shocked and embarrassed by what he saw as Ned's mockery of American electoral politics, Arthur Schlesinger announced his resignation from Revitalization Corps's advisory board following the New Hampshire primary.[73]

Despite his anemic showing, neither Ned nor his loyal band of supporters had any intentions of halting the campaign. Days after the New Hampshire primary, Russell West drove to Indiana to canvass for signatures in the hopes of getting Ned on the state's primary ballot. (He failed.) Ned, meanwhile, was making plans to secure enough signatures to get onto the Massachusetts primary ballot.[74]

First, though, Ned had a wedding to attend—his own. On March 11, Ned married Elizabeth Skinner in Hartford. The daughter of shipping magnate Edward Skinner, Skinner had spent parts of her childhood living in Ecuador and England and gone to school in London and Paris before settling in New York City as a young adult. It was there in 1965 that she met Ned while doing volunteer work for Revitalization Corps in Harlem. She later played an instrumental role in organizing Operation Suburbia. Ned extended invitations to the wedding to scores of black mothers, children, and young men and women who had been a part of the Revitalization Corps family. He hired a popular local R & B band to play at the reception. When the band failed to show up, Ned asked Hartford deejay Brad Davis to go on the airwaves and call for another band to perform in its place. Within an hour, another group had arrived and the celebration continued. Ned's mother could only watch in horror. So worried that she would utter a racist epithet at one of the guests, Ned assigned one of his sisters to monitor her throughout the evening and ensure she didn't insult anyone. "He had all of these black kids and black people running around at his reception," Earlie Powell remembers. Ned's mother, Claire, Powell recalls, "was like, 'Ned, why did you invite all of *these* people?' Ned just made it open to everybody."[75] He would not have had it any other way.

After a brief honeymoon in Quebec City, Ned and supporters were in Boston ahead of the Massachusetts primary. To Ned, Boston exemplified, more than any city in America, the "paralysis of analysis" that he claimed ailed "orthodox liberalism."[76] Here, students occupied university administration buildings and regularly held vigils and marches in opposition to U.S. foreign policy in Southeast Asia but seemed, to Ned, passive in the face of crimes against humanity in their own backyard: a profoundly segregated school system, shockingly high rates of poverty and illiteracy in black and Puerto Rican neighborhoods, entire swaths of the city where it was unsafe for a person of color to venture. That year, the NAACP filed a class-action lawsuit against the Boston public school system alleging a deliberate pattern of segregation by race in the drawing of school district lines. Two years later, U.S. district court Judge W. Arthur Garrity would rule the school system in violation of the state's Racial Imbalance Act and order the busing of students from the all-white South Boston and predominantly black Roxbury across district lines, sparking a crisis that would bring the North's forms of racial apartheid to the nation's attention. But in the spring of 1972, the day-to-day injustices black Bostonians suffered—the simmering crisis in race relations, the war at home just over the horizon—seemed far from the minds, and far down the list of concerns, of greater Boston's young, educated, white liberal population.[77]

Ned could empathize with the poor, uneducated white bigot, blinded by a hate borne of his own struggles. And even as he condemned elitism and tried to shame the privileged into sharing their wealth, he could understand the sin of selfishness. What he could not comprehend, and never accept, was the passive awareness of injustice that seemed so prevalent among the students and educators of New England's elite institutions of higher learning. To devote hours to studying, writing about, and discussing poverty but spend comparatively little time actually helping the poor? It bothered, indeed enraged, Ned to no end. As the clock ticked on the fifteen minutes he had earned by waving a rubber rat at a presidential debate, Ned was determined to make sure the public understood just what that rat was meant to symbolize.

Throughout the spring, Ned traveled back and forth between Hartford and Boston. A businessman who had read about Coll offered him an empty warehouse in Jamaica Plain for use as a campaign headquarters. He gave talks to whoever would have him: Kiwanis and Rotary clubs, high schools, and colleges. To a crowd of students at Boston University, he asked why they were on strike against the war in Vietnam and not the war on Boston's poor. "They think the Indochina war is immoral," he later told a reporter. "Well, I think it's immoral that they don't seem interested in helping poor children who can't read, only three minutes from their campus." One person who covered Ned's campaign summarized his message to audiences around the city as: "If you're against the war in Vietnam, then why aren't you fighting the war in Boston?" Ned called on students to wage a war against "ignorance, slum areas, inadequate housing and racial bias." The results of the state's primary offered little indication that his message resonated with audiences or had been powerful enough to lead them to cast a protest vote against "politics as usual." He received a total of 556 votes. Ned's presidential campaign had run its course.[78]

The Democratic Party's journey into the abyss, and the final dissolution of the New Deal coalition that had dominated American politics and defined liberalism for two generations, had not run their course. That would come in November. As Muskie tanked, the party's old guard attempted to stage an eleventh-hour coup against new front-runner George McGovern, convincing Hubert H. Humphrey to enter the race late in the primary season. His entry did little to slow McGovern's momentum or heal the party's fractures. Still, they gathered in Miami Beach that August for the ritual of nominating and rallying around the party's candidate. Ned was there too. All anyone who recognized him wanted to know was whether he had brought his rat along. He hadn't.

That fall, the open beaches movement scored its greatest victory at the ballot box when voters in California passed the California Coastal Zone Conservation Act (Proposition 20), which declared the state's coastline public land and laid the groundwork for the creation of a new state agency charged with protecting the public's right to access it. At the time, only 90 miles of the state's 1,072-mile coastline were publicly owned, and of those, only 37 miles were open to the public.[79] After several attempts to pass an open beaches bill in the state legislature had succumbed to intensive lobbying from the state's energy and real estate industries, the Sierra Club, along with a newly formed citizens group, the California Coastal Alliance, successfully gathered enough signatures to place the bill on the November ballot. They then withstood a barrage of advertising from the bill's opponents, flush with political donations from land development and oil companies, to narrowly secure a victory.[80]

Weeks before California voters passed Proposition 20, lawmakers on Capitol Hill passed and President Richard Nixon signed into law the 1972 Coastal Zone Management Act. The bill authorized $165 million in federal funds through 1977 to help states prepare and implement state-level coastal planning and management agencies. Under the act, the federal government would finance 80 percent of the cost of developing a plan that met federal guidelines and establishing an agency. States were given six years to come up with a plan before federal funds dried up. The bill exemplified Nixonian federalism, doling out federal dollars to states and localities with only minimal requirements and stipulations on how the funds were to be used. To receive funds, states were required to develop a planning agency that met broad guidelines. The very wording of the bill underscored the internal tensions and contradictions among policymakers toward coastal land use regulation. The mission of these new state agencies was to both protect coastal environments and facilitate economic development of the coastal zone. "It is of national importance," the House committee report read, "that the Federal government encourage the states to arrange for the *optimum utilization* of coastal zone resources, coupled with an *adequate protection* of the zone's natural environment."[81] On the question of who owned the beach, Congress was in no mood to render a verdict, and federal regulators had little desire to tell shoreline towns how to manage their affairs.

The Kennedys of Ned Coll's imagination never seemed more dead than on January 20, 1973, when Richard M. Nixon ascended the steps of the U.S. Capitol and took the oath of the presidency for a second time.

Instead of "Ask not what your country can do for you, but what you can do for your country," Nixon scolded citizens to stop asking, "What will government do for me," and instead ask "What can I do for myself."[82] He did not need to state to whom, exactly, he was referring. Whites and blacks alike knew Nixon was taking a shot at fighters for social and economic justice, for whom "freedom was not enough," and the nation's poor and downtrodden, who might have still held out hope for a federal government that cared about their needs and stood by their side. Nixon assured his broad base of middle-class white supporters that they had done enough; they had nothing to feel guilty for; whatever problems blacks and other marginalized groups still faced were theirs to solve alone. The time had come for them to return to the task of taking care of themselves, bettering their own communities, securing their own rights and interests.

"What can I do for myself?" Selfishness, narrow-mindedness, disregard for society. What Ned held as anathema was now being praised as virtue—indeed, the highest form of citizenship—from the occupant of the highest office in the land. And the people for whom he had dedicated his life to advocate and serve were fast becoming the foil for a resurgent Right, who held their fight for justice and equality in contempt, and, as Nixon's campaign had shown, were prepared to deploy a host of racially coded appeals to white racist sentiments to accumulate political power.

It was winter in Hartford, and Ned was back in his office, surrounded by piles of donated clothes, the thermostat set so low one could see one's own breath. There were no reporters calling to hear the opinions of the always quotable young man who had upended the Democratic primary nearly a year ago. The circus had left town; poverty, joblessness, failing schools, malnourished children, a racist police force, and a corrupt housing authority remained. Ned's decision to sink substantial time and money (far more than the $100 he had initially projected) into a symbolic run for president had momentarily raised his public profile and drawn some added attention to the work Revitalization Corps was carrying out in cities and campuses across the country. But his erratic, comical behavior in New Hampshire seemed to overshadow whatever message he had hoped to convey. Ironically, the earnest young man who had envisioned his candidacy as striking a blow against the insidious spread of cynicism and apathy among America's youth would come to exemplify to pundits and the public alike just how farcical American politics had become. In his most private moments, Ned had to wonder if his sincere attempt to draw national attention to the plight of the ur-ban poor would go down as a mere stunt, the answer someday to a trivia question. Who was Ned Coll? He was, as Hunter S. Thompson put it, "the anti-rat candidate."[83]

SIX

Who the Hell Invited That Guy?

Shortly after having received his property tax bill from the town of Madison in 1973, Dr. Hiram Birnbaum placed a call to Revitalization Corps's headquarters. The respected local physician, small business owner, and real estate investor did not fit the profile of someone who called the Corps seeking help, except in so far as Birnbaum believed he was the victim of discrimination—in his case, at the hands of anti-Semitic local officials. Over the past several years, he had been locked in a bitter dispute with the town's Board of Selectmen and Planning and Zoning Commission over several of his real estate holdings and business interests. In 1970 Madison's zoning board turned down his request to build an apartment complex on some property he owned in town.[1] (Like most shoreline towns, Madison had strict zoning regulations. And like other wealthy municipalities in the state, Madison's prohibition on the construction of multi-family units and regulation on minimum lot sizes had played an instrumental role in keeping the state's poor and lower-income population locked out of suburban and shoreline housing markets and concentrated in inner cities.) Next, the zoning board rejected without explanation Birnbaum's request for a special exemption to build a golf driving range on a seventy-five-acre tract located on the town's outskirts. The final straw came in February 1973, after the town had reassessed local properties and mailed out updated property

148

tax bills. Even though the seventy-five-acre tract remained undeveloped woodlands and Birnbaum's plans for a driving range were still being contested in court, town assessor Philip Nedovich nevertheless saw fit to reclassify the property from forest land to commercial, resulting in a $14,220 increase in its assessed valuation. Other properties Birnbaum owned in town saw similarly sharp increases.[2]

Birnbaum did not reach out to Ned for advice on contesting his tax bill. Rather, he wanted Revitalization Corps's help in exacting revenge on the local government—though that's not how he put it to Ned when he finally reached him on the phone. Instead, he couched his appeal for help in the form of a generous offer. For a nominal fee, Birnbaum proposed to rent to Revitalization Corps a twelve-cabin motel that he owned in Madison for the upcoming summer of 1973. There, Ned could set up a headquarters, bus children from Hartford to the shore throughout the summer season, and—most important—secure dozens of beach passes under a provision in the local beach ordinance that allowed nonresidents staying in hotels to receive day passes to the town's resident-only public beach.[3] What better way, Birnbaum surmised, to ruin summer for the smug local officials who had thwarted his business interests at every turn and routinely mistreated and disrespected the town's small Jewish community than to extend an open invitation to that professional troublemaker and his band of ghetto children and welfare mothers from Hartford.

Ned had grown accustomed to receiving gifts from wealthy benefactors seeking to unload excess items or unwanted property and secure a tax write-off. But this was different. The very nature of Birnbaum's offer and the motives behind it set the stage for what would be the most contentious summer yet on the Connecticut shore and would turn the quiet town of Madison into an unexpected battleground in the broader struggle over race, rights, and opportunity in 1970s America.

Based on Ned's recent actions, Birnbaum had good reason to think that he would come to Madison that summer fixing for a fight. By the fall of 1972, it was clear that Ned was losing the war on apathy. President Richard Nixon had defeated his Democratic opponent, George McGovern, in the largest landslide in the nation's history. That same month, bus drivers for the Connecticut Company, the private contractor providing bus services for Hartford, New Haven, and Stamford, went on strike over low pay and working conditions. Bus service for three of the state's largest cities ground to a halt. Over seventy-five thousand daily riders, mostly poor and elderly, were left stranded, just as another bitterly cold New England winter approached. The state's governor, Thomas Meskill, however, refused to negotiate with the union representing the workers or offer more than a verbal promise of better wages once the drivers returned to their jobs. Revitalization Corps immediately responded to the crisis, setting up a ride-sharing program and having a team of volunteers drive people to jobs, grocery stores, and doctors' appointments.

While some white suburban families lent their cars and time to assisting the city's poor and others pressured the governor to take action, the vast majority of the city's suburban commuters remained coldly indifferent to the crisis. Their apathy fueled Ned's anger, frustration, and willingness to adopt extreme, confrontational tactics. As the strike entered its second month, Ned and fellow Corps volunteers and activists staged a protest at the state capitol, where they called on Meskill to intervene. With dozens of protestors by his side, Ned marched into the state capitol armed with a list of demands he planned to present to the governor. When they arrived at the governor's office, Meskill's secretary informed them that the governor was away on official business. As they milled about in the hallway contemplating their next move, Ned caught the governor out of the corner of his eye as he attempted to sneak down a back stairwell. "There he is," Ned shouted, as he began to race toward Meskill.[4] At that moment, a plainclothes officer who was monitoring the crowd grabbed Ned by the arm. Before turning to look, Ned clenched his fist, punched the cop in the gut, and kept running before being tackled and handcuffed by the officer. Arrested and charged with second-degree assault on a police officer, Ned remained undaunted. Out on bail and with a felony charge hanging over his head, he returned to the state capitol, this time to give a press conference and to present the governor a gift: a pair of red children's sneakers, a symbol of Meskill's cowardly "flight from the people" and in reference to his small stature.[5]

After a winter of battling the state's governor, Ned's thoughts turned to the summer and to resuming his fight for the public's right to the shore. And thanks to Birnbaum's generous offer, Revitalization Corps had its base of operations. Before the completion of the Connecticut Turnpike in 1958, Madison had changed little over the previous half-century. It was, like many of its counterparts along the central and eastern half of the state's shoreline, a small summer cottage community that briefly came to life each summer but remained quiet and sparsely populated throughout much of the year. Beginning in the early 1960s, though, the town's year-round population grew rapidly as the turnpike made shoreline towns attractive—and feasible—places to live for professionals working in New Haven and Fairfield County. By 1968, the town's year-round population was four times greater than it had been on the eve of World War II. Most of these new arrivals worked in other cities; as early as 1964, the Connecticut Department of Labor found, less than one-half of the wage earners in Madison worked in Madison; conversely, less than 20 percent of those who worked in Madison lived in Madison, an indication of the rapid appreciation of area real estate, which had priced out many of the people who worked in the local service trades. Both figures would continue to fall in the years ahead.[6]

Changes in the town's social composition and demographics naturally had an impact on its politics. New year-round residents of Madison often came with the explicit intention of securing for themselves homes that would appreciate in value and, for their children, good, well-funded schools. Many of these younger families also brought a new spirit of civic and social engagement to the town and, through their organizational life, looked for ways to make the community more involved in addressing the pressing social issues facing the nation. Other new residents, on the other hand, saw themselves as refugees from dying cities, determined to insulate themselves and their new communities from the problems from which they had fled. As Madison's year-round population swelled, the town's older residents mobilized against the threat of higher taxes and the increased presence of "outsiders." During these years, they began forming new political organizations; the Madison Property Owners Association and Madison Taxpayers Association took shape, their names a clear reflection of their members' interests and anxieties. Meanwhile, the families who came from New York City to their summer cottages along the town's shore each summer, who belonged to the tony

Madison Beach Club and who lived in a world all their own, remained strictly concerned with ensuring that their summers remained free of conflict or disturbance.[7]

Beneath the town's placid surface, Madison's year-round residents harbored sharply different views on the town's future and its role, as a wealthy, all-white community, in addressing the problem of racial inequality in Connecticut and the nation. Even the town's treatment of its sewage reflected larger debates over race, class, and growth within the community: as the town's growing population stretched the septic tanks attached to homes and businesses beyond capacity, contaminating the soil and polluting nearby bodies of water, local officials steadfastly refused to consider the construction of a public wastewater treatment plant. One reason not far from opponents' minds: the absence of sewer lines served as an effective prophylactic against the threat of higher-density, low- and moderate-income housing.[8] Residents who wanted to make the town more welcoming to people of different races and backgrounds had to tread carefully. The most modest gesture toward those less fortunate threatened to spark outrage among an increasingly vocal and organized minority.

That day came in the spring of 1970, following the town school board's decision to participate in a program aimed at providing quality education to a select number of students from underserved urban school districts. The brainchild of a group of professors and administrators at Dartmouth University, "A Better Chance" (ABC) placed small numbers of talented students from poor urban school districts into elite prep schools and public high schools in the Northeast. Under the model, roughly ten or so students moved into the school district, lived in a communal home under the supervision of parent volunteers, and attended the local public schools. In 1963 ABC received seed funding from the Rockefeller Foundation and in the coming years expanded the program nationwide. ABC scouting agents visited underfunded urban schools across the nation in search of students whom guidance counselors had identified as "deserving" of the opportunity to acquire the type of high school education previously available to privileged white children only.[9]

After hearing of the program, Madison residents Ken and Marty Jansen, along with a group of other parents in town, began holding meetings and drawing up plans to bring ABC to Madison. They formed a local chapter of the national organization and quickly raised over $10,000 in pledges from area residents, enough to qualify for a matching grant from Dartmouth that would pay for all expenses for the first year. All signs indicated that this would be the type of measure that would enjoy broad support among the community. Asking schools to accept only a handful of carefully screened students and requiring little else from the towns that hosted them, ABC had aroused little to no opposition from residents of the other towns where it had placed students. Coming at a moment when Northern-style school segregation practices had become the subject of unprecedented scrutiny and legal challenge, a program like ABC—with its decidedly modest aims and implicit assumptions about the superiority of predominantly white schools—tended to generate far more skepticism and hostility from figures in the civil rights and black power movements than from the residents of the affluent towns it asked to play host. In February 1970, ABC's national director Tom Mikula, along with four students who had previously participated in the program, spoke to students at Madison's Hand High School, as well as to members of the community, about the program and why it was worthy of their support. Mikula began his address to the students assembled in the school gymnasium by invoking the recently released findings and dire warnings of the Kerner Commission. "We have heard the National Advisory Committee on Civil Disorders predict that there will be two societies—one white and one black—and we take its predictions seriously." He then tried to rouse his audience from its complacency. "The responsibility to make changes in our society rests on those of us who have 'made it.' " A rousing applause and a few cheers followed.[10]

While billed as an information session and open discussion, to John Milum, a Madison resident and parent of school-age children, it seemed more like a pep rally. And he was in no mood to cheer along. He had "moved to Madison to avoid [the] problems" that seemed to plague inner-city schools, and now Madison's school board was welcoming *those* people and *their* problems with open arms![11] Milum was livid. As he discussed his views with fellow residents, he soon learned that many others shared his misgivings. Despite its small scope, ABC nevertheless promised to bring a group of teenagers from low-income urban neighborhoods into a town that was wealthy and overwhelmingly white (of the town's 9,768 permanent residents in the 1970 census, only 17 persons were black) and into a school system that, because of its location and the other structural barriers in place, enjoyed virtual immunity from the threat of court-ordered integration. By the time Madison's school board gave its blessing to the ABC program, though, there were plenty of signs indicating that the Civil Rights Movement was marching toward their doorsteps. District-wide school busing plans were being implemented in cities across the country, and calls had already begun to expand busing programs to encompass metropolitan areas. Later that summer, the NAACP would file a lawsuit against the state of Michigan challenging the constitutionality of municipal school districting schemes that effectively segregated students by race. Closer to home, a report issued that year by the South Central Connecticut Planning Agency (SCCPA) seemed to suggest that Madison should (or would) become the future site of low-income housing developments aimed at addressing the extreme concentration of the state's minority population in its inner cities. New Haven seemed closer than ever.[12]

"They're not going to do it if I have anything to say about it," John Milum said of both the SCCPA's supposed plans and ABC's impending arrival.[13] Linking the prospect of underprivileged students in Madison with the threat of low-income housing, he went door to door, asking residents to sign a petition to place a (nonbinding) referendum on the ballot in the upcoming April election that would ask voters to state their support for or opposition to ABC. He adorned the side of his pickup truck with a sign reading "Oppose ABC."[14] Fellow residents like Georgette Cutting were eager to join the fight. The mother of three commuted to work in New York City, spending up to four hours in her car each day so that her children could attend school in Madison and not be exposed to, in her words, "urban decadence."[15] Ensuring that her children would not attend the same schools and live in the same neighborhoods as *those* people was the reason she spent so many hours in her car, and she was determined to ensure that her sacrifices were not in vain. She helped coordinate the petition drive, penned biting criticisms in the local newspaper, and delivered long addresses to crowds of supporters and opponents.

Cutting and other vocal opponents of ABC tapped into these families' fears of losing what they had so recently gained. First we allow ABC students into our schools, she warned; next it will be zoning changes that will allow low-income housing, then heavy industry. Eventually, "there will no longer be any reason for my return to Madison each day. Madison will have lost its individuality, and peace and serenity will be no more." ABC did not equip disadvantaged children for success in life, critics charged; it merely bred "troublemakers." Not only that, these and other affirmative action educational programs dispensed unearned gifts to undeserving recipients, in the process robbing Madison's children of their birthright. Just look at the colleges and universities, where "for some ridiculous reason the doors [are] open to them even if they aren't qualified." Blacks have "been given more opportunity to attend colleges today than my own children," Cutting stated. And now they asked to be welcomed into our town and attend our local schools! "These changes are being planned in the name of PROGRESS," she remarked. "But is it really? I recognize it as urban decay, spreading like a cancer into our suburban areas."

Others echoed Cutting's sentiments. "Let us not be hypocrites," Theodore S. Cole implored fellow townspeople. "Many people moved to Madison to escape the problems and ills of the cities." Why would we want to invite those problems into our community? It defies logic! Our children, Rita P. Juzwiakowski argued, certainly have little to gain from the experience, contrary to what some white liberal integrationists might contend. "If you really want to teach [our kids] to know all types of people[,] take a trip to New Haven some afternoon with your daughter or son. . . . Look around, listen to the nice garbage that pours out of their mouths as they call to their girlfriends. See how they deliberately block the elderly so they have to walk around them, not to mention their complete arrogance to the city police department. Is this the fellow American you want your daughter to walk hand in hand with? Or your son to hang around with?"[16]

Horror stories of other towns that had welcomed ABC students into their schools soon began to spread around town. In Hanover, New Hampshire, it was rumored, the students morphed into angry radicals soon after arriving in town. They acted sullen and hostile toward their fellow classmates and refused to stand for the Pledge of Allegiance or take part in normal school activities. They even cheered for the opposing school at sports events! What's more, they had come to expect free clothes, sports equipment, books, and school supplies from local merchants. The five girls who attended the elite girls' school in Littleton, New Hampshire, St. Mary's-in-the-Woods, were so ungrateful, it was said, that it upset and disturbed their fellow classmates. They didn't enjoy skiing, complained about the narrow curriculum and its inattention to the black experience, and called the white students "fake" and "sheltered."[17] And these were just the rumors that found their way into print.

Along with the thinly veiled racism and fear mongering, voices opposed to ABC also condemned the manner in which the program was implemented. Why don't we, the residents and parents of Madison, get to have a say in whether we want this program or not, some asked. They are using *our* tax dollars to educate poor kids from the ghetto without *our* consent. By mid-April, the letters to the editor section of the *Shore Line Times*, which typically took up no more than one column on the opinions page, soon stretched over three or more pages in each issue.[18] One of those voices expressing opposition and ginning up fears was Hiram Birnbaum, who compared ABC to the quota systems that used to limit the number of Jews accepted into elite universities and medical schools, and he warned that it threatened to lead the nation down the path of Nazi Germany.[19]

Opponents did everything they could to undermine support for ABC and sabotage its fund-raising efforts around town. They cynically quoted from statements by urban black leaders and activists who were critical of the program for its shortcomings and unintended consequences for urban school districts. They circulated glowing descriptions of inner-city programs such as Harlem Prep as a better alternative for disadvantaged students.[20] Milum got the local chapter of the American Legion to rescind its offer to let ABC use the town's Legion Hall for a fundraiser.[21] They lobbied the town's Planning and Zoning Commission to remove a provision that allowed for the furnishing of room and board to groups of eight or more persons for philanthropic, educational, or religious purposes.[22] They even got the local public library to stop distributing a pamphlet about ABC (prepared by local high school students) because it cast the program in a positive light.[23]

ABC's supporters were caught completely off guard. They struggled to dispel myths, counter unsubstantiated rumors, and appeal to Madison's better angels. The town's first-term first selectman, Howard Hopkins, who had expressed his "overwhelming approval" of ABC, believed that fellow Madisonians would see, like he did, that they had to do their part in the struggle for racial equality and equal educational opportunity. "It is an opportunity, a responsibility, indeed a duty, Madison has to support this project." We should not only allow ABC to come to Madison, Hopkins said. We should "welcom[e] it here."[24] One ABC director expressed his disbelief at the level of fear and hostility toward the plan. "All it is is eight 15-year-old boys who need help."[25] The students who stood poised to share classrooms with the incoming students offered the loudest voices of support and the most stinging critiques of the town's insularity. "The anti-septic gauze surrounding our segregated haven," Hand High School student council president Chris Weiss wrote, "must be torn open."[26] Many preferred, instead, to allow it to fester a while longer. The debate over ABC had become a referendum on the administration of racial liberalism and the preservation of local control. And in this and other shoreline towns in Connecticut, preserving local control was paramount.

One week before Madison was to vote on the referendum, Hopkins called a special town meeting aimed at clearing up any confusion and countering the spread of misinformation by opponents. Over nine hundred people poured into the high school gymnasium on a Friday evening. A local reporter said it was the largest crowd ever assembled for a Madison town meeting. Tensions ran high, not only over the issues at stake, but also over who could express an opinion. ABC opponents were particularly incensed at the number of students who were admitted. A town meeting, they contended, should be open only to taxpaying citizens of voting age. Since the students didn't pay taxes and weren't old enough to vote, their views were irrelevant and should not be heard. Before the meeting even began, the anti-ABC faction forced the removal of a class of eighth graders from Madison's middle school who had come for a civics lesson and were seated in the front rows. Once the meeting began, Hopkins gave what one report described as an "eloquent plea for overwhelming approval of ABC." It would prove to be the last moment of civility that night. Georgette Cutting read aloud an eighteen-page stemwinder denouncing every aspect of the program. ABC supporters serenaded her with jeers, heckles, and coughing fits throughout her speech. When Chris Weiss arose to speak on behalf of his fellow classmates in support of the program and students' stake in the debate, he was shouted down and subject to a cascade of derogatory remarks from the anti-ABC faction. Another student in attendance commented afterward that both sides "acted worse than we do at our assemblies," which, he added, "can be pretty bad."[27]

In late April, voters overwhelmingly approved the referendum expressing the town's opposition to ABC and calling on the Board of Education to rescind its offer of support. Milum was jubilant. "The silent majority has spoken, and I'm proud to be a part of it." Hopkins was crushed. "I am very much distressed at the results," he told a reporter. "Apparently the majority of the voters didn't understand our national problem concerning integration and the part Madison plays in it."[28] Town counsel Philip Costello, meanwhile, expressed his bemusement at the entire referendum campaign, pointing out that the vote would have no effect on whether ABC came to town or not. And indeed, ABC officials simply ignored the vote and moved ahead with plans to enroll the students in the fall, and neither the Board of Selectmen nor the Board of Education had any power to prevent them from enrolling. By law, any person of school age residing in town could attend Madison's public schools.[29]

For opponents, the referendum was intended to pressure ABC into abandoning its plans. ABC had indicated from the outset that it did not intend to implement its program in any town where it was not welcome. But local supporters dismissed the results of the referendum as unrepresentative of the views of the townspeople. Only one-half of all registered voters had cast a ballot; presumably, supporters argued, those who didn't vote supported the program. "If people in Madison don't like our ABC kids," ABC president Thomas D. Clifford told reporters, "they should just ignore them."[30] Many who had initially supported ABC, though, now expressed reservations about going forward out of concerns for the psychological well-being of the ABC students, who were poised to move into a community that had just voted, by a wide margin, against their arrival. But Clifford remained insistent that the students would be coming to Madison in the fall.

The school board, on the other hand, began to waver. Milum and the anti-ABC forces began calling for members' impeachment if they didn't take immediate action. Hopkins and the town's Board of Selectmen passed two resolutions urging the school board to withdraw its endorsement and for ABC sponsors to abandon the project. But the school board had never granted its approval; it had just passed a motion expressing members' support for the program's aims. The school board, instead, worked to financially cripple ABC and force it to cease operations in Madison. On the basis of an untested legal theory that in cases "where there is proof that the sole purpose of a child coming into a town is for education," in June it voted to charge each ABC student an $850 annual tuition fee to attend the public high school. Town officials, meanwhile, began doing anything in their power to undermine ABC's operations. That summer they turned down ABC's request to hold a fund-raising jazz concert at the Madison Surf Club. (They later reversed the decision after being warned by town counsel Costello that it could expose them to a civil rights lawsuit.) That fall, eight ABC students settled into their new surroundings as program officials battled with the school board in court over the legality of the town's tuition scheme.[31]

The fight over ABC and the injection of stridently anti-liberal and thinly veiled racist elements into local politics polarized the town, generated a wave of negative publicity from across the state, and put everyone on edge. Days after the vote, a rumor spread through town of an impending attack by the New Haven chapter of the Black Panther Party, set to coincide with the protests scheduled in New Haven for May Day. The rumor supposedly originated with an FBI source, who purportedly warned local law enforcement that Madison would be "lucky if [it] was not wiped off the face of the map."[32] Word of an impending attack in retaliation for the ABC vote quickly spread around town. In anticipation, the police department purchased $1,436 in riot control equipment and spent $1,302 more on overtime pay. Officers were equipped with night sticks, gas masks, tear gas launchers, smoke grenades, and helmets. The department stationed officers around the high school campus. It set up a bivouac area at the nearby Hammonasset State Park. It coordinated with area ham radio operators in case the Black Panthers succeeded in sabotaging normal lines of communication. In the end, nothing happened. There were no May Day protests in Madison, and no armies of black radicals marched into town ready to exact revenge.[33]

At that spring's high school commencement, valedictorian Peter Swift lamented the town's "unwillingness to accept reality," as he put it, and its resistance to change. What, Swift wondered, were the people of Madison so intent on protecting and preserving? As he looked out at the audience, he saw so many consumed with anger, gripped with paranoia, stewing in frustration, and filled with emptiness. The lesson, if not the answer, seemed clear. "Contrary to popular belief, happiness is not three cars, a house you can't afford, a broken marriage, and an alcoholic son." If the ABC program was a test of whether the people of Madison were ready "to accept reality," Swift concluded, then clearly it had failed.[34] While some looked down in shame, others furrowed their brows in anger as they were forced to sit through another hectoring lecture delivered by an idealistic youth unwise to the ways of the world. The only thing clear to the town's "silent majority" was that it had not spoken loudly enough.

For twenty years Vera Dallas had worked as the executive assistant to Madison's first selectman. More than any person in town hall, Dallas understood how Madison operated. Nevertheless, when she announced in 1971 her plans to run against Hopkins, her boss, for first selectman, many were surprised. Few initially gave her much of a chance of winning, especially Hopkins. But the battle over the ABC had convinced Dallas that the town needed, more than anything, someone who was unafraid of standing up to critics and defending the town's autonomy from neighboring cities and the designs of liberal social engineers. That fall, while Hopkins ran what even he described as an unusually lackadaisical campaign, Dallas went door to door, telling voters of her deep roots in the community and determination to defend the town's character— like a mother would that of her child. She employed the rhetoric ABC opponents had used so effectively the previous year, promising to use her administrative skills to ensure that no outside group would be able to come in and dictate to the townspeople what was best for them.[35]

Fresh in many voters' minds was another liberal organization that had come to town, uninvited, that summer, with the intent of forcing racial diversity and urban life down their throats. On August 3, a Revitalization Corps bus filled with forty-eight children had arrived at the entrance to the Madison Surf Club, the main public beach. Town officials had caught wind of Ned's plans to come to Madison earlier in the week and tried to convince him to delay for a week so that they could find families willing to host a child. They were surprised when Ned rebuffed their offer, stating that "he did not wish to work through either town officials or churches, but directly with the people."[36] "We are concerned about the children," First Selectman Hopkins tried to explain. "How marvelous," Ned smirked. "What have you done for them?"[37] Hopkins reluctantly agreed to allow the group of children to visit.[38] For weeks afterward, locals complained bitterly at having been ambushed by Revitalization Corps and its army of "ghetto youth" as they tried to enjoy their afternoon on the beach.[39] It was, many grumbled, another instance of local officials capitulating to the demands of an outside group who had come seeking to force residents to become more engaged and more concerned with other people's problems.

That fall, Dallas narrowly defeated Hopkins.[40] Hopkins retired from public life and, as one of the reporters who covered him during these years later wrote, "retreated to his home overlooking the Sound to lick his wounds."[41] Dallas, meanwhile, followed through on her promise to defend the town against all uninvited comers. Once in office, Dallas adopted a policy of strict scrutiny of any offers of federal or state assistance and massive resistance to any attempts to force the town to open its beaches to the general public. "Let's be cautious," she warned her constituents, "that we are not trapped into using federal money in any way, shape, or form to help pay off debt for purchases of our beaches or for their operation or maintenance."[42] Residents came to talk of federal funds as a "Trojan horse," an insidious scheme to undermine local autonomy dressed up as an act of generosity.[43] Going it alone was a small price to pay to prevent hordes of slum dwellers from descending onto their beaches each summer.

As she entered her first summer as first selectman, Dallas publicly let it be known that unlike her predecessor had done, no invitations to the town's beaches would be forthcoming while she was in office. On July 5, Dallas penned an open letter to Ned in which she reminded him that the town beaches were the "private property of the residents of Madison" and informed him that she had instructed local police officers to enforce local beach ordinances and treat Revitalization Corps as they would any other illegal trespassers. Copies of her letter, which were sent to all area media outlets, became a hot news item and established Dallas's credentials as a defender of shoreline towns' privacy. Dallas appeared on several local television shows where she explained and defended the town's position. She also took the opportunity to attack Ned personally and denounce the mission and tactics of Revitalization Corps. She called the Corps's strategy of making unannounced visits to beaches and pressuring families into hosting children "terrible" and a threat to the health and safety of the children. Dallas denied that the race of the children had anything to do with her position. She claimed she was simply acting out of concern *for* the children. I have "strong convictions about placing children on the beach," she stated, and just want to avoid any child's having a "traumatic experience" as a result of being placed in a stranger's home for a weekend.[44]

In response, Ned said the people of Madison were utterly ignorant of the realities of daily life in America's inner cities, and he called Dallas's sudden concern for the health and safety of urban black youth highly disingenuous. "If people were really concerned" about their well-being, "they would have contacted us with offers to bring the children out." If they so objected to Ned's "abandoning" children on the beach (a charge he repeatedly denied, citing the numerous parents and volunteers who accompanied the children on these trips), then why did no one complain about the numbers of Madison parents who dropped their children off at the beach in the morning, "expecting the guards [would] babysit" them?[45]

With her unequivocal opposition to Revitalization Corps, Dallas became a hero to aggrieved shoreline residents across the state. Madison resident Robert L. Adams praised Dallas for fighting back against Ned's effort to "invade our town beaches" and refusing to submit to these forms of "social and racial blackmail." Echoing the sentiments of Connecticut's—and the nation's—silent majority, Adams added, "I am fed up with the arrogance and intolerance of pseudo-liberals who simply because someone disagrees with them can only resort . . . to refusing to allow their opposition to speak." Other town officials also rushed to Dallas's defense and worked to shift the discussion from race to town finances. Madison had a right to keep nonresidents off its beaches because the town "has appropriated and expended large sums of money to purchase beach facilities for its residents," a statement by the Republican Town Committee read.[46]

Emboldened by Dallas's line in the sand and the plaudits it garnered from voters, officials in other shoreline towns began to openly denounce Ned and promise to resist his entreaties. Following the release of Dallas's open letter, Old Saybrook first selectman Raymond Kotowski announced his support of the "stand taken by [Dallas] in barring all persons who are non-residents from using the beaches in her town" and planned to do the same should Coll attempt an "invasion." In Madison, public support for Dallas was strongest among year-round residents, those who were less likely to belong to a private beach or sailing club and who were more likely to visit town beaches exclusively during the summer. Conversely, wealthier residents and summer cottage owners tended to view Dallas and her supporters as unnecessarily provocative.[47]

Dallas had no defense, though, against an aggrieved businessman and property owner hell-bent on exacting revenge on the town. The following spring, Revitalization Corps announced plans to spend the summer in Madison—at Hiram Birnbaum's invitation. Ned dubbed the cluster of cabins that would house up to sixty children at a time "Peace City" and erected large signs advertising Revitalization Corps's mission in front of the property on Boston Post Road, the main road leading into town.[48] Legally, there was nothing Madison officials could do to prevent Birnbaum from renting his cabins to Revitalization Corps, and there was nothing stopping Ned from demanding beach passes for his guests. "I guess we are all shocked," Selectman Willard Hathaway said when he heard the news.[49] Everyone knew Birnbaum had rented the cabins to Revitalization Corps as retaliation against the zoning board's unfavorable rulings.[50] Selectwoman Betty Hudson tried to be diplomatic. "[I see] no problem" with Revitalization Corps coming to town, she said, "if it is handled properly, which will be the crucial key."[51]

Ned, too, expressed hope that no one in Madison "gets hysterical" over their arrival.[52] In an appearance on the television program *Face the State* on station WTIC in late May, he also left no doubt as to his purpose and gave the people of Madison a good taste of his combative style.[53] Never one to mince words, Ned came on the popular public affairs show and immediately attacked the station's ownership over its coverage of the Vietnam War and the Watergate scandal and its inattention to Hartford's poor. "The best thing that's happened to this station," he told moderator Dick Bertel, "is the fact that it's been sold." (Months earlier the *Washington Post* had announced that it had purchased WTIC for $34 million.)[54] But he didn't stop there, landing blows against the

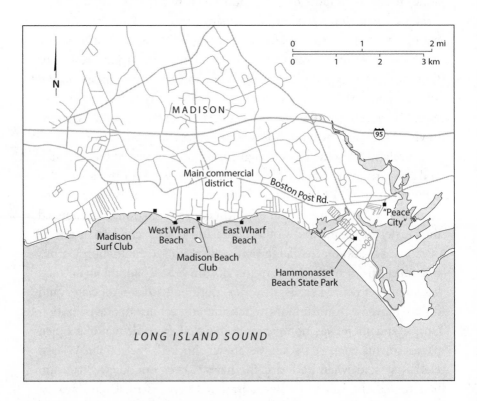

Madison, Connecticut.

city's banks and insurance companies, the chamber of commerce, his arch-nemesis Governor Meskill, and the "indifferent, disconnected" white families of Hartford's suburbs. As one report described it, "He got everyone but the archbishop."[55] By the end of the program, Bertel, who was described as "the type of man who gets angry every other year or so," "lapsed into a finger-waving flurry" at his guest, to which Ned calmly responded, "You can't take it, can you?"[56] To viewers in Madison, it was Ned's statements on his plans for the coming summer that proved most disconcerting. He charged Madison and other shoreline towns with "usurping" public land. "That land from the water and up to the high-tide mark" belongs to the public. "We're trying to open up that shoreline."[57] He brushed aside the charge that had now become a staple of his critics, that he was abandoning children and using them to advance his own political cause. "The people who are abandoning those children are the people who have blinded themselves to the fact that children need extended recreational facilities."[58]

When the cameras stopped rolling, Ned strolled out of the studio and to his car, adorned with an "Impeach Meskill" bumper sticker.[59] He could barely contain his enthusiasm at having taken on the state's media establishment in such a brazen fashion. "Somebody's head is going to roll, babe," he said as he walked out onto the city street. "They're going to say, 'Who the hell invited that guy?'" Back at his office on the North End that evening, he fielded numerous calls from supporters who expressed their appreciation of his daring attacks.[60]

Madison's Board of Selectmen knew what was in store and was desperate to minimize the expected fallout. As Ned and other volunteers prepared the cabins at Peace City for the summer, the board held closed-door meetings with town counsel Costello to discuss the town's legal options. They settled on a strategy of bureaucratic delay and intentional mismanagement. Henceforth, the entire Beach and Recreation Commission must approve every application by hotel operators for guest beach passes. In the past the town's recreation director alone approved such requests. An application lacking sufficient information would not be considered.[61]

When the decision to place authority over beach passes in the hands of the Beach and Recreation Commission was announced, town recreation director Bill Jones likely breathed a sigh of relief. The young African American was just two years into his new job. Jones was not only the first black person to occupy any position in town government, but also his family of four constituted, upon their arrival in 1971, nearly 20 percent of the town's permanent black population. Peace City promised to single-handedly triple the number of African Americans in town and threatened to set off another round of racial conflict pitting ambivalent white liberals against the town's vociferous "silent majority" just as the ABC students were returning to their respective cities for the summer. But if Jones harbored any hopes of remaining in the shadows during what was sure to be a summer of discord, he would soon find that when Revitalization Corps came to town, no one was safe from scrutiny, especially those who tried to remain on the sidelines.

Anne Loiseau and Suzanne Picard were typical of the cadre of volunteers Ned had recruited to join Revitalization Corps: young, college educated, idealistic, committed to social justice, and brought up in the Catholic Church. Loiseau had joined the Corps in 1969, shortly after she had arrived in Hartford as a student at St. Joseph's College, a small Catholic school on the city's northwest side. She was a shy eighteen-year-old from Waterbury with a passion for helping the needy. When she first arrived at Ned's office, she told him she'd do whatever they needed, just so long as she didn't have to speak in public. Of course, within a week, Ned had arranged for her to talk to a group of one hundred high school students. Eventually Loiseau dropped out of college and began working for Revitalization Corps full time, where she remained for the next nine years.[62] Picard also came from a devout Catholic family and had grown up in the small Connecticut town of Colchester, where her father owned a pharmacy. She began working for Revitization Corps soon after Loiseau.[63] In the spring of 1973, the two women moved to Madison to help coordinate efforts at Peace City that summer. There, they suffered a steady stream of verbal abuse from passersby, who would shout "nigger lovers" and other racial epithets out of their car windows at whoever happened to be outside of the cabins.[64]

On the morning of Friday, June 1, Loiseau and Picard awoke at dawn, dressed, and headed over to the cabin that served as the Corps's main office. As they would later tell police investigators, shortly after they had entered the kitchen, two white men—described as in their late twenties, clean shaven, and neatly dressed—leaped out of the cellar doorway and pounced on Loiseau. First, they punched her in the stomach and said, "You've been here too long. We people in Madison don't want you here, so you have to leave." One of the assailants then picked up a shard of broken glass and ran it across Loiseau's cheek, leaving a two-inch-long surface scratch. They threatened more harm to her and her family if the Corps didn't leave Madison immediately. One of the assailants punched Loiseau in the stomach a second time, and then both fled out of the cabin's back door. As the assault was taking place, Picard crouched in an adjoining room and placed a call to Madison police shortly after the attack. Three squad cars responded. Later that day, Dr. Birnbaum came and treated Loiseau's wound.[65]

From the outset, Madison police and local reporters seemed more interested in scrutinizing the two women's accounts than in finding the perpetrators. The cops could barely contain their contempt for Corps workers. During the investigation, one of the officers remarked that it "couldn't [have] be[en] Madison boys" who attacked the young women. "They would have really done a job on her."[66] Articles in the local *Shore Line Times* zeroed in on aspects of the investigation that seemed to cast doubt on the victims. There was no indication of forced entry, crime scene investigators reported. They found no footprints outside the cabin despite the ground's being wet with morning dew. Guests staying at the neighboring campground and a group of six men drinking coffee at a stand across the street had observed nothing suspicious around the time of the alleged assault. Investigators claimed to have found no fingerprints on the glass shard. The police told reporters that Picard "showed a definite reluctance to sign a written statement after being told a false statement could result in arrest." She did eventually sign her statement. Investigators publicly asked both Loiseau and Picard to submit to a lie detector test.[67]

Ned was incredulous. He was sure the Madison police could not be trusted to carry out a thorough and unbiased investigation. "I have no confidence whatsoever . . . in the integrity or competence of leadership of the Madison Police Department," he told reporters assembled on the grounds of Peace City. He issued a $500 reward for information leading to the capture and arrest of the assailants. He called for the state police and FBI to intervene and advised the women not to submit to any lie detector test administered by Madison police. Both Ned and Loiseau pinned the blame for violence against Corps volunteers on town officials, who, Ned charged, had "creat[ed] an atmosphere where [Peace City] is fair game." Given the inadequate police protection before the assault and the lackluster investigation and inconsistent reports that followed, Ned wondered aloud if he was living in Connecticut or Mississippi. And indeed, the police investigation raised an equal number of red flags. The complete lack of fingerprints on the weapon, despite its having been handled by both Loiseau and Picard after the alleged attack, suggested that it had been wiped clean subsequent to having been entered into evidence. It was later revealed that investigators did not do a full search of the crime scene or collect evidence until two days after the crime allegedly took place.[68]

Not just in Madison but statewide, media coverage of the incident was shaped in large measure by the media's impressions of Revitalization Corps and Ned Coll. While shoreline towns gave it scant coverage or cast doubt on the allegations, in urban media markets, the story received front-page coverage in newspapers and was the lead story on television and radio broadcasts. Tellingly, Hartford's WTIC, the station Ned had lambasted during an appearance weeks earlier, did not report on the story.[69] Facts of the case aside, Ned's penchant for drawing media attention through outlandish protests left him vulnerable to charges of fabrication and public skepticism. Despite intense and hostile interrogation from local investigators, though, neither Loiseau nor Picard ever wavered in their allegations. Eventually, both of the women agreed to take a lie detector test administered by the state police, and they passed it. But the case remained unsolved.[70]

Following the events of early June, the mood at Peace City darkened, and relations between Ned and town officials quickly deteriorated. Despite calmly assuring Ned back in April that there would be "no problem" getting beach passes for his guests, the town repeatedly refused to approve the Corps's permit application. First, officials returned his $150 check and application due to "insufficient information."

"But they won't tell us what the insufficient information is," Ned fumed. Subsequent attempts to fulfill the newly written and (Ned suspected) intentionally opaque and cumbersome application failed for reasons ranging from failure to specify the room rate for the cabins to not having the proper lodging license. The time between each submission and rejection also grew longer, while the answers Revitalization Corps received from persons at the Beach and Recreation Commission became more vague and misleading. When Ned would call and ask about the reason for the delay, someone would tell him to await a call from Chairman Robert Wigham "asking for further clarification." One day they'd tell him the application had already been mailed back; the next day they'd say it was still sitting on Wigham's desk awaiting his attention. What's more, other branches of local government seemed to be joining in what Ned described as a campaign of intimidation and harassment.

Beginning in the summer of 1973, tensions escalated between Revitalization Corps and local law enforcement in Madison, Connecticut, over accessing the town's beaches. *Photo © Bob Adelman. Courtesy Bob Adelman.*

The town's health director informed Ned that any child seeking a guest beach pass needed to pass a physical exam beforehand. The town's zoning enforcement officer began issuing the Corps fines for a sign atop the roof of the main cabin that exceeded the legal size limit by three feet.[71]

Already six weeks into the summer campaign and with little to show for it, Ned's frustration at Madison's intransigence threatened to boil over. Matters came to a head at the end of June, when Ned announced plans for a series of protests throughout the town over the Fourth of July weekend. Local officials and business owners pleaded with Ned not to disrupt the holiday festivities. "The Fourth of July is a special holiday," an editorial in the *Shore Line Times* read, "celebrating one of the more precious and ennobling privileges of mankind: freedom." Among others was the freedom to "use the available facilities of one's town, such as beach and recreation facilities, but with the responsibility to use these facilities within the limitations and restrictions governing their use agreed to by taxpayers." But Ned was having none of it. "The attitude of town officials is an insult to the memory of James Madison."[72]

It was a Fourth of July the people of Madison would not soon forget. Unable to swim at town beaches, the children and mothers who came from Hartford instead celebrated America's independence by picketing in front of the beach's entrance; in front of churches whose ministers and congregations, Ned charged, "have supported racism"; and in front of the homes of members of the Beach and Recreation Commission and Board of Selectmen.[73] On Sunday morning, July 1, Ned and an estimated one hundred demonstrators staged a pray-in in front of the town's Congregational church. During the demonstration, the church's minister approached the protesters and, as Earlie Powell recalls, said, "I don't want to ever see you on my property again. . . . You stay up in Hartford." Powell shot back, "Excuse me?!?! I'm not on your property. I'm in the street, and I'm staying right here. . . . I can hold this sign, and . . . [if] you don't like what the sign says, that's too bad." Describing the encounter, Powell said, "Oh my God that priest was so red; he was so mad. He could've hurt somebody."[74]

Afterward, the protesters marched to the front entrance of the Madison Surf Club. There, hostilities quickly escalated. Standing at the beach entrance was Bill Jones, the African American recreation director charged with enforcing local beach ordinances. Black mothers and teen-agers from Hartford viciously taunted Jones as a stooge and Uncle Tom. "Why don't you change your color, man?" one shouted. Another begged Jones to "Let us in just for today, only 15 minutes, so we can show our black faces over there." Madison police, expecting no more than thirty protesters, quickly found themselves overwhelmed by the large and vocal crowd. The cops seemed to be looking for an excuse to pounce. Ned later charged one officer with "trying to provoke me into a physi-cal attack." Some beachgoers shouted racial epithets and made other derogatory comments about blacks' supposed laziness and dependence on government handouts. Many simply avoided the spectacle altogether and stayed home for the day. Later in the afternoon, a group of twenty-five Corps protesters descended on Dallas's home. Seeking to broker a tentative peace deal, Dallas invited eight in, including Ned, but the group left without any agreement.[75]

For local merchants and hotel operators, the holiday weekend was nothing short of a disaster. All reported sharp drops in sales on what was traditionally the busiest weekend of the year. Many openly feared that the continued standoff between Revitalization Corps and the town over the beach passes threatened to damage the town's image and "cause tourists to by-pass Madison" for other towns further down the shore. Ned promised to do his part, threatening to make Madison "the most embarrassed town in the [E]ast" if it didn't grant Peace City its duly allotted beach passes. Even as area businesses begged local officials to reach an accord, few selectmen were in any mood to capitulate to Ned's demands. Selectman George Egan bitterly denounced Ned as "an insult to the black community of America," adding, "and I am a liberal."[76]

Following the Fourth, Madison's Beach and Recreation Commis-sion held an emergency Friday evening session (appropriately at the Madison Surf Club) to consider Revitalization Corps's request for seventy-eight beach passes. Ned sat in the audience, flanked by the still-bandaged Loiseau and two female Corps volunteers. Across the room sat Bill Jones. News reporters and television crews were on hand. "Let me tell you, that meeting smoked," Ned recalled. Board members grilled Ned on whether the Deluxe Motel was operating as a "legitimate motel business." They asked him whether it had any paying guests staying at the motel, whether it advertised in any publications, what rates it charged. Finally, Wigham turned to the real issue at hand: "You were quoted in the July 5th edition of the *New Haven Journal Courier,* 'We're going to get on those beaches, there is no way we won't get on those beaches.' Further, that you plan to continue and expand efforts to gain beach access for the poor. Sunday, July 1, you harassed residents and employees of this town with demonstrations and other tactics. What assurance do you give that these tactics will cease if passes are granted?"[77]

"Since when [does] people standing up for their rights [constitute] harassment in America?" Ned shot back. "A person is not breaking the law by standing up for his rights, is he?" Wigham continued to press Ned on whether he would cease his protests if the town granted his request. Ned promised only to "follow the Constitution." Later, the meeting adjourned to the cabins on Boston Post Road, where board members inspected the grounds and poured over the Corps's records, ostensibly to determine whether the cabins qualified as a motel and were thus eligible for guest passes. Upon returning, the board went into a closed session. Ned and a crowd of supporters, along with television crews and news reporters, waited outside. Ned entertained the crowd and fed the jukebox a steady supply of quarters.[78]

At 11 p.m., board members filed back out into the main hall and took their seats. Robert Wigham began to read a prepared statement. "Based on information provided verbally and a visual inspection of records, we grant the Deluxe Cabins 9 beach passes." Wigham didn't get a chance to finish reading his statement. The moment he uttered "9 beach passes," Ned jumped to his feet and angrily denounced the decision. As Dallas banged her gavel and called for order, Ned marched toward her, finger wagging, and challenged her to a public debate. When she refused, he denounced her and two other selectmen as bigots. Dallas adjourned the meeting, and board members made a hasty retreat to the parking lot. Things got worse. Out in the hallway, Ned spotted Bill Jones and unleashed a vicious verbal attack. As one report described it, "Jones stood back, his arms up, 'hit me, hit me,' he told Coll." Squad cars arrived on the scene. "But the moment passed, and the crowd, as if sensing the futility of it all[,] broke away."[79]

Board members, appalled at Ned's theatrics, were just getting warmed up. The following day, Wigham told reporters that Ned's "outlandish behavior and abusive language . . . leads me to seriously question the legitimacy of his motives." "Whenever the TV cameras were on," Wigham continued, "Mr. Coll would leap to his feet and interrupt the proceedings with a diatribe against the commission, the town officials and the citizens of Madison. I truly wish that the people who[m] Mr. Coll claims to represent could observe his actions and tactics[,] which appear to be designed to achieve notoriety for him at the expense of those loftier goals which are the stated objectives of the Revitalization Corps."[80] Seemingly lost amid the flurry of insults and counterattacks was the fact that Revitalization Corps had actually achieved a fairly sizable concession from the board. Had Ned not interrupted Wigham's prepared statement, he would have learned that in granting Peace City nine adult passes, it had, in effect, agreed to allow up to forty-five children on the beach at any one time since five children under the age of twelve could accompany every adult without requiring their own separate beach pass. It was far short of the seventy-eight passes Ned had initially demanded, but it was a concession nonetheless.[81]

After the Fourth of July, Madison residents grew more openly confrontational toward Revitalization Corps and proudly defensive of their exclusionary measures. The following weekend, resident Tom O'Donnell walked the beach distributing flyers calling on fellow residents to stand in support of Dallas and fight back against Ned's vicious attacks. "When I was a combat advisor in Vietnam," he said, "I found that sometimes you really have to fight for the things you love or you will lose them. I feel that Ned Coll's description of the town of Madison ("the biggest slum I've ever been in") may be a futuristic vision of things to come if he is allowed to coerce the town into a state of compassion out of fear. . . . It is time for the people of Madison to take a stand. . . . It is time to show that 'all people' have civil rights . . . and if it is necessary to defend these rights—we are ready to do so!"[82]

Ned's encounter with the people of Madison only fueled his desire to openly confront and publicly challenge exclusionary practices along the shore. Later that summer, he announced plans to storm the beach at

Fenwick, home to Katharine Hepburn and an assemblage of old moneyed families with deep roots in the state. "We want to challenge these people morally and socially."[83] Fenwick tried to outmaneuver Ned through generosity. Days after Ned first mentioned possibly targeting Fenwick next, borough warden Charles E. Brainerd extended a public invitation to Revitalization Corps to visit the town's beach. On July 20, Ned brought a bus filled with seventy children to Fenwick, passing through the gated entrance and disembarking onto the sandy beach fronting some of the grandest seaside mansions on the East Coast. Some of the children of Fenwick families came down to play games, give swimming lessons, loan bikes, and act as hosts for the day. "This isn't something new to us," Brainerd commented. "The people of Fenwick have invited blacks and other disadvantaged people to their homes for years."[84] The key word here was "invited." Ned was under no illusions as to Brainerd's intentions. At the end of what Fenwick's wardens later described as a "success in all respects," Ned let it be known that he did not confuse such acts of generosity with the granting of rights.[85] When asked if Fenwick's gesture had convinced him to abandon his plans to stage a surprise landing on the borough's beach at some future date, Ned replied, "No."[86] The wealthy people of Connecticut could not simply buy or donate Revitalization Corps into complacency, however much they tried.

As the summer of 1973 drew to a close, residents of the state's Gold Coast towns had good reason to fear that it might be the last they would enjoy to themselves, among themselves. On September 4, the day after Labor Day, the Connecticut Civil Liberties Union (CCLU) held a press conference in which it announced the details of its impending class-action lawsuit against towns that restricted the use of their public beaches to residents only. On behalf of the people of Connecticut who did not live along the shore, the CCLU planed to sue the town of Fairfield in state Superior Court and argue that the town's restrictions on public beach access violated the Fourteenth Amendment's equal protection clause and constituted an overextension of the powers granted to municipalities by the state. The next round in the battle for the beach would be waged in the courts.[87]

SEVEN

Freedom of Beach

By the early 1970s, a growing army of activists and litigants, clad in sandals and swimsuits, pitchforks in one hand and briefcases in the other, assembled at the gates of private and quasi-private beaches across coastal America. Between 1964 and 1974 federal and state courts decided at least twenty-six cases involving disputes over public rights on beaches. Hundreds of others were filed and countless others threatened. On October 29, 1973, the Connecticut Civil Liberties Union followed through on its announced plans and filed a lawsuit against the town of Fairfield over its beach access restrictions in state superior court.

The CCLU chose Fairfield not because its regulations were the most restrictive. In fact, anyone could technically use the town's beaches. But only residents could buy an annual pass that allowed them to park at the beach or obtain a one-day pass at a steep discount. And since the only practical means for persons to reach the beach was by car, these parking restrictions effectively barred nonresidents, all the while allowing local officials to claim that Fairfield's beaches were open to all comers. Rather, the CCLU chose to target Fairfield because it had been among the most solicitous of federal aid. In the previous two years alone, Fairfield had received three federal grants totaling $85,000 for erosion control.[1] On this count, it seemed, the law was clear. "When State or Federal funds are used by counties or municipalities for acquisition, development, or operation of [beach] facilities, local residency restrictions are prohibited," the authors of the 1969 report of the U.S. Commission on Marine Science, Engineering, and Resources (a.k.a. the Stratton Commission) wrote. [2] American taxpayers helped to pay for these facilities, CCLU lawyers planned to argue, so they had every right to use them.

Neighboring Greenwich knew this moment was coming, and it was ready. For nearly a year, officials in Greenwich had made it known that an attack on another shoreline town's exclusionary policies would be considered an attack on their town. In 1972 the city's first selectman, William Lewis, promised that Greenwich would fight any lawsuit against any Connecticut town's public beach access restrictions "all the way to the U.S. Supreme Court if necessary."[3] These were reassuring words to a community that was fast becoming a fortress of extreme wealth and privilege surrounded by urban poverty and decay. Over the years, the western edge of Connecticut—a state that did not have an income tax until 1991—had become a magnet for a class of high-level executives who worked in Manhattan but wanted to avoid paying New York State income taxes. On weekends, Greenwich families traveled to Manhattan and strolled through its parks, toured its museums, and partook of the city's robust public life. Back home, though, they worked tirelessly to make the town as unwelcoming to its neighbors as possible. In Greenwich, the neighbors were people from Port Chester, New York, a dying manufacturing town suffering from overcrowded housing, failing schools, and dismal public services that, by the mid-1970s, was among the growing number of "suburban . . . ghettos, surrounded by more affluent white communities" in the Northeast.[4]

Greenwich held the dubious distinction of having the most exclusionary public beaches in the state, explicitly closed to nonresidents and difficult even for guests of residents to enter. While other towns pleaded that the cost of beach maintenance and upkeep necessitated prohibitive access and parking fees for nonresidents, Greenwich was unabashed in its exclusionary aims. When asked to explain why, in 1958, the town doubled the price of admission for guests of Greenwich residents, First Selectman Griffin E. Harris said simply that it was meant to "discourage out of towners" rather than to produce more revenue.[5] Fairfield's

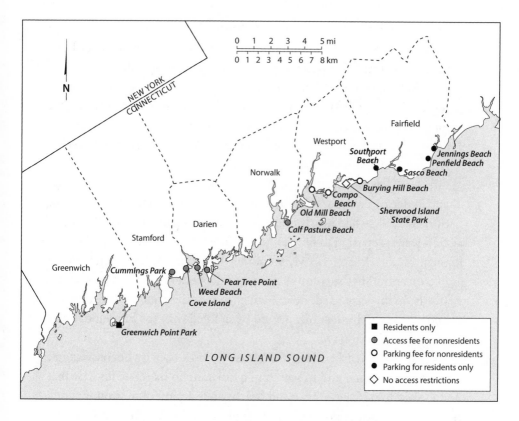

Names, locations, and legal status of public beaches
along Connecticut's Gold Coast.

beach access restrictions were relatively moderate in comparison. From
Greenwich's perspective, a decision striking down Fairfield's beach ordinances would inevitably result in its own being declared unconstitutional. So within weeks after the CCLU had held its press conference,
Greenwich's town counsel William Mottolese placed a phone call to his
counterpart in Fairfield, Noel Newman, to let him know that Greenwich
planned to join Fairfield as a co-defendant and lend its considerable
resources toward protecting the state's sand curtain.[6]

Recent decisions in neighboring state courts gave the CCLU legal team
hope and residents and officials in Gold Coast towns cause for concern.
In New York and New Jersey, rulings by the states' supreme courts had

removed a number of exclusionary devices from coastal towns' arsenals and provided civil liberties groups and open beach activists with a blueprint for overturning beach access restrictions nationwide.

Situated on the Atlantic side of Long Island, Long Beach, New York, was once thought to be the next Atlantic City. By 1970, those dreams had long been forgotten. Large hotels still lined the town's four-mile-long boardwalk, but now they were home to senior citizens, welfare recipients, and, increasingly, mental patients recently released from area sanitariums. Downtown storefronts stood empty, the buildings abandoned and in decay. Two years earlier, tensions between the city's black population and police had nearly erupted into a full-scale uprising. Town officials were preparing to file a lawsuit against the Nassau County Department of Social Services over what they believed was a deliberate policy of concentrating the county's poor and dependents in the municipality. It was, many suspected, no coincidence that the county's most racially and ethnically diverse town would be saddled with the burden of housing society's castoffs.[7]

A town that had long fashioned itself as socially liberal was in a reactionary mood and in search of a quick fix to its many ills. For that, it looked to its long, white sand beach, once a symbol of promise and a glamorous future, now just another place where the dregs of society— hippies, the homeless, kids from the ghetto, anyone with enough money for a train fare from New York City—came to hang out. The Long Island Railroad had a terminal right next to the beach, making it a convenient, and popular, summer destination for New Yorkers who had grown tired of Coney Island and who didn't own a car, a requirement for reaching the Robert Moses–designed state beach on Long Island. Isaac Dubow, recently elected the town's city council president, promised to make the beach great again by closing it to outsiders. In November 1970 the city council passed a law banning all nonresidents outright from the town's beachfront. It hired extra police officers to patrol the beach in blue shirts and pith helmets during the summer months. The town also ended a charitable program that had brought disadvantaged youth to the shore each summer.[8]

Across this and other Northeastern suburban counties, fear of urban populations and taxpayer resentment over public spending were

running high, and public beaches and parks offered a convenient, highly
symbolic vehicle for channeling voters' exclusionary sentiments. The
following year Nassau County executive Ralph Caso announced that all
beaches and parks in the county would be open to taxpaying county residents only. To gain admission to county parks, pools, and golf courses,
residents had to obtain a separate photo ID card, called a "leisure pass,"
from the county executive office.[9] Signs that read "Proof must be shown
of name and address" were placed throughout the county's parks system. The policy came to be known as the Caso Doctrine, a defiant attempt to narrow the very definition of who constituted "the public,"
turn public spaces into quasi-private facilities, and make local tax contributions akin to membership fees. Caso and Dubow's exclusionary
populism was wildly popular among voters. "Closing our beaches has
made this city a more desirable place to live," Dubow boasted. "I see
families on the beaches now. Real estate values are going up."[10] "Our
facilities are already overcrowded and overutilized, and we have all we
can do to preserve the best recreation facilities for our own residents,"
Caso added. "We must remember that it is our residents who pay for
them and maintain them through taxes."[11]

The hanging of sand curtains gave good copy, but as the civil liberties attorney Lawrence Sager pointed out, it was a poor solution to the
problems that ailed this and other middle-class white suburban towns.
"Long Beach is a city trying to overcome its problems with one law," the
young law professor who specialized in challenging exclusionary zoning
and land-use laws remarked. "Drug use won't stop with the closing of the
beaches. And it's a geographic absurdity. Four miles of beachfront serve
a community of 70,000 residents in the summer when those beaches
can hold up to 150,000 people."[12] Such steps were not about protecting
the beach from overuse or maintaining law and order. They were simply
another means "by which white suburbs manage to erect barriers to inner-city residents, thereby cementing residential segregation."[13] Moreover, it was, Sager argued, unconstitutional. While Dubow was touting
the new law, attorneys at the New York City office of the ACLU were
planning to challenge it in court. They latched on to a case already filed
by Paula and Albert Gewirtz, owners of a doughnut and knish stand
on the boardwalk whose business had suffered a 60– 90 percent loss

Even Neptune was not exempt from residents-only beach
ordinances, as seen in a political cartoon that appeared in the June 2,
1974, issue of the *New York Times. Courtesy Edward Sorel.*

in seasonal revenue as a result of the beach's new access restrictions.
Seeing this as an opportunity to challenge the constitutionality of banning nonresidents from public spaces and fearing that the case would be
tossed due to the plaintiffs' lack of standing (the Gewirtzes were town
residents themselves), the ACLU added a New York City resident to the
case and shifted focus from the law's harmful impact on local businesses
to its arbitrary discrimination against a class of people.[14]

In twelve days of hearings before the New York State Supreme
Court, Sager made the case that the town's beach access restriction violated both the equal protection clause of the Fourteenth Amendment
and the public trust doctrine. He began by arguing that the land in question belonged to the state, which held it in trust for the general public.
He showed that the dry sand beach sat on top of tidal lands that had

been filled in by erosion-control projects. These public works projects did not, however, alter the legal status of the land underneath, which still belonged to the state under the court's interpretation of the public trust doctrine. A city, Sager argued, cannot simply take land held by the state by dumping sand onto it. If the court accepted the argument that the sandy beach belonged to the state, then, Sager argued, the town's beach access restriction constituted a clear violation of due process and equal protection.[15]

Sager hoped the case could breathe new life into the public trust doctrine, but the court opted to decide the case on much narrower grounds. It ruled that the beach ban was unconstitutional but only because the beach had been expressly dedicated to the general public. Since the city had, from the beach's opening in 1936, made it available to the general public, it had, in effect, created an "irrevocable public trust."[16] The court avoided addressing the public trust doctrine entirely.

The New Jersey Supreme Court was not so shy. That same year, it ruled in the case of *Neptune City v. Avon-by-the-Sea* that the public trust doctrine required beaches to be open to all citizens "on equal terms and without preference."[17] The case stemmed from a decision by the coastal town of Avon-by-the-Sea to institute a differential fee scale for nonresidents seeking to use the town's public beaches. After the state's legislature had begun allowing cities to collect user fees from beachgoers to defray maintenance costs in the 1950s, towns up and down the Jersey shore began charging higher fees for nonresidents as a way to curtail summer crowds and, especially in the case of cities near large urban centers, keep "undesirables" out. In 1970 Avon doubled the price of a seasonal beach pass for nonresidents from $10 to $20 and raised daily rates for nonresidents from $1.25 to $2.25. Most affected by these new charges were the residents of neighboring inland Neptune City, who lacked their own stretch of shore. Neptune City residents Evelyn Irons and Lilyan Burke sued Avon, arguing that the town lacked the authority to charge differential fees for access to state-owned land, that it violated the equal protection clause, and that they had a common law right to access navigable waters under the public trust doctrine. Their attorneys also asked the court to consider the question of who belonged to the class of taxpaying contributors to the beach's construction and maintenance. They presented evidence showing the extent that federal and state tax dollars had contributed to the beach's construction and maintenance over the previous half century. Between 1920 and 1968, the state of New Jersey had devoted more money to anti-erosion projects along the state's shoreline ($26.8 million) than had all the coastal towns combined ($22.2 million).[18]

In a 4–2 decision, the state supreme court ruled in favor of Neptune City and offered the most robust, expansive interpretation of the public trust doctrine of any court in the nation's history. In his majority opinion, Justice Frederick W. Hall ruled that "while municipalities may validly charge reasonable fees for the use of their beaches, they may not discriminate in any respect between their residents and non-residents." Rather, the court "must take the view that the public trust doctrine dictates that the beach and the ocean waters must be open to all on equal terms and without preference."[19] The court ruled that the rights covered under the public trust doctrine included bathing, swimming, and recreation, not just fishing and navigation. And it cast doubt on the legality of cities' exorbitant daily access fees, which seemed likely designed with discriminatory intent.[20]

The decision went far beyond what the plaintiffs had expected or sought. And its wider implications were clear to both supporters and opponents of beach access restrictions nationwide. In wealthy seaside communities, the Avon decision, as one report put it, was "about as welcome as a shark scare."[21] Coming on the heels of the Long Beach case, the rulings by two state supreme courts, as Wallace Kaufman and Orrin Pilkey later wrote, "resounded across suburban shorefront America like a double-barreled shotgun."[22] For civil liberties attorneys in Connecticut, these decisions, and the courts' recognition that all citizens helped pay for the beaches through federal and state contributions, became the blueprint for challenging residents-only beaches. For Gold Coast residents, the decisions in New York and New Jersey only heightened anxieties over the poisoned chalice of federal aid.

For the people of Greenwich, the question was not whether federal or state intervention in shoreline affairs was desirable but rather the extremes to which town officials should go in defending its residents-only beaches from the threat of legal challenge. At the same time as the CCLU was preparing to file its suit in state court, Republican first selectman Bill Lewis was locked in a surprisingly tight race for reelection against his Democratic opponent, Frank Mazza. Registered Republicans outnumbered registered Democrats in Greenwich by nearly three to one. The GOP had held the first selectman's seat and controlled town hall for the past sixty-seven years. But in recent years, voter unrest over the Republican majority's failure to control development and manage the influx of new businesses and industries into Fairfield County had led some to speculate that a Democratic upset was in the offing.[23]

Leaving nothing to chance, Lewis played the beach card. At a rally at the Greenwich Civic Center in late October, Lewis accused Mazza during his time on the Board of Selectmen of having advocated for the use of federal funds to acquire several acres of beachfront property on Great Captain's Island. If we had followed Mazza's advice, Lewis charged, "we would [have] open[ed] up the floodgate to anyone in the country to use our parks and beaches." The crowd booed and hissed. Lewis delivered another blow. "If you want to share your beaches and parks with everyone in New York and Connecticut"—cries of "No!" cascaded through the hall—"then my opponent is your man."[24] The following day one-half page ads began running in the *Greenwich Time* stoking voters' fears of an open beach and touting Lewis's record of defending "Greenwich Beaches and Parks for Greenwich People!" "Do you want *outsiders* using *your* beaches and parks?" one ad asked.[25] Another included a picture of the fence that surrounded a town beach and the sign "Restricted / Greenwich Residents Only." Below it read, "Maintain the Greenwich Tradition!" along with a reminder of the stakes. "See what happened to Fairfield because they used Federal and State money."[26]

Voters needed no reminder. The CCLU's lawsuit against Fairfield seemed to validate defensive localism even as it demonstrated the need for collaboration among exclusive municipalities. "The suits say [if] you took federal and state money for beaches and parks, whether it was two or more, [then] . . . all of the town's beaches and parks should be open to the general public," Lewis warned. "I do not want to take the chance of having our already overcrowded beaches . . . inundated with people from this whole region."[27]

To African Americans living in Greenwich, terms like "outsiders" had long been understood to be euphemisms for "black people." It was, as the Greenwich NAACP chapter president George Twine described it, the "magic word" that local white officials and citizens alike used when referring to people of color, its meaning and intent painfully obvious yet plausibly deniable.[28] Lewis's Democratic opponent, meanwhile, characterized Lewis's "scare tactics" as a sign of desperation, a way to, as Mazza charged, "cover up failures of his Republican administration."[29] Lewis, he charged, was deliberately misleading the public as to the nature of the lawsuit against Fairfield. "The CCLU basis [sic] their suit on the premise that Fairfield's beach parking policies violate state law and the equal protection clause of the U.S. Constitution."[30]

But voters perhaps understood all too well what a decision against Fairfield foretold. If the courts found its comparatively moderate mechanism of exclusion (high parking fees for nonresidents) to be unconstitutional, Greenwich's flagrant exclusionary policies would be unlikely to withstand a future legal challenge. On November 6, Lewis coasted to reelection by only a slightly smaller margin than two years earlier. "They lied on the beach issue," Mazza fumed. "It was strictly a scare tactic."[31] And it had worked.

Open beach proponents in Congress could not have picked a worse moment to draw the nation's attention to the problem of beach access. On October 23, 1973, the House of Representatives began holding hearings on a proposed National Open Beaches Act. Texas congressman Bob Eckhardt, the bill's lead author, had lined up a slew of legal experts, coastal scientists, and conservationists who were prepared to speak on behalf of the bill to the American public. But when the time came, the nation's attention, and that of virtually everyone on Capitol Hill, was focused instead on the constitutional crisis unfolding in the White House and the war raging in the Middle East. Five days earlier, President Nixon had ordered U.S. attorney general Elliot Richardson to fire the special prosecutor investigating the Watergate affair, Archibald Cox. Richardson, as well as his deputy secretary, William Ruckelshaus, refused to carry out the order and resigned in what the press dubbed the Saturday Night

Massacre. On the first day of hearings, Arab and Israeli combatants announced a cease-fire in the Yom Kippur War.

For lawmakers and the public alike, the problem of beach access could not have seemed less urgent. One of the main experts called to testify in favor of the bill, the eminent legal scholar Charles Black, could not even muster the time to draft a written statement. "Anybody who holds himself out as a constitutional law academic by trade has been rather busy the last few days," he told committee members apologetically. Supporters of the bill tried to make the case that open beaches were good for society and the environment and counter the prevailing assumption that greater public access would lead to greater environmental harm. To the contrary, this bill "would [not] only guarantee the public's free and open access to the beaches," Texas assistant attorney general Terrence O'Rourke argued, "it would also preserve the beaches." "Had the coastlines been under public ownership," Brent Blackwelder of the Environmental Policy Center added, "th[e] pressure for federal aid [for erosion control projects] would not have arisen, and the coastlines would not be viewed as being 'in jeopardy' of destruction." Opponents of the bill, meanwhile, claimed it was unnecessary, counterproductive, and cost prohibitive. Nixon-appointed heads of numerous federal agencies lined up to register their opposition to the bill. "We cannot agree, as a matter of law, that the public is entitled to the free and unrestricted right to use the beaches of the United States as a common," deputy assistant attorney general Walter Kiechel Jr. told lawmakers. The bill could meet its objectives, he added, only through mass acquisition of coastal property, "by purchase, condemnation, or otherwise. The costs would be astronomical."[32] The two days of hearings generated minimal press coverage, and the bill, for the fourth consecutive session since Eckhardt's arrival in Congress, failed to make it to the House floor.[33]

Back in Hartford, Ned's message of civic engagement and sacrifice failed to resonate with a white middle class suddenly preoccupied with economic insecurities. In March 1974, OPEC lifted its embargo of oil shipments to the United States, but in the meantime, the price of oil had skyrocketed from three to twelve dollars a barrel. The nation's economy remained in the grips of stagflation, and the presidency was unraveling.[34] When Ned and other Corps workers went door to door in West Hartford that spring, looking for people willing to lend their time to tutoring youngsters, painting dilapidated houses on the North End, or taking one or more kids with them down to the shore some weekend, they found few takers. "Enthusiasm? Not exactly," Sam Blumenthal, president of the Tumblewood Country Club, said in response to a reporter's question about his members' reaction to Ned's solicitation of support. "There's a basic coldness in this town," Ned moaned, "a tremendous lack of spirit." Revitalization Corps had set as its goal to enlist five thousand volunteers in West Hartford that summer. By late June, they had found only fifty or so persons willing to volunteer.[35]

As his public profile grew, Ned began receiving invitations to speak across the state. He never turned one down. But the arduous schedule was beginning to take its toll on him physically. In June, Ned suffered a seizure and collapsed on stage while delivering the commencement address to students at Torrington High School. He was helped off the stage to a waiting ambulance. Later, he chalked the episode up to his having not eaten that day. He had no intentions of slowing down. Ned would not be enjoying any R&R this summer, and until the state awoke to the problems facing the urban poor, neither would those families fortunate enough to own a cottage along the shore.[36]

Plans for the Corps's most audacious, headline-grabbing protest against private beaches yet, scheduled for the Fourth of July, went forward. Earlier, Ned and a couple of his volunteers had traveled down to Madison in the Corps's ramshackle conversion van to scope out possible locations to launch their operation. There, they met with one of the town's most famous residents: Constance Pignatelli. The former wife of Italian Prince Guido Pignatellia di Montecalva, Princess Pignatellia (as she was still known in Madison) lived in a seaside mansion in Madison with her daughter, Maria Elena Pignatelli. Both of them were sympathetic to the Corps's objectives and agreed to assist it in its latest plan.[37]

Back in Hartford, around sixty-five mothers, volunteers, and children assembled at the Corps's headquarters at 8 a.m. on the Fourth. Some began painting protest signs, others prepared food, and a group of young men helped load three outboard motorboats onto the roofs of the vans. On these days, Ned acted, as one reporter described, like "a young infantry lieutenant about to send his troops into a battle that was somehow going to be fun no matter who got hurt."[38] When everything was packed, Ned called into the headquarters for everyone to load up and file out. Their destination: the Madison Beach Club. The means of attack: amphibious invasion. Base of operations: Pignatelli's private beach, located adjacent to the beach club. Before they departed, Ned placed a call to the airfield where the plane and the parachutist he had also enlisted for the mission were set to depart. The banner was secured, and parachutist Peter Gruber was ready to go. He had already notified members of the media. Reporters for the *Hartford Courant* and *Boston Globe* were already awaiting Ned's arrival.

"A good tactic," Saul Alinsky advised, "is one that your people enjoy."[39] On the ride to the shore, the kids could barely contain their excitement. It would be a Fourth of July to remember. The mothers seemed more anxious, fearful of being arrested, despite Ned's assurances that so long as they kept their feet firmly planted on the wet sand, they were doing nothing illegal. Along the way, the vans shared the road with some of the thousands of travelers who were going in search (many in vain) of a place on the shore to enjoy the holiday. Rocky Neck State Park reported over fourteen thousand people (two thousand over capacity) on its beach that day. Sherwood Island had over thirty thousand people (five thousand over capacity). And Hammonasset had to turn away over five thousand persons over the course of the day. Revitalization Corps, in contrast, planned to enjoy the holiday at a much more spacious and less crowded stretch of shore.[40]

The caravan reassembled just outside of Madison before beginning the last leg of the journey, through downtown, just as the streets began to fill with holiday traffic. They made it through downtown without incident, turned off Boston Post Road onto Island Avenue, and headed toward the shore. As the Long Island Sound came into view, the vans pulled into the boat landing, fortuitously located adjacent to the private club whose festivities they would soon be crashing. They had little time to waste; police officers would soon be on the scene, and surely they could come up with something Ned was in violation of. Ned and one of his assistants leapt out of the van and began unfastening the boats and dropping them into the water. Someone else hung a ladder off the pier. Once everything was in place, Ned and seven Corps volunteers scurried down the ladder and into the boats. The sun was shining, the skies were clear, and the members of the exclusive Madison Beach Club, who underwent a rigorous vetting process and paid a $300 annual membership for days like this, were trickling out onto the beach and planting themselves underneath one of the club's neatly arranged green sun umbrellas.

Just before noon, club members looked up to see Gruber, a thirty-three-year-old member of the Wings of Orange, a parachute team based in Orange, Massachusetts, leap from three thousand feet and begin his slow descent onto the Pignatelli's beach. Kids on the beach were cheering, their parents giving Gruber a round of applause. What a pleasant surprise, some thought, a nice start to a festive day. But just as Gruber was taking his bows, three boats appeared, all headed toward the club's shore. The lead boat cut its engine before reaching the shore. Ned, with an American flag attached to a pole, leapt off the bow and began marching, MacArthuresque, toward the beach. Stopping just before he reached the dry sand, Ned shouted, "Happy Fourth of July everyone!" and defiantly planted the flag in the sand.[41] Moments later, the plane that Gruber had parachuted from began circling overhead, carrying a banner that read, "Free America's Beaches."[42]

Club members stared in disbelief. This was an ambush. Mothers scooped their children off the beach and made a hasty retreat to the clubhouse. The club's secretary, James Hooper, sprinted down to the beach and asked Ned just what was going on. Ned pointed over to the boat landing, where more than fifty children stood. Ned asked Hooper if they could walk across the club's lawn and onto the beach. Hooper refused, informing Ned it was against the club's policy. That's fine, Ned replied. By then, Madison police officers had arrived on the scene and were spread out across the club's property. Denied permission to enter the club's property, Ned signaled to Corps workers to begin loading children onto the three motorboats from the landing. Over the next couple of hours, the boats made dozens of trips to and from Pignatelli's landing, dropping off parents and children, who then walked along the shore onto the club's beachfront, careful to remain in the wet sand. As they waded along the shore, parents carried banners that read,

Ned Coll and children from Hartford coming ashore at the private
Madison Beach Club. *Photo © Bob Adelman. Courtesy Bob Adelman.*

"God's beaches belong to everyone" and "Patriotism means helping, not
hoarding."[43]

Ned called up to the clubhouse and asked whether the members
assembled on the front porch preferred to "stand up there like kings or
come down and have a positive weekend and an afternoon of friendship."[44] He got no response except for a few muffled, half-hearted heckles from people not accustomed to being on either side of a public protest. He asked if they cared to join in the singing of "Our Country 'Tis of
Thee."[45] He got no takers. The children seemed oblivious to the standoff
on the shore. They came to have fun. Their pleasure was their protest.

It was not only disorienting to see poor people of color in this
setting, but it was also, for the club members, deeply unnerving to see
them so carefree, at leisure, picnicking on their beach, enjoying themselves, even inviting them (and their children) to join. The *Boston Globe*
described a bizarre scene. As black children played and laughed in the

water, white parents and "club personnel tried to keep members['] children away"—from doing what they ostensibly brought them there to
do: play in the water with other children.[46] By exposing the club members' cowardice, the protest, Ned believed, had achieved an important
objective. The black children who had come from Hartford's housing
projects that day saw, as he put it, "whites who are powerful running
their asses into the [club]house, and we've taken over their beach for
the afternoon." They got to see that "the emperor has no pants! . . . Activism is empowering!"[47] As they prepared to leave, Ned asked Hooper
if he could at least allow the children to walk through the property to
the road, where the vans were waiting to transport them home. Hooper
refused. They exited through the Pignatellis' property instead.[48]

   "Coll has surpassed himself in the art of staging spectaculars,"
the editorial page of the New Haven Register remarked the following
day.[49] Indeed, Ned got the press coverage he wanted. He succeeded, as
one report later noted, in "embarrassing members of the country club
set, who want to sit comfortably under beach umbrellas and discuss—
not observe—the poor and oppressed."[50] He succeeded, too, in further alienating the communities whose beaches (and whose people) he
hoped to be made more welcoming to the urban poor while giving town
officials in Greenwich and Fairfield added incentive to pour their resources into fighting the CCLU's impending lawsuit. Critics lambasted
Ned for "adding heat where light is needed," for "spread[ing] confusion
and consternation when understanding is called for," and for wasting
money that could have been "expended . . . on some needy youngsters"
on ego-gratifying "hijinks."[51] Ned, his critics charged, seemed intent on
upending the laws and traditions that had shaped the culture and society of the Connecticut shore for nearly a century.

   To these criticisms Ned replied: guilty as charged. As he drew
closer to the bastions of real wealth and power in America, he grew
less interested in fostering interactions across the class and color line
and more intent on smashing those barriers, less concerned with exposing underprivileged children to white suburban culture and more
determined to expose, to the wider public, the racism and callousness
of the nation's elite. The more resistance and avoidance he encountered
from the people he was trying to reach, the more times he saw privileged

whites retreat to the comforts of a private clubhouse at the mere sight
of poor people, the more determined Ned became in manufacturing
situations whereby upper-class whites' prejudices would become readily
apparent to the general public and the cherished traditions of privileged
white society would be subject to public scrutiny in a way that the more
crude forms of racism practiced by the white poor had been throughout
the black freedom struggle. He wanted to render visible what money
and power had succeeded in disguising. He wanted the public to see
what he had seen in the eyes of white mothers who had grabbed their
kids by the arms and dragged them into the clubhouse, lest they begin
playing with a black child. He wanted people to see the ugliness, the
unspoken prejudices, and internalized assumptions of superiority that
saturated elite white culture. More than anything, Ned wanted to upend
the rituals of *noblesse oblige* that had allowed elite New England society
to remain not merely complacent to the deprivations of others, but had
also lulled it (and the general public) into thinking that it was contribut-
ing, in a meaningful way, to helping those less fortunate.

Like those canned stories that run in newspapers each holiday, reports
of Connecticut's lack of publicly available beach space had become, by
the mid-1970s, a spring ritual, dusted off and updated by reporters just
ahead of the summer season. In the spring of 1975 came stories of local towns opening up stretches of shore previously deemed unfit for
bathing to meet demand. The new proposal on the table among policymakers was the conversion of the notorious Silver Sands State Park—a
garbage landfill and breeding ground for rats since its acquisition by the
state in 1960—into a beach.[52] Talk of limiting the power of towns to
exclude nonresidents, or of private homeowners to prevent the public
from reaching the public portion of the shore, had become the third rail
of Connecticut politics.

That spring Roy Bongartz came to Hartford to write a profile of
Revitalization Corps's beach protests for the *New York Times* Sunday
Magazine. He arrived just as Ned was planning the first beach invasion of the season: a return visit to the Madison Beach Club. On a Sunday morning in late May, some 65–70 kids and a half-dozen mothers
filed onto a bus in front of the Corps's offices on the North End. As

they drove south, Ned barked out instructions to the kids on how they should safely, and quickly, exit the bus and reach the private beach (this time, they would climb over the massive stone pier that blocked public access on one side of the club's beach), and to the parents on how to handle any encounters with the police. Once the bus parked at the pier, Coll shouted, "Everybody out, now, quick!" A stream of children, laughing and shouting, poured out. Ned ran ahead with a ladder, which he leaned against the rocks. As Bongartz described, "Then, like Vietnamese boarding the last plane for the States, the sun-lovers streamed up the ladder, across the forbidden privately owned pier, and lowered themselves down onto the sand on the other side."[53]

They all made it onto the beach moments before two squad cars arrived. A high school girl who volunteered for the Corps came dressed in an Uncle Sam costume. She and Alma Cotton planted the American

Revitalization Corps staff members hurriedly leading children across the private property of the Madison Beach Club and onto the wet sand portion of the shore. *Photo © Bob Adelman. Courtesy Bob Adelman.*

flag in the sand. To the tune of "This Land Is Your Land," they began singing "This beach is our beach." Club members watched from the porch, showing no emotion. One snapped photos with an Instamatic. Ned waved to the cops on the beach and wished them a nice day. One officer began shouting, "Private property!" repeatedly before another officer told him to cool it. Alma Cotton approached a couple of the club members who remained lounging under an umbrella, to engage them in conversation. The women did their best to ignore her. "That woman I talked to," she later said, "didn't look at me. Sort of mumbled something—very cold." As they unpacked their picnics, three of the young girls ran up to the clubhouse porch and begged to use the restroom. They were met with silence and blank stares. Finally, an older man said, "I can't give you permission. We can't do it." That was the extent of the two groups' interaction.[54]

After lunch, the group packed up its belongings and climbed back over the pier. But the day at the beach wasn't over. Always one to put on a good show for a reporter, Ned drove twenty miles east, to Fenwick. Upon arriving, the bus blew past the sign at the entrance to the private beach community warning that trespassers would face prosecution. As the kids streamed onto the beach, borough president Charles Brainerd came roaring down a path in his golf cart, his craggy face beet red, the white hairs on the back of his neck standing on end. Just as he was about to shout at the kids to get off the beach, Ned appeared and began marching toward Brainerd and informed him that, in fact, they had been invited—by the rogue son of one of the families who owned a cottage there. Brainerd backed up and sped off. The children serenaded the retired multimillionaire with chants of "Run! Run! Run!"[55]

"That Brainerd called the cops on us," one of the mothers remarked. "I swear something, he is going to suffer before he die!" And indeed, within minutes, police were on the scene. Bongartz described it as like a scene out of the film *Bad Day at Black Rock*. There, a standoff commenced. The police sternly warned the supposed trespassers to leave. No luck. They tried reasoning with them, even invoking the shore's history to make their case. But when one of the officers said that private beaches were a tradition dating back over three hundred years in Connecticut, one of the mothers shot back, "We had a slavery tradition that long, too." Finally, Chris Little, the person who had invited the Corps to Fenwick, strolled onto the beach to offer his guests some water. The police departed, Brainerd drove off, and soon after, Ned and the kids packed up and left too. As the bus wound its way through the village, Ned spotted Brainerd practicing his putting. "How you hitting the old ball there, Charlie?" he inquired. Brainerd waved him off. "Hey Brainerd," Alma Cotton shouted, "we're alive!"[56]

On the pages of the *Times* Sunday Magazine, Revitalization Corps's ambushing of tony country clubs and old monied families' hideaways seemed both comical and harmless—a milder, more family-friendly version of the protest strategies of New Left provocateurs like Abbie Hoffman and the yippies, whose stunts included an ambushing of Disneyland in 1970 and the raising of the Viet Cong flag on Tom Sawyer's Island. But to many readers who lived or vacationed in shoreline towns, Ned's amphibious invasions were no laughing matter. "When Ned Coll and his group pay my beach sticker costs, boat mooring costs, repairs to beaches (walls etc.) costs, school costs, property taxes, car taxes, boat taxes, various town taxes, then *and only then*, will I welcome freeloaders such as they to my town, beach and/or property," Westport's Hilaire B. Coy fumed. Were it not for his deliberate, and cynical, use of African American children as props, James J. Whalen of Forest Hills, New York, wrote, no one would pay Ned Coll any mind. "Here is another white man using black people for selfish political purposes."[57]

Ned's next campaign would test the liberalism of the family whose slain relatives had been his inspiration. For the 1975 Fourth of July holiday, Revitalization Corps loaded a bus full of kids and headed to Hyannisport, to the Kennedy compound on Cape Cod. They drove right up to the front gate and were greeted by Douglas and Rory Kennedy, children of the late Robert F. Kennedy. Ned asked for a meeting with Ted Kennedy. The Kennedy kids retreated behind the compound's gate. Four and a half hours passed. At one point, Ned led the crowd with the chant, "Hide, Ted, Hide!"[58] Finally, the senator from Massachusetts stepped out onto the driveway and briefly spoke with Ned and promised he would "speak out and speak strongly" on the issue of poverty, unequal access to outdoor recreation, and the work of Revitalization Corps.[59] He didn't invite the guests in. Later, a Kennedy spokesman came out to inform Ned that the senator would read a statement of support into the Congressional Record. It was, in the truest sense, the least he could do. As Ned later scoffed, Kennedy is "so distant from the problems of the city that he wants to bury it in the back of the Congressional Record."[60] Ethel Kennedy, Robert Kennedy's widow, was, however, moved to action, and she extended an invitation to thirty children from Hartford to spend a weekend at the Kennedy compound later that summer. She also spoke out publicly for open beach access, telling the New York Times, "I feel strongly that beaches should be open to the public. That's a basic need for all of us. They belong to everyone."[61]

As Ned staged amphibious invasions and ambushed prominent politicians at their vacation homes, attorneys for the Gold Coast towns waged a war of attrition against the CCLU. Since the initial hearing in state superior court in October 1973, the defendants had filed an endless series of motions and delays. Short of funds and woefully overmatched by the towns' unlimited resources, the attorneys for the CCLU struggled to even make all of the pre-trial hearings. The CCLU was forced to withdraw its first suit after defense attorneys uncovered a minor, but fatal, technical flaw in the charges. It filed a second suit against the towns in 1975, but the defense succeeded in getting this too bottled up in court.[62]

For the moment, it seemed, the people of Greenwich were safe, their beaches secure. The Gold Coast's legal team had outmaneuvered a beleaguered CCLU riven by internal squabbling over legal strategies and organizational priorities. Ned, however, was invulnerable to the divide-and-conquer strategies. When it came to organizational tactics and priorities, he refused advice, made no compromises, and brooked no challenges to his authority. Corps staff members either followed his lead or left the organization. But as long as Ned kept devising ingenious strategies for exposing the racist attitudes and practices of elite white America, raising awareness of the plight of America's poor, and sparking a wider public discussion of inequality, many stuck around, waiting to see what would come next.

Next up for Ned: Greenwich, the biggest prize of all. As he had done two summers earlier in Madison, Ned found a small provision in Greenwich's beach ordinance that he could exploit. Beginning in the 1960s, as it and other Northeastern towns stepped up their restrictions on public beach access, Greenwich began restricting the number of guests that could accompany a resident. Each person who bought a beach pass was given a guest punch card with eight punches, one for each guest a resident was permitted to bring during the summer season. When townspeople complained that this law was too restrictive, the town amended it to allow for residents to bring guests up to eight days each summer but did not specify how many guests could come on a single day. Before he announced his intentions to target Greenwich that summer, Ned had made contact with a small group of supporters who lived in town and agreed to assist him in getting kids onto the beach that summer. On June 24, one of his supporters, Susan Rice, presented her beach permit and punch card to the guard at the Greenwich Point Beach. Standing behind her were sixty children and adult chaperones: her guests. As she stated, "It isn't that I want to open up Greenwich to everyone, I just want to open up a few minds. We have lovely beaches and we ought to share them with some people who have none." The following weekend, Rice brought twenty guests with her to the beach; another resident Corps supporter brought an additional thirty-seven guests.[63]

Greenwich officials were dumbfounded by Ned's audacity and ingenuity. The Board of Selectmen called an emergency meeting to amend the town's beach ordinance. Residents could bring no more than eight guests with them to the beach and had to post a $250 bond each time. Both of the new rules could be waived at the recreation director's discretion. Officials plainly acknowledged that these new rules were aimed at Revitalization Corps and that they were passed with such haste so that they would be in effect before the next weekend.[64]

The new rules succeeded in limiting Ned's ability to get kids onto the beach, but at a cost. Across the state, people reacted with disgust at the wealthy town's nakedly exclusionary measures. The *Bridgeport Post* ran an editorial denouncing Greenwich's hair-trigger reaction. "People in towns not fortunate enough to have access to clean beaches on Long Island Sound can't understand why places like Greenwich go to such lengths to exclude them." Such action, it added, "undermines their own position" and makes Revitalization Corps's calls for open beaches and universal public access seem "quite reasonable" by comparison.[65] Nor did barring Ned and busloads of black kids from their beaches buy the people of Greenwich a quiet summer free of conflict. Ned made sure of that. Stripped of his ability to provide a day at the beach for inner-city youth and a platform to protest beach access restrictions, Ned channeled his anger and indignation at any and every bastion of wealth and privilege in Greenwich he could find. He adopted a scorched earth strategy against what he publicly called the "most racist" town in the state.[66] After the new rules were announced, Ned publicly condemned the "insensitive and blatantly racist attitudes" of town officials and vowed to "expose that town to the hypocrisy it represents."[67]

Ned's summer of rage—and Greenwich's summer of shame— had just begun. For the next two months protesters fanned out across Connecticut's wealthiest municipality, targeting a host of institutions that aided and abetted racial segregation—from real estate offices to churches—and the people who Ned believed were responsible for urban decay and the hardening of the nation's wealth divide. "This is a class issue. Look at who lives at the seacoast—rich people," he explained. "Most of them made their money in the cities. Now they owe the cities something in return."[68] To make that point abundantly clear to the people of Greenwich, and to the members of the media who kept tabs on Ned's every move, he and a dozen or so protesters stood outside the Greenwich commuter rail station on weekday mornings as white executives boarded trains bound for Manhattan, chanting and carrying banners that read, "Share the Summer," "Cocktail Bigots," "Money without Class," and "Backwich."[69] They were there again in the afternoon when those same executives returned home.

Greenwich residents struggled to claim the moral high ground. The local clergy issued a statement in support of the beach access restrictions and claimed they were nondiscriminatory.[70] In response, protesters began assembling in front of area churches on Sunday mornings, where they greeted parishioners with the chant, "Take down the cross," and held signs that read, "Store your wealth in heaven, not on the beaches."[71] "It's time for Christianity to come to Greenwich," Ned shouted. "Christ himself couldn't get to the beach with the 12 Apostles. All he'd be able to swing is eight of the 13."[72] Before long, clergymen from Hartford and New York joined Revitalization Corps in protests. On the

morning of July 20, Hartford priest Patrick McGillicuddy stood in front
of Christ Church in downtown Greenwich. "It's a shame," he said, "that
the clergymen here support discriminatory regulations and support
laws infringing upon the common good and discriminate against the
poor. Then they have the audacity to say they are Christians."[73] "Can
it be that the clergy in this town believes the disadvantaged should stay
in the slums while the advantaged enjoy recreational facilities alone?"
Ned's Greenwich ally Susan Rice asked.[74]

For many people in Greenwich, none of this made sense. This was
a community, after all, that had been one of the largest supporters of the
Fresh Air Fund. In the mid-1960s upwards of seventy Greenwich families hosted children from the inner city at their homes during the summer. Soon after the assassination of Martin Luther King Jr. on April 4,
1968, the town launched a summer camp for Harlem youth called "The
Youth for a Cool Summer." "I guess we all felt a little guilty," the camp's
co-director, Mrs. John B. Caron, remembers. Each summer, Greenwich
turned the playfields at three of its elite private schools into "resort areas for the underprivileged" and provided 60–80 inner-city kids the
chance "to experience the kind of life Connecticut boys and girls take
for granted." Hadn't we done enough? many asked. What more does
Coll want?[75]

What Ned and the mothers and children from Hartford wanted
was to be treated as fellow citizens, not charity cases. What they wanted
was the right to enjoy outdoor public space as they pleased, when they
pleased, on their own terms, to not have to wait for an invitation to
enjoy places they had every right, as citizens, to occupy. They wanted
rich white folks to stop treating civil rights as acts of generosity and
benevolence. And they wanted the people of Greenwich—and the nation—to recognize the relationship between exclusionary suburbs and
dying cities, to see the injustice of a community that derived much of its
wealth from a city—New York—but whose residents hired high-priced
tax accountants to find ways to avoid supporting and then—as that city
teetered on the edge of bankruptcy and living conditions in its poorest neighborhoods deteriorated—worked to distance itself even further
from its people and its problems.

Greenwich's leading citizens tried to remain aloof to Ned's blistering attacks and implored fellow townspeople not to take the bait. The local newspaper, the *Greenwich Time,* coached its readers on how to respond to protesters. "The watchword is to keep cool, resist emotionalism, ill-tempered attacks or ill-chosen arguments that critics can seize on to foster the let-them-eat-cake image Mr. Coll will be laboring gleefully to propagate." The town's "tormentors seek to depict [us] as smug, intransigent, selfish and imperious." Don't provide these "social activist provocateurs" the ammunition they so desire.[76]

These guidelines would prove to be hard to follow. The town's wealthiest families were incensed at what they saw as nothing less than an assault on the very idea of rewarding success and achievement. "If towns and then individuals must give up the rights they have earned and paid for, worked hard and enjoyed, just because [some] fanatical 'do-gooders' come around and make a lot of noise about *their* 'rights,'" Dorothy M. Wright fumed, "what is the sense of even trying any more? Are our rights any less, simply because we may have a prettier town, nicer facilities and home and perhaps a bit more money—all of which we have worked for—than these people from the cities?"[77] It was this sense of outrage at the audacity of the poor to challenge their exclusive right to enjoy the fruits of their wealth that white male executives tried to keep bottled inside as they pushed past groups of protesters on their way to the train station and that their wives tried hard not to express whenever they spotted Ned and his followers as they ran errands during the day. Some, though, couldn't resist speaking their mind. One shouted to Ned, without a hint of irony, as he boarded, "Go home to Hartford and take care of your beaches."[78] Others stopped to talk to the reporters who were on hand to cover the protests. The consensus was that Ned had succeeded in hardening local opinion on the beach access issue—decidedly in favor of greater restrictions. On one occasion, a purportedly intoxicated man began attacking a group of protesters in town. On another occasion, a large wooden crucifix that protesters had planted in the sand below high tide was torn down and broken in two.[79]

Such outbursts from Greenwich residents, though, were rare. Try as he might, Ned could not elicit the type of reaction from townspeople that might turn public opinion decisively against Greenwich. More disconcerting, he did not receive a warm welcome from Greenwich's African American community. Shortly after Ned announced his summer campaign against Greenwich, he visited an overwhelmingly black housing project in town on a Thursday evening, looking to drum up support. A reporter for a local radio station accompanied Ned, hoping to interview black residents and get their views on the beach access issue. Tenants did not appreciate Ned and a reporter with a microphone knocking on their doors at 9 p.m. on a weeknight. Within an hour, the Greenwich Police Department received calls reporting that someone was harassing residents. When police finally arrived, they found Ned surrounded and being yelled at by a crowd of fifty angry tenants. The Greenwich chapter of the NAACP issued a statement denouncing Revitalization Corps for presuming to speak on behalf of the town's black population. "We question the motives," chapter president Bernard Fisher said, "of paternalistic liberals who force a cause on people without consulting them." Fisher made it clear that his organization opposed the town's actions, calling the new restrictions on guests "a form of subtle racist tactics." But Ned's "barn-storming, abrasive rabble rousing tactics," Fisher remarked, had only served to "incite and antagonize people and move us further away from a solution."[80]

By then, many people in Greenwich were convinced that Ned did not seek a solution, just media attention. On that count, Ned had scored some notable victories. In mid-July, the *New York Times* ran a five-page story on Revitalization Corps's beach campaign in the Sunday Magazine. When Ned staged an amphibious landing on a Greenwich town beach on the morning of July 30, a cameraman and reporter for CBS News were there to capture it. That night, the beach access controversy in Greenwich was the lead story on the CBS *Evening News*. A national audience watched as Ned and three dozen "Hartford-area ghetto children" climbed across a rocky groin and onto the Greenwich Point Beach, where they unfurled a banner reading "Free America's Beaches." "It's not just the Greenwich beach you're talking about," Ned told viewers, "you're talking about that whole shoreline where a small percentage of wealthy people control that shoreline and the average factory worker gets on the highway and tries to go to a Connecticut state park on a Sunday afternoon and it closes very early, like on 4th of July, and he can't even bring his children in to use the shore, and that's wrong." From their beach chairs, young white mothers and older couples struggled to mask their anger and contempt. "So what are you going to do? Every time it's low tide trudge in?" a woman barked at Ned, a Catholic priest, and some young Corps volunteers. "You've got your own state park! You're just trying to get in, because it's private. You got to make your little point."[81] After the cameras had stopped rolling, police officers descended and arrested Ned on third-degree criminal conspiracy to trespass. (The state declined to press charges.)[82]

In Hartford, the office of newly elected governor Ella Grasso was busy fielding phone calls and processing letters from angry constituents on both sides of the beach debate. As public unrest grew louder each summer, the legal status of beaches was, as one official in the DEP acknowledged, "becoming less of a seasonal issue" and increasingly tied to larger debates over zoning and land use policy, environmental management and protection, poverty and wealth inequality, and society's obligations to underprivileged children.[83]

After cautiously avoiding the issue for the first two months of summer, in early August Grasso embarked on a tour of the state's shoreline, ostensibly to search for possible sites the state could acquire for public beaches and solutions to endemic overcrowding at the three state-owned beaches. Standing before a crowd of reporters at the Hammonasset Beach State Park, the first stop on the governor's tour, Grasso drew her own line in the sand and let it be known where she stood. "Private property is inviolate," she reassured residents of coastal towns and members of private beach associations. Public access to private beaches "is up to the people who own the land and their willingness to make it available." That same principle, she added, applied to public beaches owned and administered by shoreline towns. "Town beaches are the property of towns just as private beaches are private property." "This was a comforting note for hundreds of Connecticut families to whom a 'place at the shore' had become a status symbol and a long cherished dream as well," the *Meriden Journal* wrote. In the end, Grasso's beach tour was more notable for what she refused to consider than for what she actually proposed. Her only proposal was to add more parking spaces at existing state beaches. Befitting her image as an austere penny-pincher and proponent of government downsizing, Grasso concluded that the only solution to the pitiful amount of publicly accessible beach space was for the state "to try to make sure every square inch of what we now own is utilized efficiently."[84]

"Your stand against these blatant over-takers is to be applauded," Wayne Mitten of Wallingford wrote Grasso.[85] Branford resident Alice H. Camp told Grasso, "While I sincerely regret that many are not as fortunate as I, I am reassured to read of your views on maintaining private property. My parents worked long and hard to buy this land, build the cottages and give us the opportunity of using a small but private beach."[86] Others thanked Grasso for protecting the shore from the people and problems of the city. "I do not want Ned Coll bringing the ghetto to me," Mike McKay of Uncasville told Grasso. Please, he begged, "stop Ned Coll from importing trouble."[87] Critics such as CCLU executive director William Olds said that Grasso was "pandering to those town residents who prefer to erect barriers with the intent of keeping out minorities and low-income persons."[88] Rocky Hill resident Richard Peene told Grasso her "position on state beaches is the worst kind of bigotry, economic [sic]."[89]

In response to Grasso's beach tour, Ned conducted one of his own. His began on the front lawn of the governor's summer cottage in Old Lyme. There, he told reporters, he was "pretty disappointed and disgusted" with Grasso's statements. "She sold poor and working-class people down the river, or maybe I should say down the Sound." Referring to the notorious leader of Boston's anti-busing campaign, he added that the governor was "becoming the Louise Day Hicks of the Connecticut shoreline." Even some of Ned's supporters believed this personal attack on a moderately liberal governor who was trying desperately to appease warring factions was out of line. Hartford resident and Coll family friend Alexis Hook castigated Ned for his "unjustified smear" of the governor, which, she added, did more to hurt Ned's reputation and set back his cause than tarnish Grasso.[90]

In terms of socioeconomic background and racial attitudes, the shoreline community that most closely approximated Hicks's "Southie" was the decidedly working-class, unpretentious Sound View. Situated

within Old Lyme, Sound View differed markedly from its neighbors to
the east and west. After having acquired and subdivided several sections
of the Old Lyme shore in the early 1900s, developer Harry Hilliard set
aside the area that came to be known as Sound View for what he termed
the "unorganized public."[91] In his will, Hilliard specified that this beach
was to remain free of barriers or obstructions, and he prohibited the
town from enacting any ordinances that would restrict its use to Old
Lyme residents. As the surrounding area became home to some of the
state's more exclusive summer cottage communities, Sound View developed a reputation as a raucous retreat for working-class white ethnics
from neighboring towns and cities. During World War II, it attracted
scores of sailors stationed in nearby New London and soldiers from the
army barracks at Niantic, who frequented the bars and honky-tonks
that lined Sound View's main drag. In the summer of 1943, a sailor stationed in Groton raped and murdered a young woman who had accompanied him to the beach; afterward, the base commander declared
Sound View off limits. Its seedy reputation outlasted the war, and the
community's alienation from the rest of Old Lyme hardened. Summer
residents complained of infrequent policing, negligent enforcement
of parking regulations, and public drunkenness. In 1968 the town attempted to wipe Sound View off the map through a $4 million federal
redevelopment grant that would have enabled the town to clear all 482
lots in the area and replace them with 92 larger lots and more expensive
properties.[92] Old Lyme voters, however, rejected the measure, fearing
that acceptance of federal dollars would lead to federal control of the
shoreline. Better to contain the rabble to a single area than risk exposing
the entire shore to an invasion of the masses. Ironically, Sound View's
beach was widely considered the most beautiful and stable of any along
Long Island Sound. With only minimal littoral drift, it required little
maintenance or sand replenishment while enjoying an unmatched view
of the mouth of the Sound.

    Whenever an attempt to access a neighboring private beach went
awry, Ned could always count on bringing his busload of kids to Sound
View, which he did often. Ned loved talking up the working-class Italian American families who owned modest cottages and operated summer food stands and arcades in Sound View and contrasting the open

arms that kids from Hartford received there with the cold stares and callous rejection they found elsewhere on the shore. In his rosy depictions of carefree, peaceful afternoons at Sound View, where local vendors handed out free snacks while working-class white kids shared their summer with inner-city black and brown children, Ned seemed to want to will his vision of bringing urban blacks and working-class whites together into being.

The white families who lived and vacationed at Sound View saw these occasions differently. They welcomed busloads of children from Hartford because they had no choice. The beach was open to the general public. Rather than run them off, town officials were on record as having recommended that Revitalization Corps go there. "Ned Coll is welcome at Sound View anytime," Old Lyme first selectman Maurice McCarthy told the press, as Ned planned one last visit to Old Lyme that summer. But while they lacked the power to exclude, the people of Sound View made it clear that if they could, they would. Their racial animus toward blacks was only matched by their hostility to condescending white liberals who sought to speak on their behalf. After Ned had praised the people of Sound View as exemplars of humanitarian spirit of the white working class to reporters, resident Russell Carlo shot back. "Be assured, Mr. Coll, that the 'lower middle class resort' as you described us would have loved to have evicted you if we could." Calling Coll the "Pied Piper of the Ghetto," Carlo went on to draw a sharp distinction between the hard-working Italian Americans of Sound View with the "undeserving" black poor of Hartford. We "[don't] live off welfare; nor did our ancestors come over to this country looking for a hand-out"—the implication being that African Americans' ancestors, brought over in chains and held in captivity for two centuries, did—"nor did we seek to force ourselves or our children on other than [our] own property. We worked our way for the right to own beach property."[93]

As the summer of 1975 drew to a close, the two Republican candidates for Greenwich's first selectman in the primary election, held on the first Tuesday of September, fought to claim the most extreme position in favor of restricted beach access and in opposition to Ned Coll. Candidate Rupert Vernon made beach exclusion a centerpiece of his campaign.

Campaign flyers included a photo of Vernon standing knee-deep in the waters off Greenwich Point Beach, talking to bathers. Greenwich has every right to exclude nonresidents from its beaches, he reassured voters. His opponent, Clifton D. Crosby, Vernon charged, was soft on the beach issue, citing Crosby's questioning of the timing of the town's decision to tightening restrictions immediately following Coll's arrival in June. Crosby disavowed his previous statements and in speeches stressed to voters, "I have from the beginning advocated strong action" against efforts to circumvent the town's residents-only beach policy. Vernon easily defeated Crosby in the primary and strolled to victory over his Democratic opponent in the fall election.[94]

For voters in Greenwich and their open beach opponents statewide, the issue of beach access was about more than just the beach. Because the legal status of beaches was so ambiguous and the line dividing public space from private property on the foreshore so imprecise and subject to interpretation, how one defined a beach came to encapsulate a larger set of beliefs about what constituted property, what belonged to the public, and where individual rights ended and social obligations began. Indeed, the question of public beach access, and the powers beachfront homeowners and municipalities held, became a referendum on the meaning and tangible expression of freedom itself.

At the beach, the idea of freedom was made manifest; in those coveted sands it took on a physical form. Likewise, what people saw as threatening or fulfilling their notion of freedom became projected onto the outsized, often outrageous, persona of Ned Coll. To folks like Pearl and James Stevenson of Madison, Ned's actions constituted no less than an assault on "many basic fundamentals of the American way of life and the responsibilities of an American citizen."[95] To the editorial board of the New London Day, Ned was "attacking the most sacred of those truths we hold to be self-evident—the right to own property."[96] That Ned was teaching children to disregard private property rights and feel entitled to enjoy facilities for which they hadn't help pay raised the stakes even higher and allowed his opponents' contempt to run deeper. "He is teaching," E. D. Turner fumed, "that the right way to obtain creature comforts in this world is to infringe upon the rights of others and to invade their privacy and property. . . . Every property he seeks to invade represents someone's hard work, planning, and perseverance. . . . We should teach our children to be producers, not parasites."[97] Coll is setting a "terrible example" for the state's youth, Grace A. Enright of Cos Cob wrote. "He is encouraging disregard for the natural rights of ownership." He is teaching the poor to covet thy neighbor's goods, to hate those who strive and succeed.[98] Ned is instilling in those poor children, Virginia Diehl wrote, a poisonous "what's yours is ours" attitude.[99]

To these objections Ned responded, "What's yours *is* ours." Those beaches belong to us. To those claiming Ned was seeking to infringe upon private property rights, he simply replied, "You bought stolen property."[100] And to those who said he was teaching impressionable children to disrespect private property, Corps volunteer Julie Pokorny replied, "We do teach our children to respect private property. But we feel it's also important for them to know that public property . . . belongs to them as well as every other citizen of Connecticut."[101] The key for Revitalization Corps and open beach advocates was convincing the rest of the state's citizens that they had a stake in this fight, too, and that the fight for public access was about more than everyone's right to enjoy a day at the beach. It was also about the fate of the shoreline itself and the dire ecological condition of the body of water it surrounded.

EIGHT

Saving the Shore

These people in Fairfield County!" Ned shouted in disgust as he barreled down the road back to Hartford. There was no way of getting to them and no way of getting around them either. His passenger, Rob Carbonneau, knew his home state and its exclusive shoreline well. The West Hartford native remembered the kids in his elementary school whose parents owned summer cottages and who casually talked about going down to "*our* beach" on weekends, and he had wondered how it was that someone could own a beach. It was, he thought, like trying to claim ownership of the air we breathed. After leaving the state to attend college in Massachusetts and graduate and divinity school in New York City, in 1977 Rob returned to Hartford to complete his pastoral training as a Catholic Passionist priest on the city's North End. He had read about the work Revitalization Corps performed and was struck by Ned's dynamism and the "charismatic dimension of [his] message" and felt that it suited the Passionist order's mission to understand and alleviate the suffering of others.[1]

Beginning in the spring of 1977 and continuing throughout the summer, Rob took the bus from the monastery in West Hartford to the Revitalization Corps's headquarters, where he served as coordinator of social services and informal spiritual adviser to the devoutly Catholic Ned. On this afternoon, though, Rob assumed the role of chief strategist. From the passenger's seat, he turned and asked, "What do you ultimately want to get out of this, Ned? You keep talking about how you feel like you're not being listened to in Fairfield and they don't like you." Well, isn't this an "issue [that affects] the whole state?" Ned nodded in agreement. "If mean high tide is public land, why don't you bring attention [to the public's rights] by walking the whole shoreline? . . . If this is a statewide issue, shouldn't it be a statewide issue?" With that suggestion, Rob recalls, Ned "got so excited" that he "almost dr[ove] off of the road." "That's a great idea!" Ned exclaimed. "And I remember thinking, 'Oh no. What have I just said?'"

Three days later, Rob was standing beside Ned on the steps of the state capitol building as he announced plans to walk the entire 250-mile-long shoreline to draw public attention to the injustice of its inaccessibility. The public was ready to take notice. Revitalization Corps's beach invasions had revealed the extreme lengths to which coastal communities would go to keep the general public off their beaches. To a growing segment of that general public—meaning, everyone who didn't live or own a summer cottage on the shore—Ned seemed almost reasonable by comparison. "What many of us would like to see is simply free access to the admitted public domain with a bit of dry terra firma to park one's posterior on," West Hartford resident David Aliski commented in a letter to Governor Grasso. "No one suggests that cottages and land be confiscated, that property rights are ignored or anything of that sort. The cottage owners would have the right to come to the beach and enjoy the public domain, too. They simply could not exclude the rest of us from what is ours as well as theirs."[2] "Any person who has a shore cottage," Stan E. Sales of Meriden argued, "has a right to live there, but does not have the right to fence in the shoreline from outsiders. This body of water should be free for all to enjoy, no matter if it's in Connecticut, Massachusetts, Rhode Island, New York or New Jersey."[3]

In fighting to keep people off the shore, the people of coastal Connecticut were slowly—but inexorably—destroying their prized possession. By the late 1970s, the environmental health of Long Island Sound had reached crisis stage. Its waters suffered from overpollution; its shoreline was mangled and deformed by decades of haphazard, ecologically insensitive, and environmentally unsustainable patterns of development. And thanks to the obstructionist tactics of coastal legislators, who devoted their time in Hartford to fighting against the creation of a statewide coastal regulatory agency, the state was virtually powerless to do anything about it. In walking the state's shoreline, Ned told the pool of reporters assembled on the capitol steps, he aimed to bear witness to the corrosive effects of exclusion on society. What he would also find was just how destructive these exclusionary land-use practices were on the shoreline itself.

Long Island Sound is a "cesspool." "The water is a pea green. It has a smell you would not believe. It's between Chlorine and Crap." "Not only is it horrible to look at, but the stench at times is horrendous." "This is one of the worst places I have ever been in." "If we don't watch ourselves, we'll have another Lake Erie." These were some of the frank observations offered by a group of students at the University of Bridgeport after a semester of studying the Sound in fall 1973. Their professor forwarded their reports to the state's governor, Thomas Meskill.[4]

The reasons for the Sound's sordid environmental condition were many: pollution from waterfront industries, sewage from the largest metropolitan area in the United States, trash dumped carelessly from the decks of boats, oil spills that were happening with alarming regularity. During the first six months of 1973 alone, the U.S. Coast Guard reported more than 170 oil spills near the Connecticut coast.[5] But perhaps the biggest threats facing the Sound were from those who clamored to live and play along it and keep others from doing the same. Over the previous decades, officials in many of the state's shoreline municipalities had generously granted building permits for lots located dangerously close to the water and along fragile and highly mobile sections of the shore. When pressed by their constituents to protect "their" stretch of shore from erosion, these same officials had issued bonds to build jetties, groins, and seawalls, providing short-term relief to endemic problems that inflicted immediate and long-term damage on the coastal ecology as a whole.[6]

Despite significant population growth in the decades following World War II, most of the towns along the central and eastern portions of the state's coast continued to lack municipal sewage treatment facilities. As growing numbers of homes in shoreline towns were converted from seasonal to year-round occupancy, septic tanks malfunctioned with greater frequency, causing dangerously high levels of sewage to seep into Long Island Sound. Failing septic tanks caused once robust shellfish beds to suffer sharp declines in productivity. During the 1974 summer season, dangerously high levels of pollution forced the state health department to ban the harvesting of clams, oysters, and mussels for the stretch of shore between Madison and Old Lyme.[7]

By the late 1970s, officials in the state's Department of Environmental Protection identified failing septic systems, in addition to other byproducts of overdevelopment, as one of the main causes of the water quality problems along much of the state's shoreline.[8] In 1978 environmental engineers found that failing septic tanks had contaminated the soil of over 2,100 acres in the town of Clinton.[9] Despite such findings, shoreline towns ardently resisted sewage and wastewater treatment systems. Reliance on septic tanks became a strategy for limiting growth or, rather, growth of a certain kind. For towns like Madison, Clinton, and Old Saybrook, the absence of wastewater treatment systems provided an extra layer of protection against the forced introduction of public housing or low-income multi-unit residential properties. Even if open housing advocates succeeded in overturning exclusionary zoning restrictions in the courts, so the thinking went, the absence of basic infrastructure needed for higher-density development ensured these towns would remain exempt. But in a monumental victory for fair housing advocates, and an ominous development for exclusive municipalities nationwide, in 1975 the New Jersey Supreme Court declared exclusionary zoning ordinances unconstitutional in *Southern Burlington County NAACP v. Township of Mount Laurel*. In ruling that local zoning boards "must consider the welfare of citizens beyond its borders and provide housing for all classes," the court specifically singled out such excuses as "lack of sewers and water" as insufficient. Like the New Jersey high court's 1972 ruling in *Neptune City v. Avon-by-the-Sea* that exclusionary beach ordinances violated the public trust doctrine, the decision had no direct bearing on zoning laws in Connecticut but nevertheless established a legal precedence that might influence state courts in the future. In the wake of the decision, suburban municipalities in Connecticut held meetings where legal experts explained the case's implications to anxious white homeowners.[10]

While the waters of Long Island Sound suffered from pollution, the shoreline bore the scars from decades of rampant and uncoordinated overdevelopment. Jetties and groins constructed by individual property owners robbed neighboring areas of sand, disrupted natural processes of erosion and accretion, and instigated rapid changes to the shape and ecology of the shoreline, often with devastating consequences for coastal habitats. In towns such as East Haven, shoreline property owners waged relentless, if futile, battles against nature as they attempted to halt erosion and protect their homes from slipping into the Sound. Fearing the sea and the state, vulnerable shoreline communities demanded, on the one hand, federal and state aid to protect their homes, while, on the other hand, they resisted the expansion of the state's environmental regulatory powers out of concern that it would force them to abandon their homes. In East Haven's Momauguin neighborhood, severe erosion had turned its shoreline, which as late as the 1950s sported a sandy beach, into a jagged wall of boulders that grew higher and wider with each passing season by the mid-1970s. But residents nevertheless resisted calls to condemn and retreat, convinced that the dire warnings of coastal engineers masked ulterior motives. "Don't you realize the beachfront is gold-plated?" one homeowner commented. "There is no more beachfront left on the East Coast." As soon as our property is condemned, he added, "The profiteers are going to come in, make a dollar, and walk out." Meanwhile, "With the money you get for your homes, you won't even be able to afford gasoline."[11]

More than perhaps any type of land, shorelines respect no political boundaries and demand a regional approach to regulation and management. "Shoreline problems are interstate problems," a 1968 report by the President's Council on Recreation and Natural Beauty bluntly stated. Each shoreline is "part of an interrelated natural system; change in one part affects other parts."[12] "Because the problems and values of [these ecosystems] transcend local boundaries," an editorial published in *Life* magazine that same year concluded, "their protection can be guaranteed only by federal standards, binding on the states."[13] Yet at the dawn of the decade, the federal government played virtually no role

in protecting coastal environments or managing coastal land-use practices. Aside from military installations, the only signs of federal power
and authority in coastal America were the various beach replenishment
and shoreline armoring projects being carried out by the Army Corps
of Engineers, often at the behest of local and state governments. The
fate of coastal America instead lay in the hands of local officials, who
were notoriously parochial in their interests and highly susceptible to
the entreaties of developers, who exploited their thirst for property tax
revenue and vague promises of job creation to get projects approved,
regardless of environmental impact.

As coastal populations swelled and the pressure to develop shoreline property intensified, the problem of local control and need for regional planning authorities grew more evident. "Coastal land-use decisions affecting millions [are] in the hands of small-minded small towns,"
the writer Charles Bonenti bemoaned.[14] Total control over coastal
land-use policies by local governments, the authors of the 1969 Stratton
Commission report concluded, posed one of the greatest threats to the
sustainability of these fragile ecosystems. "Rapidly intensifying use of
coastal areas already has outrun the capabilities of local governments
to plan their orderly development and to resolve conflicts. The division
of responsibilities among the several levels of government is unclear,
and the knowledge and procedures for formulating sound decisions are
lacking."[15]

The 1972 Coastal Zone Management Act (CZMA) established, for
the first time, a set of federal standards for managing coastal land use
and protecting coastal ecosystems. But it tried to do so by accommodat-
ing, rather than undercutting, local governmental power. An exemplar
of President Nixon's "New Federalism," which called for transferring
greater power to states and localities to carry out federal policies and administer federal programs, the CZMA tried to strike a balance between
federal standards and local administration. Instead of federal control of
coastal areas, it offered states grants to establish and implement coastal
management plans of their own, as long as they conformed to a set of
federal guidelines. Proponents of the CZMA hailed it as a necessary and
long overdue measure that would address the dire situation facing the
nation's coasts without disturbing the balance of powers between Wash-

ington and state governments and without disrupting the thriving (if often seasonal) economies that had taken shape in coastal America over the previous decades. Critics charged that placing ultimate authority in the hands of state governments constituted one of the act's chief weaknesses and that its stated desire to protect coastal environments and promote economic development was contradictory and bound to result in the latter taking precedence over the former.[16]

Connecticut would put the act's strengths and weaknesses to the test. When Republican state senator George Gunther introduced a bill to create a statewide coastal zone management council to formulate a coastal zone management agency, he was forced to respond to critics, who called it an attack on local autonomy.[17] "I'm one of the strongest advocates of local autonomy," Gunther fired back. Shoreline public officials weren't convinced. "I feel that such a Council could and would usurp the powers of shorefront municipalities over our tidal waterfront land," Clinton first selectman Margery C. Scully warned Governor Meskill. "I also feel," she added, "that this Bill is just one more overt attempt to establish State zoning; and as with other Councils and Development Corps implies that local planning and zoning, recreation and conservation agencies, as well as the executive branch of the town, are incapable of making the right decision as to the highest and best use of our tidal shore and harbor front land. It takes common sense and vigilance on the part of local officials to guard against their growth and development . . . not State or Federal agencies or councils."[18] Stamford's superintendent of parks and natural resources, Edward A. Connell, who was also the architect of the town's 1964 ordinance that effectively banned nonresidents from town beaches, emerged as a caustic opponent of statewide coastal management and led the charge to kill the bill and scuttle any efforts to impose outside authority on local shoreline practices. He implored Meskill to oppose the legislation, calling it "a gratuitous assertion by the self-appointed preservers of the American environment that the rugged citizens along Long Island Sound are no longer capable of planning their own communities."[19] He issued a call to arms to the people of the shore to join in resisting "the efforts of the Superplanners to dominate the future land use of the State." "It is time for those with the salt spray in their nostrils to challenge the New Breed, fresh from Urban Planning courses in New York and Boston."[20] What animated these fears? Madison's Vera Dallas made it plain: a statewide coastal management agency will, she predicted, "pave the way for opening beaches throughout the state."[21]

The Connecticut Coastal Zone Management Committee, not surprisingly, identified political parochialism as the main threat to a healthy and sustainable shoreline. In its preliminary report to the state legislature shortly after the passage of the CZMA, it noted, "In too many cases, decisions for the establishment of policy and for changes in land use have been—and continues [sic] to be—the sole responsibility of individual municipalities. There is often no requirement and no incentive to consult other, even neighboring communities affected by proposals for development."[22] Private beach associations, many of which functioned as separate government entities and jealously guarded the powers vested in them by the state legislature, exacerbated the problem of localism. "Some towns have as many as 12 to 15 different bodies . . . which influence or have a voice in a particular decision such as development along the coastline."[23] By one estimate, there were roughly five hundred individual administrative and regulatory agencies in Connecticut that were making independent decisions that affected the coast.

In this political environment, lawmakers in Connecticut and neighboring states had long struggled to establish effective interstate regulatory bodies to manage and protect Long Island Sound. The first attempt was made in 1969, when New York congressmen Ogden R. Reid and Lester L. Wolff called for the formation of an intergovernmental agency, later known as the Long Island Sound Study Group, to conduct a comprehensive investigation of the Sound's environmental, recreational, and industrial uses and conditions and produce a report outlining a set of policy recommendations for sharply reducing pollution and maximizing the Sound's social, economic, and environmental assets.[24] The proposal received strong support from Connecticut senator Abraham Ribicoff, who secured congressional appropriations to carry out the study. By the time it began its work in 1972, the New England River Basins Commission, the agency charged with coordinating the project, had a $13.5 million budget and a twenty-three-person committee appointed by the governors of Connecticut and New York and comprised of environmentalists, commercial and sport fishermen, businessmen, boating and swimming enthusiasts, civic leaders, and waterfront property owners.[25]

As public concern over the fate of the planet and awareness of the destructive effects of unchecked development grew, lawmakers in Hartford and Washington took action. In 1969, Governor John Dempsey signed the Tidal Wetlands Act. This piece of legislation, along with the 1972 federal Clean Water Act, proved effective in protecting what remained of the state's coastal wetlands. Prior to the passage of the Tidal Wetlands Act, the state was losing roughly 253 acres of coastal wetlands annually to development. By the late 1970s, that number had been reduced to less than one acre per year.[26]

The state's success in protecting coastal wetlands did not, however, signal greater cooperation between shoreline governments and state and regional authorities on coastal matters. Despite the Long Island Sound Study Group's best efforts to accommodate the interests and prerogatives of local governments, release of an initial draft of its report in January 1975 sparked an immediate outcry. In response, committee members cut entirely or watered down recommendations that Connecticut work to acquire private property for public use and use the power of eminent domain to provide easements to the shore. The release of the final report later that summer garnered little fanfare and even less hope that it would lead to substantive action.[27] Weighing over five pounds and having taken five years and $3 million to complete, the final report's size and cost belied its substance and significance. It confirmed what Ned had been shouting for the past five summers: the state suffered from "a serious shortage of general public lands along the shores of the Sound," and, as a result, "large concentrations" of "low and moderate income families" were "recreationally deprived." Making the Sound more accessible to the general public, the report's authors argued, was not simply a matter of fairness and equal opportunity, but was also deeply tied to its environmental fate. "People who cannot see or reach the Sound to enjoy it cannot be expected to care about what happens to it or pay for its clean-up with their tax money. The Sound must be opened to provide more ways for more people, both city residents and suburbanites, to reach and enjoy it."[28]

But while the report was unequivocal in its call for greater public access, it avoided issuing any policy recommendations that might meet that objective. Instead, the report simply called on New York's and Connecticut's elected leaders to support the principle of public access. On the question that roiled local communities and consumed the energy of activists and civil liberties groups on both sides of the Sound, the study's authors could only say, "Both state legislatures should declare it to be official state policy that the century-long trend of reduced public access be reversed."[29] Even this general statement in support of public access alarmed shoreline homeowners. Ribicoff tried to calm their fears, reassuring critics that "access to the [S]ound is going to remain a low priority item until we have dealt with more urgent problems, like pollution control and flood control."[30] "Not a damn thing will be done" to implement any of the report's recommendations, George Gunther scoffed. The hefty document "will probably be used to press flowers."[31]

In Washington, meanwhile, the proposed National Open Beaches Act was on life support. Texas congressman Bob Eckhardt continued to introduce the bill at the start of each congressional session but never succeeded in getting it out of committee and onto the House floor for a vote. Open beach advocates achieved a modest victory when, in 1976, Congress passed a series of amendments to the CZMA, including a requirement that each participating state include "a planning process for the protection of, and access to, public beaches and other public coastal areas of environmental, recreational, historical, aesthetic, ecological, or cultural value" and authorized federal grants to cover 50 percent of the cost of acquiring land and providing easements for the public to access the shore. The amendment aimed to incorporate some of the general principles of the proposed open beaches act into the CZMA and respond to the protests waged by Revitalization Corps and other groups. But it was a weak mandate. Congress shied away from requiring coastal states to provide certain protections or meet specific standards for coastal accessibility and instead included a vaguely worded requirement that each state include a "plan for that State with respect to these matters."[32]

As lawmakers in Washington equivocated, parents and children in Connecticut searched, often in vain, for a place to lay down their towels on a hot summer day. For those who were not fortunate enough to live in a shoreline town or own a summer cottage on the shore, that meant going to Hammonasset State Park. But by mid-decade, the largest and most centrally located of the three state beaches began to show signs of overuse. Visitors to Hammonasset scrambled to claim a place to lay a blanket on a beach that was described as jam packed, "wall to wall," worse than "Fort Lauderdale at Easter." Not only was the park often filled beyond capacity before noon on summer weekends, but also those who made it past the gates found much to be desired. "It is physically impossible to put a blanket down without lying on debris washed up from the tides," Hartford resident Marion T. Nelson fumed after a trip there in the summer of 1976. "I don't feel as Ned Coll does that private beaches should be open to the public, but I do feel the state owes it to the taxpayer to keep [the state beaches] in good condition."[33]

Following Governor Grasso's 1975 summer tour of the coast, calls for the state to lift restrictions on public use of the undeveloped Bluff Point intensified. The eight-hundred-plus acre site was one of the last undeveloped portions of the state's shoreline. According to one description, it seemed "to more properly belong to Nantucket than to southeastern Connecticut."[34] At the foot of the bluff a sandspit shaped like a quarter-moon jutted four thousand feet out into the Sound. Its pristine, seemingly untouched appearance masked a contentious, colorful human history. Beginning in the late eighteenth century, horses, sheep, and cattle grazed on the expansive grounds before the site fell into disuse throughout the latter half of the nineteenth century. In 1927 the state announced plans to acquire the site and designate it as a state park for the poor. "It was," as one local article described it, "to be a place where the poor could come bask in the sun and cool off in the waters. A place where mill workers from the north could shed the grime of their labors."[35] But before the state could put its plans into effect, the Great Depression hit, followed by the devastating hurricane of 1938, which laid waste to most of the structures scattered across the site.

When the state revisited the site in the early 1960s, all of the properties had been abandoned, and much of the eight hundred acres and five-mile-long shoreline had been ceded back to nature. The perfect location, the state's then governor John Dempsey thought, for a new,

modern state park.[36] In 1963 the state began acquiring the land via condemnation and hired an engineering and architectural firm to draw up
plans for what officials in the DEP hoped would become the "Coney
Island of Connecticut."[37] The design called for a concrete path along the
beach, extensive dredging off shore, and the reshaping of the beach to
accommodate sizable summer crowds. Critics panned it as an "ecological nightmare" that would inflict devastating and irreversible damage to
one of the most beautiful, scenic areas of the coast and one that had become popular among hikers and bird watchers. State officials ultimately
rejected the plan as "too grandiose."[38]

In the wake of the Bluff Point proposal, conservation groups
sprang into action and lobbied the state to protect the area's flora and
fauna, native species, and habitats from further damage. Foremost
among their demands was the closing of the roads and a ban on motor vehicles. In 1975 the Bluff Point Advisory Council, which had been
charged with determining the best use for the site, recommended it be
designated as a coastal reserve.[39] By making Bluff Point a coastal reserve,
conservationists could ban the use of motor vehicles, prevent construction of buildings on the grounds or docks and boardwalks along the
shore, and place strict limits on its use by visitors—including its beach,
which, without the use of a car or a boat, was practically inaccessible.
It was, advisory council members and supporters argued, the only way
to save the beach and preserve the area's highly fragile ecosystem. "If
you open up the area to car[s] all the way down to Bluff Point," council
chairwoman Sidney Van Zandt argued, "the beach might last three to
seven years . . . before [it] separates from the mainland."[40] "There's a
very tenuous environmental balance at Bluff Point," DEP commissioner
Stanley Pac, expressing support for the proposal, added, "and I wouldn't
want to see a big beach or a boardwalk or anything built there."[41] In
June 1975 Grasso signed into law a bill making Bluff Point one of two
coastal reserves in the United States (the other is Point Lobos Reserve in
Monterey, California).[42]

Residents of Groton, where Bluff Point was located, were incensed.
Despite enjoying twenty-six miles of shoreline, the town lacked any
public beaches. Aside from Bluff Point, all of its sandy shores were in the
hands of private beach associations. "The people of Connecticut . . . are

panting for access to a small slice of [the] Connecticut shoreline," the editor of the *Norwich Bulletin* fumed. But when one became available, the state deemed it "too good for people other than bird watchers and nature trail afficionados."[43] Where was Ned Coll when the fate of Bluff Point was being decided? "Surely the poor urban population that Coll claims to represent would enjoy the beach at Bluff Point far more than a tiny beach in Madison." Or where was the CCLU, which "has been so vocal about opening the tiny number of town beaches to state residents, yet has totally ignored the miles of Bluff Point beach that are being kept from the people."[44]

Even as the exclusive beach communities surrounding Groton put up fences, hired security guards, and (in the case of one community) created a year-round police force to protect their beaches from outsiders, with the state's move to designate Bluff Point as a coastal reserve, area residents blamed environmentalists for making the shore inaccessible to the public. The people who wanted to protect the environment— not the truly wealthy—became the new "elite." The protections of rare and native plants and species, Thomas R. Truscinski argued, are "simply excuses to save Bluff Point as a playground for the few."[45] When a state senator from Groton tried to introduce a bill that would have given local residents a special exemption to use the beach indefinitely, officials in the state's DEP office warned that it violated the Interior Department's non-exclusionary policy for facilities acquired and developed with federal funds and, if passed, would force the state to forfeit over $2.5 million it had already received for the site's acquisition.[46] "[DEP's] logic is that they'll lose federal funds because it will exclude people as a town beach," an incensed Groton mayor Betty Chapman fumed. "But right now it is as exclusionary as it can get."[47] The bill never came up for a vote, and following the 1976 summer season, the beach at Bluff Point was permanently closed to the public.[48]

On the morning of July 21, 1977, they assembled at the Connecticut– Rhode Island border: Ned, his longtime associate Anne Loiseau, and a new ally, Brother Rob Carbonneau. "With colorful rubber boats and backpacks that made it look like a technicolor commando raid," a reporter on hand to cover the start of the walk wrote, "Edward T. 'Ned'

Left to right: Ned Coll, Anne Loiseau, and Rob Carbonneau during their walk along the entire Connecticut shoreline in the summer of 1977 to protest its inaccessibility to the public. *Copyright © 1764–2017. Hartford Courant. Photo: Tom Condon. Used with permission.*

Coll plowed into the Pawcatuck River"—and dove, yet again, headfirst into the bitterly contentious, and far from resolved, battle over the fate of the state's shoreline. As they began their 250-mile-long walk, Ned unfurled a banner that read, "Taxpayers Trail." When, a few miles into their journey, a man came out of his beachfront home and shouted that the three were trespassing and he planned to summon authorities, Ned replied, "No, we're not. This is state land, and our taxes are used to clean this water."[49]

"In the beginning it was sort of nice," Rob recalled. "It was scenic . . . and enjoyable." That didn't last long. On day two, they encountered their first major obstacle—Stonington Harbor—which they attempted to cross in rubber rafts. "It was very, very cold, and Anne had hypothermia." As they struggled to keep warm, Rob realized, "Oh my goodness, this is dangerous. And we've only just begun." The three soldiered on. After recuperating at the home of one of the several shoreline families who had agreed to host them, they set out again. The following day, they reached the shores of Groton Long Point, one of the hundreds of private beach associations they would pass on their journey. "Oh, Groton Long Point," Ned muttered. "This is going to be interesting." But rather than cold stares, to Ned's astonishment, a group of people standing on the beach greeted the weary, sun-baked trio with a round of applause.[50]

More hazards lay ahead. A submarine narrowly missed their raft as it crossed the mouth of the Thames River near New London. They were forced to paddle through the wading pool at the Millstone Nuclear Power Station in Waterford. "In retrospect, that was probably not a smart thing to do," Rob later remarked. They continued to encounter some hostility from shoreline homeowners but were more struck by the number of people who expressed their support. "People are coming out of their houses," Ned later commented. "Some nice people let us pitch a tent on their lawn. . . . Others brought us food for lunch."[51]

As they discovered, shoreline communities were often just as divided on the question of beach access as the rest of the state, and they saw Ned's walk as an opportunity to draw attention to the flagrant violations of the public's rights being committed by their neighbors. Along Old Lyme's shoreline, the group navigated a "maze of early erector-set fences and pedestrian-blocking out-croppings of stone and boulders" that, as one critic observed, "subvert[ed] the tenets of law, fairness and decency."[52] Local residents who did not belong to one of the several beach associations along the town's shoreline agreed, and on the day the three arrived at Old Lyme hung a sign over one of the fences that extended out into the water that read, "Welcome! Ned Coll, this is another illegal Monster Fence—We wish you can do something about! [Signed] Residents without Access to the Beach." Earlier that summer, the Old Lyme Shores Beach Association had placed a chain-link fence atop the rock jetty that marked its boundary with the neighboring Old Colony Beach Association. The fence, which extended forty feet beyond the high-water mark, aimed to prevent nonmembers from hiking along the shore. "We have people on the beach who just don't belong here," Old Lyme Shores board member Edward Flanigan explained. Members of Old Colony claimed the fence was illegal and posed a danger to children and others who might attempt to climb over, burrow under, or wade around it. Old Lyme Shores officers claimed that since the DEP had approved construction of the jetty thirty years earlier, they were well within their rights to place a fence atop it. DEP officials disagreed, noting that the permit did not grant permission for a fence, not to mention that the jetty was meant to halt erosion, not bar outsiders. In July it filed a lawsuit against the beach association seeking to have "Old Lyme's Berlin Wall" (as it came to be known) removed.[53] After the DEP sued, the association agreed to tear down the portion of the fence that was indisputably beyond the high-water mark and thus on public lands. But it subsequently built another fence ten feet from the jetty that DEP officials said complied with state regulations. "It's even worse now," one Old Lyme resident said in disgust. "It looks like they're trying to keep sharks in a cage." "This thing reminds me of a concentration camp," another remarked.[54]

When Ned, Anne, and Rob arrived on the shores of Westbrook, a beachfront homeowner came out to welcome them and extend an offer to camp on his beach for the night. As they soon learned, the homeowner was in a dispute with a neighbor who was trying to build a massive wall along his property line and onto the beach. At Sachem Head, the three walked across a private beach that had been opened to the public out of spite. The previous year Steven Leninski, a Holocaust survivor who had made a fortune as an antiques dealer and real estate investor, purchased several cottages in the private beach community with the intent of winterizing and reselling them. When his neighbors objected and succeeded in getting the town of Guilford to rule him in violation of a local zoning ordinance, Leninski promised retaliation. He painted an American flag on the side of his seaside cottage and posted a large sign in the front yard welcoming the "huddled masses to the pristine shores of the town's choicest beach property." He began receiving threatening phone calls. Vandals attempted to set fire to his home. A neighbor told him, "Leninski, you finally met your match. We're going to chew you up, spit you out, and nail you to a cross." In response,

Leninski planted a large crucifix in his front yard. After his neighbors took him to court, charging that his impromptu "public beach" violated zoning regulations, Leninski turned an undeveloped lot he owned on the street into a parking lot for visitors. "I hope he drops dead," said one neighbor, before adding, "We just want to keep things happy and pleasant."[55]

A foul, unpleasant mood hung over the shore. People who enjoyed luxuries few could imagine instead squandered their good fortune and leisure time on petty acts of spite and elaborate forms of retaliation. Meanwhile, the public—and the shore—suffered. When the hikers reached the town of Branford, they found another sign posted to a fence jutting out into the water asking for Ned to help get it removed.[56]

As the group reached the final leg of its journey—the Gold Coast —random acts of kindness gave way to unbridled hostility. As Rob quickly learned, "the people in Fairfield County *really* did not like Ned." In the town of Fairfield, an overzealous lifeguard shouted at them to leave and threatened to call the police. Ned responded in kind, and a shouting match ensued. It only got worse from there. Further along the shore, an angry motorboater sped dangerously close to them at a high speed as they walked through shallow water. "This is why you walk the whole state," Rob thought to himself. Ned got into another heated argument with a beachfront homeowner, and blows were exchanged. "It was intense." Sporting his Roman clerical collar, Rob tried, at times, to be the peacemaker. "Ned, you don't have to be so obtuse with these people," he remarked. "You don't have to fight with everybody. . . . We're tired; we're walking; let's just keep walking."[57] But Ned could not just keep walking. He could not let it go.

Twelve days and 250 miles later, Ned, Anne, and Rob reached the New York State line. Their feet were covered in calluses, and Ned was sporting a black eye from an assault by a beachfront homeowner and four stitches on his face from a fall. They were sunburned and weary but eager to tell their story to the pool of reporters that were awaiting their arrival. Fittingly, residents of the Hawthorne Beach subdivision in Greenwich summoned police officers to remove two reporters who had parked along a private road shortly before the three arrived. Another middle-aged woman berated the reporters for giving Ned the attention he craved. "If you birds [reporters] would just ignore that bird [pointing at Coll]," she shouted, "he would just stew in his own juices." Instead, reporters listened as Ned described the litany of social and environmental injustices that they had encountered on their journey; the "hundreds of stone, concrete, steel, and wooden jetties that provide no right-of-way for the public"; and the lack of racial diversity among the people who lived along the Sound. "From Rhode Island to the middle of Fairfield County we honestly saw fewer than 20 black and Puerto Rican citizens on the shores of this state." What belonged to the people was instead, as Ned put it, "a private swimming pool of the very, very rich." "Our segregated shoreline is an insult to our Bill of Rights." "It's not meant for big yachts, but for little children."[58]

Thanks to the publicity resulting from the walk, the DEP took immediate action to remove some of the illegal shoreline obstructions Ned had uncovered. Within months, DEP commissioner Stanley Pac announced that henceforth, the state would no longer approve permits for new jetties or repairs to existing ones unless they provided a means for the public to traverse them. More jarring to residents of shoreline towns, the DEP also announced that it planned to reexamine the legality of nonresident beach access bans.[59]

For Rob Carbonneau, the walk was a journey of discovery—about his state and its people, about Ned, and about activism. He was surprised—and struck—by the amount of support they had received from shoreline residents. "A handshake, a wave, a glass of iced tea, or a bed at night in their home, greatly humbled us," he later wrote. "I feel closer to Connecticut, its people and its coastline."[60] Ned, however, felt even more estranged from his home state and exhausted from the battle. Ned's style of activism was like that of a boxer who was determined to knock out his opponent in the first round. Once he saw the "prejudice of the person, he just attacked the prejudice," Rob explained. Ned's fight with the people of coastal Connecticut was now entering the eighth round. It remained unclear who was winning on points, but it was clear, to Rob at least, that Ned was no closer to scoring a knockout. "Protesting is hard. It's hard work. Why are you in a fight if the energy is the protest? . . . Ned was right, but [when it came to the people who lived along the Gold Coast] he didn't know how to bring [them] onto his side in a participatory way." He didn't know how to work the ropes. He could only attack.[61]

That fall, as the temperature dropped, Ned's thoughts turned to the long, cold New England winter that lay ahead. The previous winter, extremely cold temperatures had led to massive shortages in home heating oil across the Northeast, which, combined with the nationwide energy crisis, had sent fuel prices skyrocketing. As state lawmakers struggled to respond to constituents' desperate demands for relief, Revitalization Corps launched Operation Fuel, a program that delivered emergency fuel aid to needy families via fuel banks established throughout the state. As Ned solicited funds from businesses and corporations and pressed lawmakers to provide additional emergency fuel aid, Corps staffers like Anne Loiseau and a team of volunteers responded to callers who phoned in to a twenty-four-hour hotline at the Corps's headquarters. From January through March 1977, Corps volunteers worked for 1,540 consecutive hours responding to calls and coordinating the delivery of heating oil to desperate families.[62]

Another winter loomed, and state lawmakers still had not come up with a plan to help the state's poor pay for home heating oil, which continued to escalate in price. No aid, it seemed, was forthcoming from Washington either, where President Jimmy Carter told a shivering nation to don a cardigan and learn to live with less. His feet still callused and his calves still sore, in October Ned embarked from the state capitol on a 340-mile walk to the nation's capital, seeking, as he put it, to "raise consciousness" in the cities and towns along the eastern seaboard of the struggles of New England's poor to stay warm each winter and to call on the president and Congress to devote $50 million toward helping the poor pay heating bills that winter.[63] When he returned to Hartford later that month without any guarantee of funds, he turned his attention toward the governor's office, which also seemed indifferent to the crisis that lay ahead, content to rely on Ned to drum up private donations.[64] In response, Ned lambasted Governor Grasso for her apparent indifference to the poor. In November Revitalization Corps staged demonstrations in front of the governor's executive mansion in West Hartford. In December Ned followed Grasso to Boston and protested outside the Boston University Law School, where she was giving a speech, telling reporters he was there to call attention to what he said was her "racist attitude" toward the poor.[65]

Rather than try (as her predecessor, Thomas Meskill, had done) to run from Ned, Grasso instead tried to utilize him. In the fall of 1976 she appointed Ned as an unpaid "Special Adviser" to the governor, giving him, as Ned later bragged, a "direct feed" to her on the problems facing the state's poor. She even arranged to have Revitalization Corps move into a new headquarters on the North End, an unused state office building that the state leased to the Corps for one dollar for five years.[66] It was a brilliant strategy for neutralizing a vocal critic. "I've never seen anything work as good as that," former Revitalization Corps worker Russell West remarked. "Ned wanted publicity; he wanted titles; he wanted his picture to be taken and his voice to be listened to. She gave him some sort of recognition; he grooved on that."[67] The following spring, Grasso announced plans to bus over seven thousand children from low-income inner-city families to the state's beaches that summer.[68] Grasso's strategy for neutralizing Ned worked like a charm. Overnight, he went from condemning Grasso as a racist to extolling her virtues and defending her record.

Grasso's handling of Ned spoke to her cautious political instincts. As the public clamored for a resolution to the conflict, Grasso offered only modest, piecemeal proposals. Rather than risk alienating shoreline voters and summer homeowners by attempting to acquire private property or create public access points to the shore, she instead opted to try to engineer more space on existing state beaches. At Rocky Neck State Park, Grasso's task force on beaches recommended a massive beach nourishment project that would increase the beach's size by over 50 percent and its capacity by 6,600 persons.[69] Coastal scientists called it a colossal waste of money and effort, noting that because of the shape of the shoreline and flow of the currents, much of the sand pumped from the Sound's bottom would, in short order, be washed away. Meanwhile, efforts to halt erosion on the beaches at Sherwood Island State Park inadvertently threatened to rob neighboring municipal and privately owned beaches of their sources of sand. After the state constructed a rock jetty at Sherwood Island, the resultant change in littoral drift along the shore led to the rapid erosion of neighboring Compo Beach. A storm that struck the coast in the fall of 1977 washed away a fifteen-foot section of the beach and brought high tide within a few yards of several homes.[70]

In January 1978 the General Assembly began debate over the Connecticut Coastal Area Management bill. The state had just over a year to hammer out a bill to establish its own coastal management program if it wished to remain eligible for federal funding under the CZMA. The bill introduced that winter took a carrot-and-stick approach to coastal municipalities. It authorized each of the state's thirty-six shoreline towns to develop its own coastal management plan as long as it met certain state and federal guidelines. If a town failed to do so, the state would step in and take control of its coastal zone. Even as state lawmakers structured the bill in a manner that preserved, as much as possible, local control, many representatives of shoreline towns wanted to kill the bill in its entirety and prevent the state from joining the CZMA compact. The towns of Old Saybrook and East Lyme emerged as centers of resistance. East Lyme first selectman George Seebeck denounced the bill as an "administrative nightmare" that would reduce local officials to "impotent observers" of coastal management policies.[71] Representatives of beach associations objected to the bill out of fear that it would effectively nullify their zoning powers and place them in a subordinate position to the municipalities that would manage the coast. The Connecticut Conference of Municipalities, in turn, criticized the bill for giving too much power to the state DEP commissioner.[72]

"The main dispute over the Connecticut legislation," the *New York Times* noted, "arises from the fear of coastal towns that they will lose control over their own shorelines, and particularly municipal beaches."[73] Critics interpreted portions of the bill as empowering the DEP to override any local planning and regulatory decisions. As the General Assembly debated the bill, Ned continued to apply pressure to state lawmakers. On July 12, 1978, he staged a protest outside the office of the state attorney general, Carl Ajello, calling on him to withdraw sales tax exemptions from towns that denied the public access to their beaches.[74] Days later he staged another, shorter, hike along the shore to call attention to violations of the public's right to the shore. Along with Loiseau and Alma Cotton, he walked from Black Point in Niantic to Griswold Point in Old Lyme; along the way, they reported to have found twenty-five state coastal permit violations. "We learned a lot and the public is learning a lot," Ned said, about "how people are being treated as second-class citizens because of a lack of enforcement of state law."[75] Public opinion polls continued to show that a majority of the state's citizens agreed with Ned on the issues, even if they disagreed with his tactics.

In this hostile political climate, shoreline towns were determined not to cede any power to state officials. Supporters of the bill conceded that given the strong "opposition to the program" among legislators in southeastern Connecticut, it stood little chance of being passed before the end of the 1978 legislative session.[76] When it became evident that giving the DEP final authority over planning and zoning decisions was a nonstarter for coastal legislators, the bill's sponsors proposed instead a nine-member coastal area review council, whose members would represent state, regional, and local public and private interests, to resolve disputes between state and municipal officials over coastal management and development proposals. While environmental groups howled, claiming the state's chief environmental regulatory body had essentially abdicated its powers, shoreline town officials remained unsatisfied. "I don't want to see the state and federal governments coming in and telling us what zoning we can do and what we cannot do," Waterford first selectman Lawrence J. Bettencourt commented.[77] These revisions did nothing to address that fundamental objection. Nor could any proposal that hoped to meet federal criteria. At its core, the CZMA sought to bring an end to the uncoordinated, fragmented system that afforded shoreline towns and beachfront property owners total local control over coastal management.

In the fall 1978 elections, candidates for office in coastal districts made the pending Connecticut Coastal Management Act a centerpiece of their campaigns. In the assembly district that encompassed Waterford, Republican candidate and local real estate agent Frederick T. Davis ran a single-issue campaign against the bill, which he called "dangerous for Waterford." His opponent, Democrat Janet Polinsky, succeeded in defeating him by stressing her own opposition to the bill and her belief that "People in local communities know what's best for them."[78] In the state's Second Congressional District, Democratic candidate Christo-

pher Dodd (the son of former U.S. senator Charles Dodd) nearly tor-
pedoed his campaign with an offhand remark about the legal status of
beach property. In an August 29 story that appeared in several shoreline
newspapers, Dodd was quoted as saying, "These beaches don't belong
to the people who live in these towns." He added, "I respect the right of
people to own private property, but I do feel that it denies other people
the right to access these facilities, and we should do more about it."
The comments set off a firestorm. The Westport Council of Beaches
released a statement attacking Dodd as "support[ing] the philosophy
of Ned Coll in opening up private beaches." Caught off guard, Dodd at
first responding by saying, "I don't even know Coll's philosophy and I
never raised his name." But as criticism mounted, Dodd called a meeting with a group of fifty state representatives, members of local beach
associations, and politicians from shoreline towns in Old Lyme's town
hall. Dodd disclaimed any intention to interfere with property rights on
the shore. He assured them, "I'm not for confiscating private property
or suggesting private property be subject to trespass." His comments
were, he explained, merely a statement of general principles, not policy
prescriptions. He stood by his belief that the state should do more to
acquire shoreline property available on the open market, but he rejected
the use of eminent domain to do so. "Honest to God, I didn't believe
these ideas would be so revolutionary."[79]

As Dodd learned, even the slightest nod to the public's right to
the shore was enough to send many coastal residents into hysterics and
political adversaries scrambling for ways to exploit their fears. Weeks
before the November election, Dodd's Republican opponent, Thomas
Connell, mailed voters small bags of sand with a note attached that read,
"Take a look at this tiny bag of sand. It may be all that's left of your beach
if Chris Dodd has his way."[80] Dodd won the election, but his so-called
gaffe would dog him for years to come.

Supporters of the state's coastal area management bill refused to
give up or allow their opponents to run out the clock. In January 1979
they completed a comprehensive revision of the bill. Its most significant
change was the elimination of a passage that stated, as a general policy,
the state's desire to "encourage public access to the waters of Long Island
Sound and to encourage recreational opportunities within the coastal

area." Seen as too open to interpretation, the bill's critics demanded that it instead say, "To encourage public access to the waters of Long Island Sound by expansion, development and effective utilization of state-owned recreational facilities." In short, dump some more sand on the beaches at Hammonasset, Rocky Neck, and Sherwood Island State Parks.[81]

Four years, $1.4 million in federal funds, and five revisions later, in the spring of 1979 the General Assembly was ready to vote on the bill. On May 31, 1979, the state senate overwhelmingly passed the bill by a vote of 33–1, and Grasso signed it into law soon after. Critics still railed against the legislation. Edward Connell called it "a completely unnecessary, vague and atrociously-verbose document designed to substitute a new cult of Paradise-on-Earth dreamers . . . for the good burghers of Madison, Waterford, Darien, and other shore towns between Stonington and Greenwich as decision-makers for the use of tidal property."[82] In fact, it was the weakest coastal management bill passed by any state at the time. It stripped the DEP of any power to compel towns to act on its recommendations or guidelines, though it did retain the power to sue towns for egregious violations of the law. Many believed that the law failed to meet the minimum standards set by the federal government and feared that the state would be forced back to the drawing board. The National Resources Defense Council threatened to take the state to court in order to prevent a newly created state agency from receiving federal funding.[83]

The state had its coastal regulatory agency and a plan, however inchoate, to save the Sound. Shoreline towns and beach associations, meanwhile, survived the storm with the private status of their beaches intact. The Connecticut shore was poised to begin a new chapter in its relationship with the state and its people. It would do so, though, without its moral conscience, Ned Coll, by its side.

NINE

Go Home, Ned

H istory," Ned Coll predicted at decade's end, "will record
that in 1979 our national character was challenged. . . . History will also judge our reaction—our courage versus our
paranoia, our confidence versus our despair, our creativity
versus our stagnation, our sense of purpose versus our sense of greed."[1]
In the decade that followed, Americans' pursuit of material wealth—
greed—became synonymous with the nation's sense of purpose and the
wellspring of its creative energies.

Greed found a welcoming home on the Connecticut shore, where,
in spite of the previous decade's victories in the struggle for environmental conservation and protection, real estate development along
fragile, ecologically sensitive shorelines surged, state regulatory agencies
dawdled, and the wealth and income disparities between and among
the state's coastal and inland populations grew. The new state agencies
tasked with protecting coastal wetlands from development and facilitating public access to the shore suffered from budget cuts and staffing
shortages. In Washington, a new administration hostile to the very idea
of environmental protection staffed federal agencies with persons whose
chief qualification was their opposition to the very mission of their office. Overworked and understaffed regulatory agencies were little match
for wealthy property owners and large-scale real estate developers, who

brazenly began beachfront construction projects without approval by
the state's Department of Environmental Protection and then strong-
armed state officials into granting permits afterward. As a new class of
home buyers settled along the state's shoreline, a new layer of social and
economic stratification began to emerge, this one between the upper-
middle-class families who had owned summer beach cottages for generations and a new class of the super-wealthy, who built ostentatious
seaside mansions.

   In Hartford, the manufacturing plants that had brought hundreds
of thousands of African Americans to New England and fueled the city's
economy throughout much of the twentieth century closed or moved
operations to the suburbs. In suburban Hartford, a new process of
black ghettoization was under way. Throughout the 1970s, as blacks in
Hartford fought to realize their dreams of good schools, safe neighborhoods, the financial security that suburban homeownership promised,
and the civil right to equal housing opportunities the 1968 Fair Housing
Act provided, the city's real estate industry adopted new strategies for
racial containment. As early as the 1960s, real estate agents began the
practice of steering black home seekers to the suburb of Bloomfield,
located north of the city (and adjacent to the North End). By the early
1970s, speculators were profiting handsomely from black demand and
white fears, playing up the threat of an imminent "invasion" of blacks
to convince whites in Bloomfield to sell their homes at below-market
value, then turning around and reselling these homes to black families
at a significant markup. By 1973, the twin practices of "blockbusting" (as
this practice came to be known) and racial steering in Bloomfield had
become so egregious that the U.S. Justice Department, responding to a
complaint filed by fair housing advocates, brought charges against seven
Hartford real estate firms for violating the Fair Housing Act.[2]

   While white families fled, Ned and his wife, Elizabeth, moved
in. Shortly after their marriage in 1972, the couple bought a home in
Bloomfield and began raising a family. Unlike many other suburbs
that experienced an influx of African American families in the 1970s,
Bloomfield ultimately did not experience a wholesale exodus of its white
population. Through a host of innovative public policy strategies and

the vigilant efforts of local fair housing organizations, the city achieved a remarkable degree of integration and stability in its housing markets. Dubbed an "All-American City" for its unprecedented level of racial diversity, Bloomfield allowed Ned and Elizabeth to provide their two children, John and Elizabeth, the type of integrated environment that Ned had devoted his life toward achieving, even as residential patterns throughout the rest of the state and the nation remained starkly divided along racial lines.

Back in the city, Revitalization Corps found itself performing a form of triage on a battered and neglected neighborhood: tutoring children stuck in failing schools, helping a tenant struggling to pay rent, pressuring a landlord not to initiate an eviction, helping a mother whose son had just landed in jail, helping an out-of-work father find a job. Ned used his power of persuasion—his willingness to make some noise—to compel employers, landlords, and law enforcement to cut someone a break. But this lone activist, waging a case-by-case war on poverty, was no match for the structural forces that conspired to marginalize and exclude Hartford's urban black and Puerto Rican poor from the region's economic prosperity. Ned remained dogged in his quest to expose the children of the North End to a world beyond the ghetto's walls, to show children like Lebert "Gee" Lester that, as he put it, "there was a better way . . . that people lived differently, not everyone is on welfare, not everyone is in public housing, not everyone is really poor. You don't have to come from a privileged side to make things better for yourself."[3] "We gave [Ned] hell," remembers Warren Hardy, who grew up on the North End in the late 1970s and early 1980s. "We gave him above and beyond hell. And it never stopped him. It never fazed him. He continued to move forward with what he had in mind."[4]

But the neighborhood, and the city and state, had moved on. Blacks on the North End had grown tired of relying on a white liberal activist, no matter how sincere and committed, to be their mouthpiece, their liaison to the city's power structure. In the housing projects, a new generation of black women had taken the lead in fighting to defend public housing from disinvestment and public attack. Revitalization Corps, meanwhile, struggled to attract a new wave of younger volunteers and steadily lost its longest-serving ones. Critics did not fail to note Ned's "thinning cadre of activists" on hand at his various protests, which became increasingly scattershot and hard to take seriously.[5]

Along with his influence in the community, the city, and across the state, Ned's physical health began to deteriorate as he struggled to control his epilepsy. His personal life began to unravel. And habits and actions that had once seemed eccentric—calculated, even—now seemed, even to his supporters, increasingly unhinged, reckless, and counterproductive. For all his enigmatic qualities and his stubborn resistance to align himself with other movements, Ned Coll—and the shore he had spent a decade fighting to open to the public—came to embody both the splintering and disintegration of racial and social justice movements and the triumph of individualism over communalism and wealth over commonwealth in the 1980s. Ronald Reagan's America had little patience for the hectoring diatribes of an increasingly lonely, isolated activist seemingly stuck in the past, still waging a class war that had already been lost.

In the immediate aftermath of Ned Coll's walk along the state's shoreline in the summer of 1977, a sea-tide change in the state's attitudes and policies on beachfront access and coastal environmental protection seemed under way. Months after Ned and his companions reached the state's western border, DEP commissioner Stanley Pac announced new, tougher policies on jetty permits, promising not to grant permits for any shoreline barriers or physical alterations that were meant to keep outsiders off beaches.[6] For shoreline town residents who had become fed up with the exclusionary antics of beachfront property owners, Ned Coll had become somewhat of a folk hero for the little guy and gadfly-for-hire. When, in the spring of 1979, the residents of Old Lyme decided to fight against the attempt by a beachfront bar to erect fences that extended into the waters on both sides of its property, thereby obstructing the public's ability to hike along the shore, they called on Ned to come down and stage a protest. He happily obliged.[7]

Racial tensions in the state remained high, with beaches and places of public recreation a flashpoint of conflict. In small towns and suburbs, African Americans who attempted to purchase homes found themselves subject to unrelenting harassment and sporadic acts of terrorism. During the late 1970s, the Connecticut Commission on Human Rights and Opportunities (CCHRO) found a "significant increase" in incidents of racial terrorism and mounting evidence of white supremacist organization recruitment in the state. The Department of Public Safety reported seventeen cross burnings in the state in 1979 alone. It estimated that there were upwards of three hundred members of the Ku Klux Klan living in the state and identified an active chapter in Danbury. The investigators partially attributed the increase in racist attacks to white economic insecurity and fears of downward mobility. In East Haven, a working-class, heavily Italian American suburb of New Haven, white homeowners waged a dual campaign—one to save their homes from falling into Long Island Sound as a result of erosion, the other to keep black people from buying homes in their neighborhoods. The former entailed constant pressure on local and state lawmakers not to condemn their properties and instead fund increasingly expensive shoreline stabilization projects; the latter was a sustained campaign of violence and intimidation against African American families who attempted to purchase homes in the East Shore neighborhood. Black civil rights groups reported several incidents of harassment and assault on black beachgoers at New Haven's Lighthouse Point Park, including an unprovoked attack on a busload of black children attending a church picnic on the beach. On another occasion, a gang of white youths severely beat an African American man as he tried to change a flat tire on his car in an all-white neighborhood. Town officials failed to investigate many of these incidents and ignored the pleas of black residents for protection. The town's mayor refused to even acknowledge receipt of a letter from a local civil rights organization detailing the horrific acts committed against black residents and the toll these had inflicted on parents and children. After several attempted fire bombings, repeated slashings of tires on cars, and the tossing of rocks through windows of homes, and the steady drumbeat of crowds of white youths chanting, "Get out, nigger!" outside of their residences, most of the families who had moved into East Shore had, by the end of the decade, retreated to neighborhoods in the city.[8]

Outside of Bloomfield, blacks struggled to buy homes and gain acceptance in the suburbs and smaller towns of central Connecticut.

In the mid-1970s, Lebert Lester Sr. and his family bought a home in the town of Cromwell with the help of Lester's employer, Gardener Nurseries, which co-signed the mortgage. At the time, only five other black families lived in the town. The Lesters' new neighbors were far from welcoming. "When we got that house out there, man, that was some more trouble," Lester's son Lebert ("Gee") recalls. Neighbors forbade their children from playing with Gee or any of his six brothers and sisters. In school, the seven siblings experienced a profound sense of alienation from classmates and discriminatory treatment from teachers. Then, on the afternoon of January 2, 1976, a fire broke out in the family's home. Everyone inside escaped without harm. A small child at the time, Cecil Lester still vividly recalls seeing his older brothers rush into the blazing house in a desperate attempt to save the family's two pet dogs, Yoggie and Poochie. They were able to retrieve only one of them. To the Lesters, it was clear the fire was deliberately set by someone who hoped to force them out of the neighborhood. Local law enforcement conducted a perfunctory investigation, but no arrests were made. Town officials offered to help the Lesters find another home in town. They refused and instead moved back to Hartford's North End, eventually settling into a home on Main Street across from Revitalization Corps's headquarters.[9]

The Lester family's brief residency in Cromwell and hasty retreat to Hartford were indicative of white resistance and black ambivalence to efforts to diversify the state's small towns and rural areas. Between 1950 and 1970, the state's African American population became increasingly concentrated in its six largest cities: Bridgeport, Hartford, New Haven, Norwalk, Stamford, and Waterbury. By 1978 these cities housed 87 percent of the state's black population but less than one-third of its white population. Conversely, over two-thirds of the state's white population lived in towns with miniscule minority populations.[10]

Decades in the making, by the 1970s the state's segregated landscape seemed immune to any attempts to counteract. In 1969, a group of Hartford's leading corporate executives embarked on a plan to relocate, en masse, the North End population to a planned development located outside of the urban core. Dubbed the Greater Hartford Process, the plan called for the total dismantling and redevelopment of the city's North End and relocation of twenty thousand of its residents to a "new town" located in an outer suburb of Hartford. Seeking to prevent a frenzy of land speculation and forestall local resistance, officials tried to keep the location of the "new town"—slated for the small, nearly all-white town of Coventry, located fifteen miles east of Hartford—a secret until the group had acquired the land. Over the next four years, the group spent over $8 million acquiring real estate in Coventry. Blacks in Hartford, meanwhile, expressed anger over their exclusion from the Hartford Process's planning and deliberation, while suburban whites feverishly speculated and worked to uncover the location of the planned development. When, in January 1973, Governor Meskill prematurely revealed the location of the new town, Coventry residents rose in opposition while local officials announced their refusal to cooperate. Soon after, the Hartford Process shelved the project. In place of dispersal, it focused on containment of the ghetto. As revealed in an internal memo leaked to the press in January 1975, officials in the Hartford Process proposed instead to "consolidate the welfare dependent elements" of the city's black and Puerto Rican populations in depressed neighborhoods, create an additional buffer between the North End and downtown by tearing down housing projects located closest to the city's center, and reduce Puerto Rican in-migration. The memo's disclosure sparked massive protests. An estimated one thousand demonstrators formed a human barricade around the city's new civic center, forcing the city to cancel its grand opening ceremony.[11]

Like their shoreline counterparts, suburban municipalities embraced localism whenever the threat of integration seemed most acute. When in 1977 officials in HUD criticized the town of Manchester over its failure to provide low-income housing, as specified in grants it had solicited and received from the federal agency, residents promptly voted by a 3–1 margin to withdraw from the program. The move sparked a lawsuit from the U.S. Justice Department over violations of the Fair Housing Act. As they maneuvered to limit federal or state control, white suburban homeowners and officials dismissed critics in a manner that echoed criticisms offered by shoreline towns over beach access policies. Just as the public beaches of Gold Coast towns were open to all who could afford to live there, "Anyone who can afford to move to West Hartford is welcome to do so, regardless of background," West Hartford mayor Ellsworth Grant said in response to critics of the town's exclusionary zoning ordinances. And just as opening up the beaches to all comers threatened to destroy sensitive coastal habitats, as defenders of exclusionary beaches claimed, the high-end real estate markets of West Hartford, town councilman Lauchlin McLean explained, "[are not] suited to low and moderate income housing from a practical standpoint."[12]

The small numbers of African American families who lived in some of the state's more affluent cities and towns were constantly reminded that their local governments functioned to keep their presence to a minimum. In Greenwich, tensions between the city's African American residents and local officials came to a boil in 1979. Fittingly, the conflict was sparked by an action by Greenwich officials aimed at protecting the residents-only status of the town's beaches. In 1979 Congress earmarked $25,000 of an $845,000 community block grant designated for Greenwich toward the renovation of a community center located in the black neighborhood of Pemberwick. Town officials refused to accept it. Albert F. Varner Jr., the Republican candidate for first selectman, argued that acceptance of the federal funds for a public recreational facility might jeopardize the status of town beaches. Richard Blumenthal, U.S. attorney for the District of Connecticut, tried to reassure Greenwich officials that the community block grant would not expose them to a lawsuit, but to little effect. "Any grant which even remotely threatens continued local control of beaches will not be tolerated," the *Greenwich Time* thundered. "We should not be tricked by the argument that we are only getting our tax dollars back," Greenwich resident Charles H. Granger warned. Ultimately, the board voted to accept the block grant on the condition that the $25,000 set aside for the community center was removed.[13]

Blacks in Greenwich were outraged. The local chapter of the NAACP called for a public forum with the Republican candidates who had led the opposition. Before an audience at a local AME church, candidates Varner and Rebecca Breed responded to pointed questions about their motives for opposing federal funds for the community center. Pointing an accusatory finger at the two candidates, resident Bernice Norwood Napper commented, "When we talk about building housing, we say we're afraid of letting certain kinds of people in. When we talk about beaches, we say we've got to keep certain kinds of people out. My question is, who are you talking about when you say 'certain kinds of people?'" NAACP member George Twine asked Varner, "You say we'll open the gates to outsiders. What outsiders are you talking about? Who are the outsiders when the average span of residency in Greenwich is 4½ years?" Squirming in his seat, Varner feigned ignorance at what Twine was implying. Twine persisted in his interrogation. "You know what I'm asking," he told Varner. "I don't believe I do, George," Varner replied. NAACP branch president Bernard R. Fisher broke the stalemate. "It's the people you talk about in the back rooms but not at public meetings," he told Varner. "You know it. We're talking about black people." Breed expressed shock at the accusation. "You seem to say we're saying something else, that we're camouflaging something else."[14]

That was exactly what they were saying. For the next hour, black residents stood before the candidates and told of their own experiences of racial discrimination in their search for housing, for employment, and in places of public recreation. Soon, white residents began to speak out against the town's decision to sacrifice a community center so as to protect its exclusionary beaches. Greenwich resident Michael McDermott characterized it as a cynical political ploy aimed at winning an election by playing to voters' fears. "As a life-long Republican, I must express my shock, dismay, and anger at the blatant, shoddy attack on the Pemberwick community."[15]

McDermott should not have been shocked. Playing the "beach card" had, by 1979, become a familiar political tactic of Republican candidates for local and state office. One year earlier, Congressman Chris Dodd had seen his campaign nearly derailed over comments suggesting that the state's beaches belonged to the general public. Two years later, James Buckley, his opponent in the race for one of the state's U.S. Senate seats, repeatedly invoked Dodd's comments on beach access. In television spots, Buckley plastered Dodd's statement—"Those beaches don't belong to the people who live in those towns"—across viewers' screens, citing it as evidence of the Democratic candidate's "lack of regard for property rights."[16] In radio spots, Buckley intimated that Dodd favored federal control of beaches, and he promised to defend beleaguered shoreline communities from "outside forces."[17]

It was, to be sure, a desperate tactic from a losing campaign. In November, Dodd coasted to victory. But it once again placed Dodd on the defensive and underscored the degree of paranoia among shoreline communities in regard to the threat of public beach access. Indeed, shoreline communities had come to treat any outside aid for anything having to do with the coast or recreation with suspicion. In January 1981, Madison's Board of Selectmen was faced with the question of whether to accept a five-year, $50,000 federal grant for coastal management. "We've never taken any state or federal funds that have anything to do with our coastline," Selectwoman Betty Young told fellow board members. "If we accept this federal aid, I'm afraid of what we might get in return." Despite assurances from the state's Coastal Area Management director Arthur Rocque that the federal or state government had "neither the power nor the inclination to open local beaches to out-of-town residents," and even though opponents of the funding conceded that the chances it would force open the town's beaches were "one in a million," they voted to reject the grant. No amount of aid, First Selectman John Phillips commented after the vote, was worth the loss of local control over the beach.[18]

On New Year's Day 1980, hundreds of bleary-eyed Americans dragged themselves out of bed, bundled up, and headed to the beach. They came to commemorate the start of what conservation groups had dubbed the "Year of the Coast," a year-long campaign to draw public attention to the dire state of America's coastlines and spur action against unregulated and environmentally reckless development. In a speech to the nation the previous fall, President Jimmy Carter had endorsed the call to action and pledged to push for new legislation aimed at coastal protection and preservation. In total, Americans staged thirty separate hikes along sections of the nation's shores. Later that year, organizers held a Sandcastle Day, where participants were encouraged to build sandcastles in the shape of beach houses and condos near the water's edge to demonstrate the hazards of building in the coastal zone, and—borrowing a page from Ned Coll's playbook—they held a Coast Discovery Day, where families were encouraged to bring underprivileged inner-city children with them to the beach.[19]

But while many participants stressed positive action and took a light-hearted approach to the public demonstrations, others viewed the state of America's coasts as a matter of dire concern. Instead of celebrations and festivities, as Year of the Coast organizers had planned for the upcoming year, "What might be more appropriate would be a chain of flaming beacons down each coast as a signal that America's shores are under siege," *Boston Globe* columnist Ian Menzies argued. "This shouldn't be a story of pretty pictures, of sun and sand and waving beach grass . . . but of raw, floating sewage, tar balls and oil slicks, litter-strewn beaches and eroded dunes, overdevelopment and 'keep out' signs."[20] Indeed, signs of progress in the struggle to save America's shores were hard to find. Eight years after the passage of the CZMA, only nineteen of the thirty-five states and territories eligible for federal assistance had adopted a federally approved coastal management plan.[21] Like in Connecticut, beachfront homeowners and residents of shoreline towns led the opposition to the creation of state regulatory agencies and, following their creation, exploited their weaknesses. By providing numerous incentives for states to "delegate as much responsibility to local government as is possible," the CZMA had hoped to foster cooperation between state coastal commissions and shoreline municipalities. In practice, however, this federal approach to coastal management simply gave local governments more tools to resist and evade state regulators, who, as Army Corps of Engineers assistant counsel Martin R. Cohen remarked, "tend to view the commissions as 'no growth' planning agencies imposed upon them." As a result, Cohen noted, "It is not unusual to find that the state commissions are unaware of local development in the coastal zone." The 1976 amendments to the CZMA, meant to encourage greater public beach access (and placate the demands of open beach advocates) by providing states with funding to expand public beaches, had also failed to penetrate America's sand curtains. Five years later, Congress had yet to fund the program.

By year's end, few Americans were still aware that it was the Year of the Coast. The sole legislative achievement was Congress's reauthorization of the CZMA for another five years. And that fall, voters elected a new president, Ronald Reagan, who had made no secret of his contempt for federal agencies interfering with local prerogatives and, upon assuming office, made the defunding and dismantling of the Office of Coastal Zone Management one of his environmental priorities.[22]

While conservative Republicans in Washington led the push to roll back environmental regulations, in Connecticut, it was the state's Democratic governor Ella Grasso who frustrated efforts to implement and enforce coastal management policies. Her administration's adversarial stance toward environmental regulation was well known. In 1976 the director of the DEP, Joseph Gill, was forced to resign after lawmakers in the General Assembly uncovered an internal memo that recommended the firing of "econuts" and the dismantling of many of the DEP's regulatory and enforcement units.[23] From its inception, the state's Coastal Management Program had struggled to enforce new environmental protections in the face of concerted opposition from the dying port cities and polluting industries located along urban waterfronts, whose dire predictions of shuttered factories, idle shipyards, and long unemployment lines had gained a sympathetic hearing by the Grasso administration. The obstructionist tactics of towns like Madison made the task of coordinating local governments all the more difficult. Nevertheless, by the early 1980s, the fledgling state agency had scored some small victories over recalcitrant towns that had refused to review coastal development plans and over developers who had resisted including public walkways and easements in proposals. But as the pressure to develop coastal real estate intensified, the office found itself increasingly overwhelmed. From 1977 through 1986, the number of applications for shoreline construction projects in the state jumped 62 percent. Whereas in 1983 the state had reviewed applications for 57 major shoreline development projects, in 1986 it received 320 proposals.[24] But while the DEP's workload increased, during these years the number of state employees reviewing coastal development proposals shrank. By 1988, the state had only two employees handling the more than 350 applications it received each year, down from the five staffers who had handled the 50 or so applications submitted annually at the beginning of the decade. This was by design. Under Stanley Pac, the DEP made a conscious decision in the 1980s to scale back its efforts at regulating coastal development and instead redirected its energies toward inland water diversion projects.[25]

Chronically understaffed and under intense pressure to speed up the application approval process, the Office of Coastal Management struggled to adequately scrutinize applications. Numerous projects were approved without alternative proposals by the state that would have minimized environmental damage. In one instance, state regulators hastily allowed a prominent real estate developer to remove 4,500 cubic yards from the mud flats at the mouth of the Connecticut River so that he could build a dock long enough to accommodate his 120-foot-long power yacht. Not content to wait for state approval, some large-scale developers moved ahead with coastal development and then strong-armed state regulators to approve a project after its completion. By 1988, according to one estimate, 8 percent of all shoreline building permits were being granted after the projects had already been completed.[26]

While the diminished state agency was good for developers, it was devastating for the state's fragile—and dwindling—coastal wetlands. Prior to 1970, coastal development had resulted in the loss of over one-half of the state's thirty thousand acres of tidal wetlands.[27] The destruction of these valuable ecological habitats led the state to enact a robust wetlands protection program that was credited with dramatically slowing wetlands losses during the 1970s. But as increased pressure to develop coincided with the DEP's decreased oversight capacity, wetlands losses mounted. By the mid-1980s environmental conservation groups began calling attention to what the local director of Greenwich's wetlands agency called "undetected nibbling" of coastal wetlands by property owners and developers, in particular in the vast amounts of coastal wetlands acreage that state regulators had yet to map and record.[28]

As developers nibbled away at coastal wetlands, polluters carelessly fouled the waters. Beginning on July 6, 1988, medical waste began washing ashore on beaches from Connecticut to New Jersey. Shocked bathers arrived on beaches to find "vials of encrusted blood and needle-tipped syringes." Coming at the height of the AIDS epidemic, that summer's infamous "syringe tide" (as the press dubbed it) sent beach towns along the Connecticut shoreline into panic and led to mass closings of beaches. On July 24, Greenwich closed its beaches after bathers found medical waste off Byram Beach. By summer's end, medical waste had washed ashore at beaches in eight other shoreline towns in the state.

All told, health officials recovered over two thousand syringes. Federal investigators later determined the trash had come from the overflowing Fresh Kills Landfill on Staten Island.[29]

"The longer you worked for [Ned], the more bitter would be the falling out," Russell West explained. "And indeed that was the way it was with me as well." After working for Ned throughout the early to mid-1970s, West had had enough. "Ned was going further and further afield, more and more over the edge of the precipice, and he was getting more and more Catholic and more and more in your face." When West told Ned he was leaving the organization, Ned offered him a payment to convince him to stay. "When I told him I didn't want his check, [that] I was go-ing to be quitting the organization . . . he became furious and he tore [it] up into a hundred pieces."[30] West didn't see Ned again for another twenty-five years.

By the early 1980s, most of the Revitalization Corps chapters around the country had quietly folded. All of the other members of the team Ned had built over the previous decade had already left. Just days before the 1979 Christmas holiday, Anne Loiseau told Ned that she would be leaving to begin a three-year mission in Venezuela for the Catholic Foreign Mission Society. Loiseau had been working for Revi-talization Corps since 1969, far longer than anyone else. "Ned had a ten-dency to burn through people very, very quickly," as West put it, "but not Annie." She had been at Ned's side for every initiative, and every controversy, of the past decade. She had the scars to prove it. "Anne and I were extremely close," Ned explained. "Anne knew what shit was. And she was a lot younger than me but she was extremely savvy." Though Loiseau eventually moved back to Connecticut, married, and started a family, she never worked with Ned again and did not respond to re-peated requests for an interview for this book.[31] Her departure marked the end of an era.

Just weeks after Ned lost his longest-serving associate, the *Hart-ford Courant* commemorated Revitalization Corps's fifteenth anniver-sary with a less-than-flattering profile of the enigmatic activist. Based on interviews with a range of local leaders and North End activists, the article painted a picture of a figure who was increasingly out of step with the times, stuck in an imagined, idealized past, when, as he put it, "government and religion seemed relevant. There was an electricity in the air; there was a feeling we could solve some of the problems facing society." But while Ned waxed nostalgic, others poked holes in his mythologized career. Ned, critics contended, had always seemed more focused on generating headlines than achieving results. He prized self-promotion over coalition building. His scattershot, seat-of-the-pants approach to community service and engagement had left a long trail of incomplete initiatives and unfulfilled promises. Ned, other North End leaders commented, "doesn't represent their people," and "his efforts to help the city poor aren't as successful as others might believe." Others dismissed his efforts to generate publicity for his various initiatives as mere "gimmicks" that invariably lacked any "meaningful follow-up" and said his unpaid position in the Grasso administration amounted to little more than "free office space."[32]

Almost as if on cue, Ned's first public action following the profile article was perhaps his most impulsive yet. In late January, he summoned reporters to a press conference held in the office building he was renting from the state for one dollar a year to announce that he was resigning his unpaid advisory position in the Grasso administration. He then proceeded to attack the governor in characteristically personal terms. "She has no gut feeling for the poor or the working class," he told the assembled audience. "Whatever she's done in the area of human services you could put on the back of a stamp." "She doesn't think of people in Hartford or other cities as people." Ned never specified what triggered him to resign his ceremonial post and denounce the governor as a stooge for the state's "very, very wealthy." His exodus from the executive branch barely registered with the governor, who never provided an official comment on the matter. He got to keep the office at 2250 Main Street, where Revitalization Corps remained for years to come.[33]

Ned was in desperate need of a new audience, a new community in need, and a new adversary. That spring, he found his audience on Harvard's campus, his community in a desperately poor housing project and middle school in Boston's Brighton neighborhood, and his adversary in U.S. district judge W. Arthur Garrity Jr. The previous fall, Ned had launched a campaign to recruit college students to volunteer in the city's public schools and housing projects. He found an ally in Dean Yarbrough, the principal of Mead Middle School in Brighton, who welcomed Revitalization Corps volunteers into his classrooms. Set among rows of burned-out apartments, adjacent to the Fidelis Way housing project, and with the spires of Harvard's River Houses visible in the distance, Mead Middle School epitomized the vast disparities between and close proximity of wealth and poverty in the city. That December, Judge Garrity ordered the struggling school, which operated at half capacity, to be closed at the end of the school year.[34]

Mead Middle School's uncertain future underscored the impossible choices facing the federal judge who had, for over a decade, supervised the city's tortured struggle to desegregate its public schools. While its heavily black and poor student body—and the school's isolation and history of underachievement—seemed to exemplify all of the problems that integration promised to alleviate, the school had nevertheless become a center of community life and point of pride for its current and former students, parents, and teachers. Its new principal had vested the school with a new sense of mission, and the presence of the wily activist from Hartford, and, soon, a weekly stream of tutors from the Ivy League school across the river, had seemed to breathe new life into the aging building and had made Mead a place worth saving.

When he wasn't hunched over a wobbly desk in an aging classroom in Brighton helping a student with a math or reading assignment, Ned was prowling the magisterial halls and manicured lawns of Harvard's campus, seeking to inspire (or shame) students of the nation's most elite university to "give a damn" about the poor. He crashed student organization meetings. He marched into dining halls, climbed on top of tables, and gave impromptu speeches, where he told of the horrific conditions in many of the city's public schools and housing projects. "It's a goddam pit," he shouted. "And it needs your help." Ned's "gruff manner" and "creative obscenities" immediately captured the attention of students, who seemed to enjoy hearing him denounce their school's elitist culture, and made him a popular topic of conversation on campus that spring. They called him "the Evel Knievel of activism." The *Harvard Crimson* ran a couple of articles on the wild-eyed activist who seemed to be popping up, unexpectedly, all over campus and who could always be counted on, at the very least, to say something outrageous. "I used to think Harvard was full of shit," he told one student organization. "Now I can smell it." The crowd erupted in laughter. "The more you learn about Ned Coll," a student writing for the *Crimson* commented, "the more you are certain he is a lunatic."[35]

The "lunatic" still possessed the gift of persuasion. By March, he had recruited forty students to volunteer in the Fidelis Way projects. He has "definitely tapped some sentiment here" and forced students to "think about important questions," one student remarked. Revitalization Corps began running a shuttle bus to Brighton from Harvard Square on weekdays. Each afternoon, Ned would canvass Harvard Yard and try to recruit others to come along. One story recounted in the school newspaper typified his method of recruitment. A student tour guide was leading a group of prospective students and their parents on a campus tour. As they gathered in front of the statue of John Harvard on the Yard, Ned leapt forward, brushed the unassuming guide aside, and commanded the crowd's attention. "Folks, Harvard really is a great school," he bellowed. "You have a tremendous city here, filled with arts and culture, all at your fingertips. But Boston is also recognized as the most racist city in America, and poverty exists here rivaling any in the nation." Parents gasped. Some grabbed their children and pulled them close, perhaps fearing that the slightly disheveled, apparently unhinged speaker might lunge at them or take one of them hostage. Ned then pointed to the idling bus filled with student volunteers parked in Harvard Square. "These students here are about to go out to a housing project across the river to tutor 12-year-olds who read like six-year-olds should. Any of you want to come along?" By then, some of the parents and prospective students had fled the scene; the tour guide had gone in search of campus police. One precocious high school–aged girl, however, asked, in jest, "Is there any money in it?" Ned winced and, for a moment, it appeared as if he might actually lunge at her. His rage at such crass displays of self-interest burned deep. Instead, he just hissed, "Jesus, she's perfect for this place," and walked away.[36]

Throughout the spring, the fate of Mead Middle School hung in the balance. As resistance mounted, Garrity became cagey about which schools would ultimately be forced to close. On March 21 Garrity's office released a list of schools to be closed that surprisingly did not include Mead. Parents and teachers were relieved, but doubts remained. In late March, Ned went to the federal courthouse and demanded to see Garrity. One of his staffers assured Ned that Mead would remain open through the following school year. One week later, though, Mead was back on the chopping block. Garrity released a statement saying that the school had been "omitted inadvertently" from the previous list. The Boston School Committee and school superintendent Robert Wood immediately appealed the decision. Ned was apoplectic. Upon hearing the news, he rushed to the courthouse and attempted to storm Garrity's office. Before he had gotten past the secretary, two federal marshals tackled him. Ned was arrested and charged with breach of peace. In May the U.S. Court of Appeals issued a stay of Garrity's order. Mead would remain open at least one more year. Ned returned to Hartford.[37]

The same day that federal marshals arrested Ned in Boston, doctors in Hartford performed a hysterectomy on Governor Ella Grasso. A month earlier, the governor had been diagnosed with ovarian cancer.[38] At the time, women diagnosed with the highly aggressive form of cancer had a survival rate of under 15 percent. Grasso tried to shield from the public the seriousness of her illness and conduct the affairs of her office on a reduced work schedule. By midsummer, her political maneuvering at the Democratic National Convention, where she attempted to convince President Carter to release his delegates and allow an open convention, had led many to believe that she was fully recovered and ready to resume work full time. "She's back in the harness," one Democratic insider commented.[39] Hope for a recovery was quickly dashed. In November, Grasso was readmitted into the hospital, where tests revealed that the cancer had spread to her liver.[40] Doctors gave her weeks to live. For weeks afterward, she tried to continue performing her duties from a hospital bed as rumors of her impending resignation swirled. Finally, on December 5, 1980, Grasso announced her resignation. On December 31, 1980, her lieutenant governor, William O'Neill, was sworn in as the state's eighty-fourth governor. Grasso died on February 5, 1981.[41]

Five days before Grasso succumbed to cancer, Ned's mother, Claire, passed away. Seven months later, his father, Daniel, died.[42] As he mourned his parents' deaths, Ned's own health was deteriorating. Physically and mentally, he was a wreck. He began suffering epileptic seizures with greater frequency. As his star faded, Ned grew increasingly focused, indeed obsessed, with generating headlines and remaining on the public's radar. The previous spring, a reporter in Boston had agreed to do an interview. Against his doctor's advice and family's wishes, Ned sped up to Boston to meet with the reporter. There, he suffered a massive seizure. In the emergency room doctors summoned a priest to administer last rites. His wife, Elizabeth, along with longtime Corps volunteer Alma Cotton, rushed to the hospital. Ned's condition stabilized, but when he returned home, he was placed on a heavy regimen of drugs to treat his epilepsy. As before, he neglected to take his medications, eat properly, or rest. Soon, the seizures returned. His family begged him to heed his doctors' advice, but to no avail. Instead, he became even more stubborn and defiant and—to those closest to him—intolerable.

In 1984, Elizabeth filed for divorce. Ned moved out of their Bloomfield home and into a small cabin on a lake in the town of Barkhamsted. Friends and associates worried about him. Felton Rockcliffe, who had grown up on the North End, had ridden on buses to the shore as a child, and had received tutoring lessons from Revitalization Corps as an adolescent, became a full-time Corps staffer in the early 1980s and, as Ned's health worsened, assumed a leading role in administering the organization's programs. He begged Ned to "take better care of himself." His public appearances became less frequent and increasingly bizarre and discomforting. Gone were the biting jokes and sharp wit, replaced by anger and incoherence. "That's quite a parking lot you have here," he sarcastically remarked to an audience of students at a West Hartford high school in 1985. "More nice cars in that lot than in half the city of Hartford." As the students fidgeted in their seats, Ned—invited to speak to encourage the students to volunteer and assist the poor—proceeded to attack the students for their class privilege and sense of entitlement. It did not go over well. "I feel like I had to defend myself," one student remarked. "He accuses us and is condescending." "His message is a guilt trip. He has no right to make me feel guilty. We're here to help."[43]

Ned wasn't cut out for the 1980s, a decade when many former activists who had come of age in the 1960s retreated to the suburbs, played the stock market, and went corporate. Others lost their minds. As greed became good, government bad, and the market the ultimate arbiter of value (and values), Ned's strident denunciations of Americans' worship of the "god of materialism," his message of communalism, and his efforts to awaken a spirit of social activism fell on deaf ears or, worse yet, were subject to mockery and derision. In Reagan's America, the idea of devoting a couple of hours a week, much less a year or more of one's life, to community service seemed both quaint and a waste of time and energy. Even those sympathetic to Ned's ideals and mission advised that he stop with all of his activism and agitation and instead get a *real* job. "I like Ned Coll," one former Corps volunteer commented. "But he should upgrade from the '60s and come into the '80s. The street activists of the '60s are now lawyers and journalists and working from within. He should, too."[44]

That ship had sailed long ago, perhaps on the day when Ned had quit his job at an insurance company, drained his bank account, and dedicated himself to fulfilling President Kennedy's vision for America, as his young mind understood it at the time. Now, twenty years later, a middle-aged Ned Coll was still working to build a more humane, involved citizenry, still fighting to make public officials more accountable to the public, and public places more public. He kept fighting, but it was clear that he was losing. If the 1970s saw America in retreat from the ideals of the "new frontier," the 1980s marked its complete and unequivocal repudiation of it. The America that elected (and reelected) Ronald Reagan as president also had little patience for the likes of Ned Coll. Admonishments—to do more for others, to stop acting with selfish disregard for the poor—that used to elicit moments of introspection or generate feelings of guilt now just pissed people off.

Ned continued to denounce elitism and issue threats of direct action against exclusionary practices. But the recipients of his attacks began to notice that Ned no longer followed through on his plans. In the mid-1980s, Ned announced plans to resume his assault on the state's privatized shoreline with plans to file a class-action lawsuit. "We are going to bring the shoreline question of public access, one way or the other, definitely into the courts this summer," he promised in May 1986.[45] These were idle threats. No lawsuit was filed. Local officials in shoreline towns increasingly paid him no mind. Locals along the shore began to refer to him in the past tense, "the guy who brought the black kids down here," as a sales clerk in the town of Niantic put it. "Whatever happened to Coll? You don't hear much about him any more."[46]

On the North End, Ned still retained the loyalty of mothers whose children he helped feed and educate and those whose lives he helped repair. People like Jimmy Martinez, a former heroin addict who, after serving fifteen months in jail, managed to get clean and became a field worker for Revitalization Corps. Kids like Gee and Cecil Lester, who were among the hundreds of children who came to Revitalization Corps's offices— for tutoring, for a meal, and, increasingly, for safety from the streets.[47] "[The address] 2550 [Main Street] was a place where you could go, it was safe, and you knew you was gonna get something to eat, and then there was just always the activities, something positive to [do]." For Jose Vasquez, who grew up in Stowe Village in the early 1980s, one of four children in a home beset by poverty, alcoholism, and abuse, Revitalization Corps and its white director offered refuge from an American society unabashed in its contempt for the poor. "At an early age as a child, I felt the rejection when I would go shopping at stores with my mother" and white customers looked in disgust as she counted her food stamps. "I felt inadequate. Especially around Caucasians. . . . But when I met Ned Coll, I didn't feel any of that. I felt loved."[48]

But love alone could not bring back jobs or repair the tattered remains of the welfare state. While Hartford's booming, prosperous suburbs enjoyed the fruits of federal and state investment and business relocation, its inner city bore the scars of decades of disinvestment, depopulation, demolition, and isolation. Throughout the 1980s, scores of the city's largest manufacturers and employers closed or relocated. By 1990, the city had shed over seventeen thousand manufacturing jobs over the previous two decades.[49] Due to the metro area's failure to build a public transportation infrastructure to accommodate the migration of people and jobs outside of the central city, new jobs in the suburbs remained out of reach for the urban poor. The city of Hartford was home to one-fifth of the total population of the greater Hartford metropolitan area but to 90 percent of the region's welfare recipients and two-thirds of its unemployed. It had one of the highest infant mortality rates of any city in the nation and the highest percentage of children living in hunger of any city in the United States. As the Reagan administration presided over draconian cuts to anti-poverty programs and aid to cities, officials in Hartford struggled to make up the difference and found little assistance from their suburban neighbors, which, thanks to the state's tradition of local autonomy in fiscal matters, enjoyed exclusive control over local tax revenues.[50] It was instead forced to rely on revenue from property taxes in a city in which roughly one-half of all property was exempt from taxation and from regressive sales taxes, a situation that inflicted a heavy burden on the city's poor. Prior to the state's adoption of an income tax in 1991, Connecticut had the highest sales tax of any state in the nation (8 percent) and imposed the fifth heaviest tax burden on its poor population. The city's public housing projects became sites of extreme poverty. By the early 1990s, over two-thirds of all adult males in Stowe Village were unemployed. Hartford's housing authority compounded the suffering of its tenants. It enforced steep fines for tenants who failed to keep the hallways outside of their apartments clean, and tenants often learned of such fines only after having traveled across town to the housing authority's offices on the city's south end to pay their rent. "If they didn't have the exact rent, if they had a fine for their hallway or something, [housing authority officials] wouldn't take the rent," one former Revitalization Corps volunteer recalls. "I couldn't believe what people had to go through."[51]

As rural and suburban Connecticut fortified barriers to its housing and job markets, the poverty rates in its three largest cities—Hartford, New Haven, and Bridgeport—soared, and the lives of the poor became more isolated and, to the state's sizable affluent white population, even more invisible. During the 1980s these three metro areas became—and remain—home to some of the highest concentrations of white affluence (defined as areas with at least 90 percent white population and median household income at least four times the federal poverty level) and racially concentrated poverty (defined as areas where less than one-half of the population is white and at least 40 percent live below the poverty line) in the nation. By the mid-1980s, 25 percent of Hartford's population lived below the poverty line. In Hartford's suburbs, by contrast, over 97 percent lived above the poverty line. In the Capitol Region as a whole, the city of Hartford constituted only 17.4 percent of the total population but 61.5 percent of its families living in poverty. Forty percent of all Hartford children lived in poverty.[52]

As rates of unemployment in the city's black and Latino neighborhoods skyrocketed, housing projects like Stowe Village became home to a thriving illicit drug trade. Morning, noon, and night, customers flocked to the housing project. "[White] people come . . . from out of town in their Subarus, at all hours," one Stowe Village mother remarked in disgust. Dealers enlisted young children as drug runners. "One of my friends, his older brother was one of the drug dealers, and what he was doing was if you had a bike, he would give you a brown paper bag . . . and he would ask you to ride it somewhere," Gee Lester remembers. "Depending on how far you ride, you would get twenty, fifty, or one hundred dollars." With the proceeds earned by transporting drugs on their bikes across town, kids as young as ten and eleven ditched Ned's "hand-me-downs" in favor of new Adidas sweatsuits and Nike sneakers and, as Gee remembers, ridiculed those children, like him, "who were [still] getting [their] clothes from . . . Ned." "That's the only way they can make money," Melissa Diaz, a sixteen-year-old Stowe Village resident explained. If they wanted a nice car, stylish clothes, jewelry—the visible signs of success in an America that was embracing conspicuous consumption and the ethos of acquisitive capitalism with a vengeance— "they don't got no other choice." Absent a massive jobs program that offered urban black and brown youth real wages and realistic prospects of upward mobility, the struggle to eradicate the drug trade was, some public officials conceded, bound to fail. "Once a young fellow gets his handful of money [selling drugs] . . . why is he going to work some hamburger joint for $4 an hour?" explained Nathanial Davis, director of public safety for the Hartford Housing Authority (HHA).[53]

"It was very dangerous," remembers Ralph Knighton, who grew up in Bellevue Square in the 1960s and returned to Hartford after college to work for the city. And nobody in charge, it seemed, was doing anything about it. "The housing authority people . . . didn't want to be bothered with that. It was just easier to put your eight hours in and go home. The same thing with the police," who seemed content to allow "the community to police itself."[54] Even as the nation's law enforcement publicly waged a war on drugs, police in Stowe Village, many believed, played an active role in the drug trade. "Kids would tell me about cops buying drugs and I'd believe them. . . . They did not feel like [the] police . . . [or] anybody had their back."[55]

North End residents implored city officials, law enforcement, and the housing authority officials to take action to combat the scourge of addiction and violence. "Stop giving these kids protection," begged Deloris Anderson, an African American mother of four who lived in a first-floor apartment in Stowe Village. "If the jail's too small, build more jails." Conditions had gotten so bad that Anderson pined for the law-and-order politics of her native Alabama. Down there, she said, "We don't play that mess. George Wallace should have been president. We wouldn't have this."[56] Stowe Village had become such a thriving, open market, and attracted buyers that ranged from businessmen in suits to suburban teenagers to homeless addicts, that when the commissioners of the Hartford Housing Authority pulled up to the front of the housing project in their government-issued cars for a monthly meeting with the tenants' association in the fall of 1986, they were greeted by a solicitous salesperson. "That was the last straw," Hartford Housing Authority chairwoman Curtissa Cofield promised. "Tenants had been complaining. After people tried to sell drugs to the commissioners, we couldn't pretend we didn't know about it, or didn't see it."[57] Afterward, the HHA began initiating eviction proceedings against families of people arrested on drug-related crimes. While the knee-jerk policy resulted in mothers and children being tossed out on the street, it did little to slow sales or even chasten dealers. When a group of twenty tenants, flanked by twelve police officers, led a march against drug peddling and violence through the dilapidated housing project in the summer of 1989, they were greeted with laughter and heckling from neighborhood dealers and runners. As the marchers chanted, "No more drugs," a group of teenagers chanted back, "More drugs, more drugs." In the middle of the procession, a young white man drove up to the front of the housing project and, seemingly oblivious to the heavy police presence that afternoon, attempted to make a purchase. As the *Hartford Courant* reported,

"Police put the out-of-town man in a cruiser and questioned him as the marchers filed past them."[58]

The city's drug epidemic touched every family. Two of Gee's cousins became addicted to heroin. Gee's mother, he recalls, "would sneak them into the house and give them shelter. She would feed them. Anything she could to help them; she always try to help them. . . . This guy would be laying in the street and she would go in her car and pick him up and bring him to our house." Revitalization Corps kept its doors open and its programs running, even as the number of older children and teenagers participating, and neighborhood mothers volunteering, dwindled.[59] The organization appeared to have reached its end when, in 1986, it was forced to vacate its offices on North Main Street and moved into another formerly vacant state-owned building on Holcomb Street, in a residential neighborhood outside of the heart of the North End.

In desperate need of a new beginning, Ned found it by way of a chance encounter at a Peace and Justice rally in the town of Norwalk in the spring of 1988. There, he met Leslie Hammond. From 1977 to 1984, Hammond had worked as a trader on Wall Street for Merrill Lynch, the fourth female member in the history of the New York Stock Exchange and first ever at her company. But after entering Alcoholics Anonymous in 1981, Hammond had grown increasingly disillusioned with Wall Street. "I saw for me that Wall Street was all about money and I just wanted to have a lot more value in my life." She walked away from her high-salaried position to take a job working for a nonprofit that delivered food to soup kitchens throughout the five boroughs of New York. But this, too, proved unsatisfying. "I always felt like [shelters and soup kitchens] were a band aid. Not that they weren't important," but it mainly consisted of "white, middle class [people] helping . . . but not really empowering." Leaving the city, she enrolled in Yale Divinity School with the intention of becoming an Episcopal priest. When Hammond first met Ned, as she later recalled, "I was immediately attracted to that energy." He struck her as someone who "was really trying to empower people. Help them, but also empower them."[60] After finishing divinity school, she began working for Revitalization Corps. In 1990, Ned and Leslie married.

That same year, bullets from gunfire exchanged between rival gangs fatally hit fifteen-year-old Coretta Pratt as she stood in front of her Stowe Village apartment. Pratt's death enraged Ned to a degree few had ever encountered before and led him to embark on a protest campaign unprecedented in its level of provocation and potential for danger. "In twenty-five years working in the North End, I've never seen anything like it," Ned remarked, feet from the chalk outline of where Pratt was gunned down. "Poverty? Sure, that's always been here. But the drugs. Everything is so wide open. They don't even try to hide it anymore." Both city officials and the executives in suits who rushed to and from downtown office towers every weekday seemed content to simply keep the drug situation contained. "These are the people least able to defend themselves," Ned raged. "But who do you think cares? Look, we're a mile from those big insurance giants who are paying for the effects of what goes on here. People who should be ashamed of themselves that all this is going on—and they're not lifting a finger to stop it."[61]

"I was a little pissed off," Ned, in a rare moment of understatement, later remarked, "because I've been tutoring these kids, and here these cats start moving in. . . . And the cops had to be looking the other way for that kind of shit to be going on wide open. Yuppies were coming in from downtown into that project to buy their drugs for the weekend. They'd go in, and it'd be like a drive [thru]. It was wide open." Worse yet, it seemed to Ned as if the people of Stowe Village had also given up and handed over control of their neighborhood to the drug traffickers. "What gets me is that everyone—even people here—think there's nothing that can be done."[62]

What Ned couldn't see—and failed to understand—was the quiet, heroic work being done by the tenants inside the project. In the face of unending violence and despair, where children went to sleep to the sounds of gunshots every night and walked past junkies and stepped on broken vials and used needles on their way to school each morning, Stowe Village tenants mobilized and organized to improve conditions from within. The tenants' association appointed building captains for each of Stowe Village's three-story complexes and placed them in charge of improving living conditions and facilitating greater participation in community life and activities among the neighbors. In the previous two

years, residents had launched fifteen social service and recreation programs. They had launched a daily after-school clean-up program involving over fifty children. Almost all of these local leaders were working
women caring for multiple children. In between working four different
part-time jobs, tenant Jewell Allen led cooking classes and coached a
girls' drill team at Stowe Village. Many of the women had lived much
if not all of their lives in Stowe Village. To them, it was home, it was a
community, and it was worth saving. "I love the people here, the kids,"
twenty-six-year-old building captain Gwen Morgan said. "I want to
help the kids. I feel I owe them something. I got so much out of Stowe
Village growing up here." The tenants' efforts included combating the
scourge of drug violence and addiction. In this, they carried out their
work in spite of the constant threat of retaliation.[63]

"If people really knew what kind of guts [it takes], and what these
women have to deal with in order to just stand up [to dealers]," HHA
director John Wardlaw commented, "they would be totally surprised."
Tenant organizers and council members pursued their own strategies for
minimizing the damage drug trafficking inflicted on families and children. Months after the city arrested one of the project's leading "king-
pins," another group emerged and assumed control over the drug trade.
Deals took place in broad daylight, often within eyeshot of seemingly
indifferent police officers. One reporter described witnessing a steady
stream of high-end automobiles, many with out-of-state license plates,
pull up to Stowe Village's makeshift drive-thru (dubbed "McDrugs"),
place their order, procure their product, and drive off while less than
two hundred feet away two police officers stood watch over two utility
workers. They were trying, one exacerbated building captain claimed,
but they were not fools. "I'm not going to get on camera and say, 'Last
week I snitched.' "[64] Black tenants drew on a lifetime of experience with
violent, corrupt cops and a racist criminal justice system in adopting
strategies of survival and modes of resistance—to traffickers and law
enforcement alike—in what outside observers glibly called a war zone.

All Ned saw, though, was a neighborhood that had lost hope and
a tenants' association that was, he was convinced, complicit in the project's thriving drug market. Energized and enraged, Ned decided it was
up to him—and only him—to be Stowe Village's savior. One afternoon

in the spring of 1990, he sauntered up to the front of the housing project, the principal site of transactions, holding a sign that read, "Drug Store's Closed" and carrying a notebook where he dutifully wrote down the license plate numbers of every one of the steady stream of cars that rolled up and consummated a deal. There he remained each day for weeks on end, sitting on a folding chair under a large umbrella, like someone camped out for a parade, as the procession of buyers came—and, once they caught sight of him, sped off. "He would all of a sudden go in buildings" as drug deals were taking place "and disrupt everything," Jose Vasquez remembers. "He was not playing. He'd get in people's faces in a minute."[65]

The reaction among neighborhood residents—all of whom knew Ned, many of whom had received tutoring lessons from him or, as children, had traveled to the beach on a Corps bus—was mixed, ranging

Ned Coll's highly provocative protests against drug trafficking in Hartford's public housing projects bitterly divided residents of the city's North End. *Copyright © 1764–2017. Hartford Courant. Photo: Sherwin Williams. Used with permission.*

from amazement, admiration, and fear for Ned's safety to anger and resentment at his tactics and dismissive attitude toward local leaders. "I finally got a night's sleep," Stowe Village resident Alfredo Rodriguez told a reporter. "The man's got guts."[66] Earlie Powell tried to dissuade him from confronting drug dealers in such a brazen fashion. "I said, 'Ned, Ned, you need to stop. Ned, it's too much.'"[67] "When Ned went to Stowe Village," Gee recalls, "I said, 'Man, they're gonna kill Ned.'" So did Vasquez. "I thought they [were] going to kill him." On one occasion, a dealer approached Ned's daughter Elizabeth, then in high school, as she walked the family's dog through the project. "He came up to us . . . and said to me, 'You better get your dad out of here, or I'm going to cut all of your dog's legs off with this machete,' and showed me the machete."[68]

Ned dismissed these as idle threats. He knew a lot of these kids who now threatened to do him harm. They were just little "punks." Besides, he hadn't come there to attack them so much as to shame and embarrass the HHA and local tenants' association for their perceived inaction. Within days, though, tenants began counterprotesting him and telling reporters that he had no clue what challenges residents faced and what measures they took, each day, to combat drug dealers and improve living conditions. As they implored Ned to go away, he shouted back, "Get out here and do something and help me."[69]

Ned's rude, condescending, accusatory manner toward members of the tenants' association enraged area residents. These working mothers, John Wardlaw fumed, "are doing things far beyond what is expected. . . . [Ned] totally disrespected the acts on the part of the minority women who are women, mothers, fathers, teachers and crime preventers. . . . Their leadership should be respected." "In the '60s, [Ned's] approach would work," HHA public safety director Nat Davis commented. "But today, you must involve the tenants." Instead, Ned ignored them. "He ignored the fact that we existed," Gwen Morgan commented. He presumed to know what was best for the poor and fashioned himself as the only person capable of saving them from themselves. "This ain't no plantation," Lucinda Thomas, the executive director of the Hartford Tenants' Rights Federation, responded. "If he can't work with us," Morgan added, "we don't need him." Several parents pulled their children out of Revitalization Corps's tutoring program in protest.[70] Ned "was

a very brave man" to go after drug trafficking in such a brazen manner, Ralph Knighton remarked. "But the fact of the matter is you're not
going to get the support because . . . those drug dollars were paying
people's rent. It was putting food on people's table. And many young
people didn't have any alternatives. They couldn't [find] work. Some of
them [didn't] know how to read and write. There were a lot of variables
that contributed to the drug trade becoming institutionalized in public
housing."[71]

If Ned seemed blind to the structural forces behind the crisis, the
local media were even more so. Local news reporters descended on
Stowe Village to cover Ned's protest but not the conditions that had fueled the rise of drug trafficking. "I [tried] to help one of those TV people
see some of the problems, like the hallways and the conditions the kids
had to live with," Leslie Hammond recalls. But "they didn't care about
that. They [only] wanted to hear about the drama between Ned and the
housing authority. . . . They loved the conflict."[72]

There was plenty of that. In mid-May, the tenants' association held
an open meeting with Ned and members of the community. Tenants'
board president Mamie Bell, who had campaigned to end drug trafficking in Stowe Village for years (her slogan: "Stowe Village, Not Drug
Village") but who was now on the receiving end of Ned's attacks, might
have thought the meeting would defuse growing tensions between Ned
and the board. She was wrong. The first person to speak that evening
was Brian Robinson of the Nation of Islam. Robinson implored the
group of thirty black tenants in the audience to stop fighting among
themselves and then denounced Ned and other white people who, he
said, didn't belong in the projects. With that, Ned shot out of his seat.
Waving his arms, with a crazed look in his eyes, he rushed toward the
podium, shouting at Robinson. "Hey, jerko! Where have you been?"
Within seconds and before Ned had a chance to take a swing at him,
the bow-tie-and-white-suit-attired Fruit of Islam surrounded Robinson
and ushered him out of the room. Ned redirected his fury at Bell, seated
in the first row. That's when things really got out of hand. As a man who
had secured his first job thanks to Revitalization Corps tried to restrain
him, Ned issued a string of obscenities and, witnesses alleged, racist and
sexist epithets directed at Bell and another female board member, Linda

Spenser. Though accounts afterward differed, Spencer claimed Ned called her a "black bitch." Gwen Morgan also alleged that in the fracas, Ned punched her. Within minutes, police arrived on the scene. Ned was arrested and charged with third-degree assault, inciting a riot, and breach of peace. Leslie Hammond accompanied Ned to the meeting and, with tears streaming down her face, watched as he was handcuffed and thrown into a squad car. Word quickly spread throughout the housing project and, before long, the entire North End, of Ned's words and actions.[73]

Ned vowed to return to the corner of Hampton and Kensington Streets (where Stowe Village was located) the following day. And he did. Hundreds of tenants streamed out of their apartments to protest drug violence *and* Ned. Dozens of children stood across the street, "carry[ing] signs protesting drugs and Coll's presence." They chanted, "Go home, Ned. Go home." Ned planted his thumbs in his ears and waved his fingers. Dozens of police officers attempted to keep matters under control. John Wardlaw begged Ned to leave. "Ned, these people are trying as hard as they possibly can. . . . They are trying to help themselves." And, he added, "They do not want you coming in here and taking over the leadership." Ned just shouted and shook his finger in Wardlaw's face, calling him and his associates at the HHA "jackasses" and "jerkos." Eventually, the longtime HHA director walked away, shaking his head in disgust. Rather than consider Wardlaw's suggestion, Ned vowed to never work with local tenant leaders, whom he disparaged as a "group of thugs." With that, Mamie Bell had had enough and feared that, as Ned continued to escalate his rhetoric, the situation could quickly descend into violence. "This is our project," she shouted. "Give us our due respect."[74]

And get out. Sheriffs served Ned with a restraining order on the street corner and physically removed him from the scene. This, Ned yelled to onlookers, was proof "they don't really want to stop the drugs." The following morning, Bell and a group of tenants were in the office of Hartford mayor Carrie Saxon Perry. "Ned Coll has disrupted our community. All we would like is to work together." "No one is against what Ned stands for," Nat Davis stressed.[75]

"Has Ned Coll flipped out?," longtime *Courant* columnist Tom Condon asked in the paper the following morning. To many readers, the question seemed rhetorical. The more pressing question was, would the North End turn on him? Had he alienated himself from the people who had stood by him? Years earlier, as Ned had struggled with his health and struggled to remain relevant, North End resident Spencer Todd had said, "Like everyone else, Ned needs love, and people to stand up for him. He gets plenty of that around here." Would he still?[76]

On that afternoon, at least, most of the people gathered on the corner of Hampton and Kensington just seemed sad and confused. Tenant Valerie Powell, one of dozens—perhaps hundreds—out on the street that day who had taken part in Revitalization Corps programs as a child, simply shook her head and said, "That's not the Ned Coll we knew years ago." In the years to come, he would drift even further from his earlier life and embark on the last, and strangest, leg of his journey, while someone else would pick up the cause of open beaches and score a remarkable legal victory.[77]

TEN

Welcome to Greenwich!

During the 1980s, Americans became less concerned with guaranteeing access to the beach and more fixated on the elusive dream of owning a piece of it themselves. This was all the better since, thanks to a series of pivotal Supreme Court decisions handed down at decade's end, access to the nation's developed shorelines seemed more elusive than ever. In *Nollan v. California Coastal Commission* (1987), the U.S. Supreme Court ruled in favor of a town beachfront homeowner who had resisted the state of California's attempt to carve a path to the Pacific coast across his property. The case concerned the extent to which the state's coastal authority, charged with ensuring the public's right to the foreshore, could force beachfront homeowners to provide easements across their property. In a 5–4 decision, the court held that when it came to beach access, property rights trumped the public interest. If California wanted to provide an easement across a beachfront homeowner's lot, it had to compensate the owner.[1]

"Hallelujah!" Madison resident Bonny Risbridger exclaimed upon hearing the news. To Risbridger and her neighbors, the ruling seemed to offer their private beach community an additional layer of protection from the threat of an invasion of the hoi polloi. Henceforth, her husband, Robert, added, members of the Seaview Beach Association need not worry about "the intrusion of the public" onto their beach.[2]

263

Four years later the U.S. Supreme Court scored another victory for beachfront property owners when it ruled in favor of real estate developer David Lucas, who had sued the state of South Carolina's coastal commission over its enforcement of a statute that prohibited him from building houses on two oceanfront lots; Lucas argued that the regulation constituted a taking of property under the Fifth Amendment. The lots in question were located dangerously close to the sea. As recently as 1968, both had been entirely submerged offshore; two years prior to the Supreme Court's decision Hurricane Hugo had inundated both lots under four-foot-deep floodwaters. Giving states the tools to prevent housing construction in such mercurial, ecologically sensitive, and flood-prone coastal areas had been the guiding principle of the federal CZMA. But in *Lucas v. South Carolina Coastal Commission,* even these modest measures seemed under attack. Though the court's decision was not as sweeping as property rights proponents had hoped—and conservationists had feared—it nevertheless seemed to endorse the legal argument that legislative attempts to place limits on the use of coastal properties and protect the public's interest in beach access and protection constituted a "regulatory taking" that required compensation. Given the value of beachfront property, this legal doctrine threatened to halt states' efforts to manage coastal land use and have a chilling effect on efforts to pass legislation in the future.[3]

While the decisions empowered coastal developers to challenge the authority of environmental regulators and emboldened beachfront homeowners to employ more aggressive forms of exclusion, they sent a clear message to the American public that the beach did not belong to it. This land was *their* land. The only glimpse the average American would get of the gilded sands of America's most exclusive beachfront properties would come courtesy of the wildly popular television show *Lifestyles of the Rich and Famous.*

During the 1980s, Connecticut rapidly ascended the ranks of the most unequal states in terms of household income and wealth in America. Between 1980 and 2012, no other state experienced a greater increase in the income gap between the top fifth and bottom fifth of its population.[4] Land-use policies and practices continued to augment social policies and reflect the state's values and priorities. The state ranked forty-ninth out of fifty in total amount of public land per capita.[5] When it came to building wealth and isolating the poor, Connecticut was without equal. By the early 1990s it held the title as the nation's wealthiest state in per capita income as well as the most economically segregated. (It was the ninth most racially segregated state.) Much of this inequality could be attributed to exclusionary local zoning ordinances, which, one legal scholar commented, "created an imbalance between the housing needs of low-income, urban minorities and the housing opportunities of their more affluent, white, suburban neighbors."[6]

Residents-only beaches helped to enhance the Gold Coast's exorbitant real estate market and reinforce barriers to affordable housing. In Greenwich, real estate agents habitually drove past the entrance to Greenwich Point Park and explained to prospective homeowners who *could* and *could not* use the beach. Keeping nonresidents off its public beach became emblematic of Greenwich's cultural identity, a marketable feature that spoke volumes about the town's overall disposition toward those who didn't belong there. Residents maintained a high degree of vigilance in policing its public spaces and ferreting out persons who didn't fit the appearance of a typical Greenwich resident. Following a ferry trip to Greenwich's Island Beach in 1990, resident Edgar D. Gates penned an angry letter to the *Greenwich Time* denouncing town officials for their seeming failure to enforce local ordinances. Gates based his conclusion on the "disproportionate number of [fellow] passengers who speak only in foreign languages" and the "several Hispanic families" he observed disembarking from the ferry afterward. "On some days at Island Beach, and even at Greenwich Point," he fumed, "the population resembles and sounds like a random sample of the visitors to the annual 'Sidewalk Sales,'" referring to a local event that drew the *rabble* to town. "It makes one wonder if our system is working according to plan." Ironically, few of the families of high-level corporate executives who moved to Greenwich in the 1980s would ever step foot on the town's beaches or any of its other public gathering spaces. Fewer still would enroll their children in the town's public school system. Their social lives revolved around country and yacht clubs, and their swimming and sunbathing was conducted strictly on private sands. Lucas Point, the beach association adjacent to Greenwich Point Park, enjoyed the exclusive use of its own private beach just down the shore.[7]

In the seventy-plus years since the state's General Assembly had passed a special act in 1919 authorizing the creation of a parks system for its residents, Greenwich had evaded any legal challenge to its beach access policies. The town's deep pockets and high-powered legal team had scared off all would-be litigants. It had, that is, until one spring afternoon in 1994, when a guard posted at the gates of Greenwich Point Park leapt out of his booth and ordered a pair of joggers to "Halt!" That winter, Stamford resident and Rutgers law student Brenden Leydon and a friend had begun running a route through Stamford and onto Tod's Point and back. But the first time the pair went on a jog after the town began stationing a guard in the spring, the two nonresidents were stopped, interrogated, and ordered to leave.[8] "At that point," Leydon recalled, "I thought it was kind of a dumb law but assumed if they were doing it, they could do it, and just found another jogging route."[9]

That fall, Leydon enrolled in a constitutional litigation clinic at Rutgers and began working on the case of Hwilda Barkawi, a Muslim woman who in 1993 had been ordered to leave a park in the borough of Haledon, New Jersey, after a resident had complained. Officers said it was because she was not a resident. When she returned the following day with her children, she was issued a $200 fine and a summons.[10] As he worked on the case, which ultimately was resolved in Barkawi's favor in 1998, Leydon came to appreciate the parallels between the New Jersey town's exclusionary practices and Greenwich's. "I started learning that what they were doing was absolutely illegal." And it fit a pattern common among wealthier enclaves located near towns and cities with large numbers of poor and people of color. "It's just wrong," he thought.[11]

The following spring, Leydon became the first person to ever file a lawsuit against the town of Greenwich over its beach access policy, setting the stage for what would ultimately become the last round in the town's long struggle to keep the general public off its public beach and the last stand in its defense of the state's sand curtain.

Greenwich Point Park offers the only unobstructed view of the Manhattan skyline anywhere in the state of Connecticut. Like the city that
towered in its distance, the town's public beach seemed to continually
generate a high degree of tension and anxiety among its users. Highly
caffeinated mothers in oversized SUVs jockeyed for parking spots.
Neighbors in the Lucas Point Association fretted over the high volume
of traffic and complained about the noise; some posted terse signs in
front of their million-dollar homes warning that any car that dared park
in front of their houses would be towed. The guard posted at the gates
learned to be vigilant in detecting intruders, whether they came bearing a borrowed pass or stowed away in someone's trunk. The people of
Greenwich did whatever it took, and went to any lengths, to manufac-
ture that elusive idyllic setting, including the use of eighteenth-century
artillery. To rid itself of Canadian geese, which took up residence along
the town's shore in 1986, the town hauled out a cannon and proceeded
to fire a series of blank shots at the flocks. "The booms," the *Wall Street
Journal* noted, "failed to budge the birds from some of America's choicest real estate." Next, they lined portions of the shore with electric fences,
traditionally used by livestock farmers on cattle, with the hope that a
few high-voltage shocks would send the geese a clear message that their
presence was not welcome. "We think of it as a behavior-modification
program," the town's chief of beaches and marinas explained. The geese
chose to stay.[12]

Greenwich's wealthiest families, in contrast, retreated to one of the
dozens of country and yacht clubs, each occupying varying degrees of
status and exclusivity. "You don't see many of the old Greenwich families down here anymore," one longtime user of the town's beach told a
reporter.[13] Or the new families. Instead, you saw the families of small
business owners, office managers, chefs, police officers, firefighters, and
schoolteachers. You might also find the children of domestic servants
and workers in the town's service industries, a disproportionate number
of them African American and Latino. Or some of the residents of the
town's 860 units of public housing, also overwhelmingly black and Latino.
While many of the folks found on the town beach on any given summer
afternoon enjoyed a degree of privilege few outside of Fairfield County
could scarcely imagine, many others lived in Greenwich to service the

luxurious needs of its upper class. Some went to work through the back entrance of country clubs, where they spent long, backbreaking days furnishing drinks and meals for club members and suffered with a smile the daily barrage of petty insults and capricious demands that flew from the mouths of drunken white male executives, haughty housewives, and pampered teenagers. On summer days the parents and children of Greenwich's "blue-collar" families "used the town beaches and other recreational centers as our only real diversion" and were acutely aware of their own exclusion from the town's private clubs.[14]

Throughout the 1980s, as the town grew wealthier and the wealthy retreated from public spaces (no matter how narrow "the public" was defined), the town beach became, in effect, the de facto country club for those residents who could not afford—or possess the right credentials, including skin color—to become members of a country club. As such, residents came to view their tax dollars as akin to membership dues, payment of which entitled their contributors to the exclusive use of those facilities they paid to support. Justifying the exclusion of non-residents on these grounds required town officials to also claim that its beach was wholly supported by local tax dollars.

Local officials continued to make a show of rejecting aid from Washington or Hartford and trumpeting its fiscal independence. Such was the case in the aftermath of a nor'easter that pummeled the state's western coast with hurricane-strength winds in December 1992, resulting in six deaths, scores of injuries, and hundreds of millions of dollars in property damage. The storm left behind a trail of devastation: over 12,000 homes severely damaged or destroyed (3,460 in Connecticut), massive beach erosion, and shattered sea walls. Barriers that had been built to delineate property boundaries and keep the public out were strewn across front yards, reduced to rubble, or simply washed out to sea. Nature, once again, had spoken. Along the Northeastern corridor, however, most municipalities were too busy begging federal and state officials for disaster relief to hear. Congress quickly responded with federal disaster aid to help communities rebuild mangled shorelines and refortify beachfront properties.

Greenwich, which suffered some of the storm's heaviest damage, would have none of it. Town officials proudly refused a $250,000 FEMA grant to repair and restore its badly damaged shoreline because it contained a provision that, town attorneys concluded, would have required it to allow access to the general public. "We have had this posture for 80 years or so," First Selectman John B. Margenot Jr. told reporters, "and if there were any possibility of there being jeopardy to our independence, we would eschew applying for Federal funds." "That would be a typical Greenwich answer," the director of the American Littoral Society, D. W. Bennett, said in response. "None of these fancy towns want the crowds. They want the beach, but they want it to themselves."[15]

Contrary to its public claims, Greenwich officials wanted the federal and state dollars, too. Over the years, Greenwich had quietly but doggedly solicited federal and state funds for a whole host of improvements to the town's beach. Since the 1970s it had benefitted, both directly and indirectly, from the EPA's multi-billion-dollar project to reduce pollution levels in Long Island Sound. It had received $42 million for the improvement of the town's sewer treatment plant, which included the extension of sewer lines to the beach. It had solicited state funds to improve the water quality of a pond on the park grounds. Indeed, Greenwich never missed an opportunity to seize outside funds or benefit from federal and state projects, even as it made a show of rejecting federal or state funding, no matter how trivial the amount, that had strings attached.[16]

Preserving the beach's residents-only status and the sense of privilege it conferred on its users helped obscure the town's stark wealth divide and assuage, if only temporarily, the anxieties of its shrinking middle class. Between 1984 and 1986, the average price of a three-bedroom, two-bathroom house in Greenwich increased at a rate of 34 percent annually.[17] By 1990, more than one-half of the town's homes were assessed at more than $500,000; just ninety-six homes in the entire city were valued at less than $100,000.[18] The high demand for properties led many middle-class homeowners to sell their comparatively modest homes to developers and relocate to less expensive neighboring towns. New entrants into Greenwich's labor market, meanwhile, found themselves unable to live in the town where they worked. In the early 1980s Greenwich dropped out of practical necessity its residency requirement for public employees. By 1988 over 50 percent of its schoolteachers, 60 percent of its hospital workers, and 48 percent of its police force lived outside of Greenwich. The town continually struggled to fill positions such as postmaster and head librarian that, whether by law or custom, demanded local residency.[19]

While it resisted measures that would have expanded the availability of less expensive housing, Greenwich remained committed to protecting those privileges conferred by residency in one of the nation's wealthiest municipalities. It had spent decades preparing for the day when someone would formally challenge its exclusionary public beach ordinance. That day came in April 1995, when Brenden Leydon filed suit in State Superior Court in Stamford over his denial of entry into Greenwich Point Park the previous summer. Leydon adopted a two-pronged attack on Greenwich's residents-only ordinance. First, he claimed that the law violated the public trust doctrine, not only because it denied the general public the right to access the wet sand portion of the beach, but also because any park, like any street or sidewalk, is dedicated for public use and cannot be restricted to a certain class of citizens. Second, he argued that the law also violated the public's right to free speech as protected under the U.S. and Connecticut state constitutions. Under Connecticut's state constitution, the government must justify any restriction on access to public space by demonstrating that activity on it would be incompatible with the intended purpose of the property.[20]

Leydon had, in the truest sense, only the law on his side. Still in law school, he leaned on the advice of his law professors to build his case, prepared for court in between studying for the bar exam, and paid for all expenses out of pocket. In contrast, Greenwich hired one of the state's most prominent attorneys, Ralph Elliot, who had led the defense team in the CCLU's aborted 1975 lawsuit. A pair of attorneys who lived in Greenwich and were managing partners at a New York City firm formed the Greenwich Point Preservation Association and raised hundreds of thousands of dollars for the legal effort. Throughout the spring, members distributed pamphlets in the downtown area. Later that summer, they began canvassing the beach to mobilize support. The town's legal team also tried to recruit other shoreline towns to join in its defense, as Greenwich had done for Fairfield when that town had faced the prospect of a lawsuit in the mid-1970s. All of them declined. Greenwich was on its own.[21]

Leydon's lawsuit generated national headlines. The case had all the makings of a David-versus-Goliath legal battle and came on the heels of a series of ugly racist incidents in the town. The previous summer, tensions between Greenwich's African American community and police had reached a boiling point after officers apprehended a white and a black teenager who were setting off fireworks in the Armstrong Court housing project.[22] Officers released the white youth to his parents while placing the black youth in jail. The incident prompted African American community leaders to accuse the town of racial bias and ultimately forced the U.S. Justice Department to intervene in mediating the dispute.

Weeks after Leydon filed his lawsuit, Greenwich's public high school was rocked by a racist scandal after it was learned that five white male seniors had successfully encoded the words "Kill All Niggers" in the school's yearbook. The message, embedded in the students' photo captions, had gone undetected until one of them bragged to friends about it. The black student body was devastated. "How are my kids going to feel when I show them my yearbook and they see how these people felt about us?" graduating senior Keyshe Ruperto asked reporters.[23] School officials scrambled to retrieve and destroy the fourteen hundred copies that had already been distributed to students and parents. The students were suspended and not allowed to receive their diplomas at commencement that spring but were ultimately allowed to graduate after undergoing what school officials called a summer racial sensitivity "boot camp" run by the former chairman of the Congress of Racial Equality (CORE) Roy Innis.[24]

Black residents expressed disgust at the light punishment for what amounted to a hate crime and the students' refusal to publicly acknowledge or apologize for their actions. "I came to this part of the country more than 40 years ago to escape these kinds of episodes," Milton Waddell, chairman of Greenwich's First Baptist Church, fumed. "I'm just stunned and shocked by all of this, though it doesn't surprise me because this is something that's been happening in Greenwich for a long time." Racism "has always been there," one longtime black resident said of Greenwich, "sometimes in subtle ways and other times—such as with this incident—in more overt ways."[25]

Indeed, the subtlety of the act seemed to typify the experience of racism in Greenwich and upper-class towns in the Northeast more generally. The Reverend Brenda J. Stiers, the executive minister of the Riverside Church of Christ in Manhattan and a Greenwich resident, called the hidden message in the school yearbook "a perfect metaphor for the town of Greenwich—like the hidden racism that is symbolized by the closed clubs and housing." It forced people, she added, to "slowly, painfully [see] that we are not this perfect little town after all."[26]

Many residents, however, were in no mood for soul searching. "They're kids. They made a mistake. They took their feelings a little too far. I don't think they should be arrested or held back from graduation," claimed Charlene Belmont, an office manager who lived in the middle-class neighborhood of Cos Cob, where the families of two of the suspended students also resided. In defending the light punishment, the superintendent of the Greenwich public schools whined that because of the negative publicity the incident had generated, "these students and their families have already paid a heavy price. They have achieved a degree of notoriety, hatred and ostracism that I would wish on no one."[27]

For Greenwich, the negative publicity continued into the summer. Over the Fourth of July holiday, the social activist and provocateur Michael Moore staged an "invasion" of Greenwich's public beach for his nationally televised FOX show *TV Nation*. In less than ten minutes of airtime, Moore encapsulated the issues and perspectives that framed Leydon's lawsuit and the decades of unrest that had preceded it. The skit begins on a basketball court in Harlem, on what comedian and *TV Nation* reporter Janeane Garofalo describes as "an excruciatingly hot day in New York City." Deciding they "had as much right to cool off at Greenwich's beach as anyone else," Garofalo and a multi-racial group of New Yorkers board a bus and head out of the city. The scene then shifts to the beach in Greenwich, where a blonde-haired, college-age woman struggles to justify the town's residents-only stance. "It should just be for Greenwich residents," she explains, "since we are the ones paying taxes on it, and living here is kind of a privilege and it ensures kinda our safety since we know only Greenwich residents are coming here."

To the charge that racism drove this policy, a white liquor store shop-keeper says, "How are they discriminating? People hired the minority to work in their home, who are very close. I mean, you can't be any closer."[28] Right?

For Garofalo and her busload of companions, the closest they would get to the beach by land was the front entrance gate. After being denied entry, the group is next shown aboard a tugboat—the stars and stripes flapping in the wind, Wagner's "Ride of the Valkyries" in the air—barreling toward the beach. One mile off shore, they climb into dinghies and begin rowing toward their destination. After a Greenwich police boat, flanked by the U.S. Coast Guard, surrounds the fleet, Garofalo leaps into the water and swims the rest of the way. On the beach, a crowd gathers. Garofalo swims ashore, introduces herself, and cheekily tells the assembled crowd that she's "come to enjoy your lovely beaches for the day." A blonde-haired, middle-aged man in a white polo shirt and tan khakis stammers, "If you like the lovely beach, why don't you buy some property in Greenwich, pay taxes, and come here and enjoy it?" A confused and distraught teenage girl asks, "Why do you have to do this on, um, our holiday?" Gesturing to fellow beachgoers, she adds, "All these people, our taxes are going . . . to this!" An older man asks why the police haven't come and arrested the trespassers yet. Gesturing wildly and jabbing his finger in Garofalo's face, the polo-shirted, self-appointed spokesman repeats, "You can just buy a piece of property and come in and live here." "With that kind of friendly attitude, I'd love to live here!" Garofalo deadpans. As she walks off the beach, wet and dejected, the crowd serenades her with jeers. A mother with her child by her side shoos Garofalo away as one would a fly at a picnic, shouting, "Go! Go! Go!"[29]

Leydon's lawsuit had put everyone in Greenwich in a foul mood, especially those who actually frequented the beach and who bristled at the press's caricature of them as being "elite." Given the town's high curve, this is understandable. Many of the people found on the beach any given summer afternoon did not belong to a country club. They likely sent their kids to public schools. Every day, they were reminded, in ways both subtle and overt, that they were *not* elite and did not belong to Greenwich's upper crust. For years, the beach had seemed to provide the town's working- and middle-class families an illusion of privilege. It was one of the few gathering places in town that obscured, rather than accentuated, the town's sharp class distinctions. To preserve its exclusivity, Greenwich stressed the beach's inclusiveness. "The wealthy people," Ralph Elliot stressed, "don't go to the beach."[30] "Contrary to what is being said, this isn't an issue that affects the wealthy, because they don't use Greenwich Point, they go to country clubs," the head of the Greenwich Point Preservation Association explained. "This is an issue that affects average, working Greenwich residents."[31] "I was born and raised here and I certainly wasn't raised with money," one resident fumed.[32]

From the outset, Leydon made it clear that his case against Greenwich was about more than a beach. It was about the wider disparities in income and opportunity between working- and upper-class Americans, the segregation of the rich and isolation of the poor. "Discriminatory access policies for public parks and beaches are completely contrary to the noble principles upon which this *nation* was founded." He bemoaned "the growing trend toward gated communities walled off from interaction with the rest of the common folk," calling it "anathema to what our nation is all about." And he called attention to the parasitic relationship between wealthy suburban enclaves and struggling cities and the fictions that sustained it. In response to those who argued that local taxpayers should get to decide who uses their beach, he said, "Everyone pays taxes. The tax rates in our urban areas are generally far higher than the rates in wealthy suburbs, but it is generally the wealthy suburbs who are screaming to keep inner-city dwellers off their precious turf. These same suburbanites don't hesitate to take advantage of urban areas when it suits them, for work or cultural activities. But when the city folk want to have a barbeque in their local park, somehow a national crisis has erupted."[33] Make no mistake, this case wasn't about fiscal priorities, or, as town officials argued, the protection of a fragile environmental resource. "It is an issue of elitism, classism and racism all rolled into one."[34]

Decades earlier, it was Ned Coll who was leveling such biting critiques at Gold Coast society. Now, it was Leydon who had become its most despised adversary, "the sand," as one commentator described, "in Greenwich's Top-Siders." Barely a week went by without some resident penning a bitter denunciation of the young attorney in the local newspaper. Like Ned, they said, Leydon was merely seeking publicity for him-self. "Everyone feels this is such a special little haven, and why should one guy, a law student with something to prove, come in and ruin it?" one resident complained. "Please, no lectures on freedom of speech. . . . Most of us know that he chose Greenwich to make a name for himself because of the Greenwich stereotype," another added. Leydon began receiving anonymous hate mail—always, he later joked, written "with good grammar"—and angry phone calls at his Stamford office. A note from a person calling himself an "Old Greenwich W[orld] W[ar] II Vet, RTM [Representative Town Meeting member], Churchgoer, Taxpayer [and] ex-Vol[unteer] Fireman" simply said, "*You* are an over-idealistic, self-important, naïve, attention-seeking asshole." He seemed shocked at "the degree of hostility that has been directed at me . . . since I started this." But he was under no illusions as to the source of locals' anxiety. "Since I filed the suit, I have had a number of Greenwich residents tell me they wouldn't particularly care if I came in, but it was who would want to come in behind me that they would be worried about." This, Leydon surmised, was a subtle reference to the comparatively large black and brown populations in the neighboring towns of Stamford and Port Chester, as well as New York City. One anonymous writer told Leydon that by pursuing open beaches, "You're affecting my kids' safety."[35]

In February 1998, the trial began in Stamford Superior Court. One of the first witnesses Leydon called to testify: Ned Coll.

While Leydon was channeling the spirit of Ned Coll, his predecessor in the fight for open beaches was on a spiritual journey that had taken him far from his roots and, many worried, far from the realm of reality. Following his arrest at Stowe Village in the spring of 1990, Ned had re-treated to his cabin in Barkhamsted. Barred from entering the housing projects by judicial order, ostracized by the community who had once supported him, he sank into a deep funk. He stopped taking the medi-cation to treat his epilepsy. While sitting at home on Pentecost Sunday 1990, he had what he characterized as a "mystical experience." Images of violence and fear flashed through his mind. "I saw events going on in this nation, good and bad, and the calling was [that] God was livid at this nation, and the thing he seemed most concerned about was our greed." He saw the Virgin Mary. The conduit for these visions—the unplugged television set in his living room—was, God told him, the culprit. Television and advertising were destroying the country, numbing its population into complacency.[36]

At that moment, Revitalization Corps became God Activism, and Ned, a prophet. He started wearing long strings of rosary beads and a large wooden crucifix that hung down to his knees. That fall, he began showing up in towns throughout Connecticut, wearing a sandwich board covered in various religious messages and Bible passages and handing out copies of his manifesto. In New London, he built a small shrine to the Virgin Mary on a downtown sidewalk, where he recited the rosary and preached his message of spiritual revitalization. "Billboards promoting liquor and smoking are saturating the neighborhoods of the poor and working class in this nation and state. The religious people . . . need to fight back." He began traveling to New York City and holding prayer vigils in front of television network headquarters.[37]

In November 1994, friends and associates feted Ned at a luncheon to celebrate Revitalization Corps's thirtieth anniversary. But Ned was in no mood to dwell on the past. When asked to speak, he proceeded to deliver a rafter-rattling speech on the evils of television. "Television is insidious and it's more addictive and more damaging than most drugs," he warned. "It's deadening us. It's stupefying us. It's dividing us. It's attacking our soul." The activist who had once railed against monied elites and apathetic suburbanites was now obsessed with the ubiquity of twenty- and seventy-inch screens in American life. "You go to a restaurant and there's a television in the background to numb you. People don't go out as much, they don't communicate as much, they don't write letters, they don't read. Their souls are subdued. We've turned away from each other."[38]

With the case of *Leydon v. Town of Greenwich* headed to trial, Leydon turned to Ned and called on him to testify about his own past attempts to stage protests at Greenwich Point Park. No amount of coaching could prepare Leydon, or the presiding judge, Edward R. Karazin Jr., or the defense attorney, John Meergergen, for Ned's appearance on the stand. Testifying for less than one hour, Ned nevertheless elicited twenty-four objections from Meergergen. Ned, in turn, expressed disgust at the entire judicial format. "I've worked in the center of poverty for thirty-four years and you folks are up here playing musical chairs." The judge and attorneys didn't know what to make of his strings of non sequiturs. The judge admonished Ned to stop giving "rambling answers." "This is not normal conversation where people just sit around a table and chat," the judge reminded the witness. In between repeated objections and lectures from the bench, Ned did tell bits and pieces of his 1970s campaigns. He told of how he became an accidental activist for open beaches: "I intended to just get people down to . . . the beach and then all of a sudden I saw the doors were closed." He recounted the resistance he encountered from local officials, the infamous assault on two of his workers in Madison, and the dire need to address the recreational deprivations of the urban poor. "If these kids aren't into the water and if they're not playing with kids, including kids in Greenwich . . . these kids are going to be playing with drugs, guns, knives. . . . It's as simple as that. It's in my gut and it's been in my gut a long time." Afterward, Ned remarked that the attorneys for Greenwich looked like undertakers.[39]

Throughout the trial, Leydon repeatedly referenced Ned's protests during the 1970s to make the case that Greenwich Point Park constituted a public forum and that, moreover, the residents-only policy served to restrict activities protected under the First Amendment. In this respect, Ned's performance on the stand—and the contempt in which he was held among Greenwich residents—undermined the town's argument that the invitation requirement provided an adequate safeguard for protecting free speech rights. Who, after all, would invite Ned Coll onto their beach? It strained credulity. Indeed, Greenwich's invitation requirement virtually assured that the beach would remain free of unpopular people and viewpoints. "Jesus Christ," Leydon later reminded Judge Karazin, "recruited the Apostle Peter on a beach," an event that "according to the [B]ible . . . took place on a beach in a Town where Christ was not [a] resident." Now, "imagine today a man in his early thirties, with long hair and a beard, wearing a robe and sandals" attempting to access the beach. "I think you could fairly predict the likelihood of his being invited in by the Town of Greenwich to mingle with its residents." Even if a resident decided to invite a long-haired radical to the beach, Leydon stressed, he or she could revoke that privilege the moment the guest stepped out of line.[40]

Ironically, the Greenwich Point Preservation Association also helped Leydon's case. Leydon subpoenaed Robert Churchill, one of the group's founders. On the stand, Leydon handed Churchill one of the flyers he had distributed on the beach and asked whether he was in fact using the beach as a venue to generate support for an important public policy matter, as protected under the First Amendment right to free speech. "They were *not* happy at all," Leydon later remarked.[41]

Later in the trial, Leydon hauled a television and VCR into court and tried to present the episode of *TV Nation* as evidence. When Karazin tried to postpone its showing until the following day, Leydon said, "Judge, I paid $170 to have this today and it's a daily rental. I'd rather not pay it again tomorrow." Karazin allowed it to be shown but then said it could not be used as evidence.[42]

While Leydon operated on a shoestring budget, Greenwich's legal team brought forth an army of well-paid experts. On the stand, Jonathan S. Falk of National Economic Research Associates predicted that a beach open to the general public would bring upwards of 1.4 million cars onto Tod's Point each year.[43] Town officials testified that they had restricted public use out of concern for the beach's fragile ecology. They also tried to argue that Greenwich Point Park was not (despite its name) a park since the state supreme court had ruled in several previous cases that public parks must be open to the general public, not members of a particular municipality. It was, they insisted, a beach. And since, with regard to beaches, Connecticut's common law interpretation of the public trust doctrine applied only to the wet sand portion of the shoreline, the town was well within its rights to bar nonresidents from the park, er . . . beach.[44]

In Judge Karazin's court, these arguments worked. On July 8, 1998, he ruled that Leydon had failed to prove that Greenwich's beach ordinance was invalid on public trust or free speech grounds. Karazin dismissed the claim that Greenwich's ordinance restricted Leydon's First Amendment rights, reasoning that "if the plaintiff truly intended to express himself on the Point, he would have been able to do so, unimpeded, if he were accompanied by a Greenwich resident."[45]

Leydon immediately filed an appeal to the state's appellate court. In briefs before the court, Leydon recounted the history of public parks in America, citing the renowned architect and urban planner Frederick Law Olmsted's vision for Central Park as a space where the rich and poor alike could come together and exchange ideas on equal footing. He referenced the litany of federal and state decisions recognizing the importance of public parks in a democratic society. He referred to the campaign of New Jersey senator and 2000 presidential candidate Bill Bradley, who launched his run for president that summer by walking along the beaches on the Jersey shore meeting with voters. He noted the recent decision by the Connecticut Supreme Court in the landmark case *Sheff v. O'Neill* (1996), which found the state's school districting scheme unconstitutional because it resulted in high concentrations of racial and ethnic minorities in underfunded urban districts. In the majority opinion, the court recognized the value of "interracial and multiethnic exposure to each other and interaction between them," as well as the "negative effects" of policies that fostered isolation and parochialism "on both groups." He mocked the town's claims that the wording of the 1919 Special Act granting it authority to maintain beaches and public parks for its citizens required that it exclude nonresidents. Why, Leydon asked, would the state grant "Greenwich and Greenwich only . . . such a privilege[?]" "The fact that the Town might be more xenophobic than other municipalities in Connecticut hardly suffices as a reason." And he cast further doubt on the town's claims that it limited access to residents only strictly out of environmental concerns, noting that Greenwich already had laws on the books "prevent[ing] any person from disturbing or harming these sensitive areas," adding that while "the Town does not post a single guard at any of these tremendously fragile areas, . . . they post two guards at the entrance to the Park who zealously enforce the residents-only requirement." In May 2000, the three-member appellate court reversed the lower court's decision, ruling that Greenwich's beach ordinance violated the public trust doctrine, which held that municipal parks are held in trust "for the general public and not solely for use by the residents of the municipality" and as such, the town was "required to allow state residents the same access to its public beaches and public parks as it offers to its residents."[46]

"The court might as well have outlawed films in Cannes," the *New York Times* wrote.[47] This decision, Greenwich resident Anita Visentin Perito predicted, is "destined to destroy the enjoyment of all Connecticut beachgoers."[48] "We moved here because Greenwich has a safe feeling and a certain beauty that we didn't find elsewhere," another resident commented. "What's going to happen when kids from other towns start showing up?"[49] That summer, a sand sculpture titled "Brendan [*sic*] Leydon's Beach" finished second in the Greenwich Point Park's sand sculpture competition. It depicted a pair of giant feet molded to look like a person buried in sand.[50]

If Greenwich was shocked, it should not have been. Legal experts roundly denounced the town's ordinance as blatantly unconstitutional and the town's defense unconvincing. "Discriminating against nonresidents is an odd way to manage public resources," Quinnipiac law professor Richard Schragger commented. "It is difficult not to share the suspicion that Greenwich simply does not want 'outsiders' to use its beaches, whether or not they are willing to pay their fair share and whether or not they would behave responsibly once they got there."[51] Praising the decision, the editorial board of the *Connecticut Law Tribune* framed the case as "both an issue of law and of social morality and equity. Municipalities are not private clubs into which one can buy membership. They are public entities created by the state. They have no more right to exclude non-residents from their beaches than they do from their municipal streets." "I always assumed I was going to win, so I wasn't that surprised by [the decision]," Leydon later told an interviewer.[52]

Greenwich's legal team readied its appeal to the Connecticut Supreme Court. Attorneys for the Lucas Point Association submitted a brief to the court arguing that opening the beach to the general public would render the easement void. "We feel that the stakes are high," association president Bob Churchill explained, "and that we are right in so many issues. We have a duty to stay the course, not just for the neighborhood but for the entire state."[53] In a separate brief, Elliot accused Leydon of attempting to import New Jersey's laws on beach access into Connecticut, a move that, if successful, he predicted, would lead to the "Jerseyfication" of the state's coast.[54]

In March 2001, the state supreme court heard the case. Later that summer, it affirmed the appellate court's decision: Greenwich could not prohibit nonresidents access to its public beaches. Whereas the appellate court determined that the law violated the public trust doctrine, the supreme court ruled that it violated the public's right to free speech, a finding that ultimately gave the decision far greater standing than it would have had had it been decided strictly on the basis of common law. Leydon spent a total of $1,200 out of pocket on the case. Greenwich's legal team billed the town over $110,000 for its work on the case.[55]

Pat Gasparino returned home from the beach that afternoon and heard the news. A friend had called and left her a voice message. "She was screaming on my machine. I just got a knot in my stomach. . . . I just think it's not fair for us as town residents to [have to] share this beach, with the public."[56] Fellow resident Wendy Spezzano called the decision "a slap in our community's face" and said it was "a very sad time in United States history, not just Greenwich and Connecticut." "Who is protecting our right not to associate with Mr. Leydon?"[57] "Nobody agrees with this decision," Ibolyas Kerekes, a Hungarian immigrant hairdresser, told a reporter as she lounged on the beach. "This will ruin our beaches. All those New Yorkers, they will come to the beach and the minute they smell money here they will come with guns and rob and kill people."[58] Bradley Brock called for an uprising: "I understand that government can expropriate your property 'for the greater good,' but I thought they had to pay you when they did that. What's Greenwich getting for the loss of control over their asset? Nothing but a lawyer bill. This is unconscionable. About time for a tea party."[59]

Greenwich's lawyers succeeded in delaying the inevitable, filing a motion for reconsideration and obtaining a stay on the decision that, they presumed, would keep it from taking effect until the end of the summer season. Critics of the town's relentless legal fight expressed their disgust. "This increasingly desperate resort to legal maneuverings to preserve a morally indefensible position reminds me of nothing more than the endless efforts in the South to resist judicial orders to overturn segregation laws," James McKean wrote. "Are we going to have our elected officials, when the last appeal has been exhausted (at our considerable expense)[,] stand at the entrance to Tod's Point, ax handles in hand?"[60] Rather than wait until the court was back in session, the justices met in conference in late August and summarily denied Greenwich's motion to reconsider. Case closed. Effective September 13, 2001, Greenwich's public beach must be open to the public.

A reporter for the *Fairfield Hour* tracked down Ned Coll for his response to the historic decision, but his mind was elsewhere. "What they're really doing is keeping Jesus Christ off their beach," he explained to the perplexed reporter. "Someday they'll be accountable for that."[61] Leydon had planned to throw a party on the beach on September 13 to celebrate, but he canceled it following the tragic events that had taken place miles away in Manhattan two days earlier. Still, he remained skeptical that the town would ever comply with the spirit of the court's decision. "The odds of Greenwich being reasonable are so low that I'd be better off playing Powerball."[62]

True to form, opponents of public access pored over the court's decision in search of possible loopholes. The Lucas Point Association considered rescinding the easement it had granted the town and instead turning the road leading to the beach into a private drive open to residents only. "We have no obligation to allow any specific person to cross our easement," association president Bob Churchill explained.[63] Ultimately, the deep-pocketed members realized the shakiness of their interpretation of the law and decided they had spent enough on fighting to protect a doomed ordinance. Local attorney Joseph McLaughlin floated a proposal to adhere only to the free speech aspects of the decision by granting free speech permits to nonresidents wishing to use the beach. Nonresidents wishing to demonstrate on the beach would have to obtain a permit between seventy-two and twenty-four hours in advance and not be allowed on the beach for more than two hours. Nor could they use that time to swim, "because," he explained, "you cannot go for a swim and carry a picket sign at the same time." Most fellow residents scoffed at the idea. Leydon called it absurd. "By freedom of speech, they were not limiting that concept to formal addresses, to people standing on the corner at Hyde Park in London giving harangues to crowds." But McLaughlin was dead serious. "If I want to demonstrate on Fifth Avenue in New York, I can do so, but I have to get a permit." "My reading of the decision is that what Greenwich has to do is have an ordinance that makes reasonable accommodations for nonresidents to come onto the beach for the purpose of expressing themselves under the First Amendment."[64]

A much easier means of exclusion remained at Greenwich's disposal. In contrast to the New Jersey Supreme Court in its *Neptune City v. Avon-by-the-Sea* decision, the Connecticut Supreme Court did not attack the use of differential fee schedules for residents and nonresidents. Towns could continue to charge nonresidents a higher fee to park and access the beach and make the process of obtaining permits as cumbersome as possible. At the time of the decision, Connecticut law professor Jeremy Paul predicted, "The reality is, as long as the parking regulations are upheld, the number of people who will actively take advantage of this [decision] is small."[65] Months after the decision, the Greenwich Board of Selectmen voted to enact a new fee schedule for the upcoming season. Nonresidents seeking to use the beach would have to purchase a seasonal pass. Price: $408 per adult, $149 per child.[66] No day passes would be made available. The outcry was immediate. Critics lambasted the nakedly exclusionary tactics on talk radio and in the opinion pages of newspapers across the state. In Hartford, State Representative Ernest E. Newton III blasted the policy as "racist."[67] "You could go to Europe or the Bahamas for that kind of money," Leydon scoffed.[68] First Selectman Richard Bergstresser feebly tried to defend the outrageous fees. "We are using verifiable numbers, methodology and accounting standards. This is not an Enron creative-accounting effort."[69] Few were buying it, though.

"It's hard to even put into words how ridiculous this proposal is," Leydon remarked. "I'm certainly going to be going back to court, and I'm confident I'll win."[70] Greenwich residents denounced the plan as unnecessarily adversarial and one that was sure to embroil the town in further litigation and negative publicity. "It was a public relations nightmare," board member Peter J. Crumbine commented. Bergstresser acknowledged, "Many residents found the plan unacceptable, and the reaction was the same in town, across the state and, indeed, around the nation."[71]

The board met again and voted to reduce the seasonal pass to $308 and agreed to sell day passes for $20 per person.[72] Seemingly unable to avoid generating negative headlines, it added a new provision requiring nonresidents to obtain a permit to use any of the town's public parks. To even use the playground on the town's common, a nonresident would have had to buy a day pass and, without one, could be subject to arrest. The prospect of a mother being hauled off to jail for bringing her kid to a playground made Greenwich "the laughingstock of the evening news." "Even residents who had backed the lawsuit were appalled."[73] The board quickly eliminated the fees for using town parks and reduced the price of one-day admission to the town beach from $20 to $10 per person. "At least we've now left the realm of the shockingly unreasonable," Leydon commented.[74]

Greenwich was still not done constructing new obstacles for non-residents. Whereas previously residents could purchase a day pass for guests at the gate, Greenwich would now require nonresidents to buy passes at one of two off-site locations in town. Town officials contended that this ruling was meant to speed the flow of traffic into the park by not requiring guards to count change. Leydon found this excuse laughable. "If their actual concern was traffic, that doesn't seem like a particularly good idea," given the number of guests who would be forced to turn around and drive back into town. "It's just doing something clearly for the only purpose of making it harder."[75] Where some found crass cynicism, others saw a strategy worth emulating. Officials in Madison adopted many of Greenwich's tactics for dissuading nonresidents from coming onto its beach. It, too, stopped selling guest passes at the gate and instead moved sales to an off-site facility miles from the beach, open only on weekdays.[76]

As it searched for new ways to exclude nonresidents, Greenwich also began to more closely scrutinize its own citizenry. The Leydon case compelled town officials to closely examine the places of residence of those who had obtained resident beach passes in previous years. In the fall of 2001, it began sending out notices to several residents informing them that they were, in fact, not residents. Michael Trager, a former vice president of NBC Sports, lived in a home that straddled the border between Greenwich and Stamford. For years, he had voted in Greenwich elections, sent his daughter to Greenwich public schools, and received passes to the town beach. In a terse letter, the town informed him that his property was not considered part of Greenwich, that he was ineligible to vote in future town elections, and that his daughter should begin reporting to public school in Stamford. Another family with three children enrolled in Greenwich public schools, including two children with special needs, similarly received a notice from the town that it had two weeks to enroll the children in a different school district. For years, Gerald Porricelli had been an active contributor to Greenwich civic affairs. But shortly after he applied for beach passes in 2001, "I received almost instant notice that I was not a Greenwich resident anymore." Porricelli petitioned the town's board of electors to hear his case for reinstatement. But public officials were in an unforgiving mood. "I'm sorry," Greenwich registrar Veronica Musca replied tersely. "[You] should have bought a house in Greenwich."[77]

The following spring, Greenwich braced for the onslaught of unwashed masses fleeing the concrete jungle. "It'll be like living on the main drag to Jones Beach," one resident predicted.[78] "They'll have to erect a bank of toll booths to let in the hordes."[79] The onerous fees and confusing rules on buying a pass proved a sufficient deterrent. A reporter on hand the first day of the 2002 season noted that few nonresidents came, "and those who did complained about the steep fees they were charged." A carload of children in tow, Manhattan resident Patricia Tuz drove onto Tod's Point, only to be told by the guard, over the sounds of a crying three-year-old, to first turn around and go back into town and buy passes at the city center. There, she shelled out one hundred dollars for ten beach passes plus twenty dollars for a parking pass. "I feel like I'm being punished," she muttered.[80] "Towns have indeed made their beaches public," *New York Times* reporter Christine Woodside wrote, "but the prices are so high and the rules about buying passes so awkward that much of the Connecticut coast remains as out of reach as ever."[81] The CCLU issued a report card on beach towns' compliance with the Leydon decision. Both Greenwich and Madison received an "F." "If it costs you $60, or you have to walk a mile to get to the beach, these are restrictions that do prohibit people with economic or physical difficulties from enjoying the beachfront," CCLU

director Teresa Younger noted. By any objective measure, exclusion by
income and inconvenience worked. Greenwich saw a net *decrease* in the
number of visitors to its beach that summer. Madison issued a total of
only eighteen day passes and twenty vehicle passes to nonresidents the
entire summer.[82]

"I'm embarrassed for my state," Woodside wrote. "The coast is
treated like a private club for those with the right credentials." What
Woodside neglected to mention, though, was that she seemed to possess the credentials needed to circumvent the law. As part of her investigation of beach access restrictions in the state, the middle-aged
white woman and her two children arrived at beaches without passes to
see what would happen. Invariably, the guards let them in. "We got in
everywhere we tried," she exclaimed, "even when we weren't supposed
to." She praised the gatekeepers, who "seemed embarrassed by the rules,
often apologized for them, and sometimes tried to help us work around
them." In Madison, she arrived without passes on a weekend, when the
only place she could obtain them was closed. The guards looked the
other way and let her in. In Stamford, the gatekeeper "waved me in"
despite her not having passes. "He saved us $20 and a trip to the Gov-
ernment Center." And in Greenwich, where Woodside was able to buy
passes at the off-site location, the gatekeeper declined to stamp them so
that she and her family could use them again. The rules, it seemed, did
not apply to everyone.[83]

Beach patrols selectively enforced many of the dizzying number of
regulations and prohibitions that town governments had enacted over
the years. Like the ban on exercise groups meeting on the beach. So un-
enforced was this ordinance that the *Greenwich Time* featured a photo of
a group exercising on the beach in 2002, never once mentioning that the
men and women in the photo were breaking the law. Area trainer Jason
Hall had used the beach for group workouts without incident until the
summer of 2005, when one of his groups, which included several black
and Puerto Rican women, showed up. Among the Greenwich residents
coming to exercise that morning were Millie Bonilla and Sheila Foster,
the wives of former New York Mets stars Bobby Bonilla and George
Foster. The Bonillas had lived in Greenwich for fourteen years; their

children attended Greenwich High School. Both Millie and Sheila were active in civic affairs.

On the morning of June 7, 2005, though, they were just two black women in exercise outfits without proper identification. The guard refused to allow them in. When the women argued back, he threatened to have them arrested. The trainer tried to continue the session with the remaining group members. The guard told him that group activities were prohibited on the beach and ordered them to disperse. They all suspected racial bias. Bonilla and Foster, along with Claudette Rothman, also African American, filed a formal complaint with the town's affirmative action office and the Connecticut Commission on Human Rights and Opportunities (CCHRO).[84]

The day after the incident, Hall contacted the town's affirmative action officer, Kelly Houston. "You know Kelly I have two groups of women down there and one group hasn't had a problem and the other has had nothing but trouble. You can imagine what the difference is between the groups can't you? Tell me I'm wrong."[85] Herself African American, Houston was married to the president of the local chapter of the NAACP. She knew the three women and had expressed interest in joining the group. "I would love to tell you, you are wrong," she wrote Hall, "but I am positive that you are not." She tried to apologize for the bigoted attitudes of town employees. "Understand this is not intentional. These men are just condition[ed] to see white people on the beach all the time. So yes, when there [are] a few (3–4) black people together they take notice." And she tried to give Hall some helpful advice. "I do think that you can use the facilities. However you will have to be discreet and if you are asked you are going to have to say you are just working out with friends. If you are doing a black group, you are going to need to cut your numbers down. Welcome to Greenwich!"[86]

Three weeks later, Houston exonerated town employees of any wrongdoing. But slowly, word of Houston's private comments to Hall had begun to leak out. The *Greenwich Time* filed a FOIA request for any messages pertaining to Hall's exercise group. The town was able to produce only messages in which Houston indicated her interest in joining. She had deleted the messages sent to Hall the day after the incident.

Finally, in early December, the newspaper got hold of Houston's correspondence with Hall.[87]

"This is really going to be horrible," Selectman Peter Crumbine commented. As town officials fretted over another blow to the town's reputation and re-acted the ritual hand wringing over being cast in "an unfair light" by the media, the women's attorney, Joseph Moniz, went on the attack. "The town should look at the substance of what was said in those e-mails and the significance of them, and not worry about when and how they were received."[88] White members of the group who were turned away that morning spoke out as well. One said she had returned to the beach on several occasions since the incident and been let in without an ID. "This is not about us," Bonilla stressed. "If they don't take us seriously, can you imagine how they treat others?"[89]

Overnight, the women became pariahs in their own community. In letters to the editor published in the local newspaper, they were called "self-centered individuals of privilege," accused of playing the "race card," mocked for failing to follow "a few simple rules," and they were told they needed to grow "thicker skin."[90] Seeking to defuse tensions and put the story to bed, the town readily accepted a settlement offer from the CCHRO that required each town employee involved in the incident, including Houston, to attend ten hours of anti-discrimination training. Throughout the firestorm, the question of why Houston felt pressure to exonerate the beach officials in spite of her personal belief in their guilt went unanswered. Perhaps the answer was all too obvious.[91]

Epilogue
Nature Bats Last

I
t was a cloudy, slightly chilly weekday afternoon in June 2009 when I picked Ned up at his office in Hartford and drove toward the coast. When we arrived in Old Lyme, the beaches were nearly empty. There was no guard asking us for our passes, no attendant checking our car for its sticker. "No Trespassing" signs still lined the beach, while massive piles of stone, amassed right to the water's edge, still marked the boundary lines of private beach associations. The sight of these barriers seemed to invigorate the sixty-nine-year-old activist. "Private beach?!?!" he shouted into the wind. "Who the fuck are they to say private beach?" As he defiantly climbed over and around barriers and sunk his feet into the private sands of communities he had battled decades earlier, Ned turned to me, flashed a mischievous grin, and said, "Let me tell you, Coll was [once] a four-letter word along this fucking shoreline, man."[1]

For many, it still is. It's been nearly forty years since Ned last staged a protest on a beach in Connecticut. And yet the image of him arriving, unannounced, with a busload of kids from Hartford still remains fresh in the minds of many who live or spend their summers along the shore. Ask a private beach association member of his or her thoughts on public beach access and you'll likely hear a reference to "busloads of inner-city kids. . . from Hartford."[2] "We have deeds to these [beaches] and we have [had] since 1921," the president of one beach association told me in 2015. "So no, we don't want buses coming down here and dropping people off at the beach. That's not how it's supposed to be."[3] In a recent survey of beach users' views on public access to town beaches in the wake of the *Leydon* decision, many respondents expressed fears "of an invasion of 'busloads' of people (most often children) who crowd and denigrate the beaches if allowed access."[4] Asked about the continued resistance of shoreline communities to public beach access, one official in the state's (renamed) Department of Energy and Environmental Protection (DEEP) explained, "The image in their minds still is busloads of people from out of town coming in."[5]

Much has changed along Connecticut's shore in the years since Ned Coll staged his beach invasions. "The traditional beach communities," DEEP coastal planner David J. Blatt explained, "are being done away with. . . . Instead of a little community of seasonal cottages, people are selling out. The beach communities are becoming more heterogeneous; they're not ethnic or regional enclaves any more. The houses are bigger. Anyone who can afford one can go there now and build something big. But one thing that's been consistent throughout all of these eras is opposition to the general public coming down."[6] And the cold shoulder given toward persons on the beach who, as one shoreline resident put it, are "obviously from outside of this area."[7] "You look at these people," one longtime homeowner in the exclusive summer beach community of Groton Long Point commented, "and you know, they're not Groton Long Point [members]. . . . [They]'re not the type who lives here. . . . I don't want to sound discriminatory, but it's just deeded and it's private."[8]

While the *Leydon* decision opened all of the public beaches in Connecticut to the public, it has had, as geographer Adam Keul observed, "a negligible effect on the social exclusivities that still govern people's experiences of the beach."[9] In practical terms, town beaches in the state's wealthiest communities remain as inaccessible as ever, as municipalities have deployed a host of subtle, but no less effective, instruments of exclusion. In Greenwich, residents can purchase season beach passes and process numerous other transactions online. Nonresidents, however, must still purchase single-entry passes in person at one of two locations in town, both still located far from the beach, and both still closed on weekends. Madison still sells season passes only to residents and taxpayers, while charging nonresidents twenty-five dollars to park on Mondays through Thursdays and forty dollars on Fridays through Sundays and holidays. In Westport, it costs nonresidents thirty dollars to park at Compo Beach on weekdays and fifty dollars on weekends and holidays. Persons from out of town seeking to use the beach find themselves forced to fork over outrageous parking fees because towns have removed or severely limited the availability of street parking near the beach. At Groton's Eastern Point Beach, the closest public parking space is a quarter-mile from the beach, with a one-hour time limit.[10]

Hostility to the public remains a defining feature of private beach associations' political culture. "Any residential development, whether it's one person or several, will fight tooth and nail against any kind of public access," according to Blatt. "One time I was even told that a lawyer's client was worried that murderers would come park there and attack people in their homes."[11] This fear of outsiders and the land-use practices it yields continues to have negative environmental repercussions. Take the controversy over a piece of land in the shoreline community of Rowayton in Norwalk, for example. In August 2013 prominent local architect Bruce Beinfield acquired a half-acre parcel of land on a narrow peninsula in the middle of Farm Creek, a tidal estuary. Soon after, local residents caught wind of his plans to build a large house on the lot, one that would obstruct many neighbors' views of Long Island Sound. "The town just rose up en masse," as one resident described it. Resistance to the plan was so intense that Beinfield abandoned his plans and entered into negotiations with the Norwalk Land Trust, which hoped to make the site a public nature sanctuary. The only problem: the property was part of the Pine Point Beach Association. When members of Pine Point learned of the land trust's plans to allow public access to the site, they scuttled the deal, citing fears that it would lead to "people . . . com[ing] in droves, or busloads . . . and devalu[ing] our properties." After the land trust backed out of the deal, Beinfield moved forward with new construction plans, this time a house that was less obstructive of other homeowners' views but that would also take up more square footage of ground and inflict potentially more damage to the tidal estuary. Pine

Point members gave their approval, while residents of Rowayton chose not to launch another campaign to save Farm Creek.[12]

While the "whites only" signs that once littered the American landscape have become artifacts of a dark chapter in our collective past, held up as reminders of what America has overcome, the instruments of segregation used in mid- to late-twentieth-century Connecticut and throughout the Northeast—and the culture of exclusion that inspired and sustained it—are still very much in operation today.[13] Over the past several decades, as declining tax revenues forced cities to close public parks, playgrounds, beaches, and swimming pools that offered low-income families affordable places of recreation, exclusive municipalities introduced new residency requirements and privatized formerly public spaces.[14] As they did, they followed Connecticut's lead and emulated its model for racial and fiscal segregation. Nowhere is the state's influence on today's "separate and unequal" America more evident than in the gated communities and private homeowners' associations that have become a common feature of upper-class neighborhoods and vacation destinations across the nation. These places have rightfully come to symbolize economic stratification and class segregation in this, our Second Gilded Age. But in Connecticut, their use as a symbol of exclusivity and mechanism of exclusion dates back to our First Gilded Age.

These trends hold ominous implications for the future of American democracy. Indeed, public space plays an essential role in a democratic society. Such spaces are, in theory, places where people of different backgrounds, races, ethnicities, and income levels come into contact with each other (what the legal scholar Gerald Frug calls "fortuitous association") and, in the process, have to learn how to get along.[15] They counteract the tendencies toward balkanization and parochialism that private venues foster and stand as a check on the dominance of the wealthy over political discourse and corporations over cultural norms in America. In an age when personal wealth closely correlates with political influence, public spaces afford marginalized voices in society places where they can go and be heard, where dissident views can be aired and nonconformist lifestyles can be expressed freely, and where a diverse nation can engage in the hard work of becoming a diverse society. That public spaces have, throughout American history, rarely been truly public and, as a result, have often failed to live up to their promise should not render their steady disappearance any less alarming.

Along with public space, America's shorelines are themselves disappearing, as the waters of the world's oceans warm and sea levels rise. In contrast to public space, this *has* generated much alarm among the people who live and own property along the shore, but—as recent events indicate—shows no sign of generating a commensurate sea change in our approach to coastal development and land-use management. In August 2011 Hurricane Irene struck the Connecticut coast, destroying over twenty-five homes in the town of East Haven, causing ten deaths, and flooding thousands of homes along the Gold Coast. The following spring, a group of state legislators, with the backing of the Connecticut chapter of the Nature Conservancy, introduced a bill that called for "a fair and orderly legal process to foster strategic retreat of property ownership, over a period of several decades" in areas along the coast that were subject to severe erosion and repetitive structural damage. Shortly after the bill was introduced, Climate Central released a report that estimated that sea levels in Long Island Sound would rise an additional twelve inches by 2050. For decades, climate and coastal scientists had been calling attention to the unsustainability of coastal development and issuing calls for a "strategic retreat" from the nation's shores, to no avail. To the contrary, the devastating storms that struck the coasts with greater frequency seemed to make homeowners and lawmakers more determined to stand their ground and hold back the sea. Outrage over the bill was immediate. State senator Len Fasano, whose district was the hardest hit by Irene, led the fight against what he called a "forced taking [of private property] by government." Lawmakers quickly backpedaled and removed any references to "retreat" from the bill.[16]

A similar pattern unfolded following Hurricane Sandy, which struck the Northeast in October 2012. Surveying the wreckage along Long Island, disaster planning specialist Irwin Redlener remarked, "There are millions of people who live in areas like this and, you know, at what point does it make sense to just call it a day and not have people live there?" Orrin Pilkey, the nation's foremost expert on the environmental impact of coastal development, called on lawmakers to take some "tough medicine" and end "this cycle of repairing or rebuilding

properties in the path of future storms." Many critics singled out the
National Flood Insurance Program and the Hazard Mitigation Grant
Programs for incentivizing development and rebuilding in flood-prone
areas. Even as government programs encouraged development in haz-
ardous areas, coastal communities' long-standing resistance to government interference—specifically concerning public beach access—
exacerbated the damage Sandy inflicted on shoreline properties.[17]

One of the areas to suffer the most damage from Sandy was Sea
Gate, a private gated community located on the western tip of Coney Island. The 850-home community was surrounded by razor-wire-topped
fences. To enter, guests had to pass through a security checkpoint. Its
streets, parks, and beaches were all off limits to the public. For decades,
Sea Gate residents had shunned federal and state aid for repairing its
severely eroding beachfront. In the late 1980s, its homeowners' association opted out of an Army Corps of Engineers project to stem erosion

The aftermath of Superstorm Sandy in East Haven, Connecticut.
Copyright © Associated Press. AP Photo/Jessica Hill.

along the peninsula out of concerns that participation would jeopardize the private status of its beachfront. Better, residents concluded, to lose the beach entirely than lose the private beach. Civil engineers cited Sea Gate's refusal to participate in past projects as responsible for the severe damage it suffered from Sandy. In its aftermath, residents who had shunned government assistance in the past came running for disaster aid. Their working-class neighbors were decidedly unsympathetic. "They seclude themselves," Cesar Catala commented. "They put their noses down at us. We get treated like we're second class, just because . . . we live in the projects and we rent." Another added, "Funny how people who segregate themselves and generally regard everyone not like them as dangerous others all of a sudden rediscover 'community' when they need help."[18]

Following Sandy, shoreline homeowners in Connecticut likewise refashioned themselves as members of the community and, in the words of one incredulous DEEP official, "deserving victims."[19] Their appeals for help resonated with state lawmakers, who rushed to ease rebuilding restrictions and loosen standards for redevelopment. In June 2013, Connecticut governor Dannel Malloy signed a law that made it easier for shoreline homeowners to get a permit to rebuild a dock or seawall and construct new flood and erosion control structures. Rather than relocate, homeowners used insurance payouts and federal disaster relief to elevate their homes.[20] Of the forty-three FEMA buyouts in Connecticut between 2010 and 2012, fewer then 20 percent were for homes situated along the shore. The most vocal defenders of homeowners' rights to return were local lawmakers in shoreline municipalities, who were, as one reporter noted, "loathe to give up the hefty property taxes on waterside and water-view properties."[21] As sea levels rise, the contentious politics and contradictory policies on shoreline development will only intensify. "People are going to want to build more walls," Kristal Kallenberg in the state's Office of Long Island Sound Programs predicts. "They're going to want to fortify [the shore]. . . . [And] how can you say no if somebody wants to protect [their property]?"[22] Especially when the property in need of protection is some of the most valuable in the state and is owned by some of its wealthiest and most influential residents.

The problem of climate change is fundamentally tied to the problem of wealth and income inequality, and few places in America better illustrate these dynamics than coastal Connecticut, America's most unequal state. Since 1977, no other state has experienced a greater increase in income inequality. Today, those in Connecticut's top 1 percent earn fifty-one times more than those in its bottom 99 percent. Much of that wealth (as well as a significant portion of its poor) is concentrated in southwestern Connecticut. Home to the Gold Coast as well as the deeply impoverished city of Bridgeport, this metro area has the widest income gap of any in the nation. If it were a country, it would be ranked the fourteenth most unequal spot on the planet, just behind Brazil. "To walk down Bridgeport's deserted Main Street, with its boarded up stores and hard-luck hotels, and then stroll down Greenwich Avenue later that day," reporter Michael Moran remarked, "is to experience different planets."[23]

"I don't think of it at all," one Greenwich resident said of Bridgeport. "I don't think I've ever even met someone from there." One would be hard-pressed to find a more fitting tribute to the tireless efforts of Gold Coast residents over the previous decades to seclude themselves from the poor, both in places of residence and places of public congregation. "It's like we're invisible," said one woman who commutes from Norwalk to her dry cleaning job in Greenwich.[24]

Beginning in the early 2000s, hedge fund managers flocked to the wealthy town situated along the state's western border. By the mid-2000s, prime office space near Greenwich's train station commanded higher rents than high-rises in midtown Manhattan. The average price for a single-family home soared to over $2.2 million. Today, Greenwich is referred to as "the capital of the hedge-fund world." Its managers control roughly 10 percent of the total hedge fund assets globally. As wealth has poured into Greenwich, its middle class has been forced out. Along the town's downtown commercial district, high-end retail stores and international brand outfits occupy storefronts that used to house local businesses. Throughout the town, modestly sized houses are being bought, torn down, and replaced by super mansions. As more and more of its schoolteachers, police officers, and other middle-class professionals are forced to commute from neighboring towns, traffic congestion and air and noise pollution have increased sharply.[25]

The beach access battles that once consumed the town and, to its critics, exemplified Greenwich's elitism barely register with a swelling class of super rich who, almost without exception, belong to private country clubs and send their children to private schools. Indeed, few of Greenwich's new residents would ever be caught on one of the town's public beaches. "The rich in Greenwich care little about the public goods that they rarely utilize," the author of a study of the impact of the hedge fund economy on Greenwich's social structure commented. They see "[t]he public facilities, services and even public places . . . [as] their charitable giving to the town in the form of local taxation." As the elite segregate themselves from the merely well-to-do, the town's middle- and upper-middle-class residents have become more class conscious and more determined to distance and differentiate themselves from the working poor.[26]

I first met Ned Coll in the spring of 2009. He was working out of a cluttered, windowless office on the fourth floor of an aging church building in downtown Hartford. No longer able to drive due to his epilepsy and recently separated from his wife, Leslie, he lived in a barren room in a boarding house near downtown during the week and arranged to have a friend drive him to his cabin in Barkhamsted on the weekends. Revitalization Corps, now renamed God Activism, existed in name only. When he wasn't in his office, often by himself, Ned walked the streets of Hartford, stopping to engage with anyone who would give him the time. Long strings of rosary beads dangled from his neck. He sometimes carried large signs adorned with Biblical passages and messages alluding to the vision of the Virgin Mary he claims to have seen on Pentecost Sunday 1990. As we walked through downtown Hartford one summer afternoon, fellow pedestrians in business suits who caught a glimpse of Ned sped up their pace and tried to avoid making eye contact. But others approached him to say hello and express their gratitude for his work. They were, invariably, black and poor. A sixty-year-old homeless African American man ran up to us to shake Ned's hand. "I always tried to get a chance to talk to you," he told him. "Why?" Ned asked. "Because you think about black people more than white people," he responded.[27]

"Listen, Ned is good people," Gee Lester explained to me as we sat in two barber's chairs in his barber shop and salon, located on Main Street in Hartford, mere feet from the former Revitalization Corps headquarters where he had spent his afternoons as a youth. "Before you were even doing this story, I said, 'You know what, Ned's gonna die [someday], and people aren't even going to know the significance of [him] and how [he] touched people's lives.'"[28] Once so skilled at commanding attention, in recent years Ned has struggled to be heard. The fetes and honors that would normally be bestowed on someone who had dedicated his life to service, someone who was once called the "conscience" of Connecticut, have not come along. Politicians who used to fear him now ignore him. Many of the businesses and organizations that once lent their support to Revitalization Corps's various initiatives have left the city or been taken over by larger corporate entities. Others had bitter fallings out and simply stopped returning Ned's calls. "Because of the manner in which he conducted business, [Ned] created a lot of enemies," Ralph Knighton commented.[29]

The former master at attracting media attention still merits the occasional news coverage but only for his increasingly unhinged behavior, not for his causes. In 2002 he gave the opening prayer at the Connecticut State Democratic Convention, during which he called the state's Republican governor, John Rowland, a "snake" and the "Prince of Darkness." "When you take a look at John Rowland's eyes, be careful you don't regurgitate," Ned said to a shocked audience, which included all of the state's highest-ranking Democratic officials, including both of Connecticut's U.S. senators. Commentators and Republican officials rushed to condemn Ned's words and called on Democrats to rebuke what Republican National Committee chairman Marc Racicot called "outrageous and politically motivated personal attacks" on Rowland. The speech made Ned a persona non grata in the state's Democratic Party.[30] Another bridge burned. Ned, for his part, was unapologetic and claimed Rowland's later conviction on corruption charges, removal from office, and imprisonment as his vindication.

In the summer of 2009, Ned was back in the news after being arrested twice within the span of one week for breach of peace, disorderly conduct, and attempted assault of a police officer. The first incident occurred at a hip, trendy cafe in a gentrifying neighborhood in Hartford, after a manager attempted to remove a panhandler. Ned, who was seated in the restaurant and talking with the panhandler, exploded. He began shouting at the manager and called him a "Nazi" before restaurant staff called the police. Three days later, he was arrested again as he attempted to stage an impromptu protest in the lobby of a downtown high-rise building against a company he believed was practicing employment discrimination. When police arrived, Ned reportedly took a swing at one of the officers and was tackled to the ground before being handcuffed. Days later, writer Richard Rapaport penned a mournful op-ed in the *Hartford Courant,* describing these latest incidents as evidence that Ned had become "a slightly sad reflection of a man who had once been a leader in the fight for equality." "That is a shame," Rapaport wrote, "because his victories are today our victories, ones that we should be celebrating together."[31]

As his circle of friends and allies shrunk, Ned clung to the relationships he had forged with the parents and children he served on the North End. People like Earlie Powell, who remains one of his closest confidants, and Gee Lester, today a successful small business owner, one of the few on the North End. On many a weekday morning, Gee arrives at his business to find Ned outside, sitting on the front stoop, waiting to come in and shoot the breeze. "The younger barbers, they say, 'Who's that white dude, man, coming here like he know everybody?' I say, 'Man, that's Ned.'"[32]

"Ned was so many things to so many people," Gee explained. Some "remember him as the guy who gave them clothes to wear to school, as the guy who gave them Christmas, as the guy who took you to the beaches, who gave you books. Ned, he was just a man of the community who was constantly doing something to ensure that [for] those in need, some of their needs were being met." One afternoon, Gee recalled, he started talking with Ned about his legacy. "I said, 'Ned, you know, they don't appreciate you. No one's given reverence to what you have done over the years.'" Why, I later asked Gee. Because "Ned is a straight shooter. Ned is not going to bullshit you, you understand? Ned will expose your intentions if [they're] not genuine from the heart. . . . He was just a genuine man."[33]

"People think of New England as very enlightened. Forget about it," Russell West scoffs. Ned "raised issues that people didn't see"—or want to see. "He saw racism where it existed, but you didn't see it."[34] Like on the state's shoreline, a place so far removed from the lives of African American and Puerto Rican children living in Hartford that it might as well have been another country. But it wasn't another country, and that, as Ned saw it, was the problem.

Or, more specifically, it was white people's problem. "Segregation and poverty have created in the racial ghetto a destructive environment totally unknown to most white Americans," the authors of the Kerner Commission report plainly stated in 1968. "What white Americans have never fully understood—but what the Negro can never forget—is that white society is deeply implicated in the ghetto. White institutions created it, white institutions maintain it, and white society condones it."[35] Ned spent a lifetime trying to understand, trying to get other white Americans to understand, and once they understood, to do something—anything—about it. The beach became his lesson plan, the exclusive towns and gated communities along the shore his classroom, the summer his school term.

By climbing over and around jetties, seawalls, and other structures that delineated property boundaries and kept "undesirables" out, Ned and fellow protesters brought the fight for racial justice to a place where, perhaps, it should have been from the start. Through his outlandish, inventive, and controversial actions, targeted at people whose hands controlled the levers of power in America—people who, by the 1970s and increasingly so in the decades that followed, disavowed bigotry but who, by their actions and inactions, did more to perpetuate inequality and stifle opportunity for people of color than all of the fire-breathing racists packed into a George Wallace rally could do combined—Ned tried to change the conversation on racism in America and shift the terrain on which the struggle for equality was being fought. He not only tried to expose the gulf that separated the world of black asphalt, broken glass, and busted dreams on Hartford's North End from the white sands, cocktail parties, and privileged lives found in places like Madison, Old Lyme, and Greenwich, but he also tried to show how the two were intimately bound together.

Revitalization Corps's protests left an indelible imprint on the state's shoreline and form an important—and revealing—chapter in the modern environmental movement. The sustained efforts of Revitalization Corps and open beach activists nationwide led to the creation of the CZMA and compelled legislators and state courts to defend the public's right to the foreshore and breathe new life into the public trust doctrine. Due in no small measure to Ned Coll's actions in the 1970s, when he turned the state's beaches into a battlefield in the fight against racial inequality and social injustice, today the Connecticut coastline is ostensibly open to all of its citizens. While for Ned, the beach was more a stage for enacting his dramatization of wealth and poverty than a cause unto itself, his fight to "free the beaches" demonstrated, more clearly than any activist or organization has done before or since, that the struggles for racial equality and environmental protection are inseparable and must be fought as one. It's a point that few activists in either movement at the time appreciated (and few still today), but it is one that future movements being waged on a warming planet will be unable to ignore.

Ironically, Ned's efforts to draw implicit connections between two issues that were often treated in isolation were matched only by his inability to work with other activists, form partnerships with other organizations, or engage in the hard work of coalition building essential to any movement's long-term success. And despite being so adept at challenging those in power to do more and so committed to securing vital resources for those in need, Ned ultimately shied away from tackling the forces responsible for the maldistribution of power and resources. In this respect, Ned Coll was truly a man of his time. For all of his idiosyncrasies and adherence to gut instincts over ideology, Ned followed a quintessentially liberal blueprint for fighting racism, one focused primarily on exposing and subjecting to public scrutiny the prejudicial beliefs and practices of individuals and communities and only secondarily on dismantling the structures and challenging the institutions that produce and perpetuate racial inequality. By bringing some of America's wealthiest enclaves face to face with a class of people—the urban poor—whom they had struggled to avoid and had worked diligently to exclude, Revitalization Corps compelled many middle- and upper-class whites to acknowledge their privileges and reassess their biases. Ned undoubtedly changed many white New Englanders' hearts and minds for the better, even as his confrontational tactics alienated many others and provided grist for anti-liberal forces whose influence has only grown stronger in the decades since.

Ultimately, though, Ned's activism, and the agency of the parents, workers, volunteers, and children who made up Revitalization Corps, could not overcome structural forces that were pushing America toward a separate and more unequal future. Their emphasis on fighting prejudice through interpersonal forms of civic engagement surely led many middle- and upper-class white suburbanites to recognize the humanity, resourcefulness, and resiliency of the poor, but it didn't spur liberal whites in Connecticut to disinvest in the material advantages of whiteness. Instead, they continue to demonstrate their agency through complacency—with, among others, a city (Hartford) that is home to one of the greatest disparities in median family income between the city and its surrounding suburbs of any metro area in the nation (making it one of the poorest cities in the nation but its metro area the second-richest in the country, just behind Silicon Valley, and fourth-richest in the world); with a school funding formula that richly rewards residents of wealthy districts while grossly underserving children of poorer ones, resulting in the state's having some of the highest *and* worst performing public schools in the country, with those at the bottom scoring below states such as Mississippi and Arkansas; with housing markets that work to concentrate the poor in places where the jobs have left; and with woefully inadequate public transportation that limits their access to the places where the jobs are.[36]

For a more overt expression of white agency, and the structural advantages that give it force, we need only look to the shore. Here, along public beaches that lack public parking; where visitors are forced to undergo a cumbersome set of procedures to acquire a beach pass; and where zoning ordinances, building requirements, and local land-use regulations make beachfront property exclusive and housing unafford-able yet always eligible for public assistance come the next major storm, we find the work of generations of activists, fighting in defense of one of the most cherished privileges wealth affords: isolation from the gen-eral public. These elaborate, ever-evolving mechanisms of exclusion are both a hallmark of extremely unequal societies and a tacit acknowl-edgment of the creative, persistent efforts of others to circumvent and tear down those barriers. They are, in effect, a tribute to the work of Ned Coll and the thousands of parents and children who invaded these shores and challenged the state's rigid class structure.

But even as wealth seems more entrenched than ever, another looming threat—climate change and sea level rise—will ultimately de-termine the fate of coastal Connecticut—and America—and render the final verdict on our separate, unequal, and unsustainable planet.

Abbreviations

Newspapers

APEP	*Asbury Park Evening Press*
BaS	*Baltimore Sun*
BCH	*Boston College Heights*
BG	*Boston Globe*
BP	*Bridgeport Post*
CD	*Chicago Defender*
CR	*Clinton [CT] Recorder*
CSM	*Christian Science Monitor*
CT	*Chicago Tribune*
FC	*Fairfield Citizen*
FH	*Fairfield Hour*
GT	*Greenwich Time*
HA	*Hartford Advocate*
HaC	*Harvard Crimson*
HC	*Hartford Courant*
HT	*Hartford Times*
LAT	*Los Angeles Times*
LCT	*Litchfield County [CT] Times*
MJ	*Meriden [CT] Journal*
MMR	*Meriden [CT] Morning Record*
MUL	*Manchester [NH] Union-Leader*
NB	*Norwich Bulletin*
NH	*Norwalk Hour*
NHA	*New Haven Advocate*

NHR	*New Haven Register*
NLD	*New London Day*
NYAN	*New York Amsterdam News*
NYN	*New York Newsday*
NYT	*New York Times*
OGG	*Old Greenwich Gazette*
RBDR	*Red Bank [NJ] Daily Register*
SLT	*Shore Line Times* [Madison, CT]
WHN	*West Hartford News*
WP	*Washington Post*
WSJ	*Wall Street Journal*
YDN	*Yale Daily News*

Archival Collections

ACLU	American Civil Liberties Union Papers, 1912–1990, Mudd Library, Princeton University
AJV	Arthur Jack Viseltear Papers, Manuscripts and Archives, Yale University Library, New Haven, CT
AR	Office of the Governor: Abraham Ribicoff (1955–1961), Connecticut State Library, Hartford, CT
DEP	Department of Environmental Protection, State of Connecticut, Hartford, CT
EG	Office of the Governor: Ella Grasso (1975–1980), Connecticut State Library, Hartford, CT
FUA	Fairfield University Archives, Fairfield, CT
JD	Office of the Governor: John Dempsey (1961–1971), Connecticut State Library, Hartford, CT
JDL	Office of the Governor: John Davis Lodge (1951–1955), Connecticut State Library, Hartford, CT
MTCO	Madison (CT) Town Clerk Office
RF	Rockefeller Foundation Archives, Rockefeller Archive Center, Sleepy Hollow, NY
SPFC	State Park and Forest Commission, Connecticut State Library, Hartford, CT
TBG	Town and Borough Governments, Connecticut State Library, Hartford, CT
TM	Office of the Governor: Thomas Meskill (1971–1975), Connecticut State Library, Hartford, CT
WC	Office of the Governor: Wilbur L. Cross (1931–1939), Connecticut State Library, Hartford, CT

Notes

Introduction

1. "Governor Says Beaches of Towns off Limits to Intervention by State," *GT*, August 7, 1975.

2. Dorothy Wright to Ella Grasso, August 11, 1975, folder Beaches, box 133, EG.

3. Roy Bongartz, "Freedom of Beach," *NYT*, July 13, 1975.

4. Tom Condon, interview by Andrew Kahrl, June 7, 2009, transcript (in author's possession); Joanne West, interview by Andrew Kahrl, March 13, 2015, transcript (in author's possession).

5. Ralph Knighton, interview by Andrew Kahrl, November 5, 2016, transcript (in author's possession).

6. Tom Condon interview; Joanne West interview; "Those Honorary Degrees," *NH*, May 30, 1991.

7. Tom Condon interview; Ralph Knighton interview; Jose Vasquez, interview by Andrew Kahrl, November 20, 2016, transcript (in author's possession); Russell West, interview by Andrew Kahrl, March 8, 2015, transcript (in author's possession).

8. Rob Carbonneau, interview by Andrew Kahrl, October 29, 2016, transcript (in author's possession); Leslie Hammond, interview by Andrew Kahrl, October 28, 2016, transcript (in author's possession); Earlie Powell, interview by Andrew Kahrl, June 15, 2009, transcript (in author's possession).

9. See Tobin Miller Shearer, *Two Weeks Every Summer: Fresh Air Children and the Problem of Race in America* (Ithaca, NY: Cornell University Press, 2017).

10. Tom Condon interview.

11. Edward Forand Jr., "Ned Coll's Journey," *HC*, June 23, 1985; "Old Lyme to Halt Corps Buses," *HC*, August 27, 1971.

12. Earlie Powell interview.

13. Lebert "Gee" Lester, interview by Andrew Kahrl, May 21, 2009, transcript (in author's possession).

14. On the formation of Connecticut's Gold Coast, see Kara M. Schlichting, "'They Shall Not Pass': Opposition to Public Leisure and State Park Planning in Connecticut and on Long Island," *Journal of Urban History* 41, no. 1 (2015): 116–42; Stephen Richard Higley, *Privilege, Power, and Place: The Geography of the American Upper Class* (Lanham, MD: Rowman and Littlefield, 1995); Marilyn E. Weigold, *The Long Island Sound: A History of Its People, Places, and Environment* (New York: New York University Press, 2004); Peter C. Patton and James M. Kent, *A Moveable Shore: The Fate of the Connecticut Coast* (Durham, NC: Duke University Press, 1992). On suburbanization in the early twentieth-century northeast, see Robert M. Fogelson, *Bourgeois Nightmares: Suburbia, 1870–1930* (New Haven: Yale University Press, 2005); Dolores Heyden, *Building Suburbia: Green Fields and Urban Growth, 1820–2000* (New York: Vintage, 2003); Kenneth T. Jackson, *Crabgrass Frontier: The Suburbanization of the United States* (New York: Oxford University Press, 1985). On the formation of private beach associations in Connecticut, see Linda B. Krause, "Coastal Districts and Associations," report prepared for the Coastal Area Management Program, DEP, December 1976. See also Evan McKenzie, *Privatopia: Homeowner Associations and the Rise of Residential Private Government* (New Haven: Yale University Press, 1994).

15. Herbert F. Janick Jr., *A Diverse People: Connecticut, 1914 to the Present* (Guilford, CT: Pequot, 1975), 74. On New Deal housing policies and post–World War II suburbanization, see Jackson, *Crabgrass Frontier;* David M. P. Freund, *Colored Property: State Policy and White Racial Politics in Suburban America* (Chicago: University of Chicago Press, 2007); Lizabeth Cohen, *A Consumers' Republic: The Politics of Mass Consumption in Postwar America* (New York: Vintage, 2003); and Kevin M. Kruse and Thomas J. Sugrue, eds., *The New Suburban History* (Chicago: University of Chicago Press, 2006).

16. Ralph Yarborough, "Introduction to the National Open Beaches Act," 91st Cong., 1st sess., *Congressional Record* 115 (October 16, 1969), pt. 22:30335.

17. House Subcommittee on Fisheries and Wildlife Conservation and the Environment, *Open Beaches: Hearings,* 93rd Cong., 1st sess., October 25, 26, 1973, 33.

18. Wallace Kaufman, "We Should Leave Our Beaches Alone," *NYN,* August 5, 1979.

19. New England River Basins Commission, *A Plan for Long Island Sound,* volume 1: *Summary,* report of the Long Island Sound Regional Study, 1975, 6. On the environmental impact of shoreline privatization and exclusion, see also American Society of Planning Officials, *Subdividing Rural America: Impacts of Recreational Lot and Second Home Development* (Washington, DC: GPO, 1976), 46–56.

20. By the time Governor Ella Grasso addressed the issue of public beach access in August 1975, nine persons in the state had drowned that summer while swimming along unsupervised stretches of shore and in dangerous bodies of water. "Heat Wave Crowds Shore, Then Eases," *GT,* August 4, 1975.

21. National Advisory Commission on Civil Disorders, *Report of the National Advisory Commission on Civil Disorders* (Washington, DC: GPO, 1968), 81. See also U.S.

Outdoor Recreation Resources Review Commission, *The Future of Outdoor Recreation in Metropolitan Regions of the United States* (Washington, DC: GPO, 1962); Margo Tupper, *No Place to Play* (Philadelphia: Chilton, 1966), 86–89; Richard Kraus, "Recreation and Civil Disorder," *Parks and Recreation* 3 (July 1967): 38–39, 48–49; Richard Kraus, *Public Recreation and the Negro: A Study of Participation and Administrative Practices* (New York: Center for Urban Education, 1968); National League of Cities, *Recreation in the Nation's Cities: Problems and Approaches,* special report prepared at the request of the Department of the Interior, 1968; National Recreation and Park Association, *Parks and Recreation in the Urban Crisis* (Washington, DC: National Recreation and Park Association, 1969); Robert Blackwell, "Urban Recreation: Perspective and Recommendation," in *Highlights 70: 1970 Congress for Recreation and Parks* (Washington, DC: National Park and Recreation Association, 1971), 203–6; National Recreation and Park Association, *Open Space and Recreation Opportunity in America's Inner Cities: A Summary of an Analysis of Low-Income, High-Density Inner-City Residents in Their Noncommercial Leisure Resources in 25 Cities over 250,000 Population* (Washington, DC: National Recreation and Park Association, 1974); U.S. Department of the Interior, *Urban Recreation: Report Prepared for the Nationwide Outdoor Recreation Plan by the Interdepartmental Work Group on Urban Recreation* (Washington, DC: GPO, 1974).

22. "Suburbs Stiffening Beach Curbs," *NYT,* July 10, 1972.

23. "Public Access to Beaches: Common Law Doctrines and Constitutional Challenges," *NYU Law Review* 48 (1973): 393n171.

24. Jason Sokol, *All Eyes Are upon Us: Race and Politics from Boston to Brooklyn* (New York: Basic, 2014), 171. On the divergent fortunes of cities and suburbs in post–World War II Connecticut, see Douglas W. Rae, *City: Urbanism and Its End* (New Haven: Yale University Press, 2003); David Radcliffe, *Charter Oak Terrace: Life, Death, and Rebirth of a Public Housing Project* (Hartford: Southside Media, 1998); Jack Dougherty, *On the Line: How Schooling, Housing, and Civil Rights Shaped Hartford and Its Suburbs,* book-in-progress, available at http://ontheline.trincoll.edu/book/; Shaun McGann, "The Effects of 'Redlining' on the Hartford Metropolitan Region," *ConnecticutHistory.org* (March 2014), available at http://connecticuthistory.org/the-effects-of-redlining-on-the-hartford-metropolitan-region/; Terry J. Tondro, "Fragments of Regionalism: State and Regional Planning in Connecticut at Century's End," *St. John's Law Review* 73 (Fall 1999): 1123–58. On exclusionary zoning in Connecticut, see Ellen Szita, "Exclusionary Zoning in the Suburbs: The Case of New Canaan, Connecticut," *Civil Rights Digest,* March 1, 1973, 3–14; Michael N. Danielson, *The Politics of Exclusion* (New York: Columbia University Press, 1976), 59–61; Suburban Action Institute, *A Study of Zoning in Connecticut,* report prepared for the Connecticut Commission on Human Rights and Opportunities (New York, 1978); and Lisa Prevost, *Snob Zones: Fear, Prejudice, and Real Estate* (Boston: Beacon, 2013).

ONE New England's Sand Curtain

1. Ann Petry, "My Most Humiliating Jim Crow Experience," *Negro Digest* 48 (June 1946): 63–64.

2. Ibid.

3. Constance Baker Motley, interview, December 18, 1987, http://www.kaltura
.com/kwidget/wid/_419852/entry_id/1_gmoj79ut.

4. Rebecca de Schweinitz, *If We Could Change the World: Young People and America's Long Struggle for Racial Equality* (Chapel Hill: University of North Carolina Press,
2009), 181.

5. See Joseph L. Sax, "The Public Trust Doctrine in Natural Resource Law: Effective Judicial Intervention," *Michigan Law Review* 68 (January 1970): 473–566; David W.
Owens, *Public Rights in Shoreline Recreation Areas: A Selectively Annotated Bibliography*
(Chapel Hill: Center for Urban and Regional Studies, University of North Carolina,
1975); David J. Brower et al., *Access to the Nation's Beaches: Legal and Planning Perspectives*
(Raleigh: UNC Sea Grant, 1978); David C. Slade et al., *Putting the Public Trust Doctrine
to Work: The Application of the Public Trust Doctrine to the Management of Lands, Waters
and Living Resources of the Coastal States* (Washington, DC: Coastal States Organization,
1997); Diana M. Whitelaw and Gerald Robert Visgilio, eds., *America's Changing Coasts:
Private Rights and Public Trust* (Cheltenham, UK: Edward Elgar, 2005); Jack H. Ar-
cher et al., *The Public Trust Doctrine and the Management of America's Coasts* (Amherst:
University of Massachusetts Press, 1994); Dennis W. Ducsik, *Shoreline for the Public: A
Handbook of Social, Economic, and Legal Considerations Regarding Public Recreational
Use of the Nation's Coastal Shoreline* (Cambridge, MA: MIT Press, 1974).

6. Brower et al., *Access to the Nation's Beaches,* 20–22.

7. Orange v. Resnick, 94 Conn. 573, 109 A. 864 (1920). See also T. Paul Tremont, "The
Status of Riparian Rights in Connecticut," *Connecticut Bar Journal* 33 (1959): 430–39.

8. Incorporating the Fenwick Association, House Joint Resolution No. 21, January
1885, *Special Acts and Resolutions of the State of Connecticut, with an Appendix,* vol. 10:
From 1885 to 1889 Inclusive, 20.

9. Linda B. Krause, "Coastal Districts and Associations," report prepared for the
Coastal Area Management Program, DEP, December 1976.

10. "Chicago Real Estate," *CT,* April 6, 1890; "Developing Land in Old Saybrook,"
HC, November 29, 1914; "James Jay Smith: Realty Developer Began Several Connecticut
Shore Communities," *NYT,* April 17, 1942.

11. "An Act Incorporating the Point O'Woods Association, Incorporated," HB605,
Connecticut General Assembly, 1925, http://powbeach.net/documents/POW%20Char
ter%20May%202010.pdf.

12. The James Jay Smith Company was the first real estate developer to implement the "club plan" in Connecticut. "Under this plan no lots will be sold to undesirable
people, for it is a prerequisite for lot ownership that one must become a member of the
club." See "New Development on Lake Hayward Attracts Buyers," *HC,* June 8, 1930.

13. "Realty Firm in Business for 70 Years," *HC,* November 6, 1949.

14. Works Progress Administration, *Park, Parkway, and Recreational Study* (1938),
116, 134, 135, 144, box 9, SPFC.

15. "State Parks Needed: Increasing Population Creates Necessity of State Parks in
Fairfield County" (1928?), folder A. M. Turner correspondence (1928–29), box 4, SPFC.

16. "Things to Think About," *SLT,* June 20, 1946.

17. "Unneighborly Westport," *HC,* June 9, 1931.

18. "Darien Moves to Keep Outsiders from Beach," *HC,* May 13, 1933.

19. James C. Kozlowski, "Can Towns Restrict Public Park Access to Residents and Their Guests?" *Parks and Recreation* 36 (October 2001), http://cehdclass.gmu.edu/jkozlows/lawarts/10OCT01.pdf.

20. See Brenden P. Leydon v. Town of Greenwich et al., Supreme Court of Connecticut (July 26, 2001), 257 Conn. 318; 777 A.2d 552; 2001 Conn.

21. Borough of Fenwick v. Old Saybrook, 133 Conn. 22 (1946).

22. An Act Concerning Public Parks and Bathing Beaches in the Town of Greenwich (April 10, 1919), *Connecticut Special Acts and Resolutions,* vol. 18, part 1, no. 124.

23. Madison Town Meeting Minutes, March 2, 1931, vol. 3, 128–29, MTCO.

24. "More Towns Are Closing Beach Areas to Outsiders," *NYT,* July 4, 1970.

25. "Beach Discrimination," *NYAN,* August 12, 1939.

26. Frank F. Lee, *Negro and White in Connecticut Town* (New York: College and University Press, 1961), 114.

27. Paul D. Dennis, "A Coast off Limits to the Poor," *NYT,* April 17, 1977.

28. House Committee on Public Works, *Area 1—Ash Creek to Saugatuck River, Conn., Beach Erosion Control Study,* 81st Cong., 2nd sess. (Washington: GPO, 1950), 36–37. See also Kara M. Schlichting, "'They Shall Not Pass': Opposition to Public Leisure and State Park Planning in Connecticut and on Long Island," *Journal of Urban History* 41, no. 1 (2015): 116–42.

29. "Friday Night Government," *HC,* August 22, 1965.

30. See W. H. Burr to W. O. Filley, October 20, 1928; May 1, 1929; and August 5, 1929, folder A. M. Turner correspondence (1928–29), box 4, SPFC; Turner to State Forestry Department, June 30, 1930, folder A. M. Turner correspondence (1930), ibid.; Turner to Filley, July 1, 1930, ibid.; Daniel S. Sanford to Lucius F. Robinson, February 3, 1931, folder A. M. Turner correspondence (1931), ibid.; Turner to Filley, July 26, 1931, ibid.; A. M. Turner, "A State Park Policy for Connecticut," April 6, 1932, Report of the Field Secretary, Sherwood Island, State Parks and Forest Commission, DEP; "Public Beach for Fairfield County Asked," *HC,* April 24, 1931; H. H. Chapman to Governor Wilbur L. Cross, November 16, 1937, folder Sherwood Island and State Park, box 399, WC. On the 1938 Great New England Hurricane, see also Peter C. Patton and James M. Kent, *A Movable Shore: The Fate of the Connecticut Coast* (Durham, NC: Duke University Press, 1992), 1–24.

31. House Committee on Public Works, *Area 1,* 22.

32. A. M. Turner to Flavel Shurtleff, June 30, 1939, folder A. M. Turner correspondence (1939), box 4, SPFC.

33. House Committee on Public Works, *Area 1,* 36.

34. Turner to Shurtleff, June 30, 1939, SPFC.

35. Memo by William S. Wise, January 29, 1954, folder Beach Erosion, box 547, JDL.

36. Norris L. Bull to the Beach Association of Connecticut, December 28, 1954, folder Beach Erosion—Proposed Legislation, box 646, AR.

37. Norris L. Bull to Senator Prescott Bush, February 3, 1955, ibid.

38. Bull to Beach Association of Connecticut, December 28, 1954, AR.

39. Joseph B. Smith to Governor Abraham Ribicoff, April 5, 1955, folder Beach Erosion—Proposed Legislation, box 646, AR.

40. Orlando Lorenzetti to Governor Abraham Ribicoff, February 15, 1955, folder Beach Erosion (Gov. Correspondence), box 646, AR.

41. Background Material on the Connecticut Beach Erosion Control Program, April 2, 1955, folder Beach Erosion Background Material, box 646, RG 5, AR.

42. Mary-Louise Quinn, *The History of the Beach Erosion Board, U.S. Army, Corps of Engineers, 1930–63*, August 1977, report prepared for U.S. Army, Corps of Engineers (Washington: GPO, 1977), 84.

43. Earl R. Gray to Governor Abraham Ribicoff, August 30, 1957, folder Beach Erosion—Beach Town Officials, Legislators, Beach Associations, box 646, AR.

44. "Friday Night Government," *HC,* August 22, 1965.

45. Krause, "Coastal Districts and Associations," 9.

46. Ibid., Appendix A; "Mother Nature Died Here: An Epitaph for Wetlands?" *HC,* March 29, 1970; "Endangered Edge of the Sea," *Life,* July 19, 1968, 4; Governor John Dempsey to Senate Committee on Interior and Insular Affairs, February 10, 1961, folder Shore Line Areas 1961–1962, box A-295, JD; "Connecticut's Beaches" (1975), folder DEP/Beaches, box 133, EG. On the environmental impact of post–World War II homebuilding, including wetlands, see Adam Rome, *The Bulldozer in the Countryside: Suburban Sprawl and the Rise of American Environmentalism* (New York: Cambridge University Press, 2001), esp. 154–65.

47. U.S. Outdoor Recreation Resources Review Commission, *Outdoor Recreation for America: A Report to the President and to the Congress* (Washington: GPO, 1962). See also Diana R. Dunn, "Leisure Resources in America's Inner Cities," *Parks and Recreation* (March 1974): 34.

48. The ORRC's mandate explicitly excluded urban areas from consideration in favor of rural and suburban populations.

49. U.S. Department of Housing and Urban Development, *Improvements Needed in Administration of Open-Space Land Program,* special report prepared for U.S. General Accounting Office, March 8, 1972, 5–6.

50. U.S. Commission on Marine Science, Engineering, and Resources, *Our Nation and the Sea: A Plan for National Action* (Washington: GPO, 1969), 7:239–46.

51. R. Sargent Shriver, "Achieving Environmental Justice," in *Congress Highlights: 1972 Congress for Recreation and Parks,* ed. Anita E. Leifer (Washington: NRPA, 1973), 12–17.

52. U.S. Department of Housing and Urban Development, *Urban Recreation: Report Prepared for the Nationwide Outdoor Recreation Plan by the Interdepartmental Work Group on Urban Recreation* (Washington: GPO, 1974), 40.

53. Ibid., 20.

54. *Gentleman's Agreement,* dir. Elia Kazan (20th Century Fox, 1947).

55. "Greenwich Tests Show Color Bias," *NYT,* July 21, 1964.

56. Jason Sokol, *All Eyes Are Upon Us: Race and Politics from Boston to Brooklyn* (New York: Basic, 2014), 64.

57. Lily Geismer, *Don't Blame Us: Suburban Liberals and the Transformation of the Democratic Party* (Princeton, NJ: Princeton University Press, 2014), 24.

58. James G. Coke and Charles S. Liebman, quoted in Michael N. Danielson, *The Politics of Exclusion* (New York: Columbia University Press, 1976), 59.

59. David L. Kirp, John P. Dwyer, and Larry A. Rosenthal, *Our Town: Race, Housing, and the Soul of Suburbia* (New Brunswick, NJ: Rutgers University Press, 1995), 47–48.

60. "Draft Zoning Laws Hit By Rights Unit," *HC,* October 26, 1975.

61. Andrew Wiese, *Places of their Own: African American Suburbanization in the Twentieth Century* (Chicago: University of Chicago Press, 2004), 227; Danielson, *The Politics of Exclusion,* 61; "The Suburbs Have to Open Their Gates," *NYT,* November 7, 1971.

62. Suburban Action Institute, *A Study of Zoning in Connecticut,* report prepared for the Connecticut Commission on Human Rights and Opportunities (New York: Suburban Action Institute, 1978), 83–85.

63. Ellen Szita, "Exclusionary Zoning in the Suburbs: The Case of New Canaan, Connecticut," *Civil Rights Digest,* March 1, 1973, 10.

64. Ibid.

65. Between 1950 and 1970, the percentage of Connecticut's black population that lived in the state's six most densely populated cities (Bridgeport, Hartford, New Haven, Norwalk, Stamford, and Waterbury) increased from 73 percent to 79 percent. By 1978, 90 percent of the state's African American population and 70 percent of its Spanish-speaking population were concentrated in central cities (areas with the least restrictive zoning ordinances). See Suburban Action Institute, *A Study of Zoning in Connecticut,* 17, 1.

66. "Darien Puts Curb on Church Camp," *NYT,* June 15, 1955.

67. Ibid.

68. Color Declared Basis of Andover Rejection," *HC,* November 2, 1963; "NAACP Leader Raps Inaction of Killian," *HC,* May 12, 1969; "Negro landowner wins Andover lake rights," *HC,* December 29, 1967.

69. "Pressures of Growth Stir Zoning Battles in Suburbs," *NYT,* May 29, 1967.

70. Georgiana Weldon, open letter, March 7, 1967, folder Zoning, box A-313, JD.

71. Harold A. Huckins Jr. to Governor Dempsey, March 30, 1967, ibid.

72. Marie Lloyd to Governor Dempsey, April 5, 1967, ibid.

73. "Pressures of Growth Stir Zoning Battles in Suburbs," *NYT,* May 29, 1967.

74. Edward Case to Governor Dempsey, March 27, 1967, folder Zoning, box A-313, JD.

75. "Compromise Reveals Legislative Failure," *HC,* July 2, 1972.

76. Thomas J. Sugrue, "All Politics Is Local: The Persistence of Localism in Twentieth-Century America," in *The Democratic Experiment: New Directions in American*

Political History, ed. Julian E. Zelizer, Meg Jacobs, and William J. Novak (Princeton, NJ: Princeton University Press, 2003), 317.

77. Margaret Weir, "Urban Poverty and Defensive Localism," *Dissent* 41 (Summer 1994): 337–42.

78. Clyde Summers to Spencer Coxe, May 20, 1969, folder 2, box 1125, ACLU.

79. "Women Barred from Beaches Threaten Action," *HC,* August 2, 1966.

80. Henry P. Bakewell Jr., letter to the editor, *NHR,* August 4, 1966.

81. Regina Beauton, letter to the editor, *NHR,* August 4, 1966.

82. "3 City Women again Refused Beach Entry," *NHR,* August 8, 1966.

83. Osmond Fraenkel to Melvin L. Wulf, April 4, 1968, folder 2, box 1125, ACLU.

84. Melvin L. Wulf to Osmond Fraenkel and Edward J. Ennis, April 2, 1968, ibid.

TWO   What Am I Doing Here?

1. "Ned Coll's Journey," *HC,* June 23, 1985.

2. Ibid.

3. *Fairfield Manor* (1960), 60–61, 90, FUA; *Fairfield Manor* (1961), 98–99, 131–32, 163, ibid.; *Fairfield Manor* (1962), 28–32, 48, 159, ibid.

4. Walter Petry, interview by Andrew Kahrl, September 28, 2015, transcript (in author's possession).

5. Ellen Kaye, "The Invasion of Old Lyme," *Harper's Bazaar,* August 1972, 108.

6. Walter Petry interview.

7. "Ned Coll: 'Crusader' on the Move Here," *WHN,* June 27, 1974.

8. Ned Coll, interview by Andrew Kahrl, May 18, 2009, transcript (in author's possession).

9. "Coll Has Lived in the Spirit of Kennedy," *HC,* November 23, 1993.

10. Ned Coll interview, May 18, 2009.

11. Earlie Powell, interview by Andrew Kahrl, June 15, 2009, transcript (in author's possession).

12. Ibid.

13. Charles S. Johnson, "The Negro Population of Hartford, Connecticut" (New York: National Urban League, 1921), 22–51.

14. "North from the Cotton Fields," *HC,* March 8, 1925; S. K. Close, "The Ties That Bind: Southwest Georgians, Black College Students, and Migration to Hartford," *Journal of South Georgia History* 15 (2000): 19–53; Thomas R. Lewis and John E. Harmon, *Connecticut: A Geography* (Boulder, CO: Westview, 1986), 70; David Radcliffe, *Charter Oak Terrace: Life, Death, and Rebirth of a Public Housing Project* (Hartford, CT: Southside Media, 1998), 59–63.

15. Johnson, "The Negro Population of Hartford," 12, 51–66.

16. Slum Clearance Study Committee, *Preliminary Survey of Housing Conditions in Slum Areas for the Purpose of Laying Out a Slum Clearance and Rehousing Program in the City of Hartford, Connecticut* (Hartford, 1934), 38; "Where Can a Negro Live?," *HC,* August 19, 1956; Radcliffe, *Charter Oak Terrace,* 4.

17. "Courts Seen Lax on Slumlords," *HC*, June 4, 1969.

18. "North End Assn. Airs Problems of Negro Area," *HC*, August 10, 1967.

19. "Negro Health Record Hit by Bulletin," *HC*, March 27, 1937; "A Challenge to Hartford," *HC*, March 29, 1937.

20. "City Slums Worse Than Last Year," *HC*, January 29, 1956; "Rat Bite Property Added to Slum Housing List," *HC*, August 24, 1962; "Health Dept. Outlines Possible Source of Russell St. Block Rash Problem," *HC*, June 16, 1964. See also Malcolm McLaughlin, "The Pied Piper of the Ghetto: Lyndon Johnson, Environmental Justice, and the Politics of Rat Control," *Journal of Urban History* 37, no. 4 (2011): 541–61.

21. Kenneth B. Clark, *Dark Ghetto: Dilemmas of Social Power* (New York: Harper Torchbooks, 1965), 27, 32–33.

22. See Federal HOLC "Redlining" Map, Hartford area, 1937, available at http://magic.lib.uconn.edu/otl/doclink_holc.html.

23. Harold Lewis Malt Associates, *An Analysis of Public Safety as Related to the Incidence of Crime in Parks and Recreation Areas in Central Cities*, special report prepared for U.S. Department of Housing and Urban Development (Washington, DC: GPO, January 1972), 3.

24. "Negro Study Urges Social Facilities," *HC*, January 18, 1945; "Civic Study Urges Action For Negroes," *HC*, January 16, 1945.

25. "The Public Housing Authority," *HC*, May 22, 1937.

26. "Board to Continue Investigation of Tenement Houses," *HC*, August 17, 1933.

27. "Cornerstone of Bellevue Square Laid," *HC*, September 29, 1941.

28. "Bellevue Square Stone Rites Set This Afternoon," *HC*, September 28, 1941; "Cornerstone of Bellevue Square Laid," *HC*, September 29, 1941.

29. "Would Halt Segregation in Housing," *HC*, February 23, 1949.

30. "Bellevue Square Tenants Hurl Charges at Authority," *HC*, May 11, 1951.

31. "The People's Forum," *HC*, February 11, 1956.

32. *1953 Supplement to General Statutes of Connecticut*, sec. 2464c and 2465c. See also Connecticut Commission on Civil Rights, *Racial Integration in Public Housing Projects in Connecticut* (Hartford, 1955), 18, 1.

33. "Exit the Benign Quotas," *HC*, March 5, 1965.

34. "NAACP Demands City End 'Benign' Housing Quota Plan," *HC*, February 17, 1965.

35. "Projects Show Rise in Non-White Tenants," *HC*, August 15, 1968.

36. "Projects See Minority Influx," *HC*, April 8, 1969.

37. See Radcliffe, *Charter Oak Terrace*, 66–67.

38. "Roaches Infest Stowe Village," *HC*, September 13, 1967.

39. Radcliffe, *Charter Oak Terrace*, 9.

40. "Stowe Village, or Mud in Your Eye," *HC*, October 29, 1951.

41. "Rats, Cockroaches, Garbage," *HC*, March 22, 1971.

42. Ida V. Carlotti, letter to the editor, *HC*, December 16, 1954.

43. Edward T. Coll, letter to the editor, *HC*, December 6, 1966.

44. Earlie Powell interview.

45. Ibid.

46. Ibid.

47. Ibid.

48. Edward T. Coll, letter to the editor, *HC*, August 29, 1964.

49. Ibid.

50. "Revitalization Corps Founded by Negro, 32," *Indiana [PA] Evening Gazette,* March 27, 1972.

51. Ned Coll interview, May 18, 2009.

52. "Ned Coll's Journey," *HC*, June 23, 1985.

53. Walter Petry interview.

54. "An Unofficial Service Corps," *BG*, November 15, 1964.

55. Ned Coll interview, May 18, 2009.

56. Ibid.

57. Edward T. Coll, letter to the editor, *HC*, July 2, 1965.

58. "One Man Can Make a Difference," *Fairfield*, Fall 1967, 9–13.

59. Ibid.

60. Ned Coll, letter to the editor, *HC*, July 21, 1967.

61. "One Man Can Make a Difference," *Fairfield*, Fall 1967, 9–13.

62. Edward T. Coll, letter to the editor, *HC*, January 7, 1965.

63. Edward T. Coll, letter to the editor, *HC*, January 17, 1966.

64. Edward T. Coll, letter to the editor, *HC*, August 27, 1965.

65. Ibid.

66. Neal Ashby, "Ned Coll's Peace Corps," *Parade*, January 23, 1966, 10.

67. Ibid.

68. Ibid.

69. "Search for Purpose: The Private Peace Corps That Ned Coll Created," *Life*, April 28, 1967, 72–75.

70. Edward T. Coll, letter to the editor, *HC*, July 2, 1965.

71. "Local Special Studies 'Revitalization Corps,'" *HC*, December 25, 1966.

72. Ibid.

73. "New Corps Program Moves Business into the Ghetto," *HC*, March 31, 1968, 1B.

74. Saul Alinsky, *Rules for Radicals* (New York: Vintage, 1971), 70, 98.

75. Riley Johnson, interview by Andrew Kahrl, June 17, 2009, transcript (in author's possession).

76. Alinsky, *Rules for Radicals,* 98, 70.

77. "'Operation Hank' Ends with Songs," *HC*, August 15, 1967; "Revitalization Corps Fans Out to Suburbs," *HC*, May 31, 1968; "Ned Coll's New Frontiers," *HC*, May 14, 1967; "Revitalization Corps," *HC*, November 20, 1968; "New Pleas Made for Children's Winter Clothing," *HC*, December 17, 1966; "Rights Group Questions Halt of Milk Delivery," *HC*, October 9, 1968.

78. Earlie Powell interview.

79. Ned Coll, interviews by Andrew Kahrl, June 21 and June 10, 2009, transcripts (in author's possession).

80. "Lull (The Talk of the Town)," *New Yorker,* November 11, 1967, 51–53. See also "A New Aid Corps at Work in City," *NYT,* December 13, 1965.

81. On the controversy surrounding the construction of the New York State Office Building in Harlem, see Brian D. Goldstein, *The Roots of Urban Renaissance: Gentrification and the Struggle over Harlem* (Cambridge, MA: Harvard University Press, 2017), esp. 88–111.

82. "Lull (The Talk of the Town)," *New Yorker,* November 11, 1967, 51.

83. Elizabeth Johnson (nee Skinner), interview by Andrew Kahrl, June 13, 2017, transcript (in author's possession).

84. "Editorial Lauds Project Started by Ned Coll," *HC,* September 8, 1967.

85. Ashby, "Ned Coll's Peace Corps."

86. Elizabeth Johnson (nee Skinner) interview; "Corps to March Nov. 17 'Day of Rededication,'" *HC,* October 27, 1968.

87. Khalil Gibran Muhammad, *The Condemnation of Blackness: Race, Crime, and the Making of Modern Urban America* (Cambridge, MA: Harvard University Press, 2010).

88. Lyndon B. Johnson, "To Fulfill These Rights" (commencement address, Howard University, Washington, DC, June 4, 1965), http://www.presidency.ucsb.edu/ws/?pid=27021.

89. "Unusual Young Man's Unique Enterprise," *HC,* October 9, 1966.

90. "Coll's Revitalization Corps Growing Despite Tiny Budget," *HC,* July 31, 1966.

91. "Lull (The Talk of the Town)," *New Yorker,* November 11, 1967, 51.

92. "Chapter Opened by Revitalization Corps in Florida," *HC,* April 4, 1966; "Revitalization Corps Launches Bridgeport Project," *HC,* June 14, 1966; "College Chapters Sought by Aid Unit," *NYT,* September 26, 1966; "Corps Opens U of H Chapter," *HC,* October 21, 1966; "Ned Coll's New Frontiers," *HC,* May 14, 1967.

93. "Students Form 'Ghetto Peace Corps' Chapter," *YDN,* November 17, 1967.

94. In the fall of 1962, the Leflore County (Miss.) Board of Supervisors halted the distribution of federal surplus commodities into the county in retaliation for black voter registration. In response, the Student Nonviolent Coordinating Committee (SNCC) launched a nationwide campaign for emergency food deliveries to the Delta region. Churches, college students, and liberal organizations delivered truckloads of food, clothing, and medical supplies to Mississippi that winter. See Charles Payne, *I've Got the Light of Freedom: The Organizing Tradition and the Mississippi Freedom Struggle* (Berkeley: University of California Press, 1995), 158–61. Smaller-scale efforts to assist the state's impoverished population, such as the one carried out by Revitalization Corps, continued for the next several years.

95. "Lull (The Talk of the Town)," *New Yorker,* November 11, 1967, 51–53; "Begin Drive for Clothes," *YDN,* November 29, 1967; "Firm Loans 11-Ton Truck for Delta Clothing Drive," *HC,* December 13, 1967.

96. "Clothing Collected," *YDN*, December 13, 1967; "To Erase the Blot of Intolerance," *BCH*, February 16, 1968; "The Revitalization Corps Aids 'Other Americans,'" *BCH*, March 26, 1968.

97. "To Erase the Blot of Intolerance," *BCH*, February 16, 1968.

98. "Operation Suburbia: Worlds Apart Meet," *HC*, August 6, 1967.

99. "Search for Purpose: The Private Peace Corps That Ned Coll Created," *Life*, April 28, 1967, 72–75.

100. "Help Children Get Fresh Air Care," *NYAN*, June 22, 1927.

101. "Americans Helping Americans," *Lexington [NC] Dispatch*, March 24, 1971.

102. "Coll's Revitalization Corps Growing Despite Tiny Budget," *HC*, July 31, 1966.

103. "Americans Helping Americans," *Lexington [NC] Dispatch*, March 24, 1971.

104. Elizabeth Johnson (nee Skinner) interview.

105. Edward T. Coll, letter to the editor, *HC*, August 24, 1966.

106. "Coll's Revitalization Corps Growing Despite Tiny Budget," *HC*, July 31, 1966.

107. "Operation Suburbia: Worlds Apart Meet," *HC*, August 6, 1967.

108. "Coll's Revitalization Corps Growing Despite Tiny Budget," *HC*, July 31, 1966.

109. "Harlem Children Get View of Suburbia," *HC*, April 2, 1967.

THREE Rats Cause Riots

1. "Militant Marches Protest River Peril," *HC*, May 15, 1969.

2. "Parents Seek to Cover River," *HC*, May 12, 1969, 32.

3. "Council for Fencing, Lowering Park River," *HC*, May 14, 1968.

4. "Tenant Representation Plan Favored," *HC*, March 12, 1969.

5. "Demonstrators March Again at Flatbush Avenue Bridge," *HC*, May 16, 1969.

6. "Parents Tired of Waiting for Lower Depth on Park River," *HC*, April 30, 1969.

7. "Parents Angered at Unkept Promises," *HC*, May 18, 1969.

8. "Dead Rats Win N.Y.C. Rent Strike," *CD*, December 31, 1963; "Slum Rent Strike Upheld by Judge," *NYT*, December 31, 1963; "Harlem Slum Fighter," *NYT*, December 31, 1963.

9. "Governor Sends 'Rat' to Wagner," *NYT*, February 26, 1964.

10. Michael W. Flamm, *In the Heat of the Summer: The New York Riots of 1964 and the War on Crime* (Philadelphia: University of Pennsylvania Press, 2016).

11. Richard Kraus, "Recreation and Civil Disorder," *Parks and Recreation* 3 (July 1967): 38–39, 48–49.

12. Diana R. Dunn, *Open Space and Recreation Opportunity in America's Inner Cities: A Summary of an Analysis of Low-Income, High-Density Inner-City Residents in Their Noncommercial Leisure Resources in 25 Cities over 250,000 Population* (Washington, DC: National Recreation and Park Association, 1974), 27.

13. Kenneth B. Clark, *Dark Ghetto: Dilemmas of Social Power* (New York: Harper Torchbooks, 1965), 31; Anthony Shaw and Porfirio R. Pascasio, "Child Pedestrian Accidents in Central Harlem," *New York Medicine* 23 (June 1967): 270–74.

14. "Poverty, Cops Blamed in Riots," *CD*, July 18, 1966.

15. "Westside Riots Parallel Earlier Outbreaks," *CD*, July 18, 1966.

16. Martin Luther King Jr., quoted in Malcolm McLaughlin, *The Long Hot Summer of 1967: Urban Rebellion in America* (New York: Palgrave Macmillan, 2014), 88–89.

17. "Program Rushed for Slum Youth," *NYT*, August 7, 1966.

18. Lyndon B. Johnson, quoted in Richard Kraus, *Public Recreation and the Negro: A Study of Participation and Administrative Practices* (New York: Center for Urban Education, 1969), 86.

19. August Heckscher, "Keynote Address: Recreation and the Urban Crisis," in *The Proceedings of the Congress for Recreation and Parks Sponsored by the National Recreation and Park Association* (Washington, DC: National Recreation and Park Association, 1967), 5.

20. Ibid., 8.

21. "NYC Keeps 'Cool Summer' Spending a 'Cool Million,'" *CD*, July 8, 1967.

22. Heckscher, "Keynote Address," 4–9; Richard Kraus, "The Park and Recreation Profession's Responsibility in the Ghetto," in *Proceedings of the Congress for Recreation and Parks, National Recreation and Park Association* (Washington, DC: National Recreation and Park Association, 1970), 169–73; Tom L. Hargett, "Programs That Work in the Ghetto and Why," in *Programs That Work—Practical Guide to Successful Public Policy for Parks and Recreation* (Anaheim, CA: National Recreation and Park Association, 1972).

23. Robert Weaver, "Ventilating the Crowded City," *Parks and Recreation* 1 (November 1966): 893.

24. Bureau of Outdoor Recreation, *Recreation in the Nation's Cities: Problems and Approaches,* report prepared for the U.S. Department of the Interior (Washington, DC: Government Printing Office, 1968), 1.

25. Kraus, "The Park and Recreation Profession's Responsibility in the Ghetto," 169.

26. Jeff Wiltse, *Contested Waters: A Social History of Swimming Pools in America* (Chapel Hill: University of North Carolina Press, 2009), 188.

27. Nanine Clay, "Miniparks—Diminishing Returns," *Parks and Recreation* 6 (January 1971): 23. See also Jane Jacobs, *The Death and Life of Great American Cities* (New York: Random House, 1961), esp. 89–111.

28. Clark, *Dark Ghetto,* 4–5.

29. Ibid., 5.

30. "Health Dept. Outlines Possible Source of Russell St. Block Rash Problem," *HC,* June 16, 1964.

31. "Poor Pay Top Prices, Say Rights Groups," *HC,* August 17, 1966.

32. Mary Frances Libassi, "The Elderly of Charter Oak Terrace" (master's thesis, University of Connecticut, 1973), 15.

33. "North End Residents, Police, Air Gripes on Ghetto Relations," *HC*, August 21, 1968.

34. "City Stores Hit by Bricks, Fire," *HC*, July 13, 1967.

35. "Discontent Explodes in the North End," *HC*, July 15, 1967; Ralph Knighton, interview by Andrew Kahrl, November 6, 2016, transcript (in author's possession).

36. "7 Accused of Tossing Firebombs," *HC*, August 17, 1967.

37. *Rat Extermination Act of 1967*, HR 749, 90th Congress, 1st sess., *Congressional Record* 113 (June 29, 1967): 19548–56.

38. Ibid.; Jimmy Breslin, "The Rats Come Every Night. . . : Takes Off Shoe," *WP*, July 25, 1967.

39. "75 Invade Capitol Hill for Rat Bill," *WP*, August 8, 1967.

40. Ned Coll, letter to the editor, *HC*, July 21, 1967.

41. Federal Housing Administration, *Underwriting Manual* (1936); excerpt available at http://epress.trincoll.edu/ontheline2015/wp-content/uploads/sites/16/2015/03/1936FHA-Underwriting.pdf; "'Reluctance to Integrate' Seen in Relocation Study," *HC*, January 1, 1964; Connecticut Advisory Committee to the United States Commission on Civil Rights, *Report on Connecticut: Family Relocation under Urban Renewal* (July 1963), 16, http://www.law.umaryland.edu/marshall/usccr/documents/cr12c76.pdf. On expressways as instruments of ghettoization, see also N. D. B. Connolly, *A World More Concrete: Real Estate and the Remaking of Jim Crow South Florida* (Chicago: University of Chicago Press, 2014).

42. Matthew D. Lassiter, *The Silent Majority: Suburban Politics in the Sunbelt South* (Princeton, NJ: Princeton University Press, 2006), 1.

43. "Coll Charges Violence in Cities Nurtured by Apathetic Suburbia," *HC*, June 23, 1969.

44. Edward T. Coll, letter to the editor, *HC*, July 21, 1967.

45. National Advisory Commission on Civil Disorders, *Report of the National Advisory Commission on Civil Disorders* (Washington: GPO, 1968), 1.

46. Ibid.

47. "New Corps Program Moves Business into the Ghetto," *HC*, March 31, 1968.

48. Edward T. Coll, letter to the editor, *HC*, March 22, 1968.

49. "New Corps Program Moves Business into the Ghetto," *HC*, March 31, 1968.

50. Ibid.

51. "A New Aid Corps at Work in City," *NYT*, December 13, 1965.

52. "Revitalization (Talk of the Town)," *New Yorker,* February 17, 1968, 26–27; "Revitalization Corps Support Urged by RFK," *HC*, February 7, 1968.

53. "Tear Gas Used in Hartford," *HC*, April 5, 1968.

54. Ned Coll, interview, May 18, 2009; "Ned Coll's Journey," *HC*, June 23, 1985.

55. "Mobs Roam North End, Set Fires: Stores Hit, Missiles Injure Two," *HC*, April 6, 1968; "John Barber Arrested, Charged with Incitement," *HC*, April 12, 1968.

56. "Marchers Mourn Fallen Leader," *HC*, April 8, 1968.

57. Elizabeth Johnson (nee Skinner), interview by Andrew Kahrl, June 13, 2017, transcript (in author's possession).

58. "Family Interaction Starts with Hot Dogs," *HC,* May 6, 1968; "Revitalization Corps Fans Out to Suburbs," *HC,* May 31, 1968.

59. "Corps Tutors Try to 'Bridge Gap,'" *HC,* July 28, 1968.

60. "Fence Demanded by Parents," *HC,* May 7, 1968.

61. Ibid.

62. "Protesting Parents Organize Campaign," *HC,* May 8, 1968; "Action Promised on Park River Hazards," *HC,* May 9, 1968.

63. "Report of Governor's Task Force on Lead Poisoning," December 1970, folder Lead Poisoning Report, box A-785, TM.

64. "Six Children from North End Affected by Lead Poisoning," *HC,* June 13, 1968.

65. "'Boilup' Draws Police," *HC,* June 29, 1968.

66. "North End Residents, Police, Air Gripes on Ghetto Relations," *HC,* August 21, 1968.

67. "Tear Gas Used in North End," *HC,* July 19, 1968.

68. "North End Curbside Ammunition Removed," *HC,* June 26, 1968.

69. "'Soul Choppers' Groove at Block Dance," *HC,* July 20, 1968.

70. "Polluted Water or Hot Summer?" *NYAN,* July 25, 1970.

71. House Committee on Government Operations, Subcommittee on Executive Reorganization and Government Research, *Preserving the Future of Long Island Sound,* prepared by Eric Mood, 91st Cong., 2d sess., 1970, Committee Print 168–71.

72. Barry S. Tindall, "From Bedford-Stuyvesant to Bear Mountain," *Parks and Recreation* 4 (January 1969): 41–42.

73. Ibid.

74. "Discrimination Charges Denied by Beach Clubs," *APEP,* July 23, 1968; "Beach Club Admissions Policies Public Test Due," *RBDR,* July 29, 1968.

75. "A Step toward Friendship," *HC,* September 29, 1968; "Meeting Sought to Air Beach Club Bias Claims," *APEP,* July 24, 1968.

76. "Parents Tired of Waiting for Lower Depth on Park River," *HC,* April 30, 1969.

77. "Governor Condemns Dams," *HC,* May 18, 1969.

78. "Parents Tired of Waiting for Lower Depth on Park River," *HC,* April 30, 1969.

79. "Parents Protest River Level, Fights," *HC,* May 8, 1969.

80. "Parents Angered at Unkept Promises," *HC,* May 18, 1969; "Park River Level Down 5 Feet," *HC,* May 30, 1969.

FOUR Let's Share Summer

1. Russell West, interview by Andrew Kahrl, March 8, 2015, transcript (in author's possession).

2. Russell West interview; "Racism Seen Adults' Problem," *HC,* October 25, 1971; Joanne West, interview by Andrew Kahrl, March 13, 2015, transcript (in author's possession).

3. "State Residents Chided on Vacation Program," *HC*, May 3, 1971.

4. Russell West interview.

5. "Revitalization Corps Outing Draws 2,000 to Seminary," *HC*, June 27, 1971; Ned Coll, interview with Andrew Kahrl, May 18, 2009, transcript (in author's possession).

6. "Suspect Bound Over in Assault on Coll," *HC*, May 28, 1969.

7. Ibid.

8. Ned Coll, interview by Andrew Kahrl, May 21, 2009, transcript (in author's possession).

9. Earlie Powell, interview by Andrew Kahrl, June 15, 2009, transcript (in author's possession).

10. David Royston, interview by Andrew Kahrl, March 11, 2015, transcript (in author's possession).

11. "Volunteer Help Sought to Take Children on Trips," *HC*, April 23, 1971; "Aid Welfare Families, Residents Are Urged," *HC*, August 19, 1971.

12. "Inner City Youth Visit Shore," *HC*, August 8, 1971.

13. "Bus Outings for Blacks Test Connecticut's Beach Rules," *NYT*, August 31, 1971.

14. "Corps to Take 20 Families on Westport Visit," *HC*, July 11, 1971.

15. Ellen Kaye, "The Invasion of Old Lyme," *Harper's Bazaar*, August 1972, 108.

16. "Shoreline Visits Sought for Poor," *NLD*, July 17, 1971.

17. "Kids from the Ghetto Welcomed to Seashore," *Milwaukee Journal*, August 23, 1971; Board of Selectmen Meeting Minutes, August 2, 1971, 96–98, MTCO.

18. Dorothy Turner, Report on Ned Coll's Activities in White Sands, folder Hartford (General), box A-729, TM.

19. "Controversy Continues about Corps' Visit," *HC*, October 3, 1971.

20. "Bus Outings for Blacks Test Connecticut's Beach Rules," *NYT*, August 31, 1971.

21. "Frightening Affair at Old Lyme Shores," *Ridgefield Press*, September 23, 1971.

22. "Visit by Children Draws Complaint," *NLD*, August 19, 1971.

23. "Bus Outings for Blacks Test Connecticut's Beach Rules," *NYT*, August 31, 1971; Mary Ann Smith, letter to the editor, *NYT*, September 8, 1971.

24. "Frightening Affair at Old Lyme Shores," *Ridgefield Press*, September 23, 1971.

25. Mary Ann Smith, letter to the editor, *NYT*, September 8, 1971.

26. Sandra Joncus, letter to the editor, *NLD*, September 2, 1971.

27. Kaye, "The Invasion of Old Lyme."

28. "Old Lyme to Halt Corps Buses," *HC*, August 27, 1971; "Influx of Children Brings Complaint," *NLD*, August 19, 1971.

29. "Old Lyme Gets Visit from Coll," *HC*, August 29, 1971.

30. "Frightening Affair at Old Lyme Shores," *Ridgefield Press*, September 23, 1971.

31. "Women's Club to Help Plan Summer Visits," *HC*, November 24, 1971.

32. "Residents Start Inner City Exchange," *HC*, July 28, 1972.

33. Earlie Powell interview.

34. "Revitalization Corps Again Plans to Bus Inner-City Youth to Shore," *NLD,* July 1, 1972.

35. Rebecca de Schweinitz, *If We Could Change the World: Young People and America's Long Struggle for Racial Equality* (Chapel Hill: University of North Carolina Press, 2009), 4.

36. See Robert C. Eckhardt, "The Texas Open Beaches Act," *The Beaches: Public Rights and Private Use* (Houston: Texas Law Institute of Coastal and Marine Resources, University of Houston, 1972); Richard J. Elliott, "The Texas Open Beaches Act: Public Rights to Beach Access," *Baylor Law Review* 28 (1976): 383. See also Gary A. Keith, *Eckhardt: There Once Was a Congressman from Texas* (Austin: University of Texas Press, 2007).

37. See State ex rel. Thornton v. Hay, 22 Ill.254 Or. 584, 462 P.2d 671 (1969). See also "Sand for the People," *The Nation,* February 23, 1970, 196; David J. Brower et al., *Access to the Nation's Beaches: Legal and Planning Perspectives* (Raleigh: UNC Sea Grant, 1978), 27–28; and Douglas L. Inman and Richard M. Brush, "The Coastal Challenge," *Science,* July 6, 1973, 20–32.

38. President's Council on Recreation and Natural Beauty, *From Sea to Shining Sea: A Report on the American Environment — Our Natural Heritage* (Washington, DC: GPO, 1968), 174–75.

39. James A. Noone, "New Federal Program Seeks to Aid States in Control of Coastal-Area Exploitation," *National Journal,* December 9, 1972, 1890.

40. Wallace Kaufman and Orrin Pilkey, *The Beaches Are Moving: The Drowning of America's Shoreline* (Garden City, NJ: Anchor Press, 1979), 236.

41. Ralph Yarborough, "Introduction to the National Open Beaches Act," 91st Cong., 1st sess., *Congressional Record* 115 (October 16, 1969), pt. 22:30335.

42. "Revitalization Corps Again Plans to Bus Inner-City Youth to Shore," *NLD,* July 1, 1972.

43. "Controversy Continues about Corps' Visit," *HC,* October 3, 1971.

44. "Shunned by Some, Corps Volunteer Finds," *HC,* July 27, 1972.

45. Earlie Powell interview.

46. "Operation Depolarization," *MJ,* July 22, 1972.

47. "Corps Wants to Put 3,000 in Shore Homes," *HC,* July 22, 1972.

48. "Corps Workers Are Asked to Agree to Polygraph Exam," *SLT,* June 14, 1973.

49. Margery Scully, quoted in "Plans for Beach Visitation Discussed," *HC,* July 20, 1972.

50. "Plans for Beach Visitation Discussed," *HC,* July 20, 1972.

51. "Inner-City Youngsters Invited August 28," *HC,* August 10, 1972.

52. Robert J. Olson, letter to the editor, *CR,* August 10, 1972.

53. "Plans for Beach Visitation Discussed," *HC,* July 20, 1972.

54. "Board Airs Corps Visits to Beaches," *CR,* July 20, 1972.

55. "Coll's Corps in the Swim This Summer," *CR,* July 27, 1972.

56. "Black Point Beach Group Will Host Youngsters," *HC,* July 23, 1972.

57. Ibid.

58. "Harris Disputes Ned Coll's Statement," *HC*, July 25, 1972.

59. "Coll Apologizes for Visit Announcement," *HC*, July 26, 1972; "Selectman Criticizes 'Ned' Coll for 'Complete Irresponsibility,'" *HC*, August 6, 1972.

60. Robert J. Olson and Dick Fortunato, letter to the editor, *CR*, August 17, 1972.

61. Paul W. Bristol, letter to the editor, *CR*, August 24, 1972.

62. Dorothy D. Reba, letter to the editor, *CR*, August 24, 1972.

63. "Confrontation at the Beach?," *CR*, August 17, 1972.

64. "Coll's Kids Get Warm Welcome," *CR*, August 31, 1972.

65. Ibid.

66. "Coll, Despite Fire, Pushing Shore Plans," *HC*, November 20, 1972.

FIVE   Gut Liberalism

1. Jules Witcover, *The Making of an Ink-Stained Wretch: Half a Century Pounding the Political Beat* (Baltimore: Johns Hopkins University Press, 2005), 110.

2. "Ned Coll, 'Crusader' on the Move Here," *WHN*, June 27, 1974.

3. "Americans Helping Americans," *The Dispatch* (Lexington, NC), March 24, 1971.

4. "Revitalization Corps a Birthday Richer," *HC*, June 23, 1971.

5. "Ned Coll Is Critical of His Role," *HC*, January 19, 1971.

6. Saul Alinsky, *Rules for Radicals* (New York: Vintage, 1971), 194, 184.

7. "Coll Charges Violence in Cities Nurtured by Apathetic Suburbia," *HC*, June 23, 1969.

8. Ned Coll, interview by Andrew Kahrl, June 10, 2009, transcript (in author's possession).

9. "Coll Charges Violence in Cities Nurtured by Apathetic Suburbia," *HC*, June 23, 1969.

10. "Revitalization Corps Founded by Negro, 32," *Indiana [PA] Evening Gazette*, March 27, 1972.

11. Jack Hatch, letter to the editor, *HC*, May 31, 1969; "Revitalization Director to Travel to Midwest," *HC*, February 15, 1970; "Humphrey Honorary Head of Coll's New Urban Program," *HC*, March 1, 1970.

12. "Group Aims to Implement Riot Commission's Plans," *NYT*, March 3, 1970.

13. "'Revitalize Urbia' Theme for Weeklong Campaign," *HC*, March 4, 1970.

14. Jack Dougherty, "Shopping for Schools: How Public Education and Private Housing Shaped Suburban Connecticut," *Journal of Urban History* 38, no. 2 (2012): 205–24.

15. See Mary Daly, "Race Restrictive Covenants in Property Deeds," October 22, 2012, http://commons.trincoll.edu/cssp/2012/10/22/race-restrictive-covenants-in-property-deeds/.

16. "Program Hopes to Aid Ghetto," *HC*, March 10, 1970.

17. "Volunteer Corps to Stage Vigil for Inner City," *HC*, March 12, 1970.

18. "Program Hopes to Aid Ghetto," *HC*, March 10, 1970; Revitalize Urbia Days, March 2, 1970, folder Revitalize Urbia Days (1970), box A-291, JD.

19. "One Man's Peace Corps," *CT*, March 13, 1970.

20. "'Revitalize Urbia' Lists Nationwide Activities," *HC*, March 15, 1970.

21. Revitalize Urbia Days, March 9, 1970, folder Revitalize Urbia Days (1970), box A-291, JD.

22. "Coll Latest Entry in Congressional Race," *HC*, April 9, 1970.

23. Campaign advertisement, *HC*, May 8, 1970.

24. "Democrats Identify Major Issues of Day," *HC*, April 29, 1970.

25. "State GOP Wary of Economy, Indochina," *HC*, May 27, 1970.

26. "Schlesinger Stumps for Coll," *HC*, October 10, 1970.

27. "Bennett Available for State GOP Bid," *HC*, June 10, 1970.

28. Evelyn J. Lavelle, letter to the editor, *HC*, May 18, 1970.

29. "Coordinator Named for Coll Campaign," *HC*, June 6, 1970.

30. Lee A. Reidy, letter to the editor, *HC*, July 8, 1970.

31. Nathaniel Hathaway, letter to the editor, *HC*, May 24, 1970.

32. "Democratic Leaders Swing Nomination to Jay Jackson," *HC*, June 22, 1970; "Coll Qualifies as Independent Candidate for Congress in 1st District," *HC*, August 30, 1970.

33. "Coll Runs as Independent after Convention Defeat," *HC*, June 23, 1970.

34. "Coll Campaign Opens 2 Offices in West Hartford," *HC*, August 23, 1970; "Coll with Small Vote May Pretend He Won," *HC*, November 4, 1970.

35. Ned Coll interview, May 21, 2009.

36. "Mayor Opposes Teen-Age Vote," *HC*, September 30, 1970.

37. "Democrats Take 4 of 6 House Seats," *HC*, November 4, 1970; "Coll with Small Vote May Pretend He Won," *HC*, November 4, 1970.

38. "U.S. Jaycees Name Ned Coll as 'Outstanding Young Man,'" *HC*, January 10, 1971.

39. "Rockefeller Grant: $9,500," June 1971, RF; "Revitalization Corps a Birthday Richer," *HC*, June 23, 1971.

40. "Rockefeller Grant: $150,000," November 1971, RF; "Revitalization Corps Gets Grant," *HC*, November 21, 1971.

41. "They Came East to Help the Poor," *HC*, May 22, 1971.

42. "Operation Suburbia Attracts Nuns to City," *HC*, June 18, 1970; "Revitalization Corps Founded by Negro, 32," *Indiana [PA] Evening Gazette*, March 27, 1972.

43. "'Ned' Coll, 32, Tries to Enter Primary," *HC*, January 6, 1972; "Coll Makes New Hampshire Primary," *HC*, January 7, 1972; "Coll Joins Presidential Primary with Unusual Political Pledge," *HC*, January 8, 1972; Russell West, interview by Andrew Kahrl, March 8, 2015, transcript (in author's possession).

44. "Coll Makes New Hampshire Primary," *HC*, January 7, 1972.

45. "Coll Joins Presidential Primary with Unusual Political Pledge," *HC*, January 8, 1972.

46. "Muskie Campaign Workers See Move by Opponents to Create Resentment," *MUL*, March 3, 1972.

47. "Coll Joins Presidential Primary with Unusual Political Pledge," *HC*, January 8, 1972; Ned Coll interview, June 10, 2009; "Ned Coll, 32, Tries to Enter Primary," *HC*, January 6, 1972.

48. "Coll Joins Presidential Primary with Unusual Political Pledge," *HC*, January 8, 1972.

49. "Americans Helping Americans," *The Dispatch* (Lexington, NC), March 24, 1971.

50. "Coll Joins Presidential Primary with Unusual Political Pledge," *HC*, January 8, 1972.

51. Hunter S. Thompson, *Fear and Loathing: On the Campaign Trail '72* (New York: Straight Arrow Books, 1973), 59.

52. "Coll Campaign Office to Open in Boston," *HC*, January 25, 1972.

53. "Coll Opens Offices for Campaign," *HC*, January 12, 1972; "Coll Joins Presidential Primary with Unusual Political Pledge," *HC*, January 8, 1972.

54. Thompson, *Fear and Loathing*, 37.

55. "Ed Coll Tough Act to Follow," *BG*, March 6, 1972.

56. "Marriage Not Slowing Activist Coll," *HC*, March 19, 1972.

57. Ibid.

58. Earlie Powell, interview by Andrew Kahrl, June 15, 2009, transcript (in author's possession).

59. "Muskie Campaign Workers See Move by Opponents to Create Resentment," *MUL*, March 3, 1972.

60. "'Relevant Religion' Not School Prayer, Is Needed, Says Coll," *HC*, February 3, 1972.

61. "Ed Coll Summarizes Policies," *MUL*, March 6, 1972.

62. "Meskill Stumps Granite State, Meets Coll," *HC*, March 4, 1972.

63. "Viet Issue Sparks Debate," *MUL*, March 6, 1972.

64. Ibid.

65. "New Hampshire Debate Offers Few Surprises," *HC*, March 6, 1972.

66. "Viet Issue Sparks Debate," *MUL*, March 6, 1972.

67. "Muskie, McGovern Clash on Finances," *LAT*, March 6, 1972.

68. "Ed Coll Tough Act to Follow," *BG*, March 6, 1972.

69. Ned Coll interview, June 21, 2009.

70. "N.H. TV Debate Has No Winner," *BG*, March 6, 1972.

71. "Political Unknown, 32, Steals TV Spotlight in New Hampshire Race," *CT*, March 6, 1972; "Ed Coll Tough Act to Follow," *BG*, March 6, 1972; "Primary Runners Ramble on TV," *Guardian* (UK), March 7, 1972.

72. Ned Coll interview, June 21, 2009.

73. Elizabeth Johnson (nee Skinner), interview by Andrew Kahrl, June 13, 2017, transcript (in author's possession).

74. Russell West interview.

75. Elizabeth Johnson (nee Skinner) interview; Earlie Powell interview.

76. "Primary Vote Seen by Coll as Symbolic," *HC*, April 27, 1972.

77. J. Anthony Lukas, *Common Ground: A Turbulent Decade in the Lives of Three American Families* (New York: Vintage, 1986).

78. "Ed Coll and His Rat Kick Off Drive in Mass. Presidential Primary," *BG*, April 5, 1972; "Ned Coll's Foe Is in City Streets," *BG*, May 14, 1972.

79. Anthony Wolff, "We Shall Fight Them on the Beaches," *Harper's*, August 1973, 56.

80. See Robert G. Healy, *Land Use and the States* (Baltimore: Johns Hopkins University Press, 1976), 80–125, and Calvin Trillin, "Some Reflections on Sand as Real Estate," *New Yorker*, November 18, 1972, 215–24.

81. Coastal Zone Management Act of 1972, Pub. Law 92–583, 86 Stat. 1280, 92nd Cong., 2d sess. (October 27, 1972). See also Robert G. Healy and Jeffrey A. Zinn, "Environment and Development Conflicts in Coastal Zone Management," *Journal of the American Planning Association* 51, no. 3 (1985): 300; David J. Brower et al., *Access to the Nation's Beaches: Legal and Planning Perspectives* (Raleigh: UNC Sea Grant, 1978), 39–48.

82. Richard M. Nixon, Second Inaugural Address (January 20, 1973), available at http://avalon.law.yale.edu/20th_century/nixon2.asp.

83. Thompson, *Fear and Loathing*, 190.

six Who the Hell Invited That Guy?

1. "Residents Discuss Gravel Pit," *HC*, July 15, 1973.

2. "3 Zoning Requests Denied," *HC*, June 6, 1971; "Property Assessments Lashed," *HC*, February 25, 1973. See also Board of Selectmen Meeting Minutes, February 20, 1973, MTCO.

3. "Corps Leases Woodland Acres," *HC*, February 2, 1973.

4. "Revitalization Corps Director Arrested," *HC*, January 13, 1973.

5. "Gubernatorial Footwear," *HC*, January 19, 1973.

6. Raymond and May Associates, "Development Plan: Town of Madison, Connecticut," report prepared for Madison (CT) Planning and Zoning Commission, 1969, 1–5; Richard Matheny, "Case Study: Pollution of Hobbit Pond (Meadowville [Madison, Conn.])," 1973, folder 29, box 54, AJV.

7. On the Madison Property Owners Association, see Matheny, "Case Study," n.p. On the Madison Taxpayers Association, see "Taxpayers Schedule Annual Meeting," *HC*, May 26, 1971.

8. See Matheny, "Case Study," n.p.

9. Ibid; "Madison Spends a Day Learning Its ABCs," *SLT*, February 26, 1970; Andrea Walton, "Building a Pipeline to College: A Study of the Rockefeller-Funded 'A Better Chance' Program, 1963–1969," *American Education History Journal* 36, no. 1 (2009): 151–69.

10. "Madison Spends a Day Learning Its ABCs," *SLT*, February 26, 1970.

11. "Pupil Housing: A Problem No One Likes," *SLT*, March 12, 1970.

12. "Milum to Oppose Low Cost Housing," *HC*, May 1, 1970.

13. Ibid.

14. "Big Turnout Expected at Polls for Boy Project Referendum," *HC,* April 28, 1970.

15. Comments here and in the following paragraph are from Georgette Cutting, letter to the editor, *SLT,* June 18, 1970.

16. Theodore S. Cole, letter to the editor, *SLT,* April 16, 1970; Rita P. Juzwiakowski, letter to the editor, *SLT,* April 23, 1970

17. Thomas A. King, letter to editor, *SLT,* April 9, 1970.

18. See, for example, *SLT,* April 16, 1970.

19. H. B. Birnbaum, letter to the editor, *SLT,* April 23, 1970.

20. "ABC Issue Moves toward April 28 Vote," *SLT,* April 23, 1970.

21. "Contract with ABC Is Cancelled by American Legion," *SLT,* April 2, 1970.

22. "Zoners Consider Amendment That May Affect ABC Plan," *HC,* April 17, 1970.

23. "Shore 'Nuff," *SLT,* April 16, 1970.

24. "Controversy over Aid to Disadvantaged Comes Up for Voter Decision Next Week," *HC,* April 19, 1970.

25. "Aid to Disadvantaged Youth Draws Vigorous Opposition," *HC,* April 18, 1970.

26. Chris Weiss, letter to the editor, *SLT,* April 9, 1970.

27. "Controversy over Aid to Disadvantaged Comes Up for Voter Decision Next Week," *HC,* April 19, 1970; "ABC Issue Moves toward April 28 Vote," *SLT,* April 23, 1970.

28. "Referendum Rejects Needy Student Plan," *HC,* April 29, 1970.

29. "Costello Reverses Decision," *HC,* July 18, 1970.

30. "Clifford to Proceed with ABC," *HC,* May 20, 1970.

31. "Five Board Resignations Asked by ABC Opponent," *HC,* July 8, 1970; "ABC Students Must Pay Tuition Says Education Board," *SLT,* June 4, 1970; "Suit Challenges Tuition Fee," *HC,* June 3, 1971.

32. "Walker Lauds Town for Crisis Readiness," *HC,* May 6, 1970; "Need for Police Public Information Stressed," *SLT,* May 14, 1970.

33. "Commissioner Defends May Day Riot Expense," *HC,* May 24, 1970.

34. "Change Necessary Says Peter Swift in Valedictory," *SLT,* June 25, 1970.

35. "Mrs. Dallas to Run for Selectman," *HC,* June 16, 1971; "Candidate Welcomes Chance to Serve," *HC,* July 14, 1971; "GOP Candidate Praised," *HC,* July 29, 1971.

36. Board of Selectmen Meeting Minutes, August 2, 1971, MTCO.

37. "Visiting Children Taken Home," *HC,* August 6, 1971.

38. "Hartford Children Will Visit at Beach," *HC,* August 3, 1971.

39. "Coll Continues Effort for Ghetto Youth," *HC,* September 4, 1971.

40. "Mrs. Dallas Wins in Close Race," *HC,* November 3, 1971.

41. June S. Rice, *One Writer's Voice* (Nashville, TN: Scythe Publications, 1996), 102.

42. "First Selectman's Corner," *SLT,* January 18, 1973.

43. "Beach Issue Can't Shake Off Problems," *HC*, March 17, 1976.

44. "Confrontation Shaping Up on Madison Beaches," *NHR*, July 7, 1972; "First Selectman Defends Beach Policy," *HC*, July 8, 1972.

45. "Letter on Beach Policy Opens Up Pandora's Box," *NHR*, July 9, 1972.

46. Robert L. Adams, letter to the editor, *SLT*, July 13, 1972; "GOP Committee Backs Selectmen's Ordinance Stand," *SLT*, July 13, 1972.

47. "Kotowski Rips Beach Use Plan," *NHR*, July 13, 1972; "First Selectman Defends Beach Policy," *HC*, July 8, 1972.

48. "Corps Rents Cabins for Madison Outings," *NHR*, May 13, 1973.

49. "Corps Leases Woodland Acres," *HC*, February 2, 1973.

50. When another local business owner got into a dispute with the zoning board, he mentioned Birnbaum's actions as a warning. "If they push me too far," Ted Cole, owner of a gravel pit in Madison, commented, "I'll destroy the value of their property. I'll put in low-cost homes. They pushed Birnbaum too far and look what happened." See "Residents Discuss Gravel Pit," *HC*, July 15, 1973.

51. "Corps Leases Woodland Acres," *HC*, February 2, 1973.

52. Ibid.

53. "Activist 'Ned' Coll Takes on the City's Establishment and Wins a Battle," *HC*, May 30, 1973.

54. "Coll Hits WTIC on Home Base," *HC*, May 28, 1973.

55. "Activist 'Ned' Coll Takes on the City's Establishment and Wins a Battle," *HC*, May 30, 1973.

56. Ibid.

57. "Coll Hits WTIC on Home Base," *HC*, May 28, 1973.

58. "3 City Women Again Refused Beach Entry," *NHR*, August 8, 1966.

59. "Activist 'Ned' Coll Takes on the City's Establishment and Wins a Battle," *HC*, May 30, 1973.

60. Ibid.

61. Board of Selectmen Meeting Minutes, May 7, 1973, 17–24, MTCO; "Board to Handle Beach Passes," *HC*, May 20, 1973.

62. Roy Bongartz, "Freedom of Beach," *NYT*, July 13, 1975, and Jackie Ross, "Mission Work Set by Corps Worker," *HC*, December 23, 1979.

63. Ned Coll, interview by Andrew Kahrl, June 21, 2009, transcript (in author's possession).

64. Ned Coll, interview by Andrew Kahrl, June 10, 2009, transcript (in author's possession).

65. "Activist Says 2 Men Beat Her in Madison," *HC*, June 2, 1973; "Coll Insists State Police Join in Probe," *HC*, June 19, 1973.

66. "Ned Coll Stepping Up Beach Landings for Connecticut's Poor," *BG*, August 5, 1973.

67. "Corps Worker Asked to Take Lie Test," *HC*, June 13, 1973.

68. "Coll Insists State Police Join in Probe," *HC*, June 19, 1973; "Alleged Assault Victim Takes Polygraph Test," *HC*, June 29, 1973.

69. "WTIC-TV Ignored Assault, Coll Says," *HC*, June 3, 1973.

70. "Alleged Assault Victim Takes Polygraph Test," *HC*, June 29, 1973.

71. "Corps Sets Protest over Beach Move," *HC*, June 30, 1973; "Coll Claims Hostility against Corps," *HC*, June 14, 1973.

72. "The Fourth of July—Freedom to Choose," *SLT*, June 28, 1973; "Corps Sets Protest over Beach Move," *HC*, June 30, 1973.

73. "Corps Sets Protest over Beach Move," *HC*, June 30, 1973.

74. Earlie Powell, interview by Andrew Kahrl, June 15, 2009, transcript (in author's possession).

75. "Access of Minority Outsiders to Madison Beach Is Disrupted," *NYT*, July 5, 1973; "Incomplete Beach Pass Application Keeps Corps Bus from Beach Sunday," *SLT*, July 5, 1973.

76. "Madison Hostelry Operators Hope Corps Issue Ends Soon," *HC*, July 5, 1973; "Officials to Consider Beach Controversy," *HC*, July 6, 1973; "Officials Visit Coll's Operation," *HC*, July 7, 1973.

77. Ned Coll interview, June 21, 2009; Beach and Recreation Commission Meeting Minutes, July 6, 1973, n.p., MTCO.

78. "Revitalization Corps Gains Beach Passes after Stormy Session," *HC*, July 8, 1973; "Officials Visit Coll's Operation," *HC*, July 7, 1973.

79. "Revitalization Corps Leases 12-Unit Motel in Shoreline Town," *HC*, May 13, 1973; "Revitalization Corps Gains Beach Passes after Stormy Session," *HC*, July 8, 1973.

80. "Revitalization Corps Gains Beach Passes after Stormy Session," *HC*, July 8, 1973.

81. Beach and Recreation Commission Meeting Minutes, July 6, 1973, MTCO.

82. "Corps-Town Activities during Week Result in Corps Use of Beaches," *SLT*, July 12, 1973.

83. "Revitalization Corps Steps Up Activities in Shoreline Towns," *HC*, July 17, 1973.

84. "Beach Owner Invites Youths, Coll to Outing," *HC*, July 19, 1973.

85. Borough of Fenwick, Meeting of Wardens and Burgesses, August 5, 1973, reel 2, TBG.

86. "Inner-City Residents Shore Outing Guests," *HC*, July 21, 1973.

87. "Town Rules on Beaches Face Test," *HC*, September 5, 1973.

SEVEN Freedom of Beach

1. "Why Us? CCLU Picks Fairfield to Sue on 'Exclusionary Beach Practices,'" *FC*, October 31, 1973.

2. U.S. Commission on Marine Science, Engineering, and Resources, *Marine Resources and Legal-Political Arrangements for Their Development* (Washington: GPO, 1969), panel reports, vol. 3, VII-247.

3. "After a Court Ruling, Clouds at the Beaches," *NYT*, July 28, 2001.

4. "What Kind of County Will It Be in '85?" *NYT*, February 27, 1977.

5. "Hiding in Car Trunks to Get into Beach, Misusing Cards Out in '59," *GT*, September 5, 1958.

6. "Greenwich May Join Fairfield in Beach Suit," *HC*, October 24, 1973.

7. "Long Beach Plans to Sue County on 'Welfare Dumping,'" *NYT*, August 15, 1971.

8. "Beach Ban Is Debated in Long Beach," *NYT*, July 21, 1971.

9. "Suburbs Stiffening Beach Curbs," *NYT*, July 10, 1972.

10. "Beach Ban Is Debated in Long Beach," *NYT*, July 21, 1971.

11. "Suburbs Stiffening Beach Curbs," *NYT*, July 10, 1972.

12. "Beach Ban is Debated in Long Beach," *NYT*, July 21, 1971.

13. "Do the Beaches Belong to the People?" *NYT*, July 30, 1972.

14. "More Towns Are Closing Beach Areas to Outsiders," *NYT*, July 4, 1970; "Beach Ban Is Debated in Long Beach," *NYT*, July 21, 1971.

15. "City Residents Excluded from Suburb Beaches," *Lakeland [FL] Ledger*, July 28, 1972; Robert C. Eckhardt, "A Rational Policy on Public Use of Beaches," *Syracuse Law Review* 24 (1973): 979; Anthony Wolff, "We Shall Fight Them on the Beaches," *Harper's*, August 1973, 55–58.

16. "Suburbs Stiffening Beach Curbs," *NYT*, July 10, 1972.

17. "Beach Limitation Voided in Jersey," *NYT*, July 25, 1972.

18. "Do the Beaches Belong to the People?" *NYT*, July 30, 1972.

19. "Beach Limitation Voided in Jersey," *NYT*, July 25, 1972.

20. David J. Brower et al., *Access to the Nation's Beaches: Legal and Planning Perspectives* (Raleigh: UNC Sea Grant, 1978), 22; Marc R. Poirier, "Environmental Justice and the Beach Access Movements of the 1970s in Connecticut and New Jersey: Stories of Property and Civil Rights," *Connecticut Law Review* 28 (1996): 776–78.

21. "Do the Beaches Belong to the People?" *NYT*, July 30, 1972.

22. Wallace Kaufman and Orrin Pilkey, *The Beaches Are Moving: The Drowning of America's Shoreline* (Garden City, NJ: Anchor Press, 1979), 243.

23. "Lewis Cites Record; Mazza Hits Errors," *GT*, October 30, 1973.

24. "Lewis Unveils Plan for Lyon Property," *GT*, October 23, 1973.

25. Campaign advertisement, *GT*, October 31, 1973.

26. Campaign advertisement, *GT*, November 2, 1973.

27. "Lewis Flays Mazza Stance on Beaches," *GT*, October 29, 1973.

28. "Twine Blasts Statement by Vernon on Denying Housing to 'Outsiders,'" *GT*, October 9, 1975.

29. "Mazza Disputes Lewis' Account of Beach Stand," *GT*, October 25, 1973.

30. Campaign advertisement, *GT*, November 5, 1973.

31. "Town Democrats Find Some Things to Cheer about in Expected Defeat," *GT*, November 7, 1973.

32. House Committee on Merchant Marine and Fishers, Subcommittee on Fisheries and Wildlife Conservation and the Environment, *Public Access to Beaches: Hearings on HR 10394 and HR 10395*, 93rd Cong., 1st sess., 1973, 119, 143–44, 166–67, 108.

33. "Beach Access Hearings Open," *Atlanta Constitution,* October 26, 1973; "Federal Unit Opposes Beach Access Proposal," *HC,* October 27, 1973.

34. See Meg Jacobs, *Panic at the Pump: The Energy Crisis and the Transformation of American Politics in the 1970s* (New York: Hill and Wang, 2016).

35. "Revitalization Corps Moving into Town," *WHN,* May 23, 1974; "Revitalization Corps Finds Lukewarm Response in Town," *WHN,* June 12, 1974; "Ned Coll: 'Crusader' on the Move Here," *WHN,* June 27, 1974.

36. "Ned Coll: 'Crusader' on the Move Here," *WHN,* June 27, 1974.

37. "Madison Beach Protest Features 3-Way Waves," *NHR,* July 5, 1974.

38. Roy Bongartz, "Freedom of Beach," *NYT,* July 13, 1975.

39. Saul Alinsky, *Rules for Radicals* (New York: Vintage, 1971), 128.

40. "The Beaches Are Still Popular—and Still Crowded," *HT,* August 8, 1974.

41. "Madison Beach Protest Features 3-Way Waves," *NHR,* July 5, 1974.

42. Ibid.; "Coll's 'Troops' Land at Club," *HC,* July 5, 1974.

43. "Coll Renews Protest of Private Beaches," *HC,* July 29, 1974.

44. "Coll's 'Troops' Land at Club," *HC,* July 5, 1974.

45. Ibid.

46. "Private Connecticut Beach 'Invaded,'" *BG,* July 7, 1974.

47. Ned Coll, interview by Andrew Kahrl, May 18, 2009, transcript (in author's possession).

48. "Madison Beach Protest Features 3-Way Waves," *NHR,* July 5, 1974.

49. "An Unfortunate Beach Protest," *NHR,* July 9, 1974.

50. "Ned Coll: The Rebel with a Cause," *NLD,* August 7, 1975.

51. "An Unfortunate Beach Protest," *NHR,* July 9, 1974.

52. "The Beaches Are Still Popular—and Still Crowded," *HT,* August 8, 1974.

53. Bongartz, "Freedom of Beach."

54. Ibid.

55. Ibid.

56. Ibid.

57. Hilaire B. Coy and James J. Whalen, letters to the editor, *NYT Sunday Magazine,* August 3, 1975.

58. "Hartford Inner-City Group Visits Kennedys," *BG,* July 5, 1975.

59. "Coll Says Greenwich Target for Next Open Beach Effort," *HC,* July 16, 1975.

60. "Hartford Youths Visit Cape Cod as Kennedy's Guests," *BG,* July 19, 1975.

61. "Poor of Hartford Invited to Share Kennedys' Beach," *NYT,* July 19, 1975.

62. "State Civil Liberties Union May Sue Us over Use of Town Beaches . . . But It's an Involved Problem," *FC,* June 27, 1973; "Bastions of Private, Town Beaches under Attack," *NLD,* July 31, 1975; "Tide Turns for Open Beaches," *HC,* August 31, 1975.

63. "New Beach Restrictions Imposed by Greenwich," *NYT,* July 12, 1975.

64. "Ned Coll Worries Shore Property Owners," *MJ,* August 5, 1975.

65. "Beaches: Restrictions," *BP,* July 27, 1975.

66. "Coll Says Greenwich Target for Next Open Beach Effort," *HC,* July 16, 1975.

67. "Town's Leaders Tighten Limits on Beach Guests," *GT,* July 11, 1975.

68. "Maybe You Can't Get Near the Water," *BG*, July 18, 1976.

69. "Commuters Ignore Coll Picket Group at Station," *GT*, July 16, 1975.

70. "Town Clergy Leaders Hit Coll's Tactics," *GT*, July 17, 1975.

71. "Coll Group Holds Vigil at 2 Churches in Town," *GT*, July 23, 1975.

72. "Coll Assails Clergy in Beach Dispute," *HC*, July 20, 1975.

73. "Coll Group Holds Vigil at 2 Churches in Town," *GT*, July 23, 1975.

74. Rev. Bradford Hastings, letter to the editor, *GT*, July 31, 1975.

75. "Camps Change Summer for Inner-City Children," *GT*, August 13, 1975.

76. "Use of Beaches," *GT*, July 15, 1975.

77. "Let's Back Mrs. Dallas," *SLT*, July 13, 1972.

78. "Beach Rule Scored in Greenwich," *HC*, July 17, 1975.

79. "Coll's Group Stirs Protest by Residents," *GT*, July 31, 1975.

80. "Black Spokesmen Hit Both Sides of Beach Spat," *GT*, July 21, 1975; "Ned Coll: The Rebel with a Cause," *NLD*, August 7, 1975.

81. "Ned Coll, Greenwich Beach Conflict," *Evening News*, CBS, July 30, 1975.

82. "State Drops Bid to Try Activist," *HC*, October 18, 1975.

83. "Tide Turns for Open Beaches," *HC*, August 31, 1975.

84. "Governor Says Beaches of Towns off Limits to Intervention by State," *GT*, August 7, 1975; "Ella Defends Private Beaches," *MJ*, August 13, 1975; "Grasso Rules Out Buying More Land for Beaches," *HC*, August 12, 1975.

85. Wayne B. Mitten to Governor Ella Grasso, August 12, 1975, folder 53a, box 133, EG.

86. Alice H. Camp to Governor Ella Grasso, August 18, 1975, ibid.

87. Mike McKay to Governor Ella Grasso, August 12, 1975, ibid.

88. "CCLU Chides Governor for Views on Beaches," *HC*, August 17, 1975.

89. Richard Peene to Governor Ella Grasso, September 4, 1975, folder 53a, box 133, EG.

90. Alexis Hook to Ned Coll, August 21, 1975, folder DEP/Beaches, box 133, EG.

91. "Hanging Out at Ghetto Beach," *HC*, August 15, 1982.

92. Doris L. Delinks, letter to the editor, *HC*, August 16, 1968.

93. Russell Carlo, letter to the editor, *HC*, September 11, 1975.

94. "Vernon Adamant on Keeping Town Beaches for Residents of Greenwich," *OGG*, August 21, 1975; "Vernon Calls Firm Beach Stand Vital," *GT*, August 21, 1975.

95. James F. Stevenson and Pearl B. Stevenson, letter to the editor, *SLT*, July 18, 1974.

96. Russell Carlo, letter to the editor, *HC*, September 11, 1975.

97. E. D. Turner, letter to the editor, *HC*, August 16, 1975.

98. Grace A. Enright, letter to the editor, *GT*, August 18, 1975.

99. Virginia Diehl, letter to the editor, *HC*, August 23, 1975.

100. Bongartz, "Freedom of Beach."

101. Julie Pokorny, letter to the editor, *HC*, August 21, 1975.

EIGHT Saving the Shore

1. Quotes in this and the following paragraph are from Rob Carbonneau, interview by Andrew Kahrl, October 29, 2016, transcript (in author's possession).

2. David Aliski to Governor Ella Grasso, August 14, 1975, folder 53a, box 133, EG.

3. Stan E. Sales, letter to the editor, *MMR*, August 20, 1975.

4. Thomas Kenney to Governor Thomas Meskill, June 10, 1971, folder Long Island Sound, box A-774, TM; Thomas J. McCormick to Governor Thomas Meskill, December 26, 1973, ibid.

5. "Shoreline in Danger," *HC*, January 27, 1974.

6. Connecticut Coastal Zone Management Committee, "Preliminary Draft Report," August 14, 1972, folder Coastal Management, box A-772, TM.

7. Ibid.; "Septic Problems Force State Order Closing Facilities at Guilford Plaza," *NHR*, July 18, 1974; "Madison–Old Lyme off Limits for Shellfish," *NHR*, July 12, 1974.

8. Connecticut Coastal Area Management Program, "Model Municipal Coastal Program," report prepared for Department of Environmental Protection, January 1979, 16, DEP.

9. "Engineers Pinpoint Septic Ills," *HC*, October 19, 1978.

10. Southern Burlington County NAACP v. Township of Mount Laurel, 67 N.J. 151 (1975); "Zoning, Housing Issue Present Conflict," *HC*, April 19, 1975; "Attorney to Give Talk on Court Zoning Case," *HC*, June 23, 1975. On the Mount Laurel case, see also Charles M. Haar, *Suburbs under Siege: Race, Space, and Audacious Judges* (Princeton, NJ: Princeton University Press, 1996), and Douglas S. Massey et al., *Climbing Mount Laurel: The Struggle for Affordable Housing and Social Mobility in an American Suburb* (Princeton, NJ: Princeton University Press, 2013).

11. "East Haven: Demolition in Momauguin," *NHA*, May 30, 1979.

12. President's Council on Recreation and Natural Beauty, *From Sea to Shining Sea: A Report on the American Environment—Our Natural Heritage* (Washington, DC: GPO, 1968), 174–75.

13. "Endangered Edge of the Sea," *Life*, July 19, 1968, 4.

14. "Maybe You Can't Get Near the Water," *BG*, July 18, 1976.

15. U.S. Commission on Marine Science, Engineering, and Resources, *Our Nation and the Sea: A Plan for National Action* (Washington: GPO, 1969), 49.

16. Ibid., 1890; David J. Brower et al., *Access to the Nation's Beaches: Legal and Planning Perspectives* (Raleigh: UNC Sea Grant, 1978), 40–43.

17. See Dan W. Lufkin to Governor Thomas Meskill, February 28, 1973, folder Coastal Management, box A-772, TM.

18. Margery C. Scully to Governor Thomas Meskill, February 16, 1973, ibid.

19. Edward A. Connell to Governor Thomas Meskill, March 17, 1973, ibid.

20. Edward A. Connell to Julius M. Wilensky (mayor, Stamford), March 17, 1973, ibid.

21. "Coast Panel Faces Opposition," *HC*, April 1, 1973.

22. Connecticut Coastal Zone Management Committee, "Preliminary Draft Report."

23. Linda B. Krause, "Coastal Districts and Associations," report prepared for the Coastal Area Management Program, DEP, December 1976, 25.

24. Thomas J. McCormick to Governor Thomas Meskill, December 26, 1973, folder Long Island Sound, box A-774, TM.

25. New England River Basins Commission, "People and the Sound: A Plan for Long Island Sound," report for the Long Island Sound Regional Study, 1975.

26. Kenneth J. Metzler and Ralph W. Tiner, *Wetlands of Connecticut: State Geological and Natural History Survey of Connecticut* (Hartford: Department of Environmental Protection, 1991), 83–84, 88.

27. "Ribicoff States It Would Be Tragic If Report on Sound 'Gathers Dust,'" *GT*, July 29, 1975.

28. New England River Basins Commission, "People and the Sound," vol. 1, 22, 6.

29. Ibid., 6.

30. "Ribicoff States It Would Be Tragic If Report on Sound 'Gathers Dust,'" *GT*, July 29, 1975.

31. "Study of L.I. Sound Lists 31 Proposals," *HC*, July 29, 1975.

32. *Legislative History of the Coastal Zone Management Act of 1972, as Amended in 1974 and 1976 with a Section-by-Section Index*, 94th Cong., 2d sess., December 1976 (Washington: GPO, 1976), 759; Brower et al., *Access to the Nation's Beaches*, 39.

33. "Pressure Rises in the State to Get More Public Beaches," *HC*, August 27, 1972; Marion T. Nelson, letter to the editor, *HC*, July 21, 1976.

34. "Bill Aims at Preservation of Long Island Sound," *HA*, August 17, 1977.

35. "A Pretty Expensive Backyard," *NB*, August 17, 1980.

36. Governor John Dempsey to Members of the U.S. Senate Committee on Interior and Insular Affairs, February 10, 1961, folder Shoreline Areas (1962), box A-295, JD.

37. "After 47 Years—We Still Wait," *NB*, January 25, 1974.

38. Thomas R. Truscinski, "Bluff Point—Coastal Reserve or Public Park?" April 12, 1977, folder Bluff Point (General), State Parks and Forest Commission Historical Files, DEP.

39. "10 Residents Selected for Bluff Point Study," *HC*, November 2, 1972.

40. "Plan Would Open Beach to Cars," *HC*, March 9, 1976.

41. "Bill Aims at Preservation of Long Island Sound," *HA*, August 17, 1977.

42. "House Passes Bluff Point Reserve," *HC*, May 1, 1975.

43. "After 47 Years—We Still Wait," *NB*, January 25, 1974.

44. "No Room at the Beach," *NB*, July 6, 1974.

45. Truscinski, "Bluff Point—Coastal Reserve or Public Park?"

46. "Beach Issue Can't Shake Off Problems," *HC*, March 17, 1976.

47. "Gill Won't Back Beach Bill," *HC*, March 5, 1976.

48. "Beach Issue Can't Shake Off Problems," *HC*, March 17, 1976.

49. "Coll Launches Beach Assault," *HC*, July 22, 1977.

50. Rob Carbonneau interview.

51. "Coll, Companions Encounter Friends, Foes on Shore Hike," *HC*, July 23, 1977.

52. Edward W. Hobb, letter to the editor, *NLD*, August 14, 1978.

53. "Fence Causes Feud between Beach Groups," *HC*, July 20, 1977; "Fight Looms over Fences," *HC*, May 13, 1979; Edward T. Coll, "The Shoreline Trek: Signs, Shouts, and Many Fences," *HC*, August 30, 1977.

54. "Old Lyme Group Erects Second Fence," *HC*, August 6, 1977.

55. "A Private Beach for Public Use," *HA*, August 24, 1977.

56. Coll, "The Shoreline Trek."

57. Rob Carbonneau interview.

58. "'Ned' Coll Ends 12-Day Shore Trek," *HC*, August 2, 1977; "Coll Finishes Coastline Walk in Connecticut," *NH*, August 2, 1977.

59. "New Shorefront Jetties Must Offer Public Way," *HC*, November 1, 1977.

60. Rob Carbonneau, "A Walk Remembered," *HC*, August 4, 1978.

61. Rob Carbonneau interview.

62. "Fuel Help Offered to Needy," *HC*, Jan 30, 1977; "Family Gets Fuel Oil After Heatless Week," *HC*, March 20, 1977; "Operation Fuel Finishes Work," *HC*, April 4, 1977.

63. "Coll Plans to Walk to See Carter," *HC*, October 8, 1977.

64. "Operation Fuel—Now!" *HC*, November 6, 1977.

65. "Grasso Speech Faces Protest," *HC*, December 11, 1975.

66. "Governor Appoints Coll Unpaid 'Special Adviser,'" *HC*, September 18, 1976.

67. Russell West, interview by Andrew Kahrl, March 8, 2015, transcript (in author's possession).

68. Governor Grasso Announces $60,000 Program to Transport Urban Young People to State-Owned Parks and Shoreline Beaches during Summer, April 21. 1977, folder Env.-State Beaches/Shore Parks, box 620, EG.

69. Jack Curry, Review of Governor Grasso's Task Force on Beaches, July 9, 1976, ibid.

70. Richard S. Gibbons to DEP, August 8, 1977, folder State Parks and Forest Commission, Historical Files (Sherwood Island Landfill), DEP; Alfred M. Freedman to DEP, ibid.

71. "Coastal Management Plan Feared," *HC*, March 1, 1978.

72. "Shoreline Dilemma Deepens," *HC*, July 29, 1978.

73. "Controlling Connecticut's Coast," *NYT*, March 21, 1978.

74. "Coll Steps Up Shore Protest," *HC*, July 12, 1978.

75. "Coll Claims Laws Violated at Shore," *HC*, July 17, 1978.

76. "Coastal Management," *NLD*, June 2, 1982.

77. "Coast Management Program Criticized at Public Hearing," *HC*, November 4, 1978.

78. "Candidates Oppose State Intervention," *HC*, October 29, 1978; "Mrs. Polinsky Returned to 2nd Assembly Term," *HC*, November 8, 1978.

79. "Beach-Access Questions Prompt Dodd Answers," *HC*, September 10, 1978; "Dodd Tries to Calm Storm Brewed by Beach Comments," *HC*, September 9, 1978.

80. "Connell Sends Tiny Bags of Sand," *HC*, October 21, 1978.

81. See Marc R. Poirier, "Environmental Justice and the Beach Access Movements of the 1970s in Connecticut and New Jersey: Stories of Property and Civil Rights," *Connecticut Law Review* 28 (1996): 719–812.

82. "Atrociously-Verbose Document," *HC*, April 7, 1979.

83. "Coastal Management," *NLD*, June 2, 1982.

NINE   Go Home, Ned

1. Edward T. Coll, "The Corps at 15," *HC*, July 12, 1979.

2. For this and the following paragraph, see "Residents Tell Rights Agency of Racial Real Estate Reports," *HC*, July 13, 1972; "An All-American City Strives to Maintain Racial Diversity," *NYT*, October 22, 1989; Jack Dougherty, "Shopping for Schools: How Public Education and Private Housing Shaped Suburban Connecticut," *Journal of Urban History* 38, no. 2 (2012): 211–16. See also Jack Dougherty, *On the Line: How Schooling, Housing, and Civil Rights Shaped Hartford and Its Suburbs,* http://ontheline.trincoll.edu/book/.

3. Lebert "Gee" Lester, interview by Andrew Kahrl, May 21, 2009, transcript (in author's possession).

4. Warren Hardy, interview by Andrew Kahrl, October 31, 2016, transcript (in author's possession).

5. Don O. Noel Jr., "The au courant *Courant,*" *Columbia Journalism Review* 20 (January–February 1982): 5–6.

6. "New Shorefront Jetties Must Offer Public Way," *HC*, November 1, 1977.

7. "Fight Looms over Fences a 'Small Berlin Wall' in Old Lyme," *HC*, May 13, 1979.

8. Connecticut Commission on Human Rights and Opportunities, *Report of Incidents of Cross Burnings and Vandalism Motivated by Racial and Religious Prejudice in Connecticut* (Hartford: Connecticut Commission on Human Rights and Opportunities, 1980), 10–11.

9. Lebert "Gee" Lester interview; Cecil Lester, interview with Andrew Kahrl, June 8, 2009, transcript (in author's possession). "Fire Damages Second Floor of Dwelling," *HC*, January 3, 1976.

10. Suburban Action Institute, "A Study of Zoning in Connecticut," report prepared for Connecticut Commission on Human Rights and Opportunities, April 1978, 17.

11. Kenneth J. Neubeck and Richard E. Ratcliff, "Urban Democracy and the Power of Corporate Capital: Struggles over Downtown Growth and Neighborhood Stagnation in Hartford, Connecticut," in *Business Elites and Urban Development: Case Studies and Critical Perspectives,* ed. Scott Cummings (Albany: State University of New York Press,

1988), 299–332, and Clyde McKee and Nick Bacon, "A Tragic Dialectic: Politics and the Transformation of Hartford," in *Confronting Urban Legacy: Rediscovering Hartford and New England's Forgotten Cities,* ed. Xianming Chen and Nick Bacon (Lanham, MD: Lexington Books, 2013), 219–35.

12. "Suburban Blacks Welcomed, but Stereotypes Remain," *HC,* October 9, 1988; "Rights Official Terms Grant's Remarks Elitist," *HC,* October 2, 1973.

13. "RTM Accepts Block Grant Funds," *GT,* October 10, 1979; "Issues of Blacks, Housing Spark Debate during Forum," *GT,* October 11, 1979; Charles H. Granger, letter to the editor, *GT,* October 10, 1979; "Assessing Fairfield County's Housing Bind," *NYT,* December 2, 1979.

14. "Issues of Blacks, Housing Spark Debate during Forum," *GT,* October 11, 1979.

15. Michael McDermott, letter to the editor, *GT,* October 12, 1979.

16. "Dodd, Buckley Trade Charges," *NYT,* October 12, 1980.

17. "Coll Defends Dodd, Buckley on Race Claim," *HC,* October 18, 1980.

18. "Officials Wary of Federal Controls As They Consider Coastal Funds," *HC,* January 10, 1981; "Madison Board Says No Thanks to U.S. Money," *HC,* January 21, 1981.

19. "1980 Is 'Year of the Coast' As U.S. Aims at Prudent Use Plan," *CSM,* January 1, 1980; "America's Abused Coastline: A Drive Is Launched to Save an Endangered Natural Treasure," *Time,* September 15, 1980, 28–29; "Beach Walks Staged in Effort to Save Nation's Coastline," *NYT,* January 2, 1980; "Sandcastles with a Message," *CSM,* August 5, 1980.

20. "Heed the SOS—Save Our Shores," *BG,* March 3, 1980.

21. "1980 Is 'Year of the Coast' As U.S. Aims at Prudent Use Plan," *CSM,* January 1, 1980.

22. "Coastal Programs Face Cut," *NYT,* April 26, 1981.

23. Connecticut General Assembly, *An Investigation of the Department of Environmental Protection,* December 21, 1976, 4, https://www.cga.ct.gov/pri/docs/1976/An%20Investigation%20of%20the%20Department%20of%20Environmental%20Protection%20(1976).pdf. See also "DEP Denies Penning Hatchet Plan," *HC,* June 15, 1976.

24. "Prosperity Taxes Shoreline Ecology," *HC,* July 26, 1987.

25. "Developers Whittle Coastal Wetlands," *HC,* October 30, 1988.

26. Ibid.

27. "Prosperity Taxes Shoreline Ecology," *HC,* July 26, 1987.

28. "Developers Whittle Coastal Wetlands," *HC,* October 30, 1988.

29. "Mystery of Fouled Beaches," *NYT,* July 25, 1988; "As Beaches Empty, Crowds at Pools Grow," *NYT,* August 7, 1988. See also Barbara Ehrenreich, *The Worst Years of Our Lives: Irreverent Notes from a Decade of Greed* (New York: Pantheon, 1990).

30. Russell West, interview by Andrew Kahrl, March 8, 2015, transcript (in author's possession).

31. Ibid.; "Mission Work Set by Corps Worker," *HC,* December 23, 1979.

32. "After 15 Years, Ned Coll Is Still Dedicated to Same Ideals," *HC,* January 6, 1980.

33. "An Angry Voice for the Poor," *HC,* March 9, 1980.

34. "Challenging Boston's Students," *BG,* October 28, 1979; "School Closing Plan Heads for Court," *BG,* December 1, 1979.

35. "Rekindling Concern," *HaC,* March 3, 1980; "Harvard Volunteers Tutor in Brighton," *HaC,* March 6, 1980.

36. "Harvard Volunteers Tutor in Brighton," *HaC,* March 6, 1980.

37. "Coll Arrested in Boston after Protest Attempt," *HC,* April 4, 1980; "Activist Is Arrested at Garrity's Office," *BG,* April 4, 1980; "Charge against Coll Is Found Justified by U.S. Magistrate," *HC,* April 18, 1980; "Coll Defends Court Action," *HC,* April 18, 1980; "Court Stays Garrity's School Closings," *BG,* May 1, 1980.

38. "Grasso's Operation Was Hysterectomy," *HC,* April 6, 1980.

39. "Grasso: Playing Presidential Politics," *HC,* August 3, 1980.

40. "Tests Disclose Governor Suffers Cancer of Liver," *HC,* November 26, 1980.

41. "Governor Grasso Resigns, Citing Illness," *HC,* December 5, 1980; "Brief, Somber Ceremony Heralds Turnover," *HC,* January. 1, 1981; "Grasso Dies; State Mourns," *HC,* February 6, 1981.

42. "Claire Coll, Mother of Activist, Dies," *HC,* February 1, 1981; "Daniel B. Coll Dies," *HC,* August 29, 1981.

43. Edward Forand Jr., "Ned Coll's Journey," *HC,* June 23, 1985.

44. Ibid.

45. "Privately Owned Shore Property: Should Public Have Access?," *HC,* May 25, 1986.

46. Forand, "Ned Coll's Journey."

47. Ibid.; "Students[,] Tutors, and More, to City Children," *HC,* October 22, 1983; "Corps Hopes UConn Visit Will Inspire City Youths," *HC,* November 12, 1989.

48. Jose Vasquez, interview by Andrew Kahrl, November 20, 2016, transcript (in author's possession).

49. See "Connecticut Reports Continued Drop in Factory Jobs," *NYT,* December 5, 1982; "Terry Corp. Shuts Plant; 340 Workers Displaced," *HC,* July 2, 1987; "P&W to Lay Off 185 at East Hartford, Rocky Hill," *HC,* October 17, 1987; "Electronics Plant in Hartford to Close; 500 Will Lose Jobs," *HC,* March 10, 1989; "Hamilton Standard to Lay Off 100 at Windsor Locks," *HC,* October 12, 1990. On poverty in 1980s Hartford, see also "Hartford's Poverty Line: Threshold of Desperation," *HC,* February 27, 1983; "Burgeoning Progress Leaves Legacy of Lost Opportunity," *HC,* February 28, 1983; "Poverty Puts Different Face on City," *HC,* March 1, 1983; Louise B. Simmons, *Organizing in Hard Times: Labor and Neighborhoods in Hartford* (Philadelphia: Temple University Press, 1994), 3, 6.

50. "Beneath the Skyscrapers—A Disparity in Wealth," *HC,* September 9, 1984; Vicki Kemper, "Operation Urban Storm," *Common Cause Magazine* 17 (July/August 1991): 10–16, 39–40.

51. Kemper, "Operation Urban Storm"; Leslie Hammond, interview by Andrew Kahrl, October 28, 2016, transcript (in author's possession).

52. See "Connecticut Had More Concentrated Poverty (and Wealth) Than Most Metros," *TrendCT.org*, May 27, 2015, http://trendct.org/2015/05/27/connecticut-has-more-concentrated-poverty-and-wealth-than-most-metros/; "Beneath the Skyscrapers—A Disparity in Wealth," *HC*, September 9, 1984.

53. "Drug Dealers' Evictions Help City Projects," *HC*, June 18, 1987; Lebert "Gee" Lester interview; "Drugs Tearing at Inner City's Fabric," *HC*, July 10, 1988; "On the Front Line against Poverty," *HC*, June 11, 1989.

54. Ralph Knighton, interview by Andrew Kahrl, November 5, 2016, transcript (in author's possession).

55. Leslie Hammond interview.

56. "Violence Linked to Narcotics," *HC*, June 26, 1986.

57. "Drug Dealers' Evictions Help City Projects," *HC*, June 18, 1987.

58. "Soldiers in War on Drugs March through Hartford Battle Zone," *HC*, April 23, 1990.

59. Lebert "Gee" Lester interview.

60. Leslie Hammond interview.

61. "Stowe Village an Island of Fear in a Sea of Tranquility," *HC*, April 29, 1990.

62. Ibid.; Ned Coll, interview by Andrew Kahrl, May 21, 2009, transcript (in author's possession).

63. On black women's role in tenant organizing and governance in public housing, see Rhonda Y. Williams, *The Politics of Public Housing: Black Women's Struggles against Urban Inequality* (New York: Oxford University Press, 2004), esp. 155–91.

64. "Project Emerging from Dark Nights of Drug Tyranny," *HC*, June 1, 1990, and "No Major Confrontations as Drug Protest Continues," *HC*, May 19, 1990.

65. Jose Vasquez interview.

66. "Activist's Tactics Offend Residents," *HC*, May 18, 1990; Lebert "Gee" Lester interview; "Despite Errors, Coll's Basic Premise Sound," *HC*, May 27, 1990.

67. Earlie Powell, interview by Andrew Kahrl, June 15, 2009, transcript (in author's possession).

68. Lebert "Gee" Lester interview; Jose Vasquez interview; Elizabeth Coll, interview by Andrew Kahrl, October 19, 2016, transcript (in author's possession).

69. "Activist's Tactics Offend Residents," *HC*, May 18, 1990.

70. "Stowe Village Ban against Coll Lifted; Some Tenants Object," *HC*, June 19, 1990; "No Major Confrontations as Drug Protest Continues," *HC*, May 19, 1990; "Project Emerging from Dark Nights of Drug Tyranny," *HC*, June 1, 1990; "Order Bars Coll from Project," *HC*, May 26, 1990.

71. Ralph Knighton interview.

72. Leslie Hammond interview.

73. "Activist Ned Coll Arrested in Scuffle with Tenants," *HC*, May 24, 1990; "Coll Returns to Stowe Village," *HC*, May 25, 1990.

74. "Coll Returns to Stowe Village," *HC*, May 25, 1990; "Despite Errors, Coll's Basic Premise Sound," *HC*, May 27, 1990.

75. "Order Bars Coll from Project," *HC,* May 26, 1990; "Activist Coll Has Court Date Today," *HC,* June 18, 1990.

76. "Ned Coll's Journey," *HC,* June 23, 1985.

77. "Despite Errors, Coll's Basic Premise Sound," *HC,* May 27, 1990; Forand, "Ned Coll's Journey."

TEN Welcome to Greenwich!

1. Nollan v. California Coastal Commission, 483 U.S. 825, 834 (1987).

2. "Beach-Front Homeowners Laud High Court Ruling on Public Access," *HC,* June 28, 1987.

3. Lucas v. South Carolina Coastal Commission, 505 U.S. 1003, 112 S. Ct. 2886, 120 L. Ed. 2d 798, 34 ERC 1897 (1992). See also Peter Overby, "Beachfront Bailout," *Common Cause* (Summer 1993): 12; Judith A. Layzer, *Open for Business: Conservatives' Opposition to Environmental Regulation* (Cambridge, MA: Harvard University Press, 2012), 175–81; Diana M. Whitelaw and Gerald Robert Visgilio, eds., *America's Changing Coasts: Private Rights and Public Trust* (Cheltenham, UK: Edward Elgar, 2005), 2.

4. Michael Moran, "Two Sides of Connecticut's Economic Divide Reveal Price of Inequality," *GlobalPost,* January 16, 2013, http://www.globalpost.com/dispatch/news/regions/americas/united-states/121226/connecticut-economic-divide-inequality.

5. See Diversified Technologies Corp., "Silver Sands State Park Master Plan," report prepared for DEP, November. 1993.

6. David Rusk, *Cities without Suburbs,* 2nd ed. (Baltimore: Johns Hopkins University Press, 1995), 115.

7. James C. Kozlowski, "Can Towns Restrict Public Park Access to Residents and Their Guests?" *Parks and Recreation* 36 (October 2001): 44–51; Edgar D. Gates, letter to the editor, *GT,* August 3, 1990.

8. "Challenging the Kingdom of Greenwich," *NYT,* May 17, 2000.

9. Brenden P. Leydon, interview by Janet T. Klion, June 24, 2003, transcript (Greenwich Library, Greenwich, CT).

10. "Court Invalidates Borough Law Restricting Park to Its Residents," *NYT,* June 12, 1998.

11. Brenden P. Leydon interview by Klion.

12. "Where the Bosses Are: Settling in Greenwich, Conn., May Not Make You a CEO—But It Couldn't Hurt," *WSJ,* March 20, 1987.

13. "Greenwich's Shifting Line in the Sand," *NYT,* July 20, 2000.

14. James R. Maher, letter to the editor, *WP,* August 15, 1997. See also Lawrence Otis Graham, "Invisible Man," *New York,* August 17, 1992, http://nymag.com/news/features/47949/.

15. "Keeping Its Shores to Itself," *NYT,* January 8, 1993.

16. Brenden P. Leydon interview by Klion.

17. "Greenwich, Conn., Fetches High Prices from Appearance-Minded Commuters," *BaS,* May 3, 1987.

18. "Tony Town Keeps Outsiders off Beach," *WP*, August 4, 1997.

19. " 'Gold Coast' Becoming Tarnished As Real Estate Prices Soar," *HC*, January 4, 1988.

20. "Law Student Is Taking on Greenwich over Its Restricted Beaches," *NYT*, April 19, 1995; Marc R. Poirier, "Environmental Justice and the Beach Access Movements of the 1970s in Connecticut and New Jersey: Stories of Property and Civil Rights," *Connecticut Law Review* 28 (1996): 721–31.

21. "Beach Bummer," *NH*, August 8, 1997; "Storming Restricted Beaches of Greenwich," *NYT*, July 21, 1997; "Greenwich Fights Beach Lawsuit with Army of Experts," *NYT*, February 22, 1998.

22. "Racist Message Reveals Town's Rift," *NYT*, June 21, 1995.

23. Connie Leslie and Sabrina Jones, "The Shame of Greenwich," *Newsweek*, June 26, 1995.

24. "Greenwich Resents Relentless Spotlight," *NYT*, July 23, 1995.

25. Ibid.

26. Ibid.

27. "Racist Message Reveals Town's Rift," *NYT*, June 21, 1995.

28. "The 'Public' Beaches of Greenwich," *TV Nation*, 1994, https://www.youtube.com/watch?v=lMS-EfcWrSw.

29. Ibid.

30. "Beach Bummer," *NH*, August 8, 1997.

31. "Storming Restricted Beaches of Greenwich," *NYT*, July 21, 1997.

32. "Greenwich's Shifting Line in the Sand," *NYT*, July 20, 2000.

33. Brenden P. Leydon, "A Nation of Liberty, Justice and Free Beaches for All," *NYT*, June 4, 2000.

34. "Storming Restricted Beaches of Greenwich," *NYT*, July 21, 1997.

35. "Challenging the Kingdom of Greenwich," *NYT*, May 17, 2000; "Law Student Is Taking on Greenwich over Its Restricted Beaches," *NYT*, April 19, 1995; Josie Kahn, letter to the editor, *GT*, August 5, 2001; undated letter to Brenden P. Leydon, Tooher, Wocl, and Leydon LLC, Stamford, CT, cited with permission from Brenden P. Leydon; "Greenwich Resents Relentless Spotlight," *NYT*, July 23, 1995; "Tony Town Keeps Outsiders off Beach," *WP*, August 4, 1997; "Beach Bummer," *NH*, August 8, 1997.

36. "A Barkhamsted Prayer Crusade," *LCT*, April 2, 2010.

37. "Social Activist Ned Coll Using Prayer in New Campaign against Materialism," *NLD*, October 6, 1990.

38. "This Man Waged War on Television before It Was Chic," *HC*, March 24, 1996.

39. Testimony of Ned Coll in Brenden Leydon v. Town of Greenwich, February 18, 1998, Superior Court, Judicial District of Stamford/Norwalk, at Stamford, Conn., before the Honorable Edward Karazin Jr., recorded and transcribed by Donna Bonenfant; "Greenwich Fights Beach Lawsuit with Army of Experts," *NYT*, February 22, 1998.

40. Brenden P. Leydon, "Closing Argument," Brenden Leydon v. Town of Green-

wich, February 1998, Superior Court, Judicial District of Stamford/Norwalk, at Stamford, Conn., cited with permission from Brenden P. Leydon.

41. Brenden Leydon, interview by Andrew Kahrl, March 24, 2017, notes, in author's possession.

42. "Greenwich Fights Beach Lawsuit with Army of Experts," *NYT*, February 22, 1998.

43. Ibid.

44. See, for example, Hartford v. Maslen, 76 Conn. 599 (1904); Stradmore Development Corp. v. Commissioners, Board of Public Works of the City of New Britain, 164 Conn. 548 (1973); Borough of Fenwick v. Old Saybrook, 133 Conn. 22 (1946).

45. "Judge Rejects Challenge to Restricted Beaches," *NYT*, July 10, 1998; Judge Edward Karazin Jr., Memorandum of Decision, Brenden Leydon v. Town of Greenwich, July 8, 1998, Superior Court, Judicial District of Stamford/Norwalk, at Stamford, Conn., 6.

46. Brenden P. Leydon, Plaintiff's Brief, Leydon v. Greenwich (Appellate Court of Connecticut, March 1, 1999), 21–22; Brenden P. Leydon, Plaintiff's Reply Brief and Appendix, Leydon v. Greenwich (Appellate Court of Connecticut, July 21, 1999), 14; Brenden P. Leydon, Plaintiff's Post Trial Reply Brief, Leydon v. Greenwich (Superior Court, Judicial District of Stamford/Norwalk, at Stamford, Conn., March 23, 1998), 8; Leydon v. Greenwich, 57 Conn. App. 712, 750 A.2d 1122 (Appellate Court of Connecticut, 2000).

47. "Challenging the Kingdom of Greenwich," *NYT*, May 17, 2000.

48. Anita Visentin Perito, letter to the editor, *NYT*, June 18, 2000.

49. "Beach Ruling Would Degrade a Major Asset," *GT*, August 6, 2001.

50. "Greenwich's Shifting Line in the Sand," *NYT*, July 20, 2000.

51. Richard Schragger, "Towns Don't Have the Right That Greenwich Claims," *HC*, March 25, 2001.

52. "A Bad Day at the Beach," *Connecticut Law Tribune*, June 19, 2000; Brenden P. Leydon interview by Klion.

53. "A Neighborhood Holds Its Breath," *NYT*, June 4, 2000.

54. "Greenwich Cites Fear of 'Jerseyfication' in Beach Dispute," *NYT*, November 11, 2000.

55. "Beach Battle Is a Sea of Trouble," *Milwaukee Journal-Sentinel*, June 23, 2002.

56. "After a Court Ruling, Clouds at the Beaches," *NYT*, July 28, 2001.

57. Wendy Spezzano, letter to the editor, *GT*, August 10, 2001.

58. "What a Town without Pity Can't Do," *Toronto Globe and Mail*, August 7, 2001.

59. Bradley Brock, letter to the editor, *GT*, August 9, 2001.

60. James McKean, letter to the editor, *GT*, August 9, 2001.

61. "Activist Celebrates Greenwich Beach Ruling," *FH*, August 30, 2001.

62. "Is That a Welcome Mat?" *NYT*, November 4, 2001.

63. Ibid.

64. "Open Up the Beach, but to Talk, Not to Swim," *NYT*, January 27, 2002.

65. "One Man's Crusade to Open the Beaches," *NYT*, August 5, 2001.

66. "Greenwich Sets Charges for Outsiders to Use Beach," *NYT*, February 15, 2002.

67. "A Patch of Greenwich Beach Is Available to All, at $10 a Day," *NYT*, March 9, 2002.

68. "$400+ to Walk the Beach," *Oklahoma City Journal Record*, February 18, 2002.

69. "Greenwich Sets Charges for Outsiders to Use Beach," *NYT*, February 15, 2002.

70. Ibid.

71. "A Patch of Greenwich Beach Is Available to All, at $10 a Day," *NYT*, March 9, 2002.

72. "Beach Battle Is a Sea of Trouble," *Milwaukee Journal-Sentinel*, June 23, 2002.

73. Ibid.

74. "A Patch of Greenwich Beach Is Available to All, at $10 a Day," *NYT*, March 9, 2002.

75. Brenden P. Leydon interview by Klion.

76. "Towels, Sun Block and, Oh Yeah, Checkbook," *NYT*, June 23, 2002.

77. "Is It Greenwich or Stamford? Lay Your Head on Either Side," *NYT*, April 10, 2003.

78. "Beach Ruling Would Degrade a Major Asset," *GT*, August 6, 2001.

79. Ibid.

80. "Greenwich Beach Open to All, but Bring Money and Patience," *NYT*, May 28, 2002.

81. "Towels, Sun Block and, Oh Yeah, Checkbook," *NYT*, June 23, 2002.

82. "Town Beaches Still Not Open," *HC*, September 26, 2002.

83. "Towels, Sun Block and, Oh Yeah, Checkbook," *NYT*, June 23, 2002.

84. "Bias Seen in Expulsion at Greenwich Beach," *NYT*, December 15, 2005; "Players' Wives: Houston, We Have a Problem," *GT*, December 11, 2005; "Crossing a Line Drawn in Greenwich's Fine Sand," *NYT*, February 9, 2006.

85. "Players' Wives: Houston, We Have a Problem," *GT*, December 11, 2005.

86. Ibid.

87. "Bias Seen in Expulsion at Greenwich Beach," *NYT*, December 15, 2005.

88. "Players' Wives: Houston, We Have a Problem," *GT*, December 11, 2005.

89. "Crossing a Line Drawn in Greenwich's Fine Sand," *NYT*, February 9, 2006.

90. Ibid.

91. "State Offers Settlement in Bias Case," *GT*, December 22, 2005.

Epilogue: Nature Bats Last

1. Ned Coll, interview by Andrew Kahrl, June 21, 2009, transcript (in author's possession).

2. Adam Keul, "The Fantasy of Access: Neoliberal Ordering of a Public Beach," *Political Geography* 48 (September 2015): 56.

3. Jon Fuller, interview by Andrew Kahrl, March 9, 2015, transcript (in author's possession).

4. Keul, "Fantasy of Access," 56.

5. Marcia Balint, interview by Andrew Kahrl, March 9, 2015, transcript (in author's possession).

6. David J. Blatt, interview by Andrew Kahrl, March 9, 2015, transcript (in author's possession).

7. Keul, "Fantasy of Access," 56.

8. Jon Fuller, interview.

9. Keul, "Fantasy of Access," 50.

10. On Greenwich's beach access policies, see http://www.greenwichct.org/gov ernment/departments/parks_and_recreation/park_beach_tennis_passes/. On Madison, see http://www.madisonct.org/504/Beaches. On Westport, see http://www.west portct.gov/index.aspx?page=324. On Groton's Eastern Point Beach, see Keul, "Fantasy of Access," 54.

11. David J. Blatt interview.

12. "Where Norwalk and Darien Collide," *NYT*, January 19, 2014; "Pine Point Association Rejects Norwalk Land Trust's Bid for Bird Sanctuary," *NH*, June 24, 2014; "Norwalk Land Trust Postpones Vote on Nature Sanctuary in Rowayton," *NH*, July 8, 2014; "Rowaytonites Urge Commission to Keep 2 Nearwater Road Open Space, Seek Compromise As Needed," *NH*, July 10, 2014; "Controversy Roils a Serene Setting," *NYT*, September 13, 2015.

13. On the civil rights movement in the North, see Thomas J. Sugrue, *Sweet Land of Liberty: The Forgotten Struggle for Civil Rights in the North* (New York: Random House, 2008), and Jeanne Theoharis and Komozi Woodard, eds., *Freedom North: Black Freedom Struggles outside the South, 1940–1980* (New York: Palgrave Macmillan, 2003). On the privatization of public space in the post–Jim Crow urban South, see Kevin M. Kruse, *White Flight: Atlanta and the Making of Modern Conservatism* (Princeton, NJ: Princeton University Press, 2005).

14. See Regina Austin, "'*Not* Just for the Fun of It!': Governmental Restraints on Black Leisure, Social Inequality, and the Privatization of Public Space," *Southern California Law Review* 71 (May 1998): 667–714.

15. Gerald Frug, "The Legal Technology of Exclusion in Metropolitan America," in *New Suburban History*, 205–20.

16. "Compromise Sought on Coastal Protection Bills," *NLD*, April 7, 2012; "To Repair the Shore, or Retreat?" *NYT*, May 3, 2012; "Shoreline Task Force Discusses Rising Sea Levels," *NLD*, August 7, 2012; "New Laws Refocus on Coast, Easing Rules, Protecting Nature," *NLD*, July 4, 2013.

17. "After Sandy, Americans Mull Retreat from the Sea," *Ottawa Citizen*, December 8, 2012; Orrin H. Pilkey, "We Need to Retreat from the Beach," *NYT*, November 14, 2012. On the National Flood Insurance Program, see Rutherford H. Platt, "Congress and the Coast," *Environment* 27 (July–August 1985): 12–17, 34–40; Erwann O. Michel-Kerjan, "Catastrophe Economics: The National Flood Insurance Program," *Journal of*

Economic Perspectives 24 (Fall 2010): 165–86; Scott Gabriel Knowles and Howard C. Kunreuther, "Troubled Waters: The National Flood Insurance Program in Historical Perspective," *Journal of Policy History* 26, no. 3 (2014): 327–53.

18. "Enclaves, Long Gated, Seek to Let Storm Aid In," *NYT,* November 26, 2012.

19. David Blatt interview.

20. "New Laws Refocus on Coast, Easing Rules, Protecting Nature," *NLD,* July 4, 2013.

21. Jan Ellen Spiegel, "CT's Repeat Flood Damage Dilemma: Move Out or Rebuild?" *Connecticut Mirror,* October 9, 2015, available at http://ctmirror.org/2015/10/09/cts-repeat-flood-damage-dilemma-move-out-or-rebuild/.

22. Kristal Kallenberg, interview by Andrew Kahrl, March 9, 2015, transcript (in author's possession).

23. Wade Gibson and Sara Kauffman, "Pulling Apart: Connecticut Income Inequality, 1977 to Present" (Hartford, November 2012), available at http://www.ctvoices.org/publications/pulling-apart-connecticut-income-inequality-1977-present; Estelle Sommeiller and Mark Price, "The Increasingly Unequal States of America: Income Inequality by State, 1917 to 2012," Economic Policy Institute, January 26, 2015, available at http://www.epi.org/publication/income-inequality-by-state-1917-to-2012/; "Capital of U.S. Income Gap Festers amid Connecticut Mansions," *Bloomberg,* December 12, 2011, available at http://www.bloomberg.com/news/articles/2011-12-12/capital-of-u-s-income-gap-festers-amid-connecticut-mansions; Michael Moran, "Two Sides of Connecticut's Economic Divide Reveal Price of Inequality," *GlobalPost,* January 16, 2013, available at http://www.globalpost.com/dispatch/news/regions/americas/united-states/121226/connecticut-economic-divide-inequality.

24. Moran, "Two Sides of Connecticut's Economic Divide Reveal Price of Inequality."

25. Hilda Pui Lee, "The Impact of the Hedge Fund Economy on Social Structure: Housing in Greenwich, Connecticut" (master's thesis, Southern Connecticut State University, 2011); "Teardowns for Trophy Houses Rising on Gold Coast," *NYT,* January 16, 2000.

26. Lee, "Impact of the Hedge Fund Economy on Social Structure," 145.

27. Ned Coll interview, May 21, 2009.

28. Lebert "Gee" Lester, interview by Andrew Kahrl, May 21, 2009, transcript (in author's possession).

29. Ralph Knighton, interview by Andrew Kahrl, November 5, 2016, transcript (in author's possession).

30. See "RNC Asks Lieberman to Weigh in on Remarks Critical of Rowland," *NYN,* August 20, 2002; Jeff Jacoby, "The Double Standard on Political Hate Speech," *BG,* December 29, 2002.

31. "Activist Coll Arrested after Tiff at Tisane," *HC,* July 16, 2009; "Activist Ned Coll Arrested Again," *HC,* July 17, 2009; Richard Rapaport, "Rebel without a Followthrough: For Activist Ned Coll, 'Doing the Right Thing' Got Stuck on Confrontation," *HC,* July 26, 2009.

32. Lebert "Gee" Lester, interview.

33. Lebert "Gee" Lester, interview.

34. Russell West, interview with Andrew Kahrl, March 8, 2015, transcript (in author's possession).

35. National Advisory Commission on Civil Disorders, *Report of the National Advisory Commission on Civil Disorders* (Washington, DC: GPO, 1968), passage available at http://historymatters.gmu.edu/d/6545/.

36. See Jack Dougherty, "The Richest City in the Nation," *On the Line*, http://ontheline.trincoll.edu/book/chapter/the-richest-city-in-the-nation/; "Hartford 2nd Richest City in America?," *HC*, January 22, 2015; "Judge, Citing Inequality, Orders Connecticut to Overhaul Its School System," *NYT*, September 7, 2016. See also Connecticut Fair Housing Center, *People, Place, and Opportunity: Mapping Communities of Opportunity in Connecticut* (Columbus: Ohio State University, Kirwin Institute for the Study of Race and Ethnicity, November 2009), http://www.kirwaninstitute.osu.edu/reports/2009/11_2009_CTOppMapping_FullReport.pdf.

Acknowledgments

"Don't tell me there's not a movie out of this."

Ned Coll has lived a life full of drama, adventure, controversy, and intrigue. And as I learned early on in this project, no one was more aware of just how remarkable this life was than Ned Coll himself. When I first stumbled onto this story, I was in disbelief that, aside from the journalists who covered him in the 1970s and 1980s, no one had written a word on his life or that of the organization he founded and led, Revitalization Corps. So, too, was Ned, who from the moment I met him in 2009, has been generous with his time and always eager to assist me in piecing together the story of his life as an activist. I am deeply grateful for his cooperation. For helping me tell my story of Revitalization Corps, I also wish to thank Lebert "Gee" Lester, Cecil Lester, Earlie Powell, Father Rob Carbonneau, Mike Downes, Russell West, Joanne West, Jose Vasquez, Ralph Knighton, Riley Johnson, Warren Hardy, Elizabeth Johnson, and Walter Petry, as well as Leslie Hammond and Elizabeth Coll. Without their memories, insights, and assistance at different stages of the project, this book would not have been possible. For helping me to make sense of Hartford's past, one in which he played an instrumental role in documenting during his career, I wish to thank Tom Condon. I also owe a debt of gratitude to Mary Lou Fusi, whom I met as this book was nearing completion and who provided crucial insights into the social and class dynamics of her hometown of Madison, Connecticut.

This is not only the story of Ned Coll and the causes he championed. It is also the story of a place: the Connecticut shore. To tell its story and acquire a better understanding of the complex dynamics of the state's coastal environment, I have relied upon the experience and expertise of Jane Stahl, Dave Kozak, David J. Blatt, and their colleagues in the Office of Long Island Sound Programs at the Connecticut Department of Energy and Environmental Protection. In addition to sharing their knowledge, bringing numerous land-use and development issues and disputes to my attention, and reading portions of the manuscript, Dave and David have put me in touch with other experts in the field, as well as residents and officials in shoreline towns.

This entire story would have likely remained a footnote in my first book were it not for the enthusiastic response and critical feedback I received at the earliest stages of this project during a fellowship at Harvard University's W. E. B. Du Bois Institute (now Hutchins Center) in 2008 and 2009. I am especially grateful to Evelyn Brooks Higginbotham and Henry Louis "Skip" Gates for welcoming me into the community of Fellows at the Du Bois Institute, as well as the Charles Warren Center, where I workshopped an early draft of my work to an incomparable audience of scholars in U.S. history and African American studies. The feedback I received from them shaped the direction of this project in the years that followed. I wish to especially thank Zoe Burkholder, Matthew Countryman, Anna-Lisa Cox, Rachel Devlin, Tom Guglielmo, Paul Kaplan, Scott Kurashige, Hope Lewis, David Luis-Brown, Jennifer Nash, Barbara Rodriguez, Epifanio San Juan Jr., Faith Smith, and Donald Yacavone. In addition to providing invaluable feedback during our time at the Du Bois Institute, Erin Royston Battat also introduced me to her father, David Royston, who shared a long history with Ned Coll that dated back to his college years, as well as a deep knowledge of the social and legal issues that have shaped the shoreline's history. I am very grateful to Erin for her help with this project along the way and to David for taking the time to share his thoughts and recollections.

In the course of this project, I have benefited from the knowledge and professionalism of staff members at numerous libraries and archives. Special thanks to everyone who assisted me at the Connecticut State Library, Harvard's Loeb and Widener libraries, the Greenwich Library, Fairfield University's Archives and Special Collections, the University of Connecticut's Thomas J. Dodd Research Center, Marquette University's Raynor Library, the University of Wisconsin–Milwaukee's Golda Meir Library, and the University of Virginia's Alderman Library. I have depended on the hard work of a number of research assistants. Thanks especially to Miraf Bistegne, Alison Brown, Jeff Ramsey, Allison Kelley, and Julia Braxton. Research for this book has been made possible through generous support from Marquette University's College of Arts and Sciences and the University of Virginia's Buckner W. Clay Dean of Arts and Sciences and the Vice President for Research.

Over the past several years, I have enjoyed the opportunity to present portions of this work before several audiences. All of these occasions have helped to shape the project and sharpen its focus. For inviting me to share my work-in-progress, I wish to thank Northeastern University's School of Law, Interboro Partners and the BMW Guggenheim Lab in New York City, the University of Wisconsin–Milwaukee's Department of Geography, and the Monterey Institute for International Studies' Center for the Blue Economy. I also wish to thank the Massachusetts Historical Society for allowing me to workshop a paper at its Boston Environmental History Seminar, and the History Graduate Student Association at Virginia Tech for inviting me to deliver the keynote address at its annual conference.

For kindly reading and commenting on portions of the manuscript, I thank William Julius Wilson, Karl Haglund, Victoria Wolcott, Brian Purnell, Josh Sides, Brian McCammack, Martin Melosi, Molly Brady, Rich Schragger, Lawrence Sager, the anonymous readers at the *Journal of American History,* and my uncle William Kahrl. Numerous scholars have also shared their thoughts and offered their expertise on various aspects of this project. I wish to especially thank Elsa Devienne, Daniel D'Oca, Jack Dougherty, John Gillis, Andrew Highsmith, Gordon Hylton, Adam Keul, Chad Montrie, Helen Rozwadowski, Kara Schlichting, Marc Selverstone, Jason Sokol, and Yohuru Williams. My friends and former colleagues at Marquette University deserve special recognition for their kindness and support during our time in Milwaukee. Thanks especially to Sameena Mulla, Alison Clark Efford, James Marten, and Eugenia Afinoguenova. The University of Wisconsin–Milwaukee's Center for 21st Century Studies kindly offered me office space and a collegial environment to research and write during a transitional year in my career. Thanks especially to Richard Grusin, John Blum, Emily Clark, and Annette Hess. Over the past several years, the following friends and family have welcomed me into their homes and provided me meals, conversation, and rest during my research trips: Marela Zacarias, Helen Rozwadowski and Daniel Hornstein, Morgan Fritz and Keelan Diana, and Christina Kahrl and Charley Wanamaker.

Wendy Strothman took an interest in this story and has provided invaluable advice while helping to shepherd the manuscript from proposal to publication. At Yale University Press, I have been lucky to work with Jean Thomson Black and Michael Deneen. Thanks also to Bojana Ristich for her expert copyediting of the final manuscript. Lily Geismer read the entire manuscript and offered the kind of detailed feedback, constructive criticism, and expert advice that every writer dreams of receiving. I cannot thank her enough for the careful attention she devoted to every aspect of this manuscript. The final product is immeasurably improved thanks to her. In addition, I wish to thank the second, anonymous reader.

Charlottesville has been a great place to work, raise a family, and call home, thanks in no small measure to my colleagues in the history and African-American and African Studies departments at the University of Virginia. I wish to especially thank Brian Balogh, Grace Hale, Claudrena Harold, Will Hitchcock, Talitha LeFlouria, Sarah Milov, John Mason and Maurice Wallace. Kathleen Miller and Whitney Yancey have provided vital assistance and support, as have the current and former chairs of the history department, Karen Parshall and Paul Halliday, and the director of the Carter G. Woodson Institute, Deborah McDowell. Thanks also to the Miller Center for Public Affairs, especially Nicole Hemmer and Guian McKee. Our time in Charlottesville has been made so much richer and more enjoyable thanks to our friends Amy and Karl Hagstrom-Miller.

Finally, I thank my beautiful and incredibly talented wife, Aileen Sevier, who is my sharpest critic, most trusted ally, and constant source of comfort and affection, and our wonderful daughters, Elodie and Muriel. The joy they bring to my life is indescribable. My love for them is boundless.

If this book is able to convey the local nature of politics, and the power of place, it is because of what I learned growing up in my parents' household. My mother, Susan Kahrl, taught me by her own example the importance of civic engagement and of the hard work that goes into making a community. I never cease to be amazed by her energy and tenacity. My father, Timothy Kahrl, taught me to see the presence of the past and appreciate the power of storytelling. From him, I learned to always root for the underdog, to notice the interests behind every ideology, and to search for the great crimes that made every great fortune. I knew I found, in Ned Coll and the Connecticut shore, a story he would especially appreciate and eagerly shared with him drafts of each chapter as they were completed. After all this time, I still wait to hear his reaction with the same excitement and anticipation as when I was a kid first learning the craft of writing. I dedicate this book to them, with all my love.

Index

Page numbers in italics refer to figures